Liberty, Property, and the Future of Constitutional Development

SUNY Series in the Constitution and Economic Rights
Ellen Frankel Paul, Editor

Liberty, Property, and the Future of Constitutional Development

edited by
**Ellen Frankel Paul and
Howard Dickman**

State University of New York Press

Published by
State University of New York Press, Albany

© 1990 State University of New York

Printed in the United States of America

For information, address State University of New York
Press, State University Plaza, Albany, N.Y., 12246

Library of Congress Cataloging-in-Publication Data

Liberty, property, and the future of constitutional development / edited by Ellen Frankel Paul
and Howard Dickman.
     p.   cm. — (SUNY series in the Constitution and economic rights)
    ISBN 0-7914-0303-3. — ISBN 0-7914-0304-1 (pbk.)
    1. Industrial laws and legislation—United States.   2. Right of property—United States.
3. United States—Constitutional law. I. Paul, Ellen Frankel.   II. Dickman, Howard.
III. Series.
KF 1570.L5   1990
342.73'085—dc20
[347.30285]   89-21639
                                                   CIP

10 9 8 7 6 5 4 3 2 1

Contents

Acknowledgments

The editors wish to acknowledge the generous support of the National Endowment for the Humanities (Ref: GB-20081-86), and especially the encouragement of the Bicentennial Division and the Division of Public Programs. Additional support was received from the Bowling Green State University Office of University Relations, the College of Arts and Sciences, and the Graduate College. Many individuals at the Social Philosophy and Policy Center, Bowling Green State University provided invaluable assistance in the preparation of this volume; they include: Assistant Project Director Kory Tilgner, Jeffrey Paul, Fred D. Miller, Jr., Dan Greenberg, Terrie Weaver, and Tamara Sharp.

Acknowledgments

Introduction

What are economic rights and why are they important? Economic rights are the rights we all enjoy to possess, use, exchange, and otherwise dispose of our property. In the American tradition, they have been and continue to be important because they protect a sphere of privacy around each individual and give each person the rights to exercise liberty and protect life without undue interference from other people or from government.

From such stellar European thinkers as Locke, Montesquieu, and the seventeenth-century natural law theorists, our Framers drew both their inspiration and their worldview. As Jefferson argued in the Declaration of Independence, men are created by their God with inalienable rights, which governments as the artifacts of man are designed to protect but cannot legitimately destroy. If governments exceed this limited, protective role, they should be overthrown and the rights of the people restored. This was straight from the great English political theorist, John Locke. From Montesquieu, the successful revolutionaries learned that to construct a government that would preserve the rights of the people—their rights to life, liberty, and property—it must be structured in such a way that power would be divided and each organ of government would check the tendency to overreach of the others. Thus, at the constitutional convention and during the debates that ensued over the Constitution's ratification, much was heard of Montesquieu's views on checks and balances and whether a republic could succeed over such a large and diverse country with seemingly divergent interests. To overcome Montesquieu's point that only monarchy could preserve liberty over large territories, the authors of *The Federalist*—Hamilton, Madison, and Jay—repeatedly emphasized that by preserving the states and instituting a national government of only delegated and limited powers, liberty could be secured.

Beyond institutional arrangements of checks and balances, the constitutional scheme (including the original document and the Bill of Rights enacted by the First Congress) included specific clauses designed to protect economic liberties. During the nineteenth century, the task of defining the meaning of these cryptic clauses and demarcating the boundaries of these liberties from governmental interference was left to the Supreme Court of the

1

United States. The contracts clause was designed to preserve the sanctity of contract, and especially to protect debtor/creditor contracts from interference by the states, which had, during the period of the Articles of Confederation, seen fit to provide debtor relief, thereby abrogating contracts. The commerce clause was inserted in the Constitution to prevent states from pursuing a beggar-thy-neighbor policy of erecting barriers to trade in interstate commerce. It was designed to preserve a free-trade market throughout the United States. The eminent domain clause of the Fifth Amendment protects property owners from confiscations by the national government by providing that "takings" be accompanied by "just compensation" and that the power only be exercised for the "public use."

The latter half of the nineteenth century was truly a critical period for the nation. America developed from an overwhelmingly rural and agricultural country to an industrial, urban one that had survived a cataclysmic Civil War. In the wake of that war, Congress enacted and the nation adopted the post-Civil War amendments: the Thirteenth, Fourteenth, and Fifteenth. The Thirteenth Amendment emancipated the slaves and, most importantly for future jurisprudence, the Fourteenth Amendment provided that all citizens of the several states should enjoy the same privileges and immunities of citizens of the United States, that no citizen should be deprived of life, liberty, or property without due process of law, and that no citizen should be deprived of the equal protection of the laws. The Fifteenth guaranteed all United States citizens the right to vote. Over the years, on a case-by-case basis, the Supreme Court "incorporated" the provisions of the Bill of Rights into the Fourteenth Amendment through the due process clause. The significance of this line of cases is enormous, for now the rights of individuals and the limitations on the federal government also hold against the states. This development provides greater protection for individual rights, but at a price. The price is the sacrifice of states' rights and some of the protection to liberty that our Founding Fathers provided by dividing power between sovereign state governments and a national government of delegated powers.

The Fourteenth Amendment proved useful not only for the protection of the rights of minorities, but also as a vehicle for insulating economic rights from government intrusion—at least for a brief period in Supreme Court adjudication. Around the turn of the century, the Court discerned freedom of contract in the due process clause of both the Fifth and Fourteenth Amendments. With this discovery, the Court entered what has come to be known as the "substantive due process era," or the era of the Old Court. Roughly from the 1890s through 1937, the Court used its power of judicial review to overturn numerous state and federal regulatory measures that interfered—as they saw it—with economic freedom. Thus, at various times, the Court declared unconstitutional minimum wage legislation, legislation limiting the maximum hours that laborers could work, minimum price regulations, and prohibitions on yellow dog contracts (whereby employers made it a condition of employment that workers not join unions). Scholars have typically excoriated this period—the so-called *Lochner* era, after a leading case of the period, *Lochner v. New York*.[1] In that case, the Court overturned a New York State act which limited the time that bakers could work to sixty hours per week. During this era, the Court carefully scrutinized economic regulation, and found much of it wanting. It applied what has been called a means/ends test—it looked at each piece of challenged legislation and asked itself whether the government was pursuing a legitimate end and, if so, whether the means chosen were the least onerous. Under this test much economic regulation passed constitutional muster, but much did not.

Subsequent generations of legal scholars accused the Old Court of abusing its prerogative by supplanting the judgment of duly-elected legislatures with its own. Only in recent years have scholars reexamined this period with less critical eyes and seen in it something more positive: a desire by the Court to protect individual economic liberty where legislatures had overreached themselves. But this view is still very novel. The accepted view since the New Deal and the late 1930s is that the Court should show great deference to legislative judgments on matters of economic regulation. The test employed by the Court has been a very lenient one: if any rational basis can be found for an economic regulation, the Court will defer to the legislature. Under this standard, the Court has found all challenged economic regulations but one constitutional under the due process clause since 1937.

In the essays that follow, both defenders and challengers of what some have called the Court's "double standard" will have their say. Some see a "double standard" in the Court's application of this deferential, rational basis test to challenged economic regulation, while it applies a much tougher test—of strict scrutiny—where legislation impinges on First Amendment rights or on equal protection rights guaranteed by the Fourteenth Amendment. Critics of this approach wonder why freedom of speech, freedom of the press, or freedom of religion should enjoy protection while economic rights are relegated to a second-class status. Others defend the Court's preference for one set of rights over the other as establishing a wholly justifiable hierarchy of rights. Still others will reject entirely the terms of this debate and argue that the Supreme Court should always defer to legislators over the whole span of rights protected by the Constitution.

Economic rights, in recent years, have once again become a lively topic of constitutional debate, whereas they had been virtually a settled issue for fifty years. The Supreme Court in 1987, for example, saw fit to give greater protection to property owners faced with overzealous land use regulation in two leading cases: *Nollan v. California Coastal Commission*[2] and *First English Evangelical Lutheran Church of Glendale v. County of Los Angeles*.[3] This heightened concern for property rights may foretell more to come, or it may simply be an aberration; it is simply too soon to tell.

Liberty, Property, and the Future of Constitutional Development: The Essays

The contributions to this volume focus primarily on developments in the constitutional interpretation of property rights since the "shift in time that saved nine" of the late 1930s. The authors have many varied recommendations for how the law ought to develop in the future.

The collection opens with two theoretical pieces, one by the premier advocate of the public choice school and the other by one of its leading critics. James M. Buchanan's "The Contractarian Logic of Classical Liberalism" examines the possible derivation of a constitutional regime that protects voluntary exchange between individuals from either private or public interferences. For ordinary tradeable goods that are fully divisible and where exchange generates no third-party effects, a veil-of-ignorance construction generates protection of the individual freedom to exchange rights to goods. Such exchange agreements are distinguishable from agreements to exchange liberties to enter separate markets. For exchange that involves the generation of third-party effects, the contractarian logic remains, predictably, nondefinitive as concerns constitutional limits on politicized interferences.

Mark Tushnet, in his "Public Choice Constitutionalism and Economic Rights," offers a vigorous critique of the very foundation upon which public choice constitutionalism is constructed. That foundational assumption is that people act in politics to maximize their economic well-being, and from this beginning public choice develops a theory of constitution-making, legislation, and judicial review. Tushnet argues that the theories of constitution-making and legislation yield fewer interesting conclusions than proponents of public choice constitutionalism typically suggest, and that their theory of judicial review is unlikely to provide sufficient guidance to judges to be acceptable.

"Civil Rights and Property Rights," by William H. Riker, addresses the "double standard" head-on. The Court sharply distinguishes between civil rights and property rights, with the former considered "preferred." In fact, Riker argues, the two kinds of rights have similar origins and functions. They can and have been justified in similar, often identical, ways in terms of the practical and moral advantages they give to people generally and to the individual holders in particular. Riker finds it difficult to see any reason for preferring one set of rights over the other.

The three essays that follow share several features in common. First, they take up the issue raised by Riker: the question of the commensurability of property rights and civil rights. Second, each essay vigorously attacks the position of one of the leading champions of the revivification of property rights in legal circles, Richard Epstein. A lively and thoughtful response from Epstein follows.

Lino A. Graglia, in his piece "Judicial Activism of the Right: A Mistaken and Futile Hope," sees no justification for heightened judicial scrutiny of civil rights, let alone property rights disputes. Judicial review is both dangerous and not explicitly provided for in the Constitution. It would be of little significance, however, if it were confined in fact, as it is in theory, to disallowing laws explicitly prohibited by the Constitution. Judicial review as it has been practiced has little or nothing to do with the Constitution and has produced such decisions as *Dred Scott:* a dubious contribution to American society. With the 1954 *Brown* decision, the Supreme Court's role changed from being a brake on change in social policy to becoming the primary initiator of it. Because the many changes instituted by the Court have uniformly advanced the policy preferences of the Left, the Court's activist role has been enthusiastically supported and defended by constitutional law professors and other members of the "New Class." They have found the Constitution "uncertain" and urged the substitution of meaningless abstractions for the Constitution's relatively definite and knowable terms. Some conservatives, particularly libertarians, have recently joined the liberal enterprise by advocating a policymaking role for the Court. Although these proponents of judicial activism of the Right would have the Court serve different political ends, their arguments are indistinguishable from those of the proponents of judicial activism of the Left. Graglia finds Richard Epstein's *Takings* a prime example of this regrettable phenomenon.

In "Economic Liberties and the Future of Constitutional Self-Government," Stephen Macedo, contrary to Graglia, contends that bolstering judicial protections for economic freedoms would serve broad constitutional values of liberty, limited government, and public reasonableness. The constitutional case for economic liberty must, he argues, be made on complex, political grounds. This is why he finds Richard Epstein's defense in *Takings: Private Property and the Power of Eminent Domain* defective. While brilliant in execution, Epstein's case for economic liberty displays the shortcomings of an analysis that is too narrowly economic and too loosely grounded in the Constitution as a whole. For Macedo, the case for economic liberty must be squared with, among other things, the constitutional value of ongoing political deliberation, and the complexity of the Constitution's goals and its scheme of representation.

In "Tutelary Jurisprudence and Constitutional Property," Frank Michelman develops contrasting, historically inspired "classical liberal" and "republican" models of constitutional property rights, along with contrasting notions of property as a "negative" and an "affirmative" (or "welfare") right. He utilizes these concepts to explain the current, uncertain state of American constitutional-legal argument respecting the protection and distribution of property. The uncertainty can be traced in part to the inability of either the libertarian or republican vision to find definitive resolution for the conflict between affirmative and negative property claims, and in part to the continuing appeal of both the libertarian and the republican conceptions of constitutionalism. Writings of Professor Richard Epstein and opinions of Justice Antonin Scalia are used to illustrate the contrasting tendencies of libertarian and republican constitutional jurisprudence and the internal conflicts common to both models.

The final three contributions to the collection connect some of the more abstract constitutional themes discussed in the earlier essays to more practical concerns. R. Shep Melnick's "The Politics of the New Property: Welfare Rights in Congress and the Courts" examines the role of the federal courts over the last two decades in defining the "New Property" entitlements created by social welfare programs. While ostensibly engaging in statutory interpretation, the courts have grafted onto several important federal programs their own need-based understanding of welfare rights, expanding benefits and striking down a variety of eligibility requirements established by the states and by federal administrators. After examining the legal doctrines that produced these programmatic changes, Melnick scrutinizes in detail the courts' restructuring of Aid to Families with Dependent Children (AFDC). He demonstrates how the courts played fast and loose with "legislative intent," explains why Congress took so long to react, and shows how, in recent years, Congress and the president have agreed to overturn a large number of court rulings.

In "Work, Government, and the Constitution: Determining the Proper Allocation of Rights and Powers," Thomas R. Haggard examines the Court's differing approaches to the employer-employee relationship over the course of this century. He identifies the social forces and philosophical viewpoints that led the Supreme Court to recognize a constitutional right to contract for work and then to repudiate the existence of that right in favor of governmental power to regulate the work relationship. The "economic due process" cases, in which the "Old Court" wrestled with the proper allocation of these rights and powers, are examined and contrasted with modern constitutional law cases on work-related issues. Haggard concludes that in determining the proper allocation between individual rights and governmental power, we must start with the proposition that law is an instrument of social coercion and then attempt to identify the moral and constitutional limits on the use of such power.

Leo Troy's "The Right to Organize Meets the Market" traces the role of market forces in eroding the right to organize and bargain collectively granted by the National Labor Relations Act of 1935. While that act transformed labor-management relations in the United States, it inevitably collided with market forces. And the market prevailed. Structural changes in the labor market and competition, both international and domestic, have steadily eroded the size and strength of American unions. Despite the shield of economic rights provided to labor unions by the law, these new developments, which began in the 1950s, ushered in a new era of labor-management relations, one in which the nonunion sector is not only dominant but growing.

The authors in this volume were selected with the expectation that their contributions would be both provocative and diverse in viewpoint. That expectation, we believe, has not been disappointed.

Notes

1. 198 U.S. 45 (1905).

2. 107 S. Ct. 3141 (1987). The Court held that imposing an easement requirement as a condition for granting a development permit was an unconstitutional "taking" because the easement did not "substantially advance legitimate state interests." (at 3146) Thus, the majority scrutinized the rationale behind the imposition of the easement rather than simply deferring to the county's judgment. This is a reversal of long-standing judicial deference on these issues.

3. 107 S. Ct. 2378 (1978). Here, the Court held that where a land use regulation so burdens an owner's use of his land that it amounts to a taking, invalidation of the ordinance is an insufficient remedy, and the landowner must be compensated for the period in which he suffered from the effects of the ordinance. Heretofore, invalidation was considered a sufficient remedy in such cases.

The Contractarian Logic of Classical Liberalism

JAMES M. BUCHANAN

Introduction

In a paper entitled "The Utilitarian Logic of Liberalism," Russell Hardin attempted to derive elements of a liberal social order from utilitarian foundations.[1] I have deliberately borrowed the structure of Hardin's title, emended by my substitution of the word "contractarian" for "utilitarian." Without the "adding-up" possibilities provided by utilitarianism, how can the structural components of social order be related, directly or indirectly, to individualist evaluative norms on a nonprivileged basis? This question, of course, defines the whole contractarian enterprise. My purpose here is the limited one of examining the possibilities of deriving legal-political-constitutional protection for voluntary exchanges from a contractarian starting point that rejects both utilitarianism and any form of natural rights.

The analytical setting incorporates well-defined membership of persons within a polity with each individual presumed to count equally in the ultimate determination of rules. Hence, legitimacy emerges only upon unanimous consent. If agreement is to be brought within the range of the possible here, some means of bridging the gap between well-identified individual interests, which will conflict, and the common or general interest, defined by the emergence of agreement, is necessary. The veil of ignorance and/or uncertainty, accompanied by some sense of the quasi-permanency of rules and institutions, offers the only means that seems fully consistent with the contractarian perspective. The question then becomes: behind a sufficiently thick veil of ignorance and/or uncertainty, will the individual in some hypothesized constitutional stage choose to ensure protection for voluntary contractual exchanges? Or, if he chooses to protect some exchanges and not others, where and how will a distinction be made?

Initially, the specific question to be addressed seems straightforward,

9

but closer examination suggests that the basic meaning of "voluntary exchange" must be clarified. What, precisely, is involved in an exchange between two persons?

I. A Simple Example

Consider the simplest possible example in which persons A and B hold initial and fully separable stocks of two potentially exchangeable goods, Apples and Bananas. Prior to entry into a trading relation, A holds a stock of Apples; B holds a stock of Bananas.

It is semantically appropriate, as well as logically useful, to say that A has rights in Apples and B has rights in Bananas prior to entry into exchange. Indeed, without some such legal or mutually respected set of rights, trade, as an institution, would not be possible.[2] But precisely what does having rights in the initial stock of Apples allow A to do? Presumably, these rights allow A to prevent others from consuming, from eating up or otherwise using, the Apples in A's initial endowment without A's consent. Person A is protected in these respects by his rights to the Apples: person B is similarly protected in his rights to the Bananas.

As Armen Alchian emphasized in his early and seminal work on the economics of property, exchange involves a transfer of rights.[3] After a trade, there has been a shift in ownership of at least some of the Apples and some of the Bananas. Note, however, that the initial definition of rights, as such, may (but need not) include entry into potential exchange relationships. As an institution, exchange requires that there be some initial assignment of rights to goods, as indicated, but it also requires a reciprocal granting of "liberties" to enter into the "market" and to make bids and offers. Person A, in our example, holds initial rights to his Apple endowment; he does not hold any initial liberty to offer these in exchange for B's Bananas.

In the strict two-person setting, such a liberty for A will be within the sphere of authority of person B, and he may or may not grant that liberty to person A. Person B may, simply, refuse to deal with person A; B may withhold any liberty of A to enter into a bargaining process, or market. Note that such action on the part of B would not, in any way, transgress on A's rights to the Apples in his initial stock. Person B may, on the other hand, allow A the liberty of entering into the exchange process, while, at the same time, person A may allow B a similar liberty. If this reciprocal granting of liberties to enter exchange takes place, person A will make offers of Apples for Bananas, and person B will make offers of Bananas for Apples.

Exchange will take place with a resultant transfer of rights to the units of goods that change hands.[4]

This highly-stylized example may seem analytically otiose, since neither person would seem to have any possible interest in withholding the liberty of entering the exchange process from the other—at least so long as we stay within the dimensions of the two-person, two-good model and do not allow noneconomic considerations to enter motivations. I shall demonstrate, however, that the distinction between rights and liberties does become relevant in more complex models, and that the usage of these terms can be helpful in reaching a provisional answer to the basic question posed earlier. I hope to show that agreement may be reached on constitutional protection for the reciprocal exchange of liberties to contract that facilitates a voluntary transfer of rights, but that constitutional protection cannot be similarly justified for the exchange of liberties that does not facilitate any transfer of rights, even if this exchange of liberties is itself wholly voluntary on the part of the parties involved.

An alternative formulation, and one that would be more terminologically consistent with Hardin's, would include, with the set of rights to initial endowments, the ability to enter into the contracting process with parties on the other sides of potential exchanges. This formulation would have the semantic advantage of not requiring reference to liberties to enter exchanges, but it has the disadvantage of requiring that some of the rights involved in the exchange process could possibly be made inalienable (nonexchangeable). That which is defined to be a liberty to enter exchange or contract in my preferred terminology becomes that dimension of rights that are made alienable by agreement in the constitutional decision-process under the alternative terminology.

II. Enlarging the Example

Consider now an enlarged, if still highly stylized, example of potential exchange in Apples and Bananas. There are now two persons, A_1 and A_2, both of whom initially have rights to stocks of Apples. There are also, say, ten persons, B_1, B_2, . . . B_{10}; each one has initial rights to a stock of Bananas. In this trading community of twelve persons, we assume that, initially, each person has allowed every other person the liberty of entering a market or exchange relationship. Under these conditions, trade will take place as in the two-person model.

In this setting, however, we should note that persons A_1 and A_2 may well find it mutually advantageous to agree, voluntarily, on a reciprocal alienation of some of the liberties to exchange that have been granted to them by the ten persons who have rights to Bananas. Person A_1 might, for example, agree to give up any liberty of entering into a trading relationship with persons B_6 through B_{10} in exchange for A_2's agreement to give up any liberty of entering into a trading relationship with B_1 through B_5. This sort of contract may be mutually advantageous to both A_1 and A_2 because, in this way, each can achieve a monopoly position with respect to a subset of the buyers for Apples. Each of the two can thereby expect to secure a somewhat larger share of the producer's-consumer's rents in the community than that share anticipated under the competitive adjustment in the absence of the market-sharing contract. The agreement will tend to make A_1 and A_2 better off at the expense of the other ten persons who, because of their larger numbers, are assumed unable to organize a fully-effective offsetting market-sharing arrangement.

If we now introduce the contractarian-constitutionalist perspective and place any person behind an appropriately-defined veil of ignorance and/or uncertainty, it seems clear that voluntary exchanges like that between the two As just discussed would *not* be provided constitutional protection, unless the value of liberty-to-enter-agreements *as such* is assigned an evaluation over and beyond access to goods that are valued. That is to say, the legal rules chosen behind the veil would not, under standard preference configurations, allow market-sharing agreements to be enforced. Behind the veil, no person could predict his or her status as an A or B. Even in this pure exchange setting, any agreement between persons on the same side of any market will ensure that potential value will not be allowed to come into being. On the other hand, and by contrast, all agreements that result in an exchange of rights to goods and services across both sides of markets will be predicted to be value-enhancing. These latter agreements or contracts will be provided legal enforceability under the agreed-on constitutional structure.

The results here are, of course, familiar. Contracts made in restraint of trade were traditionally unenforceable under the common law. These contracts may involve market shares, as in our simple example, but they may also extend to the setting of prices, along with other characteristics of the terms on which goods and services may be offered on markets. Any such contractual agreement may be interpreted as a mutual exchange of liberties to contract with persons on the other side of markets. In the simple setting here, where we limit analysis to fully partitionable goods and services that involve no spillover or external effects, any voluntary agreement by same-side traders to give up any of the liberties of dealing with other-side traders ensures that value will be destroyed. Goods and services will be prevented from moving to their most highly-valued uses, as determined by the evaluations placed on them by the participants in the potential exchange nexus.

III. Politicizing the Example

Let us now assume that voluntary *private* contracts in restraint of exchange are legally nonenforceable within the setting of the same example—the example which includes A_1 and A_2 as sellers of Apples and B_1 through B_{10} as sellers of Bananas, with traders restricted to those trades that directly involve transfers of Apples and Bananas. The legal rules are such that the As cannot make the market-sharing arrangement previously discussed.

Suppose, however, that a majority of the combined twelve–person community imposes a governmental restriction on the exchange. Suppose, specifically, that the sellers of Bananas (or at least seven of them), a clear majority, vote in favor of changing the terms of trade so that the Apple price for Bananas is set well above that price observed under the nonrestricted competitive operation of the simple economy. This legislation will insure that the ten Banana-sellers secure a larger share for A_1 and A_2. It will also ensure that total value in the economy is reduced. Apples and Bananas will not be distributed, after trade, in such a fashion that will maximize total value in the community.

Behind a veil of ignorance and/or uncertainty as to personal identification, no person would allow the constitution to permit majoritarian political action to restrict exchanges in the manner just described (unless, of course, majoritarianism, *as such,* is positively valued). Such restriction is the political equivalent of private agreements in restraint of trade or exchange. The simple analysis here indicates clearly that the simultaneous enforcement of common-law or statutory prohibitions on private contracts in restraint of trade and of politically-orchestrated restrictions on trade is, in principle, contradictory. Emphasis on the essential similarity between private market-sharing contracts and publicly-enacted restrictions on exchange calls direct attention to potential flaws in the policy stances of both the extreme libertarians and those who oppose constitutional protection for economic liberties. The libertarian who defends private, cartel-like agreement among contracting parties on the same side of a market, so long as such agreement is voluntary, must have some difficulty arguing against politically orchestrated cartel-like restrictions in particular markets, although the political-legal enforceability of private cartel agreements becomes a critical variable in any such argument. And those who justify majoritarian political interference with free exchanges should find it difficult to defend common-law limits on restraints of trade, as well as anti-trust institutions.

IV. Extensions: Partitionable, Tradeable Goods and Distributional Norms

To this point, the analysis has been limited to very simple exchange models, with almost self-evident results. The contractarian derivation of constitutional protection for the freedom of persons to carry out ordinary exchanges of goods and services is relatively straightforward. But, as the analysis has shown, this protection cannot be extended to freedom of contracts that involve the giving up of liberties to enter the exchange process. These results emerge, however, only in the simple exchange setting that was examined, along with the implied presuppositions that include the partitionability of goods among persons, the moral acceptability of trade in such goods, and the absence of third-party or external effects generated by two-person trades. In this section, I want to retain these presuppositions while examining in some detail the distributional implications of free exchange. I want to concentrate exclusively on the effects on the contractarian calculus that distributional considerations may exert.

We may stay with the Apples-Bananas example to illustrate the conditions that must be present if distributional considerations are to be relevant for the results. If, behind the veil of ignorance and/or uncertainty, a person predicts that those who, before exchange, will be endowed with initial stocks of Bananas will be distributionally worse off than those who will have initial endowments of Apples, there may then arise some argument for asymmetrically-enforced prohibitions on restraints on trade, whether privately or publicly introduced. If Banana owners (or producers, if we extend the analysis to a production economy) are systematically predicted to be poor, while Apple owners (or producers) are systematically predicted to be rich, the person behind the veil who is unable to identify his or her own position may consider exchange or terms-of-trade interferences as one means of securing distributional objectives, even in full recognition of the potential loss in total value that any such interference will ensure.

As this example suggests, however, to associate distributional positions with the specific ownership and/or production of specific goods and services seems bizarre. Normally, there would be little or no connection between distributional position and the description of the good that is initially owned or produced. Pre-market or pre-exchange endowments may, of course, differ widely, but such differences cannot readily be associated with the terms of trade in particular markets. If this is the case, there would be little or no grounds for trying to relate interferences with markets to ultimate distributional norms. This statement does not, of course, imply anything about the appropriateness (or inappropriateness) or relevance of distributional objectives in a more general constitutional calculus.

There is one market, however, where distributional elements have allegedly been significant in offering putative justification for restraints on voluntary exchange, both restraints that emerge from privately-negotiated agreement to give up liberties to exchange and from publicly-imposed constraints on individual freedom of contract. I refer here to the market or markets for labor services, where privately-agreed restraints on exchange are widely observed to be publicly enforced (e.g., labor union contracts), and, further, where governmentally-imposed restraints supplement those that are privately sanctioned. It is necessary to examine with some care the possible contractarian basis for this apparent exception to the generalized principle of classical liberalism. Can restrictions on voluntary labor exchanges be grounded in any way on the rational choices of persons in a constitutional stage of decisions?

Consider a setting most highly favorable to the argument for interferences in voluntary exchange. Assume that persons are, at birth, physically separable into two distinct classes, those who must work for others, and those who may fill employer roles. Further assume that all workers are homogeneous, and that each worker is location–specific, and, hence, unable to negotiate exchanges with alternative employers over space. Employees, as a class, being more numerous relative to their opportunities than employers, are predicted to earn substantially less per person than employers.

In this setting, employees or workers are often said to be at a relative bargaining disadvantage, and this allegation has been used as a justification for either privately-organized restraints on voluntary labor contracts, through unions, or for compulsory governmental restrictions on the terms of such contracts. But even in this rarefied and highly unreal setting, can such restrictions be derived from a veil of ignorance-uncertainty calculus?

Consider wage negotiations, where the union representing the demands of the workers secures a wage contract that sets payment above that which would emerge in the absence of the union. Fewer workers than before can secure employment at the higher wage. But if we assume that the demand for labor is inelastic (less than one in absolute value) over the relevant range, the total wage bill may be higher. The total payment to workers, as a class, will then increase. But if this institutional change is to be supported on grounds of distributive justice, the increase in the total wage bill is not sufficient. There must also be some means to ensure that, within the class of workers, the gains are more equally shared. As noted, fewer workers will remain employed, but unless those who lose employment by the wage increase are subsidized by those who remain employed at the increased wage, the institutional change will generate undesirable distributive results on almost any criterion of distributive justice. It seems clear that wage setting, as such, without institutional guarantees as to the distribution of benefits from wages above competitive levels, cannot be derived as a consequence of the rational choice calculus of a person behind a veil, even under the most favorable and extreme circumstances postulated here.

If we introduce more realism into the model, and allow for interclass mobility, non-location-specificity, and heterogeneity among both workers and employers, any private or public enforcement of wage levels above those attained in the openly competitive market will tend to impose disproportionately greater harm on those potential workers who are precisely those held to be the most "distributionally deserving" by egalitarians. The generalized conclusion seems inescapable; the principles of classical liberalism that prohibit legally enforceable restraints on voluntary exchange cannot be challenged with a contractarian model of evaluation, even when distributional objectives are fully incorporated into the analysis.

V. Beyond Procedural Norms

To this point, my usage of the contractarian logic of classical liberalism has relied exclusively on procedural criteria for institutional evaluation. The results appear determinate only because many of the substantive issues have been deliberately avoided by the presuppositions of the analysis. I have simply presumed that all persons, whether behind the veil or aware of their place in society, agree on the definitions or classifications of "goods" and "bads." Further, I have presumed that all "goods" and "bads" are fully partitionable, both in a physical and an evaluative sense. No person is interested in the production or consumption activity of any other person with respect to any identified "good" or "bad."

It is clear that most of the issues involving the putative legitimacy of private or public restraints on voluntary exchanges arise precisely in those settings where these presuppositions do not describe reality. In the terminology of welfare economics, it is the presence of "externality," whether narrowly or broadly defined, that necessarily introduces indeterminism in any attempted normative justification for a regime of generalized constitutional-legal protection for voluntary exchange. The procedural criteria of contractarianism cannot, in themselves, be extended to the substantive issues of definition and classification—at least not directly. I shall examine the limits of these criteria below. But it remains useful to emphasize the force of the contractarian logic, even within these acknowledged limits.

Empirically, persons are observed to agree on definitions of "goods" and "bads" over wide commodity and service groupings, and, further, persons agree that individual or private preferences with respect to the consumption, production, and exchange of many ordinary goods and services are of little concern to those who are not involved in carrying out such activities. Within the domain of social interaction involving the exchange of such ordinary goods and services, the contractarian logic remains unchallengeable, although, of course, defining the limits of such domain remains formidable. Private or public restraints on voluntary exchanges in these ordinary goods and services (bread, clothing, houses, haircuts, consulting) are ruled out by the procedural criteria of contractarianism, along with the empirical observation of agreement on spheres of private action.

There exists another domain of activity within which there remains widespread disagreement concerning the appropriateness of privately-motivated exchange activity. There are activities that involve what some persons may define to be tradeable or exchangeable goods and services which other persons do not acknowledge as falling legitimately within the domain of individual choice. Examples abound: alcohol, slavery, sex, drugs, blood, body organs, babies, guns and so forth. There are still other activities that may involve goods and bads that in some circumstances are deemed exchangeable, but which may in other circumstances generate third-party or spillover effects. Is an individual to be allowed to produce and market a good, the sale and/or purchase of which is predicted to adversely affect others than the direct buyer-consumer?

Can individual liberty to enter into voluntary exchanges of goods and bads that fall into the inclusive domain of externality be derived from the contractarian calculus? If not, is there some characteristic feature of such goods and services that we may identify as offering grounds to justify departure from the general norm of protection for voluntary exchange?

It is useful at this point to recall precisely what the individual is presumed to know when he makes basic constitutional choices behind the veil of ignorance and/or uncertainty. He or she cannot identify which person in the community he or she will be, what role will be occupied, what human and nonhuman endowments will be possessed, or what preferences will be descriptive. On the other hand, the overall or general distribution of these variables among the whole set of persons in the community is presumed to be known, at least within broad limits.

Consider, in particular, the preferences for goods and services, along with the preferences for the activities of others with respect to exchanges of these goods and services. For any one of the potential markets in the domain of externality, the individual behind the veil will predict that there will be a wide range of preference patterns concerning the appropriateness or inappropriateness of entering into unhampered exchange processes. There will be persons whose preferences dictate participation in ordinary exchanges in such markets without regard to the spillover effects on others in the community. There will be others, however, who will find the existence of such exchanges to be either morally outrageous or economically damaging.

Behind the veil, the chooser cannot predict which one of these preferences will describe his or her utility function. Identification remains impossible on this as on other dimensions. The choice of institutions behind the veil must, therefore, represent some judgment as to the relative significance of the varying preference patterns, along with some estimate of the frequency distribution along the spectrum. The constitutional stage chooser must balance off the possible potential gains to those who directly benefit from the exchanges that might take place and the possible potential harms to those who would be damaged by such exchanges. There is no *a priori* judgment that can be advanced in any particular case here, and, hence, no prediction as to the precise definition of the range of goods and services that would have constitutional protection for their voluntary exchanges.

This indeterminacy cannot be avoided. We may suggest, however, that rational choice behavior at the constitutional stage must also include some prediction as to the workings of those institutions that might be constitutionally authorized to intervene in the exchange processes for goods and services falling in the domain of relevant externality. In particular, rational choice here would dictate skepticism with regard to the working of politicized majoritarian intervention with voluntary exchange. As it operates ideally, even if not in practice, majority rule tends to allow majorities with relatively mild preferences to overrule minorities that may feel intensely about alternatives. It seems likely that most of the activities that fall with a relevant externality domain (e.g., smoking) invoke mildly-felt meddlesome negative preferences. Hence, simple majorities would presumably choose to prohibit voluntary exchanges in such goods and services.

These considerations suggest that, if restraints on the voluntary exchanges of goods and services are deemed appropriate, these restraints should take the form of adjustments in the legal structure so as to make contracts of exchange non–enforceable. That is to say, the constitutional

ASK JMB

stage decision should delineate carefully those markets that fall within the domain of relevant externality. These seem to be no grounds for allowing the delineation to be made through the operation of ordinary politics. For example, contracts for perpetual servitude should be constitutionally, rather than legislatively, prohibited; contracts for the exchange of sexual services should or should not be constitutionally permissible, independently of the will of particular legislative majorities. The sale and purchase of alcohol was an appropriate constitutional issue, even if historical experience suggests that the constitutional choice made in the United States was in error. In these cases, as with all tradeable goods and services, there is a *prima facie* argument against overt politicization of restraint on the exchange process.

VI. Contractarianism and Classical Liberalism

There is little that is novel in the preceding analysis. What I have attempted to do is to stay within the contractarian model for evaluation and to examine the possible derivation of constitutional protection of voluntary exchanges between persons or organizations of persons. It seems clear that persons should be allowed, and legally protected, to engage in voluntary exchanges of goods and services that are considered to be appropriate objects for private disposition when such exchanges do not generate significant spillover harms on third parties. This protection cannot be extended to voluntary agreements in restraint of exchanges, at least within any contractarian exercise of justification. For goods and services that are deemed by some persons to be inappropriate for exchanges, or goods and services the exchanges of which are predicted to generate significant spillover damages on third parties, the contractarian model is necessarily indeterminate. No general principle may be laid down for such cases; each market must be treated on its own account, and a constitutional stage decision must weigh the predicted costs and benefits of the alternative institutional arrangements. This choice calculus must incorporate some recognition of the working properties of those institutions of politics that might be expected to operate in the absence of clearly defined constitutional-legal guidelines. The analysis suggests that a strong argument may often be adduced for locating the critical decision at the constitutional stage (rather than at any postconstitutional stage) of politics.

The contractarian logic may be compared and contrasted with the argument from rights that is often employed for a comparable purpose. In a sense, the whole contractarian evaluation commences from a presumption that individuals possess rights in the initial endowments, including talents, assigned to them. Indeed, without some such presumption, we find it difficult to define what an individual is. The contractarian cannot, however, extend the definition of rights to include the particular set of activities allowed to individuals. To take this step would remove from consideration the very issues to be analyzed, and, unless there should be some agreement on what activities are within an individual's rights, the prospects for reasoned argument are necessarily closed off too early.

The contractarian enterprise commences with the rights to initial endowments, but then aims to derive some agreed-on elements of social structure that allow individuals to use these endowments. I have suggested that the individual's rights to the personal and nonpersonal endowments in initial possession do not include the liberty to offer these rights (to goods and services) in exchange to others until and unless others grant such liberties. As I have elaborated at length elsewhere,[5] it is in the interest of every potential trader to extend such liberties of entry to all potential traders on opposing sides of markets. The order of "natural liberty" described by Adam Smith suggests that such maximal extensions of liberty should be constitutionally protected, and that this protection would emerge from agreement behind a veil of ignorance and/or uncertainty. But restraints or restrictions on the trading process through agreements on market shares, price setting, or any other of the generalized terms of trade cannot find support in the contractarian logic.

It is perhaps not surprising that the contractarian exercise yields the essential principles of classical liberalism. These principles may, of course, be justified on general utilitarian as well as contractarian grounds, and, in this application, these two philosophical approaches yield closely similar results. The advantage of the contractarian perspective has always seemed to me to lie in the potential for deriving a logic of institutional structure from the idealized choices of individuals who participate in the structure, as opposed to the equally idealized choice of an external observer who is presumed omniscient.

Notes

1. *See* Hardin, *The Utilitarian Logic of Liberalism,* 97 ETHICS, 47–74 (1986).

There are parallels as well as major differences between Hardin's analysis and my own.

The substantive results of my analysis are closer to those reached by John Gray in his more inclusive, and differently directed, paper. *See* Gray, *Contractarian Method, Private Property, and the Market Economy,* Jesus College, Oxford, 1986. Mimeo.

2. It is possible to derive the initial imputation of such rights from a contractarian logic. On this, *see* my THE LIMITS OF LIBERTY (1975).

3. *See* A.ALCHIAN, ECONOMIC FORCES AT WORK (1977).

4. The distinction between the rights of ownership and the liberties to enter exchange may seem strained in advanced societies. But, aside from the analytical usefulness for the argument here, the distinction was, presumably, relevant in the "silent trade" settings between tribes that characterized pre-exchange cultures. Such "silent trade" could never have been initiated unless tribes implicitly granted to other tribes the "liberties" of invading territorial rights to the extent of displaying wares along the shorelines. It is possible to think of intertribal relationships in which territorial rights were reciprocally respected but from which no trade could ever have emerged due to the absence of any reciprocal grant of liberties to enter potential exchanges.

5. *Towards the Simple Economics of Natural Liberty,* 40 KYKLOS 3–20 (1, 1987).

Public Choice Constitutionalism and Economic Rights

MARK TUSHNET*

In the constitutional tradition of the United States, adherents of every possible political position tend to find in the Constitution the warrant for their preferred political program. Because the terms used in the Constitution—at least those relevant to issues that are politically contentious[1]—are open to numerous interpretations, people tend to move to the more abstract level of constitutional theory to justify the interpretation that supports their program. In recent discussions, those who conventionally have been called political conservatives have drawn eclectically upon all the available theories,[2] just as those who conventionally have been called liberals have. Conservative reliance upon the theory of original intent has drawn perhaps the most attention, with conservative libertarianism running a close second. The liberal counterattack on conservative originalism has, in my view, been quite successful, at least in the forum of academic and perhaps public opinion.[3] In addition, in a culture drawn rather strongly to metaethical skepticism, appeals to moral philosophy, of the sort characteristic of libertarianism, are unlikely to succeed.[4]

Another popular theory of constitutional law has been called representation-reinforcing review. Its animating idea is that we can reconcile our commitment to judicial review with our commitment to democracy by using judicial review in the service of democracy. According to this approach, the courts should identify and remedy problems in the processes of democratic representation, but should not concern themselves with the results that fair democratic processes produce. Public choice constitutionalism is the conservative analogue of this theory of constitutional law. This essay examines public choice constitutionalism as a theory of constitutional law

* I would like to thank Bill Eskridge, Warren Schwartz, Gerry Spann, the participants in a workshop at the University of Southern California, and the participants in this volume for their comments on a draft of this essay.

and judicial review. The fundamental assumptions of public choice constitutionalism are "that persons seek to maximize their own utilities, . . . that their own narrowly defined economic well-being is an important component of those utilities," and, most important, that the preceding assumptions "apply [equally] in the political and the economic realms of behavior."[5] Public choice constitutionalism derives positive theories of constitution-making, of judicial interpretation of the Constitution, and of day-to-day politics from these assumptions.

This essay makes two general arguments. Sections I and II develop the first argument: that if we pursue the assumptions of public choice constitutionalism rigorously, the positive theories we can develop are rather weak. If we assume that people maximize personal economic well-being, we will not be able to tell with much precision what sort of constitution or judicial interpretation they will choose, while if we assume that they maximize some more broadly defined measure of well-being, precision disappears entirely. Section III develops the other general argument: that public choice constitutionalism fails to provide what an acceptable normative theory of constitutionalism requires—that is, an approach that if adopted by judges enforcing the Constitution places limits on what the judges can do in the course of limiting what legislatures can do.

The argument proceeds as follows. Relying on their assumptions, public choice constitutionalists believe that they can identify forms of "governmental failure." Just as governments properly act to remedy market failures, they argue, so should constitutions remedy governmental failure. The first section applies the same assumptions to the framers of a constitution, with particular attention to the Framers of the United States Constitution. It argues that, contrary to claims made by some public choice constitutionalists, there is little reason to believe that a constitution's framers will adopt a constitution that effectively resolves problems of "governmental failure."

Even if such a constitution is adopted, however, there will be a continuing need to ensure that its provisions are respected. The judiciary is one important institution that might serve that need. The second section argues that, contrary to some public choice claims, there is little reason to believe that judges, who on public choice assumptions are self-interested maximizers, will in fact act to ensure that the constitution's provisions are respected.

The final section shifts focus somewhat. It assumes that public choice constitutionalism is normatively acceptable, and that judges somehow can be brought to accept its premises. Nonetheless, the section argues, public choice constitutionalism is an inadequate theory of judicial review because it licenses judges to invalidate a wide range of legislation, including much that political conservatives would like to preserve. The scope of this power conflicts with another assumption of constitutionalism: that no power-holder have effectively unbridled power.

I should emphasize at the outset that one could adopt the positive theory of public choice constitutionalism at it applies to one or two of its three domains—constitution-making, judicial interpretation, or day-to-day politics—without adopting that theory as it applies to the others. In particular, there is no necessary connection between the view that day-to-day politics consists of bargaining and deal-making among interest groups—one of the conclusions of public choice constitutionalism—and the normative view that judges ought to police the functioning of day-to-day politics to ensure that the deals are in some sense fair, either procedurally or substantively.

I. The Framers as Maximizers

Readers of work by public choice constitutionalists might be struck by one common locution—the denial that their assumption that political actors are self-interested maximizers makes them Marxists, or at least "simple" Marxists.[6] In discussions of the framing of the Constitution, this locution takes the form of disclaiming that public choice constitutionalism had a precursor in Charles Beard's celebrated *Economic Interpretation of the Constitution*,[7] which made the then-heretical assumption that the Framers were indeed self-interested maximizers.[8]

Beard attempted to identify the specific array of self–interested forces in 1789. Before turning to that question, however, this essay examines the more general consequences of self-interest among the framers of any constitution. The general form of public choice constitutionalism's analysis of constitution-framing is quite familiar, at least in its normative version. The framers of a constitution know that they, and their successors,[9] will be self-interested. They know that after the constitution is adopted, they will attempt to use the public power created by the constitution to promote their own interests. Yet, the argument goes, they understand that this sort of rent-seeking behavior ultimately will cost them more than they will gain, as different groups seek, and sometimes win, advantages that are not distributed to everyone. In the absence of some external enforcement mechanism—that is, a constitution—people cannot credibly promise to refrain from such behavior, even though universal restraint is in everyone's interest. The framers therefore should want to create a constitution that makes promises to refrain from such behavior enforceable by severely limiting the opportunities for rent-seeking behavior.[10]

Perhaps the most fundamental difficulty with this argument is that framers who understand that engaging in rent-seeking behavior ultimately reduces everyone's wealth need *not* establish a constitutional system to restrain themselves. They need only refrain from such behavior. That is, if one sees long-term benefits from abstaining from certain acts, ordinary notions of rationality would lead one to abstain from those acts without placing oneself under constitutional constraints.[11]

The difficulty, of course, is that although an individual might believe it rational to abstain from the acts in question, he or she may need assurance that other people will also abstain, for otherwise his or her restraint could be exploited by others. Jonathan Macey has argued that this problem of collective action would lead self-interested framers to create constitutional constraints.[12] According to Macey, without such constraints, everyone has an immediate incentive to engage in short-term rent-seeking behavior. Characterizing this as "a classic prisoner's dilemma," Macey argues that "the dominant strategy . . . is to engage in rent seeking."[13]

This overlooks the long-term dimensions of the problem, however. In more formal terms, ordinary nonconstitutional politics involves an iterated prisoner's dilemma with no end period. In the classic prisoner's dilemma, one person can take advantage of the other's forebearance by acting selfishly—that is, by defecting from the cooperative solution. When the same situation presents itself over and over, however, defecting is not obviously beneficial, because the defector can expect that his or her partner will learn from prior rounds of the game and will no longer cooperate. Experimental evidence suggests that the best strategy when this sort of game occurs repeatedly is "tit for tat"—cooperation can be sustained by immediate but short-term retaliation against a defector.[14] Although formal game-theoretic modelling is as yet unable to establish that conclusion in complex social settings,[15] the idea that a cooperative strategy works in many situations has substantial intuitive appeal.

To see that appeal, the essence of a cooperative strategy should be spelled out. Consider people at the time of framing a constitution who believe that it is important to ensure that the government they create will not be able to introduce instability into their contractual relations. They will consider adopting a constitutional provision prohibiting the government from impairing the obligation of contracts. Should they do so? Some among them might argue that they should not, because, at some later time, they might assess the benefits and costs of impairing the obligation of contracts differently. At that later time, the costs of doing so will, of course, include a reduction in the credibility of promises that the government will not interfere with the obligation of contracts, with an attendant reduction in the value of contracts, as well as increased costs that will be incurred when people try to use the government to impair the obligation of contracts and other people resist that use. Still, the opponents of a constitutional provision will argue, it might be the case that, at the later time, the benefits of impairing the obligation of contracts might outweigh these costs, and it would be foolish to bar people from achieving a net benefit by enforcing an absolute prohibition on the impairment of the obligation of contracts.[16]

I will consider below some arguments suggesting that problems of collective action nonetheless remain. First, however, it may be helpful to consider some possible restructurings of Macey's argument. Consider a voter who sees short-term advantage in rent-seeking, but understands that engaging in such behavior will cause long-term net disadvantages, because other people will engage in similar behavior. Macey's argument needs qualification, because it seeks to impose constitutional constraints on short-term defection without explaining why the long-term perspective will not lead voters to refrain from defecting. Suppose, however, that the short-term perspective in fact overwhelms the long-term one, perhaps for reasons like those exposed by recent work in cognitive psychology.[17] If voters knew that fact, they might want to create constitutional constraints to keep *themselves*—not others—from succumbing to temptation. Such constraints then allow each to promise the others credibly that he or she will not engage in rent-seeking behavior. Yet, as Jon Elster and Thomas Schelling have shown, to call the desire to create such constraints "rational" raises the deepest questions about the very notion of rationality. It requires us to say that the calculations made at an earlier time (for example, in framing a constitution) should override the calculations made at a later one, when, at both times, the decision-maker rationally assesses all the costs and benefits of proposed courses of action. Why the earlier rational calculation should override the latter equally rational one is unclear.[18]

On a more superficial level, this reconstruction runs into self-contradiction: if short-term perspectives always dominate long-term ones, that domination will lead framers to refrain from imposing limits on their long-term behavior. The argument might be salvaged if it could be established that the time horizon of people during eras of ordinary politics was shorter than their time horizon during periods of constitution-framing; though Macey explicitly makes that assumption, he does not justify it.[19] Perhaps we could argue that time horizons get longer in crises, where crises are defined as external circumstances that overcome the cognitive distortions mentioned above. But we would need an independent theory of cognitive processes to make that argument work. In any event, as we will see, there is reason to believe that the Framers of the United States Constitution had an ordinary time horizon.[20]

Another version of the argument considers competition between ordinary politics and constitutional alternatives. There are two choices open to framers: they can adopt one of several possible constitutions, or they can continue with politics as it is. Macey, relying on work by Douglass North, argues that in the competition among possible constitutions, the one that constrains rent-seeking behavior will prevail.[21] Thus, if framers were required to select a constitution, they would choose that one. Here, too, the argument overlooks the point that framers of a constitution always act in a setting where there is already some sort of governmental order in place. Their choice is between a new governmental order and the existing one, which necessarily provides some benefits to some in the society. Once the problem is seen in this way, we once again must consider why framers, some of whom benefit from the existing system, would impose restraints on future governments that would have the effect of depriving some who presently benefit of their advantages.

Macey's arguments in favor of the proposition that the framers of a constitution would impose restraints on their future action all run into difficulty when confronted with the counterargument that framers would expect cooperation rather than a constitution to place constraints on individual behavior. The counterargument can be rejected, though, if cooperation will not occur even though it is in some sense the dominant strategy. First, political life involves more than the two parties modelled in prisoner's dilemmas.[22] Second, the complexity of political life obscures information, so that voters may not be sure who exactly has engaged in rent-seeking behavior. Here, too, the effect might be diminished by the fact that those who are harmed by particular acts of rent-seeking have an incentive to identify those who abandon cooperation to serve their short-term self–interest. Third, retaliation is costly and voters have an incentive to act as free riders, refraining from expending their own resources in retaliatory activity in the expectation that others will do so, with the result that less retaliation will occur than is necessary to ensure cooperation.

These difficulties indicate that some sort of constitution is likely to be necessary to supplement the long-term incentive to cooperate, coupled with majority rule. What can a constitution do to limit the amount of rent-seeking behavior that occurs? Roughly speaking, there are two kinds of provisions that might do the job. First, there are structural impediments to the enactment of legislation that results from rent-seeking behavior. Examples are federalism and the separation of powers. These structural impediments make it difficult to enact such legislation, because its supporters must mobilize in a number of constituencies over a relatively long period of time in order to ensure majorities in all the institutions of government. Structural impediments are attractive in constitutions, because it is possible to make them work by setting each institution within the government against the others. By letting ambition counteract ambition, as James Madison put it in *Federalist* 51, framers can obviate the need to create another institution to enforce whatever division of authority they devise. Unfortunately, structural impediments simply raise the cost of enacting legislation, not just the cost of enacting rent-seeking laws. The structural impediments make wealth-enhancing legislation such as effective antimonopoly laws more difficult to enact, and so may not be a completely attractive solution to the problem we have been examining.[23]

A second kind of provision to limit successful rent-seeking is a substantive provision barring the legislature from enacting laws that are predictably the result of rent-seeking behavior. Examples are the ex post facto and contracts clauses of the United States Constitution. Such provisions are more attractive than the substantive impediments because they are targeted at the precise problem of rent-seeking. The difficulty here is that such provisions are not self-enforcing in the way that the structural impediments can be. Framers need to create another institution to determine whether the legislature has violated one of the substantive prohibitions. As we will see in Section II, the creation of such an institution raises another set of difficult problems.

Overall, then, the public choice arguments for a constitution have some force, though not nearly as much as Macey claims. To summarize the argument so far: opportunism is constrained to some degree by self-interest directly, but indirect constraints may also be necessary. Majority rule makes pluralist bargaining and coalition-forming attractive as methods of identifying noncooperative behavior. It thereby provides one source of indirect constraint by overcoming some of the collective action problems associated with multi-person iterated prisoner's dilemmas. Because majority rule introduces new problems, though, additional constitutional constraints might usefully supplement majority rule. But to the extent that such constraints are self-enforcing, they impede the enactment of wealth-enhancing as well as wealth-reducing legislation. To the extent that they are not self-enforcing, the institution that enforces the additional constraints may introduce the possibility that there will be another form of rent-seeking behavior. It is an empirical question—and there would seem to be no evidence one could possibly gather which would decide it one way or the other—whether the costs of rent-seeking in the course of enforcing a constitution are lower than the costs of opportunism in the absence of one.

I turn now to consideration of the United States Constitution in light of the analysis developed to this point. We can begin by recalling the idea of a default condition in constitution-making, which will lead to a more directly Beardian point. Public choice constitutionalism draws some of its normative appeal from its requirement that constitutions be adopted unanimously by self-interested maximizers. In reality, of course, the provisions of constitutions are highly controversial. That is because some people believe that they will be better off with the proposed constitution, while others are satisfied with the default condition. Under these circumstances, framing a constitution is an exercise in ordinary politics, in which certain factions or interest groups seek to obtain from a restructured constitution benefits that they have been unable to obtain from the default condition. Consider the example of recent proposals to amend the United States Constitution to provide for a presidential line-item veto: the groups which favor it seek a constitutional amendment because they have been unable to muster enough political power in day-to-day politics to guarantee that Congress will act in what they view as responsible ways.

The strategy for proponents of a new constitution is straightforward. They should propose constitutional provisions that provide them the benefits they seek. In addition, they should attempt to restructure political arrangements so that, in the future, they will be more likely and their opponents less likely to prevail than under the default condition. Yet there remains a serious problem: how to get the new constitution adopted. The framers cannot use the existing forum of ordinary politics to do so, for that forum is precisely the one in which they have been unable to prevail. Thus, they must go outside the existing frame of politics.

The foregoing public choice analysis is, in its essentials, the one Beard offered. As the Framers saw it, ordinary politics in the states under the Articles of Confederation was choking off the type of economic development from which they would benefit; state governments were dominated by factions seeking to relieve small farmers of debts incurred as a result of the economic expansion in the wake of disruptions caused by the Revolution. The Framers proposed to disable the states from enacting such laws. The contracts clause did so directly. At least to some, the grant of power to Congress to regulate interstate commerce similarly disabled the states by automatically preempting state regulation of that commerce.[24] In addition, the Constitution's version of federalism and the separation of powers was designed to make it difficult for dispersed interest groups to use the power of the national government. The combination of direct disablement of state governments and hurdles to the enactment of national legislation led to a regime of effective nonregulation of the economy, which is what the Framers desired. Finally, the Framers adopted an extraconstitutional method of putting the new constitution into effect. They disregarded the limitations placed on their activities by the authorities that called the convention into being; they substituted ratification by nine states for the rule of unanimity required for amendments to the Articles of Confederation; and they sought ratification by special conventions rather than by state legislatures.

This construal of the framers' activities in public choice terms conceals two difficulties. One is easily addressed. The Constitution created a national government with substantial powers. The Framers had found themselves at a disadvantage in state legislatures. Why would they not be at a similar disadvantage in Congress? The public choice answer[25] is that a higher degree of organization and coordination was needed to gain control of Congress than of state governments: consider here the issues of the size of the House of Representatives and the staggered terms of office for the President, the House, and the Senate.[26] As Madison put it in *Federalist* 10, those with "a common motive to invade the rights of other citizens . . . will [find it] more difficult . . . to discover their own strength and to act in unison with each other. Besides other impediments, . . . where there is a consciousness of unjust or dishonorable purposes, communication is always checked by distrust in proportion to the number whose concurrence is necessary." Thus, though the Framers could not guarantee that Congress would enact laws favoring their interests, they could be reasonably confident that it, unlike state legislatures, would not enact laws harming them. Because the Framers did not need to mobilize Congress in order to advance their interests, making organization more difficult for their opponents improved their relative position.

The second difficulty is more fundamental. The direct limitations on state power can be taken as typical of the constitutional constraints on opportunistic behavior which it is the point of public choice constitutionalism to create. If cooperative behavior cannot be guaranteed by self-interest alone, cooperation must be enforced—defection and opportunism sanctioned—by some external agency. In the constitutional system of the United States, the courts have become that agency.[27] The existence of courts creates opportunities for rent-seeking, both with respect to the interpretation of the Constitution and more generally with respect to the definition of property rights in the society.[28] The next section examines the difficulties that the need for courts creates within public choice constitutionalism.

II. Judges as Maximizers

Readers of work by public choice constitutionalists might be struck by a second common observation—that judges simply have not been interpreting the Constitution in accordance with the conclusions of the public choice literature. The judges' behavior is, of course, an important positive phenomenon that the public choice perspective should be able to illuminate.

What conclusions can we draw from the assumption that judges are self-interested maximizers? The earliest work on this topic approached the question from a direction that turned out to be rather misleading. William Landes and Richard Posner argued that legislatures dominated by interest-group behavior would want to create an independent judiciary whose function would be to enforce the bargains struck in the legislature.[29] Yet, as Landes and Posner acknowledged, the very independence of the judges means that they have no obvious incentives to behave in the way that legislators want them to.[30]

Robert Tollison has augmented the analysis by treating judges as people interested in maximizing their money incomes, or at least the money under their control.[31] According to Tollison, judges will respond to the desires of legislators because the latter set the budget for the former. This argument might be supported by noting some aspects of the Constitution's treatment of judicial salaries. Under Article III, judges' salaries "shall not be diminished during their Continuation in Office." This can be contrasted, first, with the parallel provision concerning the President, whose "Compensation . . . shall neither be increased nor diminished" during his or her term of office, and, second, with early proposals to amend the Articles of Confederation to allow Congress to create a judiciary with judges whose salaries could be neither diminished nor increased.[32]

Nonetheless, as Macey has pointed out, Tollison's argument is ultimately unpersuasive.[33] First, there is another collective action problem: a legislature cannot punish an individual judge who fails to enforce legislative bargains, but must punish the judiciary as a whole.[34] Second, a budget-maximizing judge would decide cases with an eye not to the past legislature that enacted the statute (or the past Framers who adopted the Constitution) but rather with an eye to the present—or, more precisely, the next period's—legislature. Third, and perhaps most important, the argument cannot be salvaged by making it more complex. Landes and Posner argued that present legislatures would want judges to enforce past bargains. That is because present legislatures want their own promises to be credible. They want to offer their constituents the promise of continuing benefits. If present legislatures cannot ensure that their deals will be enforced in the future, they cannot offer anything of value to their constituents. However, this argument does not establish that present legislatures would rationally refrain from penalizing a court that enforced a past bargain, even though the present legislature would prefer a different deal. Such a contention rests, as we have seen, on a highly problematic conception of rationality according to which long-term or second-order preferences are more rational than short-term or first–order ones.

When judges act in response to what they anticipate the legislature will do, the purported advantages of the judiciary as a method of enforcing constraints on rent-seeking behavior decline. The judges might attempt to constrain legislatures by holding statutes unconstitutional, but the legislators can retaliate by reducing the judiciary's budget.[35] Even if we accept the public choice arguments about framing constitutions, we should note that budget-setting occurs during periods of ordinary politics, when—according to those arguments—the pressures for short-term rent-seeking behavior dominate the long-term desire to eliminate that behavior. In short, legislators will succumb to the temptation to violate the Constitution, and on Tollison's assumptions judges have incentives to let them get away with it.

Macey has suggested that judges act to maximize utility in a sense broader than money income. For Macey, utility includes "prestige within the academic and judicial communities and . . . self-image and sense of self-worth."[36] "Colleagues and academics will be quick to chastise [a judge] for a silly or erroneous decision validating or extending a pernicious interest group bargain."[37] The fulminations by public choice constitutionalists against judges who have, systematically and as a class, failed to enforce the Constitution rather strongly suggest that Macey's empirical claim is wrong—unless, of course, one gains prestige by being the target of public choice outrage, which does not appear to be what Macey has in mind.

More fundamentally, Macey's account requires that we have some theory of the sources of prestige and self-image. The most obvious candidate is that prestige and self-image are measures of approval by those currently holding power or, where it makes a difference, by the ideological successors to those holding power at the time of the judge's appointment.[38] If that is the correct theory of prestige and self-image, those qualities derive from acting in accordance with the wishes of one or another group of rent-seekers, and therefore cannot give judges incentives to constrain rent-seeking behavior. An example might come from the area of First Amendment law, where we might expect judges to rule in favor of claims supported by the "responsible" press because favorable comment in those newspapers is an important source of a judge's prestige.

There is another candidate for what judges maximize: their own power. This candidate has played an important part in discussions of the constitutional law of justiciability, which defines the occasions on which the courts will decide or refrain from deciding the merits of constitutional claims. One theme in these discussions is the erosion of the limitations the Supreme Court had, in the past, placed on itself. The erosion of justiciability restrictions might be seen as a direct result of the judges' desire to maximize their own power.[39] A somewhat more interesting suggestion is that the erosion of justiciability restrictions is designed to maintain the power of judges relative to the other agencies of government: with the rise of an activist legislature comes the rise of an activist judiciary. The idea that judges act to maintain their relative power feeds into a second theme in discussions of justiciability. In the early 1960s, Alexander Bickel described what he called the prudential aspects of justiciability.[40] Bickel recommended that courts use justiciability doctrines as devices to avoid decision on the merits in cases that were, in some sense, too difficult.

Bickel's normative orientation led him to define difficulty with references to questions of substantive law, but the prudential point can be given a positive twist. The relations between courts and legislatures, on this view, can be expected to reach an equilibrium. Avoidance devices allow the courts to maintain that equilibrium—that is, their relative power—by avoiding destabilizing decisions. Judges will use these avoidance devices when the issues on the merits are too highly contentious, in the sense that judges could expect legislatures to retaliate were the judges to decide the issues on the merits.[41] Judges treat their power to decide cases as an asset that they can use to preserve or increase their power; given the possibility of legislative retaliation, power is not always increased by exercising it.[42]

One might pursue this analysis by examining areas where the courts have enhanced their own power. For example, the courts have increasingly endorsed the use of flexible, discretionary equitable remedies for violations of the Constitution.[43] No matter what the content of a substantive constitutional provision is, judicial power is enhanced when courts have discretion to structure remedies rather than being constrained to issue a particular remedy.[44] The analysis of substantive provisions is more complex, largely because there are no obvious patterns in judicial behavior with respect to such provisions that might plausibly be connected to the desire to maximize power.

Yet the absence of such patterns is itself suggestive. Judges can enhance their power by requiring that everyone come to them for a determination that what they propose to do is permissible. On this view, judges exercise power both by prohibiting and by permitting actions, for what matters is that action cannot be taken unless the courts approve.[45] To be in a position to exercise this sort of power, though, judges must not make the law so clear that people can act with a sure understanding of what the law is. If the law is clear, no one will have to stop at courts to get the judges' approval. Thus, judicial power is maximized when the law is unclear.

To summarize, if we assume that judges are self-interested maximizers, we have little reason to believe that they will in fact enforce a constitution's provisions in ways that inhibit rent-seeking behavior. Either they will be responsive to incentives controlled by rent-seekers, or they will interpret the law to assure permanent uncertainty about its meaning.

III. Could the Courts Restrain Rent-Seeking?

Section I argued that a constitution embodying majority rule provides substantial incentives for voters to make credible promises to refrain from engaging in rent-seeking behavior. Structural impediments to legislation may raise the costs of such behavior, but they will also raise the costs of wealth-enhancing legislation. Substantive limitations on legislative power may be targeted at rent-seeking behavior. Such limitations are not self-enforcing, however. Section II argued that the agency that enforces those limitations has no substantial incentives to interpret them in ways that inhibit rent-seeking behavior. This section develops the latter point by assuming that judges wanted to inhibit such behavior and by exploring the options they have in identifying it. Moving to more directly normative concerns, here we will consider the ability of courts to identify economic legislation that results from wasteful rent-seeking behavior.

John Hart Ely's theory of representation-reinforcing review is the most prominent academic version of the theory that the Constitution should be interpreted to identify and invalidate legislation that results from rent-seeking behavior.[46] According to Ely, the courts can identify "discrete and insular minorities" who are at a systematic disadvantage in the legislative process. This disadvantage leads to the enactment of laws that do not adequately take into account the interests of those minorities.[47] Such laws can be described, alternatively, as ones that extract rents from the disadvantaged minorities.

The question then becomes: what are the criteria for identifying systematic losers in the political process? The interesting answers arise in considering the political dynamics of a pluralist system of majority rule where all relevant groups are enfranchised.[48] In such a system, every law generates people who lose in the sense that they are disadvantaged by the law—the minority that opposed enactment. That, however, is a consequence of majority rule (or, indeed, of any rule allowing the enactment of laws with less than unanimous support), and cannot in itself justify the courts' invalidation on grounds related to distortions, like rent-seeking, in the legislative process.[49] Thus, we must look for systematic losers, that is, those whose interests are undervalued across a relatively broad range of issues.

In a well-functioning pluralist system, the conditions under which there can be systematic losers are rather different than the ones Ely assumes. If every group could organize equally effectively around its interest, there would be no systematic losers. Each group would develop a hierarchy of goals and would bargain with other groups, with the result that each group would form part of a winning coalition on some of its issues and part of a losing coalition on others. For example, consider a small interest group that cares passionately about a single issue and is indifferent about every other issue. That group can win on its issue by locating some other group or coalition that is just short of a majority on its most important unresolved issue, and by agreeing to join a "supercoalition" whose program consists of the issues of the small group and the near-majority. These supercoalitions can, of course, consist of different groups at different times. The result would be a body of laws that does not systematically disadvantage any group.

There are several relatively minor difficulties with this account. First, for historical or other reasons, some groups might be what Bruce Ackerman calls "pariahs."[50] Pariah groups can be defined as those whose addition to an existing coalition leads to a net reduction in the coalition's strength, as some elements of the coalition withdraw out of repugnance at associating with the pariah group. As the name suggests, pariah groups are likely to arise in societies that disfranchise such groups. Although some pariah groups may persist for some time after enfranchisement, it seems likely that they cannot be a permanent feature of pluralist democracies. By definition, those who leave a coalition that would have become a majority with the addition of the pariah group are forgoing the opportunity to enact a policy they prefer. Some near-majority, it seems likely, will eventually understand the cost to it of treating the pariah group as a pariah rather than as another potential coalition partner.[51]

Second, opportunities for beneficial deals are not always easy to identify. Such deals involve complicated trade-offs, for example, to accomplish one goal to a substantial degree, to accomplish another to a smaller degree, and to yield entirely on a third. The complexity of pluralist bargaining means that it will work best if a specialized corps of deal-identifiers and deal-makers exists. This corps is analogous to the entrepreneurs in markets who identify unserved market demands and organize supply to meet those demands. Of course, we have a name for these specialists in organizing pluralist bargains. We call them politicians.

Third, market entrepreneurs can enter into contracts with their suppliers. These contracts mean that the entrepreneurs can guarantee delivery. Politicians, in contrast, cannot promise that their constituents will honor the deals they make. This raises essentially technological problems. For example, to the extent that trades are made simultaneously, the problem of breach is reduced. Thus, politicians can improve the process of political bargaining by enacting "Christmas tree" laws in which everyone gets his or her share at the same time, by eliminating germaneness restrictions on what a legislature can consider as an amendment to a pending bill, eliminating the rule that a statute can deal with only one subject, and the like.[52] In addition, politicians can enhance the credibility of their promises if they do not have to recur to their constituents. Long terms of office and systems of campaign financing that give incumbents advantages over challengers are devices that make it more likely that pluralist bargaining will work to the systematic disadvantage of no single group.[53]

This description of a pluralist democracy suggests ways in which it can overcome the modest difficulties discussed above. Yet there is something obviously out of focus in the description. The fundamental problem arises from the falsity of the assumption that every group is equally able to organize itself for participation in pluralist bargaining. Familiar arguments establish the assumption's falsity. Once enough people are potentially interested in organizing, each will understand (a) that any law that results from organized activity will confer benefits on everyone in the group, (b) that the benefits accruing to him or her are unlikely to exceed the direct or opportunity costs of participating in the organized activity, and (c) that he or she should therefore refrain from participating, hoping to be a free rider on the activities of others.[54] Thus, as the argument is conventionally put, large groups will be at a systematic disadvantage in the pluralist bargaining process, compared to smaller ones.[55]

I present two types of criticism of this argument. The first focuses on efforts to use the free-rider argument to establish that at least some economic regulations result from systematic distortions of the legislative process and that the courts should hold such regulations unconstitutional.[56] By developing a series of examples, I argue that the free-rider argument provides insufficient guidance to the courts. When coupled with the argument of Section II, this shows that public choice constitutionalism will not do as a theory of judicial review. In the course of discussing these examples, I raise a number of conceptual issues. For example, I suggest that the free–rider argument does not readily translate into an argument about large and small groups insofar as we are concerned with the actual operation of politics.

A classic rent-seeking statute was presented to the Court in *Williamson v. Lee Optical Co.*[57] Oklahoma prohibited opticians from fitting duplicate lenses without a prescription from an ophthalmologist or optometrist (hereafter, eye doctor). Essentially all that this statue did was to generate business for eye doctors, thereby raising the price of duplicate lenses. The rent-seeking story, of course, is that the well-organized and, relative to consumers, small group of eye doctors was able to lobby effectively for the statute, while the diffuse consumer interest could not organize as effectively to oppose it. More generally, economic regulation is producer-protective regulation.

Lee Optical suggests several difficulties with public choice constitution- alism as a normative theory of judicial review. First, it shows how broad the scope of the theory is. The statute in *Lee Optical* has two economic consequences: duplicate lenses are supplied at an inefficient level relative to potential demand, and the beneficiaries extract rents from consumers. One might frame the constitutional issue as whether the latter distributional effect is sufficient under the Constitution to justify the former inefficiency effect. Normative public choice constitutionalism answers that distributional effects are always constitutionally irrelevant or pernicious. As a matter of ordinary doctrine, constitutionally irrelevant or pernicious effects cannot justify *any* legislation.[58] Thus, normative public choice constitutionalism would find impermissible that large body of legislation whose goal is primarily distributional.[59] Second, though less significant, extant constitutional doctrine has—barely—the resources to use public choice constitutionalism as the basis for invalidating economic regulation under the due process clause. It lacks almost entirely the resources to use it as the basis for invalidating statutes whose goals are straightforwardly distributional.[60] Yet, as we have just seen, such statutes are inextricably connected to regulatory statutes, in that such statutes combine inefficiency with distributional effects. Normative public choice constitutionalism is therefore likely to be doctrinally awkward, at least in the short run.[61]

Third, and probably most important, the story underlying *Lee Optical* is more complicated than I have indicated as yet. After all, the statute disadvantaged not only consumers generally but opticians as well, because the eye doctors would be able to capture some of the profits available from the increased prices for duplicate lenses, if only because they can offer a package service (prescription plus lenses) while opticians must rely on buyers to come to them after getting a prescription elsewhere. The question, then, is: why, if at all, do eye doctors have an organizational advantage over opticians (who can, after all, claim to be serving the public interest in keeping prices down)? It may be true that eye doctors are small and well-organized relative to consumers, but it is hard to see why they would be small and organized relative to opticians.[62] Perhaps there is some hidden deal by which opticians' opposition was bought off,[63] but in the absence of such a deal the case for describing the statute as the result of systematic distortions in the relative ability to use the pluralist bargaining process is substantially weakened. Or perhaps eye doctors, being wealthier than opticians, find it easier to organize. Note, however, that if the marginal cost of organizing decreases as a person's wealth increases, and if organized groups can appropriate rents better than less organized ones, the long-term effect will be to increase the wealth of the already wealthy. This resonates with the quasi-Marxist aspects of public choice constitutionalism, and might indeed justify fairly aggressive judicial scrutiny of rent-seeking legislation.

This last point can be elaborated by considering a second example of public choice constitutionalism. The story about differential ability to organize has some appeal when told about classical economic regulation of the sort involved in *Lee Optical*. It has less surface appeal when told about so-called social legislation of the sort prominent in the 1970s. Social regulation includes antidiscrimination laws and environmental and consumer protection laws. The beneficiaries of social regulation appear to be diffuse and presumptively at an organizational disadvantage—relative to the smaller, but still large, group of businesses burdened by the regulations. How, then, can the public choice story be elaborated to account for social regulation? A standard elaboration is the "big business vs. small business" story.[64] Large businesses can hire affirmative-action officers, whereas small ones cannot; large businesses can hire enough engineers to assure compliance with environmental and consumer protection laws, whereas small ones cannot. One might account for social regulation directly under this elaboration: large businesses seek to have such regulations enacted in order to gain a competitive advantage over smaller ones. Or, more plausibly, one might argue that because big business is less disadvantaged by social regulation than small business, the total amount of opposition to social regulation is reduced, despite the organizational advantages business in general has in opposing regulations desired by large numbers of people—each of whom will, however, benefit only a small amount from the enactment of regulation.

Mark Kelman has argued that, though the "big business vs. small business" story may in the end turn out to be correct, the claim that it has already been empirically confirmed is unfounded.[65] There are theoretical reasons to disbelieve the story as a general account of social regulation. The conditions under which it is rational for large businesses to seek regulation in order to gain competitive advantage appear to be quite restrictive, largely because large businesses must expend resources to secure regulation over the opposition of smaller business and the competitive advantage might not exceed the costs of securing the regulation.[66]

It is also unclear why large businesses would have an organizational advantage over consumers, or indeed—to revert to *Lee Optical*—why producers would have such an advantage over consumers. Consider the eye doctor-optician conflict in *Lee Optical*. Perhaps there are more opticians than eye doctors. Yet it seems certain that there are enough of the latter for serious free-rider problems to arise. At this point, much depends on how one models free-rider problems. If they increase with the size of the group, large groups would face greater organizational problems than small ones, even though both types face some free-rider problems. Alternatively, if free-rider difficulties appear immediately and at their maximum when some threshold is crossed, it seems quite unlikely that eye doctors would actually have an organizational advantage. The notion of individual rationality that drives the free-rider analysis seems to me more compatible with the "threshold" model with a relatively low threshold. If so, the entire public choice story about rent-seeking behavior is likely to be irrelevant for all practical purposes, because almost all interest groups will be above the threshold and none will have a systematic advantage over any other.

In addition, the benefits of regulation, spread across the class of large businesses, are likely to be smaller relative to the size of each business, while the burdens, similarly spread across small businesses, are likely to be larger relative to the size of each. If a person's willingness to expend resources varies with the amount of benefit or burden relative to size or income, the increased intensity of opposition to regulation may compensate to some extent for differentials in ability to organize arising from size alone.

The burden of the argument so far has been that the analysis of legislation as the result of rent-seeking behavior is likely to be quite complex in many cases. That complexity may be enough to raise substantial questions about public choice constitutionalism as a normative theory of constitutional law. Complexity gives judges substantial opportunities to manipulate the analysis by making concealed or open empirical assumptions, by stressing aspects of the issue that support their preferred resolution, and by overlooking or downplaying aspects that point in the other direction.[67] Yet, if a normative theory of constitutional law lets judges do whatever they independently want to do, it has little to commend it—particularly if we assume, as in Section II and public choice constitutionalism generally, that judges, like the rest of us, are self-interested maximizers.

The problem of manipulation can be seen by using examples of left-wing public choice constitutionalism.[68] I have already used *Lee Optical* to suggest that a particular model of the cost of organizing might justify suspicion of legislation that aids interest groups composed largely of wealthy people. Claus Offe has used public choice concepts to analyze the conflict between business and labor.[69] He argues that, although business can measure its interests solely by considering profits, labor must be concerned with a range of interests, from wages to working conditions to time available for leisure. As a result, he argues, labor must organize itself internally along two lines: a bureaucratic structure concerned with rationally maximizing the goals it is given, and a democratic structure designed to communicate to the bureaucracy what the members want. Further, labor can accomplish its goals only by collective activity, which means that some sort of solidarity must be developed to replace an entirely individualist orientation. This is a difficult enough task, but, in addition, its accomplishment may be self-limiting. Offe argues that unions must be large if they are to be strong enough to carry out successful industrial action. As they grow, so does their internal bureaucracy, weakening the forces of internal democracy and reducing their members' attachment to the union. This limits their ability to carry out successful collective action.

Along similar lines but more concerned with the particular structure of American politics, Joshua Cohen and Joel Rogers argue that workers rationally choose short-term gains through collective action rather than seeking larger potential gains through broader political action.[70] The structure of United States government makes it difficult to coordinate challenges to the free enterprise system: separation of powers and federalism place substantial barriers in the way of coordinated anti-free-enterprise action. Consider, for example, how difficult it would be to develop an effective program to limit the ability of long-established companies to relocate their plants if economic circumstances, as determined by the companies' managers, warranted. The problems are most likely to be experienced by one community at a time, but localized regulations might be held to violate the commerce clause by impeding the free flow of capital and, in any event, are likely to be ineffective in light of the ability of managers to mobilize and relocate financial assets rather than plants. Securing legislation from Congress would be difficult, too, because of such characteristics of the separation of powers as the staggered terms mentioned earlier.[71] These difficulties place workers at a structural disadvantage in political contention.[72]

This example does more than demonstrate that public choice constitutionalism can be used, if one wants to, to identify systematic disadvantages in the political process of almost any sort,[73] and that it is therefore unlikely to be a suitable normative theory of judicial review. It also returns us to the Beardian theme of Section I. It confirms the view of the Framers as ordinary maximizers by demonstrating that even the structural impediments to rent-seeking legislation do not operate neutrally, but rather impede the adoption of a particular type of rent-seeking legislation while preserving the opportunities for business to secure adoption of "producer protective" laws.

IV. Conclusion

From a normative point of view, of course, the ultimate issue is always comparative: is normative public choice constitutionalism better along some dimension than the competing normative constitutional theories? Proponents of public choice constitutionalism appear to believe that their case is bolstered by the apparent scientific precision of the economic theory of public choice. That is, they claim that public choice constitutionalism is preferable at least along the dimension of precision. This essay has argued, to the contrary, that the theory is not at all precise when applied to the actual operation of politics. The public choice case for constitutional constraints other than majority rule—particularly the case for judicially enforced substantive constraints—remains to be made out. Public choice constitutionalism might be preferable on some other ground, though I must acknowledge what should be apparent, anyway: my skepticism about that claim, too. For the present, public choice constitutionalism, like virtually every other normative theory of constitutional law, provides some interesting and occasionally helpful metaphors that can assist—and mislead—us as we think about the meaning of the Constitution.[74]

Notes

1. For a discussion of this qualification, see M. TUSHNET, RED, WHITE, AND BLUE: A CRITICAL ANALYSIS OF CONSTITUTIONAL LAW 61–62 (1988).

2. Perhaps the best example of conservative eclecticism is R. EPSTEIN, TAKINGS: PRIVATE PROPERTY AND THE POWER OF EMINENT DOMAIN (1985).

3. The reference is to one reading of the constitutional significance of the debate over the nomination of Robert Bork to the Supreme Court.

4. See Tushnet, *The Relevance of the Framers' Natural Law Views to Contemporary Constitutional Interpretation,* in CONSTITUTIONALISM IN PERSPECTIVE: THE UNITED STATES CONSTITUTION IN TWENTIETH CENTURY POLITICS 182 (S.Thurow ed. 1988).

5. Buchanan, *Politics Without Romance: A Sketch of Positive Public Choice Theory and Its Normative Implications* 13–14, in 2 THE THEORY OF PUBLIC CHOICE (J. Buchanan ed. 1984).

6. See, e.g., Tollison, *Public Choice and Legislation,* 74 VA. L.REV. 339, 367 (1988). Tollison, plainly not up to speed on Marxism, says that while "simple Marxism pits Capital against Labor," public choice approaches "just stress . . . the relative costs of organizing for effective action [by] [a]ny group from any part of society. . . ." For a discussion of the conflict between capital and labor, see Section III below.

7. C. BEARD, ECONOMIC INTERPRETATION OF THE CONSTITUTION (1913).

8. For examples of the disclaimers, see Landes & Posner, *The Independent Judiciary in Interest Group Perspective,* 18 J.L. & ECON. 875, 892 n.32 (1975); Posner, *The Constitution as an Economic Document,* 56 GEO. WASH. L.REV. 4, 4

(1987). *But see* Macey, *Competing Economic Views of the Constitution,* 56 GEO. WASH. L.REV. 50 (1987) (basically approving discussion of convergence between Beard and public choice constitutionalism).

9. To the extent that the framers care about their successors, an issue that raises quite thorny problems.

10. *See, e.g.* Macey, *supra* note 8, at 74–75; Macey, *Transaction Costs and the Normative Elements of the Public Choice Model,* 74 VA. L.REV. 471, 481 (1988).

11. And, of course, if one does not anticipate long-term benefits—that is, if one thinks that one will be better off by engaging in rent-seeking behavior—one would not impose constitutional constraints anyway.

12. Macey, *supra* note 8, at 74–75.

13. *Id.* at 75.

14. *See* R.AXELROD, THE EVOLUTION OF COMPETITION (1984).

15. *See* P.ORDESHOOK, GAME THEORY AND POLITICAL THEORY: AN INTRODUC- TION 448 (1986) ("infinite repetition, preplay communication, tradition, and evolutionary selection may yield a cooperative equilibrium that requires the enforcement activities of no external agent").

16. This conclusion becomes even more plausible if the definition of an "impairment of the obligation of contracts" is contestable, as, for example, when the courts distinguish between impermissible impairments of obligations and permissible adjustments of remedies. *See* Home Building & Loan Ass'n v. Blaisdell, 290 U.S. 398 (1934). When the definition is contestable, costs will be incurred even in the presence of a constitutional prohibition, as people attempt to defend their proposals as not being within the definition of the prohibition.

17. For a survey, *see* R.NISBETT & L.ROSS, HUMAN INFERENCE: STRATEGIES AND SHORTCOMINGS OF SOCIAL JUDGMENT (1980).

18. J.ELSTER, ULYSSES AND THE SIRENS: STUDIES IN RATIONALITY AND IRRATIONALITY (rev. ed. 1984); T.SCHELLING, *The Intimate Contest for Self- Command,* in CHOICE AND CONSEQUENCE 57 (1984).

19. Macey, *supra* note 10, at 481. An alternative argument would be that, under some circumstances, short-term interests could be advanced only by adopting a constraining constitution, perhaps as a trade for particular short-term interests. It seems clear that what is interesting in this argument are the circumstances under which it would hold. Yet it is not apparent how the assumptions of public choice constitutionalism would lead to a specification of those circumstances.

20. *See* text accompanying note 24 *infra.*

21. Macey, *supra* note 10, at 482–83.

22. *See* D.MUELLER, PUBLIC CHOICE 116–17 (1979). If, however, the

constitution creates a system of majority rule, voters will have strong incentives to form coalitions. Those coalitions reduce each issue to a two-party confrontation. If the coalitions differ from issue to issue, those in the majority on a later issue can retaliate against those in a prior majority who had engaged in rent-seeking behavior so long as the earlier defectors are not themselves part of the later majority coalition. *See* M.TUSHNET, *supra* note 1, at 79. At the same time, of course, majority rule introduces opportunities for rent seeking. The existence of such opportunities makes it impossible to argue that majority rule always and only identifies cooperative solutions. Yet, as I argue in Section III, the circumstances under which rent-seeking is likely to be successful are rather more restrictive than many public choice constitutionalists have suggested.

23. Of course, if one believes that there are actually few possible types of wealth-enhancing legislation, the cost that structural impediments impose in making even these difficult to enact might be outweighed by the benefits accruing to the fact that no rent-seeking laws could be enacted either.

24. For example, both the majority and the concurring opinions in Gibbons v. Ogden, 22 U.S. (9 Wheat.) 1 (1824), agreed that Congress's power to regulate interstate commerce completely displaced state authority to do so, though they differed over what constituted an exercise of the power to regulate interstate commerce.

25. For a discussion of other arguably more plausible answers, see Tushnet, *Constitutional Interpretation and Judicial Selection: A View from* The Federalist Papers, 61 S.CAL. L.REV. 1669 (1988).

26. The framers might have thought as well that they were better able to organize nationally, but there is no obvious public choice justification for such a belief.

27. That agency could have been something other than the judiciary, but the problems are inherent in having an institution to enforce constitutional limitations.

28. *Cf.* Coleman, *Competition and Cooperation,* 98 ETHICS 76, 83 (1987) (definition of force and fraud, essential to creation of property rights, rests on collective morality). Because force and fraud are defined, for purposes of determining property rights, by some institution—the courts—opportunities for rent-seeking behavior designed to influence that institution will always exist.

29. Landes & Posner, *supra* note 8.

30. *Id.* at 886–87.

31. Tollison, *supra* note 6, at 345–46.

32. U.S.CONST. Art. III, §1; Art. II, §1, cl. 7; M.KAMMEN, THE ORIGINS OF THE AMERICAN CONSTITUTION: A DOCUMENTARY HISTORY 32, 35 (1987).

33. Macey, *supra* note 10, at 498. *See also* Eskridge, *Politics Without Romance: Implications of Public Choice Theory for Statutory Interpretation,* 74 VA. L.REV. 275, 305 n.88 (1988).

34. An individual judge might be denied promotion to a higher court—although the rate of such promotions in the federal bench is rather low to begin with so the threat of denying promotion cannot be substantial, and the salary differentials between trial level and appellate judges in the federal system are relatively small anyway.

35. Or by refusing to increase the budget in line with either inflation or an increase in demand for judicial services. *See* R.POSNER, THE FEDERAL COURTS: CRISIS AND REFORM 97–99 (1985).

36. Macey, *supra* note 10, at 498 n.80. Tollison might object to this formulation on the sensible ground that it cannot generate "testable proposition[s]." *See* Tollison, *supra* note 6, at 346.

37. Macey, *supra* note 10, at 498.

38. Section III argues that, for many purposes, there are few differences between these two groups.

39. The fact that such self-imposed limitations exist at all is discussed immediately below.

40. A.BICKEL, THE LEAST DANGEROUS BRANCH (1962).

41. For a more precise formulation, see H.FINK & M.TUSHNET, FEDERAL JURISDICTION : POLICY AND PRACTICE 321 (2d ed. 1987) ("the Court restricts standing where the public would disapprove of a conservative result on the merits, and allow[s] it where the public would accept such a result"). I should note my own skepticism about this as a positive account of the avoidance doctrines, although Justice Powell expressly referred to the possibility of congressional retaliation as a justification for them. *See* United States v. Richardson, 418 U.S. 166, 191 (1974) (Powell, J., concurring).

42. This is consistent with a casual, empirical description of the court's behavior.

43. *See, e.g.,* Milliken v. Bradley, 433 U.S. 267 (1977); Hutto v. Finney, 437 U.S. 678 (1978).

44. *See* G.MCDOWELL, EQUITY AND THE CONSTITUTION (1982).

45. An important statement of this point, though put perhaps a bit strongly, is C.BLACK, THE PEOPLE AND THE COURT (1960) (emphasizing Court's role in legitimizing statutes it does not strike down).

46. J.ELY, DEMOCRACY AND DISTRUST (1980). The analysis that follows draws heavily on M.TUSHNET, *supra* note 1, at 94–107.

47. Ely has a particular theory about how this occurs, which need not be addressed here.

48. Obviously disfranchisement makes it possible for there to be systematic losers. The remedy for disfranchisement, though, is enfranchisement—not invalidation of substantive legislation. *See* M.TUSHNET, *supra* note 1, at 83–89.

49. *But see* text accompanying note 28 *supra* (all laws characterizable as rent-seeking).

50. Ackerman, *Beyond* Carolene Products, 98 HARV. L.REV. 713, 732–33 (1985).

51. Many of the most common intuitions about discrete and insular minorities are strongly affected by the fact that such minorities historically were disfranchised. My view is that the proposition that there are few pariah groups is confirmed by casual empiricism; I find it difficult to identify pariah groups who have real political programs that are not responded to by someone. (Consider in this connection the Unification Church and the American Nazi Party.)

52. *See, e.g.,* C.NUTTING & R.DICKERSON, CASES AND MATERIALS ON LEGISLATION 300–313 (5th ed. 1978).

53. Entrenchment in office is, of course, likely to produce legislation that provides advantages to legislators as such—for example, exemptions from general antidiscrimination laws and the like. These exemptions seem to me to have a relatively small impact.

54. M.OLSEN, THE LOGIC OF COLLECTIVE ACTION (1965).

55. *See, e.g.,* Eskridge, *supra* note 33; Macey, *supra* note 10.

56. A weak version of public choice constitutionalism as a theory of judicial review might contend that in the presence of systematic distortions, courts should demand substantial justifications for the legislation at issue. Yet, if the courts have criteria to decide that laws are unjustified in these circumstances, it is difficult to see why they should not use those same criteria to assess all laws, even if they cannot identify systematic distortions. For a discussion, see M.TUSHNET, *supra* note 1, at 180–81.

57. 348 U.S. 483 (1955). For other examples, see Daniel v. Family Security Co., 336 U.S. 220 (1949) (statute prohibiting funeral directors from selling funeral insurance held constitutional); United States v. Carolene Products Co., 304 U.S. 144 (1938) (statute prohibiting sale of filled milk held constitutional; for subsequent developments, see Strong, *A Post-Script to* Carolene Products, 5 CONST. COMM. 185 (1988)).

58. A weaker formulation is that a constitutionally irrelevant distributional effect will always be overcome by any inefficiency whatever. That formulation is sufficient for my purposes as well, for inefficiency is always arguably present.

59. *See* G.STONE, L.SEIDMAN, C.SUNSTEIN, & M. TUSHNET, CONSTITUTIONAL LAW 736–38 (1986).

60. R.EPSTEIN, *supra* note 2, attempts to provide a doctrinal framework for such results, but it is universally agreed, even by Epstein, that his analysis is eccentric. *See also* Pennell v. City of San Jose, 108 S.Ct. 849 (1988).

61. Structural due process in the form of requiring that the constitutionality of statutes be determined with reference to their stated goals might defer the confrontation. *See* M.TUSHNET, *supra* note 1, at 209–10.

62. For example, organizations of both groups could provide what Olsen, *supra* note 54, calls selective benefits to their members.

63. For a discussion of such deals, see Tushnet, *Rethinking the Dormant Commerce Clause,* 1979 WIS. L.REV. 125, 137.

64. *See, e.g.,* Bartel & Thomas, *Direct and Indirect Effects of Regulation: A New Look at OSHA's Impact,* 28 J.L. & ECON. 1 (1985); Linneman, *The Effects of Consumer Safety Standards: The 1973 Mattress Flammability Standard,* 23 J.L. & ECON. 461 (1980). Both articles are discussed critically in Kelman, *On Democracy-Bashing: A Skeptical Look at the Theoretical and "Empirical" Practice of the Public Choice Movement,* 74 VA.L.REV. 199 (1988).

65. Kelman, *supra* note 64, at 260–68.

66. For a critique of this argument, see Salop, Scheffman, & Schwartz, *A Bidding Analysis of Special Interest Regulation: Raising Rivals' Costs in a Rent Seeking Society* 102, in THE POLITICAL ECONOMY OF REGULATION: PRIVATE INTERESTS IN THE REGULATORY PROCESS (Federal Trade Commission 1984).

67. Of course, the ultimate issue is comparative complexity. See Section IV.

68. *See generally* ANALYTICAL MARXISM (J.Elster & J. Roemer eds. 1986).

69. The two paragraphs that follow are taken directly from M.TUSHNET, *supra* note 1, at 104–5.

70. *See also* Oestreicher, *Urban Working-Class Political Behavior and Theories of American Electoral Politics, 1870–1940,* 74 J. AM. HIST. 1257 (1988).

71. Recent federal legislation on plant closings may undermine this argument, at least if it is taken to claim that securing such legislation is not merely difficult but is impossible. It is too early to tell, though, whether the legislation is effective. It should be noted that the legislation imposes no substantive limits on a company's ability to relocate; it only requires timely notification that relocation will occur.

72. Note how these responses combine with the public choice analysis of organized interest groups such as unions. Offe and Cohen and Rogers argue that labor is at a systematic disadvantage vis-à-vis capital; public choice theorists argue that consumers are at a systematic disadvantage vis-à-vis organized labor. The interaction

of these processes may be particularly damaging to labor, whose gains from their advantage over consumers are limited by the power of capital and are confined to labor unions and their members. This may lead consumers to see organized labor as a primary source of their problems and further weaken, or at least stabilize the weakness of, labor.

73. The degree of complexity is indicated by the fact that the discussion in this essay has not addressed any of the arguments made in Ely's presentation of the general theory.

Civil Rights and Property Rights

WILLIAM H. RIKER*

For the last half century, the Supreme Court has assumed that civil rights and property rights can be sharply distinguished, and that civil rights, the "preferred rights" of *U.S. v. Carolene Products,*[1] merit greater judicial protection than property rights. Weingast and I have already shown that the Court is unjustified in its assumption that legislatures can or will protect property rights.[2] Here I propose to show that the notion of preferred rights is in itself unjustifiable.

First, I will show that the two kinds of rights, civil and property, are indistinguishable in origin. Governments grant them for the same kinds of instrumental reasons: that is, to make some part of society work better. Of course, there is a difference in the parts of society each set of rights concerns. Property rights help us feed, clothe, and shelter ourselves well, and civil rights (like freedom of speech, voting rights, and rights to a fair trial) help us operate our politics liberally. But, since the economic and political parts of society, while distinguishable abstractly, are interlocked in practice, the rights associated with each realm are similarly intermingled in the real world.

Second, I will show that the practical and moral justifications of civil rights and property rights are about the same, which is what one would expect when there isn't any discernible hierarchy of politics and economics. Consequently, I will conclude that there is no moral or practical reason to treat one kind of rights as especially deserving of judicial protection. Indeed, from the point of view of the justifications of rights offered here, it is positively immoral to elevate one kind of rights over the other.

In developing these themes, I will first look at the origin of some civil and property rights and then consider their justifications in terms of their origins. Consequently, my justifications of legal rights will be quite unlike the justifications of moral rights in seventeenth-century social contract theories modernized today by writers like Rawls and Nozick. In conclusion, I will show how the rhetorical properties of the social contract justifications

---

* Work on this essay was facilitated by a grant from the John M. Olin Foundation.

49

have perhaps contributed to current judicial (and political) misunderstanding of legal property rights and hence to their consequent insecurity.

I. The Origin of Rights

I start with the observation that, historically, conventional rights always have grantors and grantees. This was Blackstone's notion and is fundamental in Anglo-American law, though not always in Anglo-American social philosophy.

There are devices by which philosophers have sought to finesse the existence of a grantor. One is the concept of natural or human rights, which requires no grantor except nature or God. But natural right is a moral concept, not a descriptive one. To say a right is natural (or human) is to say it is a generic quality of human beings. Given, however, that in the real world rights are defined and enforced and ignored and violated by governmental acts, this generic feature is not descriptively observable. It may well exist morally, of course, but that means natural right is a moral concept, not a descriptive one.

Similarly, the notion of a social contract conflates grantors and grantees into the same persons. That is, in this mythology, the ultimate holders grant power to rulers who in turn protect the grantors' rights, so the right-holder is thus also the grantor. But it is not usually claimed that the transition from a state of nature to a state of society is a real historical event. Rather, it is a stylized fact invented to provide a rationale for grantors to give up a valuable privilege. It is true, that, occasionally, people who are cut off from their previous membership in a society with customary legal rights recreate them constitutionally. The eighteenth-century bills of rights in America are examples, as are the more primitive constitutions of mining camps in the California gold rush.[3] Such constitutions do define rights, but they are not initial contracts in the sense of Locke and Rousseau. Rather, they are determined attempts by suddenly-isolated groups to preserve customary civility, in which rights granted by previous rulers played an important part.

True social contracts, defining previously nonexistent rights, are unknown to the historical record. And this is as it should be, because social contracts that create a society involve a logical contradiction: social values exist only in terms of society. No one wants or needs property, or free speech, or the right to vote in Crusoe-like isolation. So the motivation for seeking rights, the perception and anticipation of value, implies the previous existence of the society that a social contract is itself supposed to create. Likewise, true Lockean social contracts between an existent society and a government are historically unknown, because there is no instance of a state of nature or of a society without an existing government. Sometimes new governments replace old ones (as at the end of successful invasions or revolutions), but no contracts are made; the victors are wholly intent on seizing office. Victors may subsequently grant rights as a matter of prerogative, yet this is certainly not a social contract. Aside from moments of conquest, however, governments always exist. Even the most primitive societies always have judges who enforce a customary public law, and nonhuman primate groups always have an "alpha male." And if governments, by definition possessed of the force of society, always exist, they can hardly make enforceable contracts binding themselves with people in a state of nature.

Putting aside, then, natural rights and social contracts as justificatory rather than descriptive notions, I reiterate that rights always involve grantors and grantees. To explain the origin of any particular right, therefore, one must explain the motivations and reasoning of both parties.

The petitioners are easy to understand. Since they seek some right, they presumably feel deprived or endangered without it, and they anticipate that the right will nourish and protect them. Consequently, their self-interest drives them to petition for it.

It is not so easy to understand the grantors. At the time of the petition, the right does not exist, and it is not clear why the grantors should grant it. At the time of the grant, the society is by definition stable: that is, there is a government capable of granting rights, or petitioners would not petition for them. So the grantors, as rulers of a stable society, presumably need not respond—although there are revolutionary occasions in which only foolish rulers would not do so. Yet, for every successfully established right, rulers do respond. Why? Assuming grantors are, like petitioners, self-interested persons, then it is also necessary to assume that they grant rights because they believe the petitioners' possession of the rights will itself enhance the grantors' position.

To explain the origins of rights, therefore, we must look for self-interested motives for grantors as well as petitioners. Since the origin of many rights, especially property rights, is hidden in the past or confused by many petitions, it is not easy to identify particular motives for particular rights. I have chosen, therefore, two rights as concrete examples—one civil, one property—and I now recount their history briefly.

II. The Origin of Free Speech

One civil right with an easily-identifiable origin is freedom of speech. Its earliest form is the right of free speech for members of the House of Commons, a right that seems to have been regularly claimed in the fifteenth century, though it became clearly recognized only under the Tudors. (I attach, as Appendix I, the relevant portions of a speech in 1523 by Sir Thomas More petitioning, as Speaker, for this right in what were apparently customary terms. This full speech has been saved for us not only because of More's elegance and eloquence, but of course also because of his martyrdom.)

The outstanding feature of More's speech is his emphasis on the King's interests. In the High Court of Parliament, "nothing is entreated but matter of weight and importance concerning your realm and your own royal estate." The members are "right wise and politic," but men are wise in different ways; not all are "like well witted," and not every man is "like well spoken." Indeed, just as "much folly is uttered with painted polished speech, so many, boisterous and rude in language, see deep indeed, and give right substantial counsel." But the less well-witted and the rude and boisterous cannot be counted on to give good advice "except that every of your Commons were utterly discharged of all doubt and fear how anything . . . [they] speak, should . . . be taken." More acknowledged the King's "great benignity," yet, he said, "such is the weight of the matter, such is the reverend dread that the timorous hearts of your natural subjects conceive toward your high majesty . . . that they cannot in this point find themselves satisfied, except your gracious bounty . . . put away the scruple of their timorous minds . . . and put them out of doubt."

The price, then, of the Commons' advice is their freedom to speak without arrest. If the King wants advice, he must pay.

So, pressured regularly by their own main advisors, Henry VIII and Elizabeth did mostly grant the Speakers' petitions for Parliamentary privilege and, again constantly pressured, mostly lived up to their grants. The Stuarts were less gracious and were ultimately punished (that is, forced to flee in 1689) by their subjects for not maintaining the rights they had granted. Under the Stuarts, therefore, the parliamentary claim for free speech came to be thought of as an essential political right and was incorporated in the Bill of Rights of 1689 in this form: "the freedom of speech in debates or proceedings in Parliament ought not to be impeached or questioned in any court or place out of Parliament." From there it entered the United States Constitution, Article I, Section 6: ". . . for any speech or debate in either House, they [Senators and Representatives] shall not be questioned in any other place."

In the seventeenth century, furthermore, the parliamentary claim that public wisdom cannot be gathered without free parliamentary speech was generalized to all politicians. Thus, the public function of parliamentary speech became the public function of free political speech and, finally, in our First Amendment, the public function of free speech generally.

So the origin of this one civil right can be glimpsed in the words of

Thomas More. The motives of the "timorous" petitioners are clear enough. Can we infer the King's motives for More's argument? I think so, although More was too delicate to put the matter bluntly. Part of Parliamentary advice concerned taxes. So the King's motive for granting was to obtain, not just advice, but money. And his motive makes sense if we assume he perceived that for him to legislate and tax without rebellion, people must be able to speak freely. This seems a sufficient motive for Henry VIII and, indeed, for modern rulers.

Most civil rights have similar origins. Due process, the most ancient civil right, embedded as it is in Magna Charta alongside the even more ancient property right, was to save the barons' persons and estates from royal seizure and to save the King from abdication. The modern form of *habeas corpus* was enacted in 1679 to get Shaftesbury's bully boys out of jail and to allow King Charles II to reestablish tolerable relations with the Whig lords. Most of the other rights of our first ten Amendments were developed as solutions to similar political disputes, solutions satisfactory to grantors and grantees alike. Voting rights are only slightly different. New voters presumably benefit in obvious ways and the granting politicians expect to benefit from the support of previous non-voters. So in all civil rights, self-interested motives are easily identifiable for grantors and grantees.

III. The Origin of a Property Right

Turning to property rights, it is less easy to identify a clear-cut example like parliamentary free speech. Traders' ownership of goods in trade is surely prehistoric. Land ownership has varied widely over time and has an extraordinarily complicated history. For simplicity's sake, therefore, I will use as a paradigm one recently invented property right, namely, the right of an airline to a landing slot at an airport. The history of this right is as simple, straightforward, and easily described as parliamentary free speech.

This right came into existence on January 1, 1986, when the system of allocation of slots at the four busiest airports was changed from assignment by a committee of slot-using airlines to private possession of the right to buy and sell slots. For all practical purposes, this is a property right, although the grantor (the Department of Transportation) resisted so naming it in order to avoid the just compensation requirement of the Fifth Amendment, on the possibility that it might later be necessary to take this right back. However, the future of this property right is not clear. Will it be extended to other busy airports, will it be abolished, or will it be substantially revised? Brief though its history has been and may be, it is at present a genuine right and its known origin exemplifies the origin of other property rights.

Prior to the grant of this right, slots were allocated in each airport by a committee of users. So long as the supply of slots exceeded the demand for them, these committees had no serious problems, even though they operated by the rule of unanimity. But the supply was fixed and, in busy airports, demand exceeded it. The unanimity rule was highly inefficient, because it confirmed the enjoyment of the allocation (and committee membership) for weak airlines. This rigidity prevented adjustment to travelers' wants and restricted the growth of airlines responsive to those wants. On committees operating by the unanimity rule, there was inevitably vote-selling, which has little to do with efficiency. Airlines were of course highly motivated to chase votes because, when the committees failed to decide, the allocator by default was the Federal Aviation Administration. Airlines could thus easily conclude that it was better to pay other committee members than to risk decisions by the FAA. Typically, therefore, large airlines conceded slots to small new entrants, thus buying them off at what was often a loss of efficiency, or they refused to adjust anything at all, thereby certainly losing efficiency. All this meant that the costs of landing were more than they otherwise would be, and these costs were necessarily borne by the passengers of *all* airlines, not just the inefficient ones.

How might this inefficiency have been responded to? One way was, of course, merely to muddle through, regarding the slots as common resources and attempting to reconcile disputes by committees or the FAA. Another way was to auction the slots, thus creating ownership at a profit to the government. A third was simply to give them to the current users. The issue was much debated, different airlines and different federal agencies taking various positions.[4] Muddling through was not attractive, especially since the unanimity rule gave every airline a veto which, as noted already, was itself a salable commodity. An auction, while apparently fair to the travelers whose numbers generated the value of the slots, would certainly never have been accepted by users. They would have been forced to pay for what was currently free. Hence, no petitioners for this property right would ever have appeared if their petition had required them to substitute a costly private good for a free public good. So the only feasible alternative attractive enough to inspire petitioners was simply to 'grandfather' them in with property rights in the then-current allocations.

This is what happened in January 1986 at four airports (LaGuardia, Kennedy, O'Hare, and National). Users, now owners, had a real asset they could sell, borrow against, etc. So petitioners' motives are clear enough. The regulators' motives are equally clear: the rapid expansion of air travel following the deregulation of airlines had and has put intense pressure on the public parts of the air transport system. Its apparent inefficiency has forced federal agencies to think seriously about adjustments. Some parts of the bureaucracy, especially those most immediately concerned with the allocation of slots, were extremely loath to surrender power. Others, more politically sensitive and less deeply involved in allocation, were willing, for the sake of political peace, to create the right. In this way, they behaved quite like the Tudor kings and queens, who rid themselves of persistent and politically potent petitioners by granting their petition.

Since the creation of this right, a number of sales have occurred. Some were made merely to satisfy regulators and hence are not clearly improvements in efficiency; some have been actual economic sales and have, to some slight degree, improved service. (Obviously, much more innovation in ownership and pricing are now necessary to make the skies friendly.)

IV. The Justification of Rights

So far I have indicated that, speaking descriptively, civil and property rights originate in the persistent demands of potential beneficiaries, and in the calculations of granting officials that satisfying petitioners is less costly than resisting them. But I have not yet indicated how these legal rights might be justified in broader terms than simply the private gains of beneficiaries and officials from the grants themselves. So I turn now to the justification of rights.

The normative justification of private legal rights can be formulated as a fourfold categorization:

- the practical benefits to people generally
- the moral benefits to people generally
- the practical benefits to holders and users
- the moral benefits to holders and users.

It is possible to supply strong justifications for both civil and property rights under all these rubrics, but unfortunately the justifiers of civil rights (e.g., Justice Stone in the Carolene Products case, or Chief Justice Warren in the school desegregation case[5]) have emphasized social benefits, and the justifiers of property rights (e.g., Robert Nozick and Murray Rothbard[6]) have emphasized private benefits. Descriptively, however, civil and property rights look very much alike. It is not surprising, therefore, that the first conscious enunciation of both in English law is in Magna Charta, where they are conceptually entwined and treated identically.[7] Since their justifications are also logically similar, they should, I believe, be uttered with equal emphasis on public and private benefits.

V. The Practical Social Benefits of Rights

Generally, the practical benefits of free speech (here used as a paradigm for civil rights) are those uttered by More and often repeated by writers like John Milton and J.S. Mill.[8] To put this argument in contemporary terms, I define a notion of coherence of legislation (or indeed of any imperative sentence): an imperative is coherent if the formulation of it takes into account all relevant information, both public and private.[9] If relevant information is hidden or ignored, then the imperative may well direct actions which are impossible, or contradictory, or simply inefficient. The function of free speech is to promote coherence insofar as it is possible. Other civil rights, especially those having to do with voting and the maintenance of factions (i.e., *habeas corpus,* most of the Bill of Rights, and the Fifteenth, Nineteenth, Twenty-Fourth, and Twenty-Sixth Amendments[10]), also involve coherence and the democratic assumption that only the wearer knows where the shoe pinches.[11] Furthermore, the failure to incorporate information about dissatisfaction is precisely what links incoherence with instability and rebellion. Hence, coherent legislation and the civil liberties that provide it are the basis for efficiency and stability in government. This is their main practical benefit and justification.

The practical social benefits of property rights are likewise matters of efficiency. As in the case of landing slots, property rights have the effect of directing economic operations effectively. The basic allocation of resources takes place either in a market or with some kind of non-market direction, such as common possession or central planning. In this century, we have observed the misallocations of central planning, especially in Marxist regimes. And we have also observed what has happened when private property has been even partially restored, as in the sudden reversal of famine and hunger in China as a result of the introduction of private ownership of crops. It is an interesting case of social myopia that the Chinese now say the new policy is destroying the land, apparently quite unaware that private ownership of produce requires private ownership of land. This is the lesson of what Garrett Hardin called the "tragedy of the commons,"[12] namely that farmers overgraze and deplete common lands, destroying public capital to enhance private yields. A country can respond to this tragedy either by abandoning private ownership of the yield or public ownership of the land.

China has, for very good reason, rejected the former; so if they wish to save the soil, they must reinstate private land ownership against which their revolution was mainly directed. In Europe, the solution to the tragedy (a solution Marx totally failed to understand) was the enclosure movement: namely, the institution of private lands.

One way of viewing the tragedy is to say that farmers on common lands are able to externalize some of their internal costs of production: that is, to impose them on someone else. Harold Demsetz has argued that all changes from public allocation to private ownership involve internalization of previously external costs.[13] His main example was the creation of land ownership among Quebec Indians in the sixteenth century to avoid depleting beaver. The exact history of land ownership is unknown, though it was probably granted by tribal elders. Demsetz argued that, in general, private ownership of resources encourages each user to decide whether the income from the use is sufficient to justify the true economic cost of the resource. If the cost is free or partially free (as in common lands or, say, the labor of drafted soldiers) the user overuses the resource, thereby depleting it (as with land) or removing it from a better use (as with draftees). In either case, the existence of property rights leads to a better calculation of costs and hence to a more efficient use of resources.

The similarity of property and civil rights in terms of their practical social justification is that each encourages efficiency in political and economic institutions. It is hard to differentiate the social importance of these two kinds of structures. People want food, clothing, and shelter, and they want stable government. The absence of either one makes life nasty, brutish, and short. It is hard to see how the rights necessary for avoiding one kind of trouble are any more or less important than the rights necessary for avoiding the other kind.

VI. The Moral Social Benefits of Rights

Looking now at the moral social benefits of civil rights, the claim usually made is that free societies are morally preferable to unfree ones because free societies do not systematically oppress their subordinate members. If opposing political groups flourish, as civil rights presumably guarantee, then, by definition, tyrants or political monopolists cannot exist. Civil rights are thus a necessary, but not a sufficient, condition for equality and fraternity.

A similar claim is made for the moral benefits of property rights. If a society as a society is to display a concern for the alleviation of hunger, illness, and other misery, then it must be rich enough to do so. In a poor society, the few rich people can give alms, but only in a rich society can ordinary people accumulate resources to insure themselves against famine, and only in a rich society can ordinary people act together to display concern for health and welfare. Consider, for example, how a command economy with common possession might go about the Rawlsian task of helping the worst off. By the Marxian principles of the command economies of this century, the lot of the worst off is presumably improved by sharing in the confiscation of private goods. But with inefficiency thereby assured, the wealth and income per person declines, so the situations of the worst off from pre-confiscation times become still worse.[14] Stalin killed 20 million kulaks in the name of the "poor peasants," but the worst off then had far less food than before 1913. Less powerful command economies (that is, nations less able than Russia to take resources from colonies) are economic basket cases: Rumania, Tanganyika, Cuba, Ethiopia, Vietnam, etc. Of course, the poverty of the poorest is especially striking, because, in command economies, the rich (i.e., the public officials) always flourish. To say that the absence of property rights assures worse things for the worst off is to say that property rights are a necessary condition for a fair society in Rawlsian terms.

There is probably a close connection between a sense of fairness and a sense of fraternity in society. Indeed, they may be almost the same thing. Since civil rights are a necessary condition of fraternity and property rights of fairness, it again seems hard to distinguish between them.

As a concrete example of the interweaving of these rights, consider the confiscations in Rhode Island that so angered the framers of the Constitution. To pay off its revolutionary debt, Rhode Island in 1786 inflated its currency—a paper emission that fell to 1/6 its nominal value in six weeks. Farmers sought to use the depreciated currency to pay off private debts to merchants, and merchants responded by discounting it. Then the legislature made the currency legal tender at its face value, and merchants responded by refusing it. At that point, the legislature made refusal to accept the currency a criminal offense punishable by jail and the loss of civil rights. When judges refused to employ these punishments, the legislature set up special courts staffed by judges appointed by the legislature to enforce the law. No wonder the Framers thought that the deprivation of property and political tyranny were inseparable. No wonder they tried to guard against such oppression in the future. And how regrettable that, in this century, the courts have not remembered this inseparability, as (for example) when they consistently reject challenges to rent control laws, which are often enforced by neighborhood courts which systematically deprive landlords of fair trials.

VII. The Practical Individual Benefits of Rights

The justification of rights as individual benefits has always been in terms of the opportunity that rights give their possessors to accomplish their goals. Civil rights are a necessary condition of political participation—of the ability, that is, to be politically self-directing; property rights are a necessary condition of economic participation—of the ability to be self-directing economically. Indeed, each is necessary to the other. It is hard to see how civil rights can be sustained against a governing oligarchy if there is no one in the society to fund opposition to the oligarchs. It is equally hard to see how property rights can be sustained if owners are deprived (by, for example, limitations on campaign spending or, indirectly, by public funding of campaigns) of the right to organize politically in defense of their interests. In this sense, each kind of right buttresses the other, and the demise of either leads to the demise of both.

This is vividly clear in the case of the military draft, which simultaneously deprives the draftee of a property right in one's labor and a civil right in one's person. Many writers have interpreted the ending of the draft as the greatest achievement for civil rights in this century—certainly, it involves the most people.[15] But it is also a great achievement for property rights because it allows young men to sell their services for what they are worth, either to the military or in private trade. (It is worth pointing out that the practical social benefits were as large, perhaps, as the individual ones. Not only was the economic efficiency of the armed services enhanced, but also the efficiency of the political system was enhanced, freed as it was from the onus of draft-occasioned riots.)

VIII. The Moral Individual Benefits of Rights

The justification of rights in terms of the moral benefits to holders is the most common of the traditional justifications of both kinds of rights. Natural right theories of civil rights emphasize the personal moral development involved in self-direction. Similarly, Aristotelian justifications of property emphasize the personal moral development involved in taking responsibility for property. (Aristotle criticized Plato's communism for rulers, arguing that if the rulers didn't take care of property, they could hardly take care of people.[16])

The justification of civil and property rights in terms of the moral development of individuals has always had difficulty with the propensity of individuals to "abuse" these rights. In each case, the supposed abuse consists of the right-holder treating the right as absolute and unconditional. Thus, pornography is said to be an abuse of the right of free speech because the pornographer treats a right necessary for political freedom as an absolute license to publish whatever will sell. Similarly, expenditure on non-productive luxuries ("obscene wealth") is said to be an abuse of property rights, because the spender treats a right necessary for economic efficiency as an absolute privilege of conspicuous consumption. Of course, whether these supposed abuses are truly abuses is a matter of dispute. One man's pornography is another man's art. One man's conspicuous consumption is another man's patronage of artisans or care for an irreplaceable antique. Whatever judgment one makes, the fact that questions of abuse are troublesome is clear.

I cannot resolve this dispute here. Instead, I raise it to point out that the various methods of resolving it treat civil and property rights in the same way.

The most frequent resolution is to emphasize restrictions on rights. Interpreting them as conditional grants from rulers, it then follows that what rulers have not given, they ought to continue to control. Hence, supposedly non-political speech, e.g., pornography, is subject to regulation, as is even sensitive political speech that poses "a clear and present danger."[17] So is misused property, e.g., property used to generate external costs not subject to the discipline of the market, like pesticides on food.

The problem with this resolution is that almost any unpopular speech (like R–rated movies, perhaps) or unpopular property use (like students as neighbors) can be called an external cost. Inroads of this sort can severely devalue all rights. So an alternative resolution is to assert that rights are absolute, either by reason of inhering in humans (i.e., natural rights) or by reason of an absolute grant (i.e., in a social contract or in a bill of rights). Absolute rights, whether natural or declared, presumably cannot be regulated. It does not follow, of course, that individual right-holders use these absolute rights in ways that respect other people. So one of the moral activities of having absolute rights is learning to use them inoffensively in ways that respect the rights of others.

The dispute over the moral benefit of rights to individuals remains unresolved, but the fact is undeniable that this dispute occurs in exactly the same terms, with equivalent resolutions. That is the point of significance here. Both rights generate and induce moral development in individuals, both are subject to "abuse," and, in the end, the "abuse" is resolved in the same ways, either regulation or the inculcation of self-restraint.

Conclusion

As is apparent from this brief survey, civil and property rights have historically similar origins. They are justified in the same practical and moral terms. While they involve abstractly different realms of activity—politics and economics—these different realms are in fact inextricably intertwined in real human experience, as the examples of the military draft and Rhode Island legal tender laws indicate.

It is a puzzle, then, to explain why these rights have been treated as if they were separate. Any answer must, of course, be speculation about intellectual history. But my guess is that the rhetoric used to justify property rights in the nineteenth century brought on a separation and, furthermore, made property rights seem ignoble to people in the twentieth century.

Justifications of property rights have usually emphasized individual advantage. Social contract theories and the Lockean conception of property have been easily characterized as "possessive individualism." While these theories might emphasize benefits to people generally, their rhetoric often seemed in fact to reveal nothing but greed. Since our recent ancestors were thus educated primarily on greedy justifications of property, they saw only the greed and, not surprisingly, thought that civil rights ought to be preferred. But we can now see that greed is only a minor feature of property rights—an "abuse" like pornography. It is probably true that rich people enjoy being rich, but the rights are not primarily intended to bring about this result—although, of course, they necessarily do so. Rather, when looked at over the whole spectrum of functions and justifications, property rights are intended, just as are civil rights, to satisfy a necessary condition of a healthy society and of moral individuals. We have good evidence, furthermore, that both rights work out pretty much as intended. Consequently, it seems we ought, as quickly as possible, to erase from our law the false distinction on which the doctrine of preferred rights rests.

Appendix I

The following is from Roper, *Life of More:*[18]

"Mine other humble request, moste excellent Prince, is this: Forasmuch as there be of your comons, heare by your highe commandment assembled for your parliament, a greate number which are, after thacustomed manner, appointed in the comen house to treate *and* advise of the comon affaires among themselfes aparte; And albeit, most deere leige Lord, that according to your prudent advise, by your honorable writes euery wheare declared, there hath bine as due diligens vsed in sending vpp to your highnes courte of parliament the most discreete persons out of euery quarter that men could esteeme [meete] thereunto, Wherby it is not to be doubted but that there is a very substanciall assembly of right wise *and* polliticke persons; yeat, most victorious Prince, sith among so many wise men neyther is euery man wise alike, nor among so many men, like well witted, euery man like well spoken, And it often happeneth that, likewise as much folly is vttered with painted polished speache, so many, boystyous *and* rude in language, see deepe indeed, *and* give right substanciall councell; And sithe also in matter[s] of * great importaunce, the mynd is * often so * occupied in the matter that a man rather studieth what to say then howe, By reson whereof the wisest man *and* [the] best spoken in a whole country fortvneth among, while his mynd is fervent in the matter, somewhat to speake in such wise as he wold afterward wishe to haue bine vttered otherwise, *and* yeat no worse will had when he spake it, then he hath when he wold so glafly chaunge it; Therefore, most gracious soueraigne, considering that in *your highe court of parliament is nothing intreated but matter of weight *and* importance concerning your realme *and* your owne roiall estate, It could not faile to let *and* put to silence from the geving of their advice *and* councell many of your discreete comons, to the greate hinderaunce of the comon affaires, excepte that euery of your comons were vtterly discharged of all doubte *and* feare howe any thing that it should happen them to speake, should happen of your highnes to be taken. And in [this] point, [though your] well knowen *and* *proved benighnity puttethe euery man in ryght good hope, yeat such is the waight of the matter, such is the reuerend dread that the tymorous hartes of your naturall subiectes conceave toward your highe maiestie, our most redoubted king *and* vndoubted soueraigne, that they cannot in this point finde themselfes satisfied, except your gracious bounty therin declared put away the scruple of their timorous myndes, and animate *and* incourage them, *and* put them out of doubte. It may therefore like your most aboundant grace, our most benighe *and* godly kinge, to giue to all your comons heare assembled your most gracious licens *and* pardon, freely, without doubte of your dreadfull displeasure, euery man to discharge his consciens, *and* boldlye in euery thinge incident among [vs] to declare his advise; *and* whatsoeu*er* happen any man to say, [that] it may like y*our* noble maiestye, of y*our* inestimable goodnes, to take all in good p*ar*te, interpreting euery mans wordes, howe vnconingly soeu*er* they be couched, to p*ro*ceed yeat of good zeale towardes the p*ro*fit of y*our* realme *and* honor of y*our* royall p*er*son, the prosperous estate *and* preservation whereof, most excellent sou*er*aigne, is the thinge w*h*ich we all, y*our* most humble loving subiect*es,* according to the most bounden duty of our naturall alleageans, mosts highlye desire *and* pray for."

Notes

1. United States v. Carolene Products, 304 U.S. 144 (1937). In this case, the court upheld the conviction of a producer of filled milk (i.e., skim milk with vegetable oil added) for shipping the product in interstate commerce in violation of a federal statute. Justice Stone, for the court, asserted that "regulatory legislation affecting ordinary commercial transactions is not to be pronounced unconstitutional unless . . . it is of such a character as to preclude the assumption that it rests upon some rational basis within the knowledge and experience of legislators." Then, in a footnote, he distinguished this kind of commercial regulation (which once probably would have been regarded as a violation of the due process clause of the Fifth Amendment) from "specific prohibitions of the Constitution, such as those of the first ten amendments . . ." Of these prohibitions, he said: "There may be a narrower scope for operation of the presumption of constitutionality when legislation appears on its face to be within a specific prohibition." Out of this footnoted distinction, Stone's successors (e.g., Justice Reed in Kovacs v. Cooper, 336 U.S. 77 (1949)) erected a doctrine of the preferred position of civil rights over property rights. Many have criticized the creation of an extremely important constitutional doctrine out of a casual obiter dictum in an unthoughtful footnote, but the more intellectually shoddy action seems to me the obiter dictum itself: while referring to all the Bill of Rights, it demotes the specific prohibition in the Fifth Amendment to a place far below the specific prohibitions in the First or Fourth.

2. Riker and Weingast, *Constitutional Regulation of Legislative Choice: The Political Consequences of Judicial Deference to Legislatures,* 74 VA. L. REV. 373–401 (1988).

3. J. UMBECK, A THEORY OF PROPERTY RIGHTS WITH APPLICATIONS TO THE CALIFORNIA GOLD RUSH passim (1981).

4. D. GRETHER, R. ISAAC, & C. PLOTT, ALTERNATIVE METHODS OF ALLOCATING AIRPORT SLOTS: PERFORMANCE AND EVALUATION (1979).

5. United States v. Carolene Products, 304 U.S. 144 (1937); Brown v. Board of Education of Topeka, 347 U.S. 483 (1954).

6. R. NOZICK, ANARCHY, STATE, AND UTOPIA (1974); M. ROTHBARD, MAN, ECONOMY AND STATE (1962).

7. The crucial chapters of Magna Carta (1215) are: "39. No freeman shall be captured or imprisoned or disseized or outlawed or exiled or in any way destroyed . . . except by the lawful judgment of his peers or by the law of the land . . . 52. If anyone, without the lawful judgment of his peers, has been disseized or deprived by us of his lands, castles, liberties, or rights, we will at once restore them to him . . ." Note that in 39 the taking of property (i.e., disseizure) is nested within the taking of the person or of physical liberty and that in 52 the deprivation of lands and other rights are mentioned together.

8. J. MILTON, AREOPAGITICA (1643), in, for example, the second paragraph: "when complaints are freely heard, deeply considered and speedily reformed, then is the utmost bound of civil liberty attained that wise men look for." J.S. MILL, ON LIBERTY (1959), in, for example, the first paragraph of chapter 2: "the peculiar evil of silencing the expression of an opinion is, that it is robbing the human race; posterity as well as the existing generation; those who dissent from the opinion, still more than those who hold it. If the opinion is right, they are deprived of the opportunity of exchanging error for truth; if wrong, they lose, what is almost as great a benefit, the clearer perception and livelier impression of truth, produced by its collision with error."

9. Austen-Smith and Riker, *Asymmetric Information and the Coherence of Legislation*, AMERICAN POLITICAL SCIENCE REVIEW 897–918 (1987).

10. These amendments prohibit denials of the right to vote on account of race, sex, age (over 18), or failure to pay taxes.

11. W. RIKER, DEMOCRACY IN THE UNITED STATES 42–50 (1953).

12. Hardin, *The Tragedy of the Commons*, 162 SCIENCE 1243–48 (1968).

13. Demsetz, *Toward a Theory of Property Rights*, 57 AM.ECON. REV. PROC. 347 (1967).

14. M. WARD, THE POLITICAL ECONOMY OF DISTRIBUTION: EQUALITY VERSUS INEQUALITY (1978).

15. REGISTRATION AND THE DRAFT 61–68, 121–27, 179–84 passim (M. Anderson ed. 1982).

16. ARISTOTLE, POLITICS, bk. II, ch. 5, secs. 1–16 (1262b36–1265b40).

17. On pornography, Roth v. United States, 354 U.S. 476 (1957) and Miller v. California, 413 U.S. 15 (1973); on clear and present danger, Schenck v. United States 249 U.S. 47 (1919) and Holmes's dissent in Abrams v. United States, 250 U.S. 616 (1919).

18. W. ROPER, THE LIFE OF SIR THOMAS MORE (E. Hitchcock ed. 1935), 14–16.

Judicial Activism of the Right:
A Mistaken and Futile Hope

LINO A. GRAGLIA

Constitutional law is, as a practical matter, the product of the exercise of the power of judicial review, America's dubious contribution to the science of government. Judicial review is the power of judges to disallow policy choices made by other officials or institutions of government, ostensibly on the ground that they are prohibited by the Constitution. Increasingly it has come to be used not merely to disallow, but to impose policy choices, as in judicial decisions which effectively assume control of the operation of schools, prisons, and mental institutions.[1] The central question of constitutional law, the only question common to the myriad subjects dealt with by courts under that rubric, is how, if at all, this power in the hands of judges, and ultimately of the justices of the United States Supreme Court—officials of the federal government unelected to office and holding office for life—can be reconciled with the system of decentralized self-government through elected representatives contemplated by the Constitution and generally accepted as the essence of the American political system.

Initially, the most striking thing about the institution of judicial review is that it is not explicitly provided for in the Constitution. The somewhat comparable power of the president to veto legislation is, by contrast, specified in detail, with limits on its exercise clearly stated.[2] Given that the power of judges to question and invalidate the acts of an elected legislature was and is unknown in English law—where Parliament, not a court, is said to be supreme—and the obvious dangerousness of the power if not narrowly confined, it seems appropriate to assume that the power was never knowingly granted by those who ratified the Constitution. At the least, it is appropriate to assume, as Judge Learned Hand argued,[3] that the power is a very limited one, exercisable only in exceptional circumstances.

Alexander Hamilton argued for judicial review,[4] however, and Chief Justice John Marshall established it in *Marbury v. Madison*[5] on the ground that it was inherent in a written constitution—although other nations had and have written constitutions without judicial review—and that no more was involved than in the application and enforcement of other law by judges. Judges would simply refuse to enforce statutes in clear conflict with the Constitution—for example, Marshall said, a federal statute permitting conviction for the crime of treason on the basis of the testimony of only one witness to an act, despite the constitutional provision requiring two.[6] No policymaking power was involved, Hamilton and Marshall insisted, because, as Hamilton put it, judges were to be "bound down by strict rules and precedents which serve to define and point out their duty in every particular case that comes before them."[7]

Whether or not Hamilton and Marshall were being entirely candid, which seems unlikely—neither was overly enamored of popular government— the judicial review they described and justified would have given the courts very little additional work to do. Congress, it happens, has never passed a one-witness treason law, and the Constitution, sensibly, does not prohibit a great deal more. The Constitution, it is important to remember, is a very short document, easily printed with all amendments, repealers, and obsolete matter on fourteen or fifteen pages, and apparently quite simple and straightforward. It is not at all like the Bible, the Talmud, or even the Tax Code, extensive treatments of mysterious subjects in which many things may be found with sufficient search.

The Constitution was adopted primarily for the mundane purposes of commerce and trade: basically, to create a national common market by empowering Congress to remove state-imposed impediments to interstate trade. It was not adopted, as seems now to be generally assumed, because of a felt need to create federal constitutional rights. One can hardly call the Constitution a work of great statesmanship and foresight given that it led to the Civil War, but it has proven durable, nonetheless, primarily because (apart from creating the structure of a stronger national government) it attempted to do so little. The Constitution places very few restrictions on the exercise of the federal government's enumerated powers—even after the adoption of the so-called Bill of Rights (the first ten Amendments), which deals primarily with criminal procedure—and even fewer on the reserved general sovereignty of the states. In essence, both the federal government and the states were prohibited from passing *ex post facto* laws and bills of attainder, and the states were not to enact debtor-relief legislation. In addition, the First Amendment prohibits the federal government from abridging "the freedom of speech" or interfering in matters of religion, the Second prohibits it from infringing "the right to have and bear arms," and the Fifth prohibits it from confiscating private property. The Thirteenth Amendment freed blacks and the Fifteenth enfranchised them; most important, the Fourteenth prohibited the states from denying them basic civil rights. The Nineteenth Amendment prohibits denial of the franchise on grounds of sex, and the Twenty-Sixth (and last) Amendment prohibits denial of the franchise on grounds of age to persons over the age of eighteen.

Because the Constitution restricts policy choices so little, American lawmakers—all of whom are American citizens living in America—ordinarily have little occasion to exceed its limitations and are little tempted to do so. As a result, examples of enacted law clearly in violation of the Constitution are extremely difficult to find. Perhaps the clearest example in 200 years is Minnesota's 1933 Mortgage Moratorium Act, debtor-relief legislation clearly prohibited by the contracts clause.[8] By a five-to-four vote, however, the Supreme Court held the law constitutional, thereby missing one of its few, if not its only, legitimate opportunities to exercise judicial review to invalidate a law.[9] If judicial review were in fact what it is represented to be—judicial power to enforce the Constitution—it would be a matter of little importance or interest.

In the past three-and-a-half decades, however, the power of judicial review has arguably made the Supreme Court the most important institution of American government in terms of domestic social policy. Virtually every basic social change, as the phrase has it, in that period—regarding abortion,[10] capital punishment,[11] crime control,[12] prayer in the schools,[13] government aid to religious schools,[14] compulsory racial integration,[15] street demonstrations,[16] pornography,[17] libel,[18] sex discrimination,[19] discrimination on the basis of legitimacy,[20] and so on—has come about, not by decision of our elected legislators, state or federal, but by a majority vote of the nine justices of the Supreme Court. The Court has effectively become the initiator of change and the final arbiter on the fundamental issues that determine the nature of American society and the quality of American life.

How has it been possible for the Court to make a Constitution which imposes very few restrictions on popular government, especially on state government, a virtual straitjacket on state government? The answer, to put it bluntly, is that the Court has successfully perpetrated a fraud: the central fact of contemporary constitutional law is that it has little or nothing to do with the Constitution and everything to do with the willingness and ability of a majority of Supreme Court justices to make their policy preferences the supreme law of the land. This is sufficiently shown to anyone willing to see by the simple fact that very little of the Constitution is even purportedly involved in so-called constitutional decision-making. The great bulk of rulings of unconstitutionality involve state, not federal, law, and nearly all of these rulings purport to be based on a single constitutional provision, the Fourteenth Amendment, and, indeed, on one or the other of two pair of words: "due process"—which is said, surprisingly enough, to "incorporate" almost all provisions of the Bill of Rights, making them applicable to the states—and "equal protection." No sensible person has the slightest doubt, I take it, that Supreme Court justices do not arrive at their conclusions on enormously difficult questions of social policy by studying those four words. To speak of the Court making its controversial constitutional decisions by "interpréting the Constitution" is to speak conventionally, but also seriously to mislead the uninformed; in fact, in almost no case is any question of interpretation involved.

Judicial review has been with us, of course, from almost the beginning, at least since *Marbury v. Madison* in 1803. More than fifty years passed, however, before the Court again exercised the power to invalidate a federal statute in the infamous *Dred Scott* case.[21] In *Dred Scott,* the Court held (on no good basis) that a state could not grant state citizenship to a black, and that Congress could not limit the extension of slavery into new territories. The Civil War that this decision made inevitable is undoubtedly judicial review's most significant contribution to our history. Twenty-six years later, the Court again exercised the power of judicial review against a federal statute in the *Civil Rights Cases,*[22] now holding that Congress lacked the power, despite the Thirteenth and Fourteenth Amendments, to prohibit racial segregation in places of public accommodation. From the 1890s to 1937, the so-called *Lochner* era,[23] the Court freely disallowed state and federal economic and social regulation, including two attempts by Congress to restrict child labor.[24] If judicial review provides a necessary restraint on popular government, operating as a force for moral improvement, as its proponents proclaim, it must be because of what it has accomplished more recently.

What it has accomplished more recently is that it gave us the *Brown* decision in 1954,[25] prohibiting—in theory, though not in fact until Congress acted ten years later—legally compelled racial segregation in schools and, it soon appeared, all racial discrimination by government. The effect of *Brown*'s condemnation of a clearly indefensible and intolerable situation was to enhance the Court's status and prestige so greatly as to allow it to assume a new role in the American system of government, becoming for the first time an accelerator rather than a brake on social change. The *Brown* decision established in many minds (including, certainly, the minds of many judges) the superiority of judicial decision-making on the basis of principle to decision-making by the electorally accountable representatives of the people. If the Court could end racial discrimination in the South, what great things could it not do? And if the Court could do great things, why shouldn't it? To question policymaking by the Court thereafter was inevitably to be met with the devastating reply, "So you disagree with *Brown?*" As no one could disagree with *Brown,* no one could disagree, it seemed, that free-wheeling judicial review on the basis of principles of morality and justice was an essential corrective to popular government.

Brown provided proponents of judicial activism—constitutional law making not based on the Constitution—a club with which to beat opponents into submission even when the policies imposed on the nation by the judges, such as busing for racial balance in schools, are clearly destructive and strongly opposed by a large majority of the American people. The proponents have had strong motivation to use the club because of what judicial activism has meant in practice. The apparent invulnerability of judicial activism since *Brown* lies in the fact that, although the Court's constitutional decisions have had nothing to do with the Constitution, they have had everything to do with advancing a particular political ideology, the ideology of American liberalism, which happens to be shared by the vast majority of those in a position to defend and protect the Court by finding justification for its decisions.

One could sum up the meaning of contemporary constitutional law by saying that the American Civil Liberties Union, the paradigm constitutional litigator of our day, never loses in the Supreme Court even though it does not always win. It either obtains from the Court a policy enactment that it could obtain in no other way because it would be disfavored by most Americans—such as the ruling that government cannot not cut off welfare benefits without instituting legal proceedings[26]—or it is left where it was to try again on another day. For opponents of the ACLU's policies, however—for example, opponents of unrestricted abortion—a "victory" in "constitutional" law, translated, is to be permitted to continue to fight for their point of view in the political process. Constitutional law is, therefore, not merely a fraud, but a fraud serving a particular end: enactment of the political agenda of the Left.

Although the liberal agenda advanced by contemporary constitutional law is strongly egalitarian and antitraditionalist or countercultural, it is most strongly supported by and operates to advance the interests of a cultural elite, the so-called New Class, made up of members of academia, the media, mainline churches, and others who live and work in a world of words. This class considers itself entitled by its educational and intellectual attainments and moral insights to positions of leadership and control; it sees the fact that persons of lesser attainment get an equal or greater voice in policymaking as a major structural defect of democracy. To the New Class, government with the consent of the governed, crass majority rule, is unsatisfactory and dangerous unless substantially channeled by some arrangement for government primarily by the wise and the good—that is, by people like themselves. Policymaking by judges is, as a practical matter, as close to such an arrangement as they can hope to get in this country. Intellectual attainment and moral refinement are hardly occupational qualifications for our judges, but all or nearly all of them are at least graduates of a college and a professional school, albeit of only a law school.

The judiciary presents to the New Class the twin and unique advantages of personnel who have been processed by the educational system for twenty or more years and, especially in the federal system, who are thoroughly insulated from accountability to the electorate. The fact that judges are selected only from the legal profession, with moral philosophers, sociologists, and other advanced academic thinkers considered ineligible, makes the arrangement less than ideal, but it remains nonetheless a great improvement on majority rule. The chances that a moral philosopher's or sociologist's latest work on the need to remake America will be read by or influence a judge—whose reputation and invitations to conferences and lectureships turn largely on academic evaluations—are certainly much greater than the chances that it will influence a businessman or truck-driver.

A system of government by judges or any other supposedly enlightened elite not subject to electoral control cannot, however, be openly advocated in this country: too many Americans take seriously the notion that all citizens are entitled to an equal voice in government. Defense of policymaking by judges depends crucially, therefore, upon techniques of obfuscation and mysticism. Fortunately for this purpose, the Constitution has obtained an iconic status in American life as a quasi-sacred document. Americans can be and have been made to see it as a mysterious (like much of God's handiwork) compendium of commands and limitations on the popular will. The Supreme Court has attained a similar status as the Constitution's oracle—it is not for nothing that the justices wear robes and sit in a temple. The need, therefore, is simply to convince the populace that the Supreme Court's policy prescriptions, however unpalatable or even irrational, are commands of the Constitution beyond the understanding and impervious to the opposition of the ordinary person. It would seem to be, as the phrase used to have it, a job for Superman, but the liberals, through the efforts of such supermen of constitutional analysis as Ronald Dworkin, Laurence Tribe, Frank Michelman, and Mark Tushnet,[27] have been able to bring it off.

If the Constitution is the scripture and the Supreme Court the oracle of our constitutional religion, professors of constitutional law in our law schools and political science departments are its proselytizing arm, the ordained dispensers and justifiers of its surprising and unwanted doctrines to the masses. It is a general structural defect of our system of government that the more and the worse the law, the better it is for the lawyers, and lawyers largely get to make the law. (There is no danger that lawyers will, like the dentists who put themselves out of business by curing caries, ever be responsible for a lessened need for their services.) A more specialized defect is that the more constitutional law there is, the better it is for constitutional law professors, who, therefore, understandably are great fans of the stuff. In addition, the great majority of professors of constitutional law, like most academics, fully support the Supreme Court's political agenda. They therefore see it as their primary professional function to keep the public from understanding that constitutional law is simply a cover for the Court's unauthorized enactment of policies the public opposes.

Because the task of basing contemporary constitutional law on the Constitution is not merely herculean—as Ronald Dworkin, perhaps our leading constitutional theorist, would have it[28]—but impossible, the primary need is to make the Constitution simply go away. Thus we find professors of constitutional law literally attempting the impossible by concocting and defending "non-interpretivist" or "non-originalist" theories of constitutional interpretation.[29] We find Justice William J. Brennan, Jr., the paradigm judicial activist, openly arguing that the meaning of the Constitution is unknowable—indeed, was often unknown even to the Framers—and, in any event, irrelevant because it is the product of "a world that is dead and gone."[30]

The second task of the constitutional law theorists is to substitute for the disposed-of, actual Constitution a new, grander, and more suitably uncertain one; there must be something called the Constitution, so that the Court's policymaking may be described as constitutional law. Justice Brennan's solution, typical of the highest reaches of contemporary constitutional scholarship, is to argue that the Constitution be understood as nothing more definite than the "lodestar of our aspirations," a compendium of "majestic generalities and ennobling pronouncements [that] are both luminous and obscure,"[31] which, however, he remains able and authorized both to "interpret" and to assure their enforcement. Finally, proponents of judicial activism are invariably strong believers in principle—which judges are assumed to be peculiarly good at discovering and devoted to following—and highly skeptical of the merits of majority rule. Justice Brennan, for example, tells us, on the one hand, that the Constitution contains "great" and "overarching" principles to guide and legitimate decision-making by judges, and warns us, on the other, against the "unabashed enshrinement of majoritarianism" and "blind faith" in democracy.[32]

Judicial activism since *Brown* has been very good to liberals, uniformly moving America closer to their view of the good society, a society of, for example, unlimited abortion, readily available pornography, mandated racial and sexual preferences, and extravagant protections for the criminally accused. It is not surprising, therefore, that liberals should defend it, whatever the cost in intellectual integrity. Much more difficult to understand is the appearance in recent years of a group of judicial activists of the right, conservatives or supposed conservatives who have joined the liberal enterprise of defending a highly interventionist role for the Supreme Court in the political process, albeit in the service of different ends. Their objection to contemporary constitutional law is not that it is a ruse for the Court's enactment of a political agenda, but only that the Court has not enacted their agenda.

Why shouldn't judicial activism be made to serve conservative rather than, or in addition to, liberal causes, as it did, after all, for about forty years ending in 1937?[33] Does not the failure of four appointments to the Court by President Nixon, and indeed of seven (now eight) consecutive appointments by Republican presidents, to lessen the liberal interventionism established by the Warren Court show that it cannot be lessened—a conclusion corroborated by the defeat of the nomination of Judge Robert Bork? Perhaps the best hope for conservatives, therefore, is not to fight but to seek to capture or rechannel judicial power. This is surely the best hope, in any event, if not of true (traditional) conservatives, at least of libertarians—who also have a well-defined political agenda that the majority of the American people do not accept.

Although the liberals' objective, the powerful government necessary to impose and enforce equality, and the libertarians' objective, the least powerful government necessary to protect individual liberty, could hardly be more opposed, their arguments for judicial activism are, of necessity, identical. Because the Constitution does not place American government in a libertarian straitjacket any more than it places it in a liberal one, the libertarian objective requires, no less than the liberal one, that the Constitution be disposed of, that a Constitution more suitable to free-wheeling judicial policymaking be imagined and substituted, and that the consequent restriction on majority rule be seen not as an objection but a justification.

Recent major works urging judicial activism of the right include *Public Choice and Constitutional Economics* (1988), edited by Gwartney and Wagner, and *Economic Liberties and the Judiciary* (1987), edited by Dorn and Manne, both sponsored and co-published by the libertarian Cato Institute. Bernard Siegan's *Economic Liberty and the Constitution* (1980), a founding document of the movement, urges a revival of economic substantive due process in the service of property rights and economic freedom. Siegan's proposed return to the *Lochner* era would deprive government, state and federal, of the power to regulate business and economic affairs unless a majority of Supreme Court justices agrees that such regulation is "reasonable."

The movement's most prolific and articulate proponent, however, is undoubtedly Richard Epstein, whose 1985 opus, *Takings: Private Property and the Power of Eminent Domain,* may be taken as the bible of the movement, the authoritative statement of fundamental doctrine. Stephen Macedo's 1986 monograph *The New Right v. The Constitution*, a short statement of basic principles, may usefully be taken as the movement's manifesto, made authoritative by reason of a foreword by Epstein. Macedo, a follower of such thoroughgoing liberals as Ronald Dworkin, Walter Murphy, and Soterios Barber, nicely illustrates the congruence of judicial activism of the right and left. It will be interesting to have Macedo explain in some later work how he reconciles Dworkin's natural law egalitarianism with Epstein's natural law property rights.

Macedo begins, like all proponents of judicial activism, by finding the Constitution as written woefully deficient in meaning. Its text, he tells us, is often "uncertain," presenting, as in the case of the First Amendment, "extremely difficult problems of interpretation." The First Amendment is "relatively straightforward," however, compared to the "truly majestic generalities" of other constitutional provisions, such as the Fourteenth Amendment. The Fourteenth Amendment, in turn, is clear compared to other provisions, such as the Ninth Amendment, that have "been deemed so obscure as to wholly defy judicial interpretation."[34] From all of this, one can only conclude, it would seem, that such provisions are wholly unsuited to serve as provisions of law enforceable by judges, and could not have been intended as such. Macedo's conclusion that the Constitution therefore authorizes judges to exercise judicial review on the basis of "moral philosophy"[35] is so obviously unwarranted and inconsistent with the constitutional scheme of government as to raise doubt that this is an area subject to rational discussion. The suggestion that the nation turn to a committee of lawyers for moral guidance and binding moral judgments can only be described as bizarre. If we wanted government by philosopher-kings, we would of course turn to philosophers, not lawyers; we would provide them with facilities for philosophical investigation; and we would not embarrass them by requiring that they pretend to be interpreting the Constitution.

Macedo sees insuperable obstacles to determining the meaning of the Constitution in the only way that it can be determined: on the basis of the Framers' intent. "Whose intent is to count," he asks, "what counts as evidence of intent," and what if the intentions were "complex and conflicting"?[36] This standard argument of proponents of judicial activism fails on two grounds: we do sufficiently know the intended meaning of litigated constitutional provisions, and, if we did not, the result would be that judges have no basis for judicial review, not that they are authorized to exercise judicial review on some non-constitutional basis.

Many texts are indeed difficult to understand, but our short and simple Constitution, happily, is not one of them. We always or almost always know all we need to know about the Constitution to decide actual cases; it is almost always entirely clear that nothing in the Constitution disallows the challenged policy choice. The Court's controversial constitutional decisions are not controversial because of a disagreement about the meaning of a constitutional provision, but because it is clear that those decisions are not required by any constitutional provision. No one really believes, for example, that the states lost the power to make policy on issues of abortion because Supreme Court justices decided to take one more look at the Constitution in 1973 to see what it had to say on the subject, and discovered in the then 105-year-old Fourteenth Amendment what had never been noticed before.[37] Similarly, the states did not lose the right to make policy regarding prayer and Bible-reading in their public schools because a majority of the justices noticed for the first time in 1962 and 1963 that the First Amendment, supposedly applicable to the states by reason of the Fourteenth, deprives them of that right;[28] the states lost this authority, not because of, but despite the First Amendment, which was clearly intended to protect the states from exactly that kind of federal interference.

If, on the other hand, the meaning of a constitutional provision is, in fact, so obscure as to defy interpretation, it obviously cannot provide a basis for holding a law unconstitutional. An indecipherable constitutional provision is a nullity, not (as Macedo would have it) a grant of unlimited authority to judges to invalidate laws in the name of "moral philosophy" or the "principles of justice and natural rights."[39] It is incredible that the Framers meant to make such a grant, and, if they did, our first order of business, I would think, would be to rescind it as inconsistent with self-government. Such a grant would, in any event, deprive the Constitution of further relevance to judicial review; constitutional interpretation would play no further role in judicial decision-making, except that the decisions would still be called constitutional decisions and invalidated laws would still be described as unconstitutional.

If *glasnost* may be thought to have a place in the United States as well as in the Soviet Union, this situation, it seems, should be fully explained to the public. The public should be made to understand that a finding of so-called unconstitutionality means, not a conflict with a specific constitutional prohibition, but a conflict with the judges' understanding of moral philosophy and the principles of natural law, which is to say, with their political views. Natural law has the advantage, John Hart Ely has pointed out, of meaning whatever one wants it to mean, but the disadvantage that "everybody understands that."[40] Macedo argues as if he did not understand it.

Richard Epstein is, of necessity, also no fan of the jurisprudence of original intent. His influential book, *Takings*, rests on a somewhat more sophisticated, or at least more subdued, version of Macedo's argument against a knowable Constitution. Epstein has built a truly impressive structure of constitutional limitations out of no more material than the "takings" or just compensation clause of the Fifth Amendment—"nor shall private property be taken for public use, without just compensation"—propped up, of course, with the indispensable all-purpose Fourteenth, according to which virtually every legislative action would be challengeable as a compensable taking of property. Epstein would give judges as much to do in the name of enforcing the takings clause as Macedo would give them in the name of moral philosophy, justice, or natural law. The entire structure stands, however, on twin pillars of sand: the application of the takings clause to the states, and the divorcing of the takings clause from the Constitution by rejecting its historic, intended meaning.

That the Bill of Rights in general and the takings clause in particular was meant to apply only to the federal government, not the states, was, Epstein acknowledges at the beginning of his book, "explicitly and correctly held by Justice [sic] Marshall for a unanimous court in *Barron v. Baltimore*" in 1833[41]—which would have been an excellent place for the book to end. The notion that the Fourteenth Amendment, adopted to provide and authorize additional federal protection to the newly emancipated blacks, was meant to make the Bill of Rights applicable to the states is a notion supported by little more than the desperate need of proponents of judicial activism for additional material for obscurantism.[42] It is not credible that the Reconstruction Congress that proposed the Fourteenth Amendment meant to make a major transfer of policymaking power to the Supreme Court, or that the states that ratified it meant to make such a transfer of power to both Congress and the Court and to impose an array of new restrictions on themselves.

Epstein, to his credit, cannot bring himself to make the fanciful "incorporation" argument, even though application of the takings clause to the states is essential to his system. The result, however, is to bring forth such gibberish as: "Limitations upon the powers of the state have been answered in practice by incorporating specific provisions for individuals against the state as well, including the eminent domain clause."[43] "Since this book is a mix of political and constitutional theory," he grandly announces, "I shall follow the present law and treat the [eminent domain] clause as though it applies both to state and federal action, which is consistent with the basic Lockean design . . ."[44] Applying the takings clause to the states as well as the federal government may or may not be consistent with the Lockean design—even Locke wasn't all Epstein needs him to be[45]—but unfortunately for Epstein's argument, it is not consistent with the constitutional design, which is to place few restrictions on policymaking by the states. Epstein wants the best of both worlds: application of the takings clause to the states—essential to his system—but not the embarrassment of trying to justify that application as an appropriate interpretation of the Constitution.

A second gaping hole in Epstein's argument for judicial creation of his social utopia through the takings clause is that the clause simply does not mean what he would make of it. Epstein admits, as he must, that his view of the takings clause "does not take into account the actual historical intention of any of the parties who drafted or signed" the Constitution.[46] He expressly rejects the use of "extensive secondary material"[47] to determine the Framers' intent. At the same time, because he is a legal scholar as well as a political philosopher, Epstein purports to recognize that the view that the meaning of constitutional provisions can change over time—that it is not fixed by the intent of the Framers—is "an invitation to destroy the rule of law."[48] He attempts to avoid the resulting dilemma by arguing that "the best evidence of textual intention is the language of the text itself," which is certainly correct, and that we should look to "historical sources" only to "understand the standard meanings of ordinary language" as used in the Constitution, not to determine the actual "collective purposes . . . that secured its passage,"[49] which is nonsense.

Epstein's approach to interpretation would convert the use of language from a means of communication to participation in a dangerous game in which one's words may be given a meaning different from or contrary to the meaning one is known to intend. According to Epstein, a law may be said to be properly "interpreted" even though the effect is to produce a result known not to be the result, or even one contrary to the result, that the lawmakers intended. The mistake derives from the almost irresistible temptation to believe that words have inherent meaning—meaning apart from the communicative purposes for which they are used. The mistake is illustrated by Epstein's argument that it is possible to be loyal to a law's "text as written" without being loyal to the lawmakers' known "views of the consequences it entailed"[50]—that is, that what matters is not what the lawmakers sought to accomplish or prevent, but what can be done with the words they used. If a parrot utters the words (mere sounds apart from intent) "please kill me," we are not justified in doing the poor thing in on the ground of loyalty to his text (and certainly not on the ground of his likely view of the "consequences it entailed").

Epstein argues that to treat the takings clause as a "self-contained intellectual proposition," as having meaning independent of why or by whom it was written and ratified, is not "necessarily a rejection of the Framers' intention."[51] Not necessarily, but it certainly permits rejection of the Framers' intention. It simply makes the Framers' intention irrelevant and thus deprives the clause of fixed meaning. Epstein seems to recognize and accept this when he says, in agreement with Justice Brennan, that the meaning of "specific clauses" in the Constitution "was left to future generations"[52]— which in practice means, of course, to a majority of the justices of the Supreme Court. The result is that, in the space of six pages, he manages to talk himself out of the self-evident truth, fatal to his system, with which he began, that to leave the meaning of the Constitution to "each new generation . . . is an invitation to destroy the rule of law."[53]

That Epstein's theory of constitutional interpretation is untenable can perhaps be made clear even to him by showing that it is indistinguishable from the theory of Ronald Dworkin, his counterpart on the opposite end of the political spectrum. Dworkin and Epstein are equally enthusiastic about judicial intervention in the political process, differing only in that Dworkin would have the Supreme Court enact something like John Rawls's egalitarian program[54] on the basis that it is required by natural law (and therefore the Constitution), and Epstein would have the Court enact something like Robert Nozick's libertarian program[55] on the same basis. Dworkin's principal contribution to constitutional theory is his recommendation that courts interpret the Constitution not in accordance with what he calls the Framers' "conceptions," what they are known to have actually intended, but in accordance with their supposed "concepts,"[56] abstractions elevated enough to mean anything and thus to permit judges to enact their and Dworkin's policy preferences in the name of the Constitution.

Epstein, precisely parallelling Dworkin, would have courts decide constitutional cases not on the basis of the Framers' specific purposes, known to be very limited, but on the basis of the supposed "necessary implications derived from the constitutional text and the underlying theory of the state that it embodies,"[57] which would effectively give judges a free hand. Unsurprisingly, the "necessary implications derived from the constitutional text" turn out, according to Epstein, to deviate in no respect from Epstein's policy preferences, just as the "concepts" of the Framers happen, according to Dworkin, to deviate in no respect from Dworkin's policy preferences. Macedo makes exactly the same move from the knowable and definite to the hopelessly abstract when he recommends that courts decide constitutional cases not on the basis of the Constitution's intended meaning, which he finds unknowable, but on the basis of its "moral aspirations" and "our best understanding of justice,"[58] the functional equivalents of Dworkin's "concepts" and Epstein's "necessary implications."

Epstein has so thoroughly persuaded himself of the reality and soundness of the system he has built on quicksand that he can describe its precepts as clear constitutional commands and berate Supreme Court justices for failing to follow them. The justices, however, are perfectly aware that Epstein's constitutional commands come only from Epstein. They know, in the first place, that the takings clause applies to the states for no other reason than their totally unwarranted say-so. They are not about to overrule the "incorporation" doctrine—they find it too convenient in other respects—but neither are they impelled to take it seriously when they find it inconvenient. They also know that, in any event, the takings clause does not mean what Epstein says it means—implications that he finds necessary, others find quite avoidable. The justices are, of course, quite capable of sound constitutional interpretation on the basis of original intent when it is not inconsistent with their purposes, and they have no current purpose greatly to expand the protection given property interests as Epstein recommends.

To deprive the Constitution of determinable meaning and make it a charter for judicial enforcement of an abstraction is obviously to grant Supreme Court justices very substantial, if not unlimited, policymaking power and therefore to raise with embarrassing clarity the central question of constitutional law: how can such power be reconciled with the system of decentralized democratic government contemplated by the Constitution? Proponents of judicial activism, whether of the left or the right, deal with this problem, too, in exactly the same way. They argue, first, that judges do not decide constitutional cases on the basis of their personal policy preferences, even if they are not strictly bound by the Constitution. Judicial discretion is limited and therefore consistent with democracy, the argument goes, by a supposed requirement that judges decide cases on the basis of principle, even if not exactly on the basis of the Constitution. As a second or supplementary line of defense, they argue that, in any event, the virtues of democracy and majority rule are easily overstated—that the function of constitutionalism, after all, is to frustrate majority rule.

The fallacy of the argument that the policymaking power of judges is limited by a requirement that they decide controversial issues on the basis of principle is that no accepted resolving principle exists—or the issue would not be controversial—and that, in any event, we have no practical means of enforcing the supposed requirement. An ideal of the legal system—perhaps of any conceptual system—is to make it resemble Euclid's geometry, a system with a few self-evident, or at least generally accepted, axioms from which all further conclusions follow with certainty and predictability as a matter of logic. The ideal, unfortunately, is unattainable; we lack and will always lack the requisite axioms, or judging could be largely assigned to computers. "General propositions," unfortunately, as Justice Holmes pointed out, "do not decide concrete cases."[59]

Problems of social choice are difficult, not because it is difficult to discover the resolving principle, rule, or generality, but because we have many principles—and they, like the interests they are meant to protect, inevitably come into conflict. We have a principle protecting the interest in speech, for example, but also principles protecting interests in quiet, cleanliness, safety, and order. These interests cannot, as an economist might say, simultaneously be maximized. The unavoidable conflict of legitimate interests can be resolved only by making value judgments, by evaluating and compromising the conflicting interests. The essence of self-government is that these valuations are to be made in accordance with the collective judgment of the people, not by a king, priest, or council of sages.

Even if a dispute-resolving principle could be identified in a controversial case, we have no way of imposing a constraint on judges that they accept and abide by it. If judicial review were confined, as Hamilton and Marshall suggested, to enforcing a few well-defined restraints on government—even if they were not all quite as well defined as the two-witness requirement in trials of treason—it might be feasible to sanction judges who go beyond enforcing such restraints. Hamilton assured the ratifiers of the Constitution that impeachment would be readily available to ensure that judges do not abuse their offices.[60] Jefferson's failure to remove Justice Chase for his flagrant displays of Federalist partisanship while on the bench, however, convinced him that impeachment was "not even a scare-crow."[61] That it has remained totally ineffective is shown by our failure to bring impeachment proceedings even on the basis of the clearest examples of gross judicial misbehavior, such as the Court's contemptuous treatment of Title IV of the 1964 Civil Rights Act in the *Swann* case, Title VI in *Bakke,* and Title VII in *Weber.*[62]

Even if we were willing to impeach judges for faithlessness to the law and misuse of judicial power, as we should be, it would not be feasible or appropriate to attempt to impeach them for failing to apply such ill-defined or undefined standards as those suggested by proponents of judicial activism. Just as it is unrealistic to suppose that such nebulous standards as Dworkin's "concepts" of the Framers, Epstein's "necessary implications" of the constitutional text, or Macedo's "moral aspirations" of the Constitution limit judicial discretion, it would be improper to suggest that judges could be sanctioned for failing to abide by such standards.

The absurdity of the claim that such alleged standards limit or can be a basis for limiting judicial discretion can be illustrated by trying to imagine judges attempting to utilize them in deciding actual cases. Imagine, for example, Justices William Brennan and Thurgood Marshall cogitating on whether they should hold capital punishment unconstitutional. "You know, Thurgood," Brennan might say, "according to Professor Dworkin, holder of Blackstone's old chair of jurisprudence at Oxford and our kind of guy, we are not authorized to invalidate policy choices simply on the basis of our personal preferences. If something is not explicitly prohibited by the Constitution, that is, is not within the Framers' specific conceptions—and capital punishment, awkwardly enough, is not only not prohibited but explicitly and repeatedly provided for[63]—we ought to prohibit it only when it is inconsistent with the Framers' unspecified concepts. Where do you think that leaves us on capital punishment?" "Well, Bill," Marshall might reply, "as you know, the Eighth Amendment—applicable to the states through the Fourteenth (wink, nudge)—prohibits 'cruel and unusual punishment.' What could be crueler than killing someone? And we sure have made capital punishment unusual; indeed, we effectively abolished it for more than a decade.[64] There's no question in my mind, Bill, that capital punishment is prohibited by the Framers' concepts. What do you think?" "I think," Brennan might reply, "that as usual, Thurgood, you are absolutely right: the Constitution, properly interpreted as recommended by Professor Dworkin, clearly prohibits capital punishment. There is certainly no problem here about our substituting our views for those of the American people." One could run through this exercise again, substituting Epstein's "necessary implications" for Dworkin's "concepts of the Framers," and confidently predict no change in result.

Epstein acknowledges that his standard for judicial review permits (indeed, requires) "a level of judicial intervention far greater than we now have, and indeed far greater than we ever have had."[65] This does not mean, however, he insists, that he advocates "judicial activism in cases of economic liberties."[66] Epstein apparently believes he has discovered a Euclidean system in which judges indeed have much to do, but all of it is strictly limited by the dictates of inexorable logic. His system's axioms, unfortunately—that the takings clause applies to the states and that it has inherent meaning apart from its intended meaning—are not only not self-evidently true, but not true at all. Even if his premises were true, his "necessary implications" of the takings clause are less the result of syllogistic reasoning than of his policy preferences. A judge confined, not by the intended meaning of the constitutional text, but only by Epstein's notion of necessary implications from the text, would find himself very little confined, and a judge with as much to do as Epstein would give him would likely find it hard to believe that he is confined at all.

Proponents of judicial activism, left and right, also share a profound skepticism about, not to say hostility to, majority rule. That a high degree of judicial intervention in the political process limits majority rule should, they argue, be seen as a benefit, not a loss. The very purpose of constitutionalism, they remind us, is to limit majority will in the interest of protecting individual rights. Individual rights, of course, are unambiguously good things, the more the better, as we never tire of telling the Russians. In any event, man, according to the Declaration of Independence, is "endowed by his Creator with certain inalienable rights," rights that, we must literally thank God, are not dependent on mere majority acquiescence.

Majoritarian policymaking "has appeal under some circumstances," Justice Brennan is willing reluctantly to concede, but "it ultimately will not do," he believes, because majorities cannot be trusted.[67] Judge Alex Kozinski, a Reagan appointee to the United States Court of Appeals for the Ninth Circuit, certainly has his disagreements with Justice Brennan, but not on this point. He is equally fearful of "the unbridled will of the majority," and equally insistent that we have an "anti-majoritarian and anti-democratic" Constitution.[68] Roger Pilon, conservative scholar and member of the Reagan administration, believes that while legislatures are "the domain of interest and will," courts are "the domain of reason,"[69] a view possible only for one who has read more political philosophy than Supreme Court opinions. Denouncing "the majoritarian myth," Macedo argues that "direct democracy and majoritarianism were decisively rejected by the Framers."[70] Epstein, noting "flaws in the democratic process," argues that "the Constitution clearly does not endorse any version of popular democracy."[71] The most he is willing to concede to legislatures is that the Constitution "does not assume that [they] have no task to perform."[72]

Proponents of judicial activism are, of course, correct that the Framers of the Constitution did not set up a system of direct democracy. The Constitution created a republican system of representative democracy, with the franchise largely confined (by reason of state control) to white male property owners, and with procedures, such as bicameralism, that operate to impede lawmaking. The system was nonetheless remarkably democratic for the time, with one house of the legislature based on population and subject to biennial election. In any event, and more to the point, nothing in the Constitution or its history indicates a purpose to limit majority rule by granting policymaking power to judges. It does not even explicitly provide for judicial review, much less judicial review not based on definite constitutional provisions.

The Declaration of Independence, it is true, speaks of inalienable rights granted by the Creator, but that was a revolutionary manifesto attempting to justify defiance of law, hardly fit material for the business of judges. The Constitution, by contrast, the foundation of a government and legal system, contains no such reference. Creator-endowed inalienable rights must, unfortunately, be Creator-enforced, and the Creator's record in this regard has not been good; the grim and bloody tale that is human history indicates that would-be human rights are all too alienable. Only government-granted rights are government-enforced, and in a democracy all such grants come from no other source than the people, and they continue with the approval of the people.

There is no disagreeing with Epstein that democracy has its flaws, or with Macedo that "making government accountable to the people is not sufficient to secure either order or the protection of liberty and rights."[73] All one can say for democracy, as Churchill has pointed out, is that it is better than its alternatives, the least bad form of government—which is not necessarily to damn it with faint praise, for that is also all one can say for most human institutions and perhaps for life itself. Democracy does not make rights secure—a change in the law rearranges rights and the majority can change the law—but experience indicates that it makes them as secure as they can be made. More democracy in the sense of more immediate popular control of policymaking is not necessarily to be preferred to less, but greater policymaking power in the hands of unelected and unremovable officials of the central government is most certainly not the road to individual security.

Macedo is also correct that judicial restraint is a choice of "majority power over individual liberty,"[74] but he fails to understand that judicial activism is a choice of judicial power over individual liberty. At least for one whose sad lot in life is to study the doings of judges, the former choice seems much the better bet. Judges, political scientists should continually remind themselves, are only lawyers in robes, persons skilled only in the manipulation of language to the achievement of their ends and not ordinarily noted for moral punctiliousness. Greater individual security and liberty do not lie in the childish search for an ultimate authority better and wiser than a majority of our fellow citizens, but in recognizing and accepting that we are unavoidably in each other's hands and must therefore develop and inculcate habits of tolerance and self-restraint.

Even assuming that the Framers' intent in adopting a constitutional provision can be ascertained, why (proponents of judicial activism often ask) should that intent be determinative? Why should the people of today consider themselves bound by the views of a relatively small group of people who lived 200 years ago and were, of course, not nearly so well placed to understand the needs and problems of today? The question is a good one, but its challenge, of course, is to constitutionalism, not to the proposition that the Constitution must be taken to mean what it was intended to mean if judicial review is to be consistent with the judicial function of interpreting rather than making the law. As long as judicial review is described and justified, as it always is, as constitutional interpretation, honesty requires that it be such in fact, based on an attempt to determine the Constitution's intended meaning.

Justifying constitutionalism—the limitation of contemporary self-government by prior decision-makers—is indeed a more difficult matter. The basic theories seem to be two: an alleged need to control the worse or impassioned self by the better or calmer self, and an alleged need to correct or compensate for defects inherent in self-government. The first theory is illustrated by Odysseus ordering his crew to tie him to the mast in order to prevent him from being lured to destruction by the Sirens' song that he knew he would find irresistible. It is also illustrated by a Buddy Hackett skit in which a gambler in Las Vegas who has lost all his money is choking his wife to make her give him a cash reserve that he had earlier made her promise not to give him. Proponents of judicially-enforceable constitutionalism, such as Alexander Hamilton, generally no great fans of democracy, imagine that majorities are much given to periods of passion in which they are in need of restraints.[75] The restraints must come either from the majorities' betters—people in touch with sources of guidance unavailable to the average person—which is inconsistent with self-government under conditions of political equality, or from the majority itself during one of its better moments. The latter possibility raises the question of how the people can tell their better from their worse moments; it would seem reasonable for them to assume that their present view on any issue—always the most informed—is the better view.

If, when Odysseus hears the Sirens, he orders his men to untie him from the mast, as presumably he would, on what basis can they determine that his earlier order is more authoritative? Earlier instructions do not ordinarily take precedence over later ones from the same source. Similarly, how is it possible for today's majority to be bound by the commands of an earlier one? Why cannot a majority always simply change by majority rule any previously imposed restraint on majority rule, as was in fact done in adopting the Constitution? If the delegates to the constitutional convention could decide to ignore the unanimity requirements of the Articles of Confederation, a majority today can likewise ignore any requirement of a more than majority vote to change the Constitution.

The second justification for constitutionalism is perhaps more substantial: the view that majority rule can in some circumstances—as in the prisoner's dilemma of game theory—produce results that the majority does not want or considers less than optimal. A balanced budget amendment (a constitutional limitation on federal spending), for example, might be justified on such grounds. It may be that the constitutionally protected pursuit of self-interest through the political process will otherwise inevitably produce a higher level of public spending than the majority wants. Similarly, a constitutional limit on the number of consecutive terms one can serve in a particular office might be justified on the ground that incumbency unavoidably gives advantages unrelated to merit. Of course, the problem of how a majority or any group of people at one time can control a majority at a later time remains. If a majority of the people of a state want to elect a governor for a third term, for example, despite a state constitutional restriction, presumably they could call a convention and adopt by majority vote a new constitution without the restriction.

If one believes that majority rule is the best available alternative to settling disputes by physical force—the majority would presumably be able to exercise the greater force—and that useful principles limiting majority rule are extremely difficult to state, one is led to the view, heretical in the United States, that constitutional limitations are not generally good ideas. Even our very short and generally non-restrictive Constitution, one may note, manages to create unnecessary problems. It created such a problem when, for example, President Nixon wanted to appoint Senator William Saxbe as his attorney general. Because the pay of the attorney general had been raised in the current session of Congress, along with the pay of other federal officials, the emoluments clause[76] clearly prohibited the appointment, even though Nixon wanted it, Saxbe wanted it, and no living person objected. The incident illustrated that although real constitutional questions are extremely rare, they can arise, although not necessarily to any good purpose. Similarly, one may question the usefulness of the constitutional restrictions that make, say, Henry Kissinger and Senator Rudy Boschwitz of Minnesota ineligible for the presidency because they are not native-born, as well as those that make persons less than twenty-five years old ineligible for election to the House of Representatives.

Skepticism about the value of judicially-enforceable constitutional restrictions leads to the view that, while judges should interpret those that we have in good faith to mean all that they clearly were intended to mean, they should not be interpreted to mean more—so as to disallow policy choices the Framers did not clearly disallow. Lack of knowledge as to the intended meaning of a constitutional restriction should operate not in favor of but against its application or extension. In a democracy, that is, the presumption should be in favor of policymaking through the ordinary political process and against policymaking by judges.

The meaning of the takings clause, for example, is far from clear; analysis indicates that it is very difficult to state a sensible, administrable compensation principle[77]—but then, a large part of my point has been that it is difficult to state any sensible, administrable principle. If minimal integrity could be introduced to constitutional law, however, most of the problem would be eliminated by the recognition that the takings clause is not applicable to the states—the ratifiers of the Fourteenth Amendment did not, to say the least, clearly so provide. The clause would also cause little problem, of course, if it were treated not as a judicially enforceable provision of law, but as a moral exhortation or useful reminder to legislatures, for which role it, like most of the Bill of Rights, is better suited. In any event, the history of the adoption of the takings clause, such as it is, indicates that it was understood, like most other constitutional restrictions, to have a very limited function.[78] The federal government, the Framers probably meant only to say, should not meet its needs by a policy of confiscation.

All government acts, it turns out, can adversely affect property values, but not all diminutions of value can be compensable, as Holmes pointed out,[79] or even raise a serious constitutional question, or government would be unable to function—and unlike libertarians, most people would like government to be able to function. Some diminutions must be compensable or the clause has no meaning, but how are they to be distinguished? It appears that no real, decision-aiding rule can be stated except on the basis of administrability, and considerations of administrability may require that compensation be limited to cases where the federal government takes possession of or asserts title to property. There is little to be said for such a rule except that the alternative may be a system such as Epstein's, effectively turning vast areas of policymaking over to judges, which is to say quite enough.

The arguments of proponents of judicial activism of the right, I have tried to show, are no more valid than—indeed, are not distinguishable from—the arguments of proponents of judicial activism of the left, even if, as I believe, the right's policy preferences for individual liberty and minimal government are more consistent with the maintenance of a free and prosperous society. Advocacy of judicial activism of the left can be explained, however, (even if it cannot be justified) purely on grounds of expediency. Liberals need not really be so foolish as to believe that problems of social choice can be resolved on the basis of principle rather than by evaluating competing policy considerations, or even disbelieve generally in majority rule in order to favor a high degree of policymaking by courts. They need only know, as they do, that for four decades the courts have given them and can be expected to continue to give them what they can obtain in no other way: enactment of major portions of their political agenda. Advocacy of judicial activism of the right, on the other hand, is not only mistaken but foolish, as the right can have no similar expectation.

Justice Antonin Scalia has pointed out that the "development of lawyers (and hence of judges) through a system of generally available university education which, in this country as in others, more often nurtures collectivist than capitalist philosophy" means that defenders of economic liberty "would be foolish to look for Daddy Warbucks on the bench."[80] Academia is not only the molder of judges but also, along with the media, their source of approval and protection. Academics and the members of the media support, encourage, and defend judicial activism of the left by declaring left-wing judicial activists American heroes[81] and doing all they can to spread the myth—which some of them may even half-believe—that the resulting constitutional decisions have something to do with the Constitution. Judicial activism of the right, however, they would denounce with equal or greater vigor, and with the added virtue of accuracy, as judicial usurpation of lawmaking power inconsistent with republican self-government.[82]

Justice Scalia also argued (less persuasively) that, except for the Supreme Court's rejection of "substantive due process in the economic field" in recent decades, judicial activism of the left "might have gotten even worse."[83] It is doubtful that judicial activism of the left could have gotten any worse. A realistic assessment of the Court's work makes it impossible to believe that Justice Brennan, for example, votes in any case on any basis other than his political views. It is not imaginable to me that he would refrain from voting to enact a liberal policy because he notices other justices refraining from voting to enact conservative policies; he would no doubt see the latter votes as simply and correctly rejecting conservative policies.

Justice Scalia may be right, however, that "in the long run, and perhaps even in the short run," advocacy of judicial activism of the right may reinforce in the public mind "mistaken and unconstitutional perceptions of the role of the courts in our system,"[84] and therefore may make it harder to combat judicial activism of the left. We should oppose judicial activism, of the right as well as of the left, because whatever might be the best system of government, government by a committee of unelected and unremovable lawyers sitting in Washington, D.C. and pretending to be interpreting the Constitution must surely be one of the worst. Conservatives, at least, have no reason to believe that it is likely to be an improvement on government with the consent of the governed.

Notes

1. *See, e.g.,* Swann v. Charlotte-Mecklenburg Bd. of Educ., 402 U.S. 1 (1971) (schools); Wyath v. Adorholt, 503 F.2d 1305 (5th Cir. 1974) (mental institutions); James v. Wallace, 406 F. Supp. 318 (M.D. Ala. 1976) (prisons).

2. U.S. CONST. Art. I, §7, cls. 2,3.

3. L. HAND, THE BILL OF RIGHTS 28 (1958).

4. THE FEDERALIST No. 78 (Mentor ed. 1961).

5. 1 Cranch (5 U.S.) 137 (1803).

6. U.S. CONST. Art. III, §3, cl. 1.

7. THE FEDERALIST No. 78, at 471 (Mentor ed. 1961). "Judicial power," Marshall assured us, "has no existence. Courts are mere instruments of the law, and

can will nothing . . . Judicial power is never exercised for the purpose of giving effect to the will of the judge. . . ." Osborn v. Bank of the United States, 9 Wheat. (22 U.S.) 738, 866 (1824).

8. U.S. CONST. Art. I, §10, cl. 1.

9. Home Building Savings & Loan Ass'n v. Blaisdell, 290 U.S. 398 (1934).

10. *See, e.g.,* Roe v. Wade, 410 U.S. 113 (1973).

11. *See, e.g.,* Furman v. Georgia, 408 U.S. 238 (1972).

12. *See, e.g.,* Miranda v. Arizona, 384 U.S. 436 (1966).

13. *See, e.g.,* Engel v. Vitale, 370 U.S. 421 (1962).

14. *See, e.g.,* Wolman v. Walters, 433 U.S. 229 (1977).

15. *See, e.g.,* Swann v. Charlotte-Mecklenburg Bd. of Educ., 402 U.S. 1 (1971).

16. *See, e.g.,* Gregory v. City of Chicago, 394 U.S. 111 (1969).

17. *See, e.g.,* A Book Named "John Cleland's Memoirs of a Woman of Pleasure" v. Massachusetts, 383 U.S. 413 (1966).

18. *See, e.g.,* New York Times Co. v. Sullivan, 376 U.S. 255 (1964).

19. *See, e.g.,* Craig v. Boren, 429 U.S. 190 (1976).

20. *See, e.g.,* Levy v. Louisiana, 391 U.S. 68 (1968).

21. Dred Scott v. Sandford, 19 HOW. (60 U.S.) 393 (1856).

22. 109 U.S. 3 (1883).

23. Lochner v. New York, 198 U.S. 45 (1985) (a state may not limit employment of bakers to ten hours a day and sixty hours a week).

24. Hammer v. Dagenhart, 247 U.S. 251 (1918); Bailey v. Drexel Furniture Co., 259 U.S. 20 (1922).

25. Brown v. Board of Education, 347 U.S. 483 (1954).

26. *See, e.g.,* Goldberg v. Kelly, 397 U.S. 254 (1970).

27. *See, e.g.,* R. DWORKIN, LAW'S EMPIRE (1986); L. TRIBE, AMERICAN CONSTITUTIONAL LAW (2nd ed. 1988); Michelman, *Foreword: Traces of Self-Government,* 100 HARV. L. REV. 1 (1986); Tushnet, *Following the Rules Laid Down: A Critique of Interpretivism and Neutral Principles,* 96 HARV. L. REV. 781 (1983).

28. R. DWORKIN, TAKING RIGHTS SERIOUSLY (1977).

29. *Supra,* note 27. *See also* M. PERRY, THE CONSTITUTION, THE COURTS AND

HUMAN RIGHTS (1982); Grey, *Do We Have An Unwritten Constitution?*, 27 STAN. L. REV. 703 (1975); Fiss, *Objectivity and Interpretation*, 34 STAN. L. REV. 739 (1982).

30. Brennan, *The Constitution of the United States: Contemporary Ratification*, 27 S. TEX. L. REV. 433, 438 (1986).

31. *Id.* at 433.

32. *Id.* at 436–37.

33. *Supra*, note 23. The era ended with the Court's upholding of minimum wage legislation in West Coast Hotel Co. v. Parrish, 300 U.S. 379 (1937).

34. S. MACEDO, THE NEW RIGHT V. THE CONSTITUTION 8–10 (1986).

35. *Id.* at 11.

36. *Id.* at 11–14.

37. *See* Roe v. Wade, 410 U.S. 113 (1973).

38. See Engel v. Vitale, 370 U.S. 421 (1962); Abington School Dist. v. Schempp, 374 U.S. 203 (1963).

39. S. MACEDO, *supra* note 34, at 20.

40. DEMOCRACY AND DISTRUST 58 (1980).

41. 7 Pet. (32 U.S.) 243 (1833).

42. The Fourteenth Amendment repeats the Fifth Amendment's due process clause, but not the immediately following takings clause or any other provision of the Bill of Rights.

43. R. EPSTEIN, TAKINGS: PRIVATE PROPERTY AND THE POWER OF EMINENT DOMAIN 18 (1985).

44. *Id.*

45. For example, Locke opposed gross inequalities of wealth. J. LOCKE, SECOND TREATISE OF GOVERNMENT in TWO TREATISES OF GOVERNMENT §33 (T. Cook ed. 1947). *See* Balkin, *Learning Nothing and Forgetting Nothing: Richard Epstein and the Takings Clause*, 18 URB. LAW. 707 at 709–10 (1986).

46. R. EPSTEIN, *supra* note 43, at 26.

47. *Id.* at 27.

48. *Id.* at 24.

49. *Id.* at 27, 29.

50. *Id.* at 28.

51. *Id.*

52. *Id.* at 29.

53. *Id.* at 24.

54. A THEORY OF JUSTICE (1971).

55. ANARCHY, STATE, AND UTOPIA (1974).

56. TAKING RIGHTS SERIOUSLY 134–36 (1977).

57. R. EPSTEIN, *supra* note 43, at 31.

58. S. MACEDO, *supra* note 34, at 16.

59. *Lochner,* 198 U.S. at 76.

60. THE FEDERALIST no. 79, at 474. (Mentor ed. 1961).

61. Letter to Judge Roane (Sept. 6, 1819), reprinted in 7 WRITINGS OF THOMAS JEFFERSON 140 (H. Washington ed. 1854). "Experience had proved," Jefferson said, "that impeachment in our forms is completely inefficient." (letter to Edward Livingston, Mar. 25, 1925, *id.* at 403-4) with the result that judges are given "a freehold and irresponsibility in office." Letter to Mr. Coray (Oct. 31, 1823), *id.* at 322.

62. Swann v. Charlotte-Mecklenburg Bd. of Educ., 402 U.S. 1 (1971); Regents of Univ. of Cal. v. Bakke, 438 U.S. 265 (1978); United Steelworkers v. Weber, 443 U.S. 193 (1979). In Title IV of the Act, for example, Congress carefully defined "desegregation" as "the assignment of students to public schools . . . without regard to their race," and repeated for emphasis that desegregation "shall not mean the assignment of students to public schools in order to overcome radical imbalance." In *Swann* the Court, in a unanimous opinion by Chief Justice Burger, nonetheless upheld a district court "desegregation" order requiring the assignment of students to schools on the basis of race to overcome racial imbalance. Apart from grossly misstating the facts of the case throughout the opinion, the Court stated, without supporting citation and clearly contrary to fact, that the legislative history of the Act showed that Congress did not mean to apply its definition of desegregation to the South. *See* L. GARGLIA, DISASTER BY DECREE: THE SUPREME COURT DECISIONS ON RACE AND THE SCHOOLS (1976). In *Bakke* and *Weber,* the Court held, respectively, that the Act's unqualified prohibitions of race discrimination by federally assisted institutions (Title VI) and in employment (Title VII) did not apply to discrimination against whites. *See* Graglia, *The "Remedy" Rationale for Requiring or Permitting Otherwise Prohibited Discrimination: How the Court Overcame the Constitution and the 1964 Civil Rights Act,* 22 SUFFOLK U. L. REV.569 (1988).

63. U.S. CONST. Amends. 5, 14.

64. Furman v. Georgia, 408 U.S. 238 (1972).

65. R. EPSTEIN, *supra* note 43, at 30–31.

66. *Id.* at 31.

67. Brennan, *supra* note 30, at 436.

68. *Foreword: The Judiciary and the Constitution*, in ECONOMIC LIBERTIES AND THE JUDICIARY xv (Dorn & Manne eds. 1987).

69. *Legislative Activism, Judicial Activism, and the Declining Private Sovereignty*, in *id*. at 183, 202.

70. S. MACEDO, *supra* note 34, at 23.

71. R. EPSTEIN, *supra* note 43, at 30.

72. *Id*.

73. S. MACEDO, *supra* note 34, at 28.

74. *Id*. at 27.

75. Hamilton thought the people were subject to "occasional ill humors" which, "though they speedily give place to better information, and more deliberate reflection, have a tendency, in the meantime, to occasion dangerous innovations in the government, and serious oppressions of the minor party in the community." THE FEDERALIST No. 78 at 470, 469 (Mentor ed. 1961).

76. U.S. CONST. Art. I, §6.

77. *See, e.g.*, Michelman, *Property, Utility and Fairness: Comments on the Ethical Foundations of "Just Compensation" Law*, 80 HARV. L. REV. 1165 (1967); B. ACKERMAN, PRIVATE PROPERTY AND THE CONSTITUTION (1977).

78. *See* Sax, *Takings and the Police Power*, 74 YALE L. J. 36, 54–60 (1964).

79. Pennsylvania Coal Co. v. Mahon, 260 U.S. 393 (1922).

80. *Economic Affairs as Human Affairs*, in Dorn & Manne, *supra* note 70 at 36.

81. *See, e.g.*, J. BASS, UNLIKELY HEROES (1981) ("The dramatic story of the Southern judges of the Fifth Circuit who translated the Supreme Court's *Brown* decision into a revolution for equality"); B. SCHWARTZ, SWANN'S WAY: THE SCHOOL BUSING CASE AND THE SUPREME COURT (1986).

82. For examples of such denunciation of right-wing activism of the past, *see, e.g.*, L. BOUDIN, GOVERNMENT BY JUDICIARY (1932); H. COMMAGER, MAJORITY RULE AND MINORITY RIGHTS (1943).

83. *Supra* note 81, at 35.

84. *Id*. at 34.

Economic Liberty and the Future of Constitutional Self-Government

STEPHEN MACEDO[1]

I. Introduction

The future of economic liberty under the Constitution depends on the viability of the "double standard" that has, for nearly half a century, characterized judicial interpretations of our fundamental law.[2] The modern Court applied a searching level of scrutiny to challenged laws that interfere with a list of "preferred freedoms" (including liberties associated with speech, religion, and privacy) or that involve discrimination against "discrete and insular" minorities.[3] At the same time, and despite the Constitution's several explicit supports for economic freedom, laws interfering with economic liberties and property rights are typically subjected to a lax test designed to establish only that the merest "rational basis" exists for the law in question.[4] In applying this double standard, as I shall explain at greater length below, the modern Court ignores the Constitution's support for economic liberties, disparages the close connections between economic and other forms of freedom, and invests legislatures with an unwarranted measure of trust, trampling on a core ideal of our constitutional regime: the aspiration to reasonable self-government.

This paper examines the most important case in a good many years for expanding judicial protections for economic liberties. Richard Epstein's *Takings* is rooted in economic theory and informed by a deep suspicion of democratic politics.[5] I shall argue that while we can learn much from Epstein's work, his may not be the surest way of contributing to the future robustness of neglected freedoms. His analysis is, first of all, more an exercise in pure theory than in constitutional interpretation. In addition, the proper goals of representative government in a large and diverse society are more various than Epstein allows, and the constitutional case for economic liberty must be more complex than the one Epstein advances. Finally, political deliberation and the practice of self-government, which Epstein regards as mere costs, are inherently valuable. Indeed, since our Constitution is informed by moral aspirations (never fully achieved, but worth continually striving for), the founding document itself suggests the value of reflecting on and working toward the great ends stated in its preamble (among them justice, the general welfare, and liberty).

Confronting Epstein's argument allows us to gauge the limits of a style of constitutional interpretation that is brilliantly executed, but too strictly economic. While endorsing much of Epstein's analysis, I will argue that the case for economic liberties in our constitutional order should be considered from a more broadly political perspective. Scientific rigor and theoretical simplicity cannot be the overriding aims of an adequate political understanding of economic liberty and the Constitution.

II. The Old Jurisprudence and the New

During its so-called *Lochner* era (1897–1937), the Court attempted to develop principled ways of limiting the powers of federal and state governments to regulate the economy. Under the Fourteenth Amendment's due process clause (which says, "No state shall . . . deprive any person of life, liberty, or property without due process of law"), the old Court defined individual economic liberties that were enforceable against the states. The case from which this era of economic activism draws its name, *Lochner v. New York,* struck down a state law imposing maximum working hours on bakery employees as an abridgment of "liberty of contract."[6] But the old Court's solicitude for liberty was not confined to matters economic. It moved, albeit haltingly, toward a principled defense of the whole range of constitutional liberties, economic and otherwise. As the Court explained in *Allgeyer v. Louisiana,* in a unanimous ruling that marked the dawn of this era,

> The liberty in [the Fourteenth Amendment's due process clause] means not only the right of the citizen to be free from the mere physical restraint of his person, as by incarceration, but the term is deemed to embrace the right of the citizen *to be free in the enjoyment of all his faculties:* to be free to use them in all lawful ways; to live and work where he will; to earn his livelihood by any lawful calling; to pursue any livelihood or avocation, and for that purpose to enter into all contracts which may be proper, necessary and essential to his carrying out to a successful conclusion the purposes above mentioned. [emphasis added][7]

The old Court developed a commerce clause jurisprudence that imposed limits on Congress's regulatory powers by distinguishing, for example, between commerce and production and placing regulation of the latter among the reserved powers of the states.[8] (The clause reads: "The Congress shall have power . . . To regulate Commerce with foreign Nations, and among the several States, and with the Indian Tribes. . . .") These distinctions were swept away when the Court moved to accept the constitutionality of the New Deal. The commerce clause is now regarded as the main constitutional source of the vastly expanded powers of the federal government, including its authority over civil rights, agricultural production, and labor. While the Court's abandonment of a rigorous standard of commerce clause review earned it the applause of most commentators, we should feel uneasy with a commerce power so extensive that it sacrifices other values of high constitutional standing.

Consider the fate of an Ohio farmer named Filburn who planted 23 acres of wheat for consumption on his own farm. The New Deal's Agricultural Adjustment Act of 1938 had given the Secretary of Agriculture the power to establish quotas to help the Department curtail supply and prop up prices. Filburn was fined by the Department for harvesting in excess of his "quota," which had been set at 11.1 acres.[9] Farmer Filburn challenged the quota on the grounds that it was a regulation not of commerce, but of production entirely for his own farm needs. The Court ruled, however, that his activities "affected commerce," since excess supply constituted an "obstruction to commerce."[10]

Despite its near-universal acclaim, there are many grounds on which the new commerce clause jurisprudence can be questioned. If the Framers had wanted to grant Congress power over economic affairs generally, it would have been easier to say "The Congress shall have power to regulate the economy." That is not what was said. Furthermore, as Epstein points out, "commerce" in ordinary usage suggests trade rather than manufacturing or production.[11] The language of the clause ("with foreign Nations, and among the several States, and with the Indian Tribes . . .") does not suggest the power to reach commerce conducted wholly within one state, much less within the confines of a man's own plot of land. Certainly the domestic economy of Filburn's farm affected commerce, but what does not affect commerce? *Wickard,* in short, briskly sacrificed economic liberties closely bound up with personal autonomy and gave little weight to the importance of limiting Congress's powers.

Justice Holmes warned long ago that the logic of indirect effects on a "national market" had no intrinsic limit: "Almost anything—marriage, birth, death, may in some manner affect commerce."[12] Without defining and limiting distinctions (of the sort the Court has now abandoned) or at least a sensitivity to the tradeoffs at stake, it is hard to see why marriage, divorce, or anything you may think of should not fall squarely under federal commercial regulation.

The extremely broad interpretation of Congress's powers upheld by the post-*Lochner* Court in cases like *Wickard* was, despite the Court's effort to show otherwise, a fundamental revision of commerce clause jurisprudence. Speaking for the Court in *Wickard,* Justice Jackson sought the authority of Chief Justice Marshall's opinion in *Gibbons v. Ogden*:[13]

> Marshall described the federal commerce power with a breadth never yet exceeded. . . . He made emphatic the embracing and penetrating nature of this power by warning that effective restraints on its exercise must proceed from political rather than from judicial processes.[14]

In fact, however, Marshall's reading of the commerce power in *Gibbons* denies Congress the sort of *carte blanche* that Jackson seems eager to supply:

> It is not intended to say that these words comprehend that commerce which is completely internal, which is carried on between man and man in a state, or between different parts of the same state, and which does not extend to or affect other states. Such a power would be inconvenient, and is certainly unnecessary. Comprehensive as the word "among" is, it may very properly be restricted to the commerce which concerns more states than one. The phrase is not one which would probably have been selected to indicate the completely interior traffic of a state, because it is not an apt phrase for that purpose; and the enumeration of the particular classes of commerce to which the power was to be extended, would not have been made, had the intention been to extend the power to every description. The enumeration presupposes something not enumerated; and that something, if we regard the language or the subject of the sentence, must be the exclusively internal commerce of a state.[15]

The old Court's effort to limit the reach of the commerce power, via the commerce/production distinction and others, resonates with Marshall's opinion in *Gibbons*—an opinion attuned to the dangers of reading Congress's powers too broadly and not only too narrowly.[16]

Much more would need to be said, I realize, to justify even the general thrust of the old Court's commerce clause jurisprudence, and a good deal of the *Lochner* Court's jurisprudence was misguided. I would argue, however, that since the demise of the old Court the judiciary has too often absolved government economic actions from any kind of meaningful review.

When it comes to state regulation of the economy, the Court now often requires nothing more than the barest "rationality" to justify restrictions on individual liberty. And where legislators have not actually advanced a rational basis, the Court has simply hypothesized its own rationale, displaying little concern for the existence of evidence showing that the act is tailored to advance the hypothesized end. In cases like *Williamson v. Lee Optical* (which made it illegal for opticians to fix broken glasses while allowing sellers of ready-to-wear glasses to continue in business) and *Ferguson v. Skrupka* (allowing only lawyers to engage in the business of debt-adjusting), the Court has come close to saying that the absence of any reason for interfering with people's economic affairs is reason enough.[17] Extreme deference to legislatures is especially egregious where obvious grounds for suspicion are provided by the fact that powerful groups (optometrists, lawyers) have an interest in using the law to disadvantage competitors.

It is entirely appropriate for the Court to carefully scrutinize legislation infringing on First Amendment freedoms, privacy, and other constitutional rights. The Court's double standard is an error of omission, not of commission.[18] Economic liberties deserve some weight in the difficult process of squaring competing constitutional values. And legislative actions affecting economic interests, and not only those touching on the political process and minority rights, merit a measure of real distrust. This does not mean that laissez faire must always prevail over competing values, such as Congress's need for discretion in the exercise of its commerce power. We simply cannot, however, justify the judicial abandonment of the economic sphere to unfettered legislative discretion. A burden to justify restrictions on economic liberty ought to rest with legislators. The justifications offered should be scrutinized to ensure that a legitimate end is being pursued by carefully chosen means.

The virtual non-review of cases involving economic liberty is an unconstitutional standard. Consider four of the broad constitutional values that weigh in favor of subjecting economic regulations to a more searching level of judicial scrutiny:

1) General Distrust of Popular Legislatures

Just as we properly suspect that prejudice or personal interest often lies behind restrictions on personal liberties or the right to equal protection of the laws, so too legislative restrictions on economic freedom may often be motivated by the personal interests of powerful groups rather than by legitimate public purpose. Since power is being exercised in cases involving property regulation, legislatures have an obligation to provide reasonable justifications and evidence showing that a contested act advances the public good.

2) The Ideal of Reasonable Self-Government

It is not only important *that* courts limit the economic power of the state, it is also important *how* they do it. The losers in legislative contests over economic legislation deserve, at least, to be provided with good reasons and evidence showing that a legitimate and substantial public purpose is being served by well-chosen means. As Justice Stevens has argued, the equal protection clause should be read as imposing on legislators a pervasive duty "to govern impartially."[19]

The rule of law stands for the idea that one law applies to citizens and public officials alike, and citizens have the right to challenge the government's interpretation of that law in an impartial court. As I have argued elsewhere, implicit in the rule of law and liberal constitutionalism is the aspiration to publicly-reasonable self-government.[20] The Court must not mark off the economic sphere as a no-man's-land of unreasonableness and sheer power, a domain of arbitrary legislative discretion.

3) Limited Federal Power

The Court must fairly weigh the significance of the fact that Congress's powers are enumerated. Enumeration does not imply the legitimacy of a niggardly interpretation of powers, but it does imply that there are limits. The specific grants of Article I, Section 8, may only be the "great outlines" of Congress's powers, as Marshall argued in *McCulloch*.[21] Even on Marshall's expansive reading, however, the great ends of the federal government remain limited. The Court should insist, as did Marshall, that the commerce power is exercised only for commercial ends, and not as a pretext for non-commercial purposes.[22] It should ensure, as well, that the government's pursuit of commercial ends does not overwhelm the broad liberty and privacy interests that also find a place within the Constitution's scheme of values.[23]

4) The Connections Among Economic and Personal Liberties

The old Court had a livelier and developing sense of what is only rarely noted on the new Court: that economic and personal liberties are intertwined and mutually supporting.[24] Property rights, the freedom to engage in a particular occupation, and other economic rights converge with personal values such as the security of the home, the survival of valued communities and associations, and the pursuit of happiness in a freely chosen way of life.

I have suggested that the Court apply a heightened level of scrutiny to cases where individual economic liberty is at stake, and give greater weight than it has to the interest in economic liberty. There is no denying that the Constitution poses many difficult questions, and not only in the economic sphere. A responsible Court will not evade these questions. If the commerce power competes at some points with liberties that have constitutional status, then the Court has no alternative to striking balances and drawing lines as best it can. The old Court at least struck these balances and drew these lines with a sensitivity to the values competing with the power of the national government.

Richard Epstein would simplify the difficult process of weighing and balancing constitutional values by streamlining the purposes of constitutional government. Let us turn now to consider Epstein's position, and the costs and benefits of adopting his perspective.

III. Epstein's Way

Like Robert Nozick, Richard Epstein is concerned to restore the protection of property rights to the center stage of government activity. Nozick begins his landmark work with the maxim that "Individuals have rights, and there are things no person or group may do to them (without violating their rights)."[25] Epstein's variation on the Nozickian overture would have to read: "Individuals have rights, and no state that claims to be legitimate can override those rights without paying for it." Epstein rejects any theory, such as Nozick's, that regards

> all entitlements as absolute, so all forced exchanges are ruled out of bounds, regardless of their terms. Yet without forced exchanges, social order cannot be achieved, given the holdout and free rider problems. . . . [N]o invisible hand mechanism explains the emergence of an exclusive sovereign within any given territory,[26]

Epstein adopts the language of "natural rights," but he views rights as derivative from, rather than as side constraints upon, a consequentialist moral calculus.[27] The Epsteinian state is not committed, at its base, to the protection of rights come what may. Consequentialism does all the moral work in Epstein's theory.[28] Epstein would protect property rights because, and insofar as, they contribute to an efficient, wealth-producing market order.

Epstein legitimizes government actions that override rights by invoking the real gains that are to be had from politically "forced exchanges. . . . Autonomy must be protected by supplying the equivalent for what is lost, but it is not protected absolutely."[29] There are genuine public goods with real free-rider problems: national defense being the classic example. There are, as well, "common pool problems" of property allocation (underground oil tables, for example) which can only be efficiently dealt with by mandatory schemes. People have property rights, on Epstein's view, but they have no "holdout" rights: no rights to impede, on the basis of eccentric or perverse preferences, transactions that promise positive gains. All this reminds one of Hobbes's remarks about how to deal with people who will not accommodate themselves to society:

> A fifth Law of Nature, is Compleasance; that is to say, *That every man strive to accommodate himselfe to the rest.* For the understanding whereof, we may consider, that there is in mens aptnesse to Society; a diversity of Nature, rising from their diversity of Affections; not unlike to that we see in stones brought together for building an AEdifice. For as that stone which, by asperity, and irregularity of Figure, takes more room from the others, than it selfe fills; and for that hardnesse, cannot be easily made plain, and thereby hindereth the building, is by the builders cast away as unprofitable, and troublesome: so also, a man that by asperity of Nature, will strive to retain those things which to himselfe are superfluous, and to others necessary; and for the stubbornness of his Passions, cannot be corrected, is to be left, or cast out of Society, as cumbersome thereunto.[30]

So is Epstein soft on property rights? Far from it. He views constitutional law and politics broadly as merely an extension of a libertarian interpretation of the private law of property, torts, and contracts.

What kind of property rights do people have on Epstein's view? Complete property rights of exclusive possession, use, and disposition, including the right to enjoy both present and future productive uses. "[A]*ll* regulations, all taxes, and all modifications of liability rules are," Epstein insists, "takings of private property prima facie compensable by the state."[31]

Why conceive of property rights this way? To minimize transaction costs which impede beneficial bargains: everything is assigned to some private party. Clear lines preclude opportunities for political rent-seeking that might result from fuzzy boundary lines open to political negotiation.

When can exchanges be forced? Whenever transaction costs or holdout and free-rider problems prevent the capturing of real positive public benefits. These typically arise in the provision of a genuine public good, and in allocating rights in common pools.[32]

How, crucially, are the benefits of political action to be divided? "[I]n accordance with the size of the original contributions."[33] For Epstein, political action generates no surplus of revenue for the state to distribute according to its discretion: once the costs of state operations are funded, the benefits must be paid to property owners in proportion with their original shares. Even the power to tax for the general welfare must be interpreted, according to Epstein, in light of the theory of strict property rights informing the takings clause. Redistribution is strictly forbidden; general taxation is itself a taking, so tax-funded programs must provide "implicit in-kind compensation."[34] A tax to pay for national defense or police protection must provide "in-kind" benefits (peace and security) sufficient to compensate for the value taken. Any value generated in excess of what is required for compensation should accrue to people in proportion to their initial contributions.

To illustrate the move from a hypothetical state of nature to political life, Epstein draws two sliced pies: the smaller, contained in the larger, represents people's "natural" holdings. The larger represents the value of those holdings after the inception of the state. The slices in the larger pie are simply proportional extensions of those in the smaller pie: the government may not redistribute shares among property owners.[35] If we cannot, on Epstein's view, have a state without overriding rights, we cannot have a legitimate state without insisting that just compensation be paid *and* that public benefits accrue to taxpayers *proportionately* with their initial endowments. These two requirements are said to be implicit in a properly interpreted takings clause:

> The requirement of just compensation assures that the state will give to each person a fair equivalent to what was taken. . . . [T]he public use requirement conditions the use of the coercive power by demanding that any surplus generated by the action . . . is divided among individuals in accordance with the size of their original contributions. Each gain from public action therefore is uniquely assigned to some individual, so that none is left to the state, transcending its citizens.[36]

State action is, thus, wrapped in a tight double-knot of full compensation for takings and proportionate distribution of benefits, thus precluding a discretionary surplus. This double knot removes the opportunity and, prospectively, the incentive for rent-seeking behavior.[37]

What constitutes a legitimate public use? Take the example of a gristmill owner whose damming of a river will flood the farmer's land. A benefit is provided to the general public in the form of lower prices for a basic commodity, and the mills were obliged to process the grain of all comers on a non-discriminatory basis.[38] Furthermore, a basic resource (in this case, water) is locked in place by nature, creating the possibility of holdout problems arising from "situational necessity."[39] Granted a positive social gain, a good open to all, and a plausible case that the situation of the water is, in some sense, unique, Epstein is prepared to let the taking go forward.

The really crucial thing in such cases is that fair compensation must be provided—full compensation helps ensure that a property owner is not being simply gouged or exploited. The baseline for compensation is the property's full value, not the market price. Obviously, anyone who holds a piece of property values it more highly than the available market price.[40]

In the classic case of the mill owner flooding the farmer's land, it would be most appropriate, Epstein argues, to judicially divide the surplus generated by the mill pond between mill owners and the dispossessed farmers. The New Hampshire Mill Act of 1868, for example, required compensation to the owner of the flooded land at 50% above the market value of the land, "thus ensuring a division of the surplus brought about by the forced exchange."[41] There is no reason why the mill owner should be able to capture the entire surplus generated by the mill pond.[42]

To take another example, under its landmarks preservation law, New York City prevented Penn Central from using its air rights to construct a building over Grand Central Station. We can grant that the preservation of historical landmarks is a legitimate public purpose: preserving a unique and irreplaceable good for all. The Court, in *Penn Central,* foundered not on the public use issue, but on the question of compensation.[43] In gauging the required compensation, the Court focused not on how much value was taken by the regulation, but on whether the private owner was left with what the Court deemed a "reasonable return" on his investment and whether the regulation abrogated "distinct investment-backed expectations."[44] Peter H. Aranson has criticized the line of cases initiated by *Penn Central*: "No matter how complete or incomplete it might be, loss of value is loss of value, and if the loss is a consequence of government action, there is at least a rebuttable presumption that a taking has occurred."[45] The Court cannot turn a taking into a non-taking by arguing that a "reasonable" value was left.

To round out Epstein's theory, two supporting doctrines must be introduced: first, the police power, and second, the requirement of "proportionate impact." Although it has often been thought of as the broad power, retained by the states, to protect the "health, safety, and morals" of society, Epstein argues that the police power "qualifies the explicit text" of the Constitution and is an "inherent attribute of sovereignty at all levels of government."[46] He interprets the substance of the police power in light of his libertarian theory of private law: the police power is engaged in response to wrongful private conduct that forfeits the right to compensation.[47] And crucially, satisfying the police power allows takings without compensation: the plant that repeatedly discharges poisonous chemicals into the city water supply may be seized without providing compensation.[48]

The police power, on Epstein's view, is solely about protecting individuals from force, fraud, and nuisances;[49] it is not for promoting positive goods. Environmental legislation limiting the development of wetlands or the filling of marshes might be procuring legitimate public goods, but they are not actions against nuisances on any plausible account, so they must be paid for: "when the state wants to use private property to benefit mankind, it announces it wants to take them [*sic*], at least in part, for public use. It must therefore pay for the privilege."[50] To allow otherwise would permit the politically powerful to impose the costs of public goods entirely on a few.

This brings us to the second ancillary doctrine of Epstein's theory: the proportionate impact requirement. The public use requirement of the takings clause, on Epstein's view, applies importantly to the division of the surplus generated by any particular forced exchange. The requirement of proportionality "prevents B from using the state's eminent domain power to capture the surplus," or to garner a share of the surplus proportionately greater than others; "by controlling the disposition of the surplus it limits the scope of partisan activities."[51] Requiring that surpluses generated by government activity be divided *pro rata* in accordance with initial private holdings insures that the law cannot be used to secure special benefits for particular groups.

The government is not required to pay compensation every time it takes, taxes, or regulates. Pure public goods like national defense provide implicit in-kind compensation (in the form of peace). When implicit in-kind compensation is roughly proportionate to the original holdings,

> Each person whose property is taken by the regulation receives implicit benefits from the parallel takings imposed upon others. . . . The landowner who cannot erect a large sign is assured that his neighbor cannot put up a sign that will block his own.[52]

The implicit in-kind compensation principle is crucial because it allows Epstein to endorse, without insisting on any explicit form of compensation, general rules and regulations that work to the long-term advantage of the class burdened by the rules.[53]

Epstein wants to allow the forced exchanges necessary to provide public goods while cutting off rent-seeking by disallowing redistribution altogether. Pure public goods spread their benefits fairly evenly, so the costs should be spread evenly as well. Goods may be public in a second, less pure, sense of the term: access may be open to all, but the good is not used by all (lighthouses would be a good example). In these cases, "a system of special assessments could ensure the proper matching of costs and benefits."[54]

The trick, for Epstein, is to fashion a set of judicially-enforceable rules that preclude the incentive for injustices arising from the pursuit of gain, at the expense of others, through politics. The goal, in effect, is to cure the mischief of faction. Recall that Madison defined a faction as

> a number of citizens, whether amounting to a majority or minority of the whole, who are united and actuated by some common impulse of passion, or of interest, adverse to the rights of other citizens, or to the permanent and aggregate interests of the community.[55]

With the proportionate impact test in place, self-interested behavior would tend not toward faction but toward the promotion of the public good, because the gains of collective action would be distributed in proportion to contributions made.

It is never to be assumed that, because someone whose property has been taken is also a citizen and therefore a beneficiary of a particular government scheme, in-kind compensation is sufficient. As Epstein points out, the fact that a person whose car has been destroyed by a General Motors employee owns $100 in General Motors stock does not abrogate his right to a fair settlement of his claim.[56]

Is it possible to link various legislative packages in order to see whether imbalances in one program are offset by others? Only, Epstein argues, insofar as the legislature makes the linkage explicit, for

> each part of the package was acted on independently and bears the influence of factional efforts, which the compensation requirement is meant to combat. The abuses are additive, in fact, but they are treated as offsetting as a matter of law when the political dynamic is ignored.[57]

Apparently, Epstein's concern is not only with economic impacts, for then it would be hard to see why laws should not be linked to some degree. He is, at least instrumentally, concerned with a certain quality of political process in which factional behavior, measured law by law, is disallowed. His concern, in effect, is to control the effects of faction by rooting out at each stage of the legislative process the opportunity and incentive for what Aristotle considered the essence of injustice: *pleonexia,* or unjust grasping, taking more than one's proper share.[58]

The overall point of Epstein's takings rules is to mimic as closely as possible the incentive and benefit structure among stockholders in a private corporation.[59] Of course, given differences between citizen preferences about risk aversion and other factors, the analogy can never hold exactly. But granted these imperfections, the disproportionate impact test comes as close as possible to placing all property holders on an equal footing: all share the gains of each state action proportionately, and political association is rendered the equivalent of a non-voluntary joint-stock company:

> the disproportionate impact test creates a precise link between each individual welfare function and the social welfare function, so that the latter is simply a multiple of the former. It follows (from the simple calculus) that an individual constrained by the disproportionate impact test will necessarily maximize his own welfare if he endorses government initiatives that maximize aggregate social welfare as well.[60]

With thoroughness and brilliance, Epstein draws out the stringent political implications of his theoretical structure. All negative-sum games and all redistributive programs are rendered constitutionally suspect, along with many land-use laws, progressive taxation, and much (probably most) twentieth-century social legislation. "With the possible exception of charitable deductions, the eminent domain clause forecloses virtually all public transfer and welfare programs. . . ."[61]

Epstein would not, however, sweep away the offending programs with a stroke of the judicial pen. Serious reliance interests have developed around the programs, and people have substantially altered their savings and investment patterns as a consequence of the mass of legislation; "the error of the community hath the force of law."[62] Epstein would prevent future expansion of these programs, and pare and prune where possible: no further increases in the progressivity of tax rates should be allowed, and the whole pattern of "special exactions, like the windfall profits tax," should be struck down.[63]

IV. Wealth and Virtue

Before turning to the questions of how much of Epstein's theory is a valid exercise in constitutional interpretation, I'd like to examine the attractions and significance of his central analytic device in more detail. One striking feature of Epstein's theory of politics is that the proportionate impact rule is designed to create a pattern of incentives for political behavior that is both efficient and virtuous. More effectively than the requirement of mere generality in the rule of law, the disproportionate impact test

> prevents individuals from being singled out for special abuse. . . . So long as government action constitutes a taking *and* a giving to the same individual in the same proportions, all is well. The very generality of the rule, in Rawls's phrase, places all individuals behind a veil of ignorance so that, being benefited and burdened, they will not be able to prefer their own interests to those of others.[64]

The disproportionate impact test checks unfairness more effectively than the mere generality of laws because generalization still allows "all of the burdens to be imposed on one class and all the benefits on another, imposing uncompensated takings on a grand scale."[65] The test helps institutionalize a libertarian interpretation of the basic liberal democratic requirement to treat people as equals.

Now, Epstein's main concern is not to make the legislative process more reasonable as such, but to root out opportunities for rent-seeking—and yet the two projects seem, to a great degree, to go hand in hand. For the abuses that Epstein seeks to root out are failures to acknowledge or justify a way of treating people unequally. If politics is allowed to be a means for one group to gain benefits for itself while imposing the costs on others, we have a formula for both the inefficient provision of public goods and for a gross form of unfairness. Preserving New York City's historical landmarks may well be a valid public purpose, one that enhances the property values of everyone in the city. But surely the owners of buildings designated landmarks deserve compensation for the special burden of non-development that they are being asked to bear. Nor can we assume that "it all comes out in the wash," that one special restriction on the few for the good of the many will be compensated for by other cases in which the property owners in *Penn Central* are among the many being benefited. There is no reason to assume that governmental benefits and burdens automatically spread themselves evenly.

To assume proportionality in advance is to declare utter unconcern with exploitive laws (laws that gouge a few for the sake of many, or many for the sake of a few), and to unleash an utter free-for-all of special-interest legislation. That each dog is free to try and eat the others is poor solace for those who would rather be left alone, or for those who find it hard and costly to organize. In the face of economic injustice we can do more than hope that "it all evens out in the end." We should, with Epstein, count the courts among the institutions that properly police the process of economic regulation, insisting the legislators explicitly link programs where necessary to provide compensation for takings and ensure at least a reasonably fair distribution of benefits and burdens.

Epstein rightly notes that his proscription against disproportionate impact laws bears striking similarity to the "representation-reinforcing" theory of John Hart Ely.[66] Ely sees two legitimate aims for judicial review: first, keeping the channels of political change open, by enforcing First Amendment rights, voting rights, and other guarantees of fair political participation,[67] and second, reinforcing the representation of "discrete and insular minorities" who, though formally represented, may in fact be ignored by dominant groups in the process of forming governing coalitions.[68] Ely would have the Court police the representative process to ensure, in effect, that all groups in society are represented, really and not only formally, in the process of policymaking.

In effect, Ely's substantive vision of a well-working democratic process goes beyond interest-group pluralism: not only must every group have access to the process of group bargaining, but they must also actually be represented in the final product of legislation. That is to say, the implicit vision of a well-working polity is Rousseauian: the legislative will must be general, it must will the good of all.[69] The end-product of the process must actually speak, as it were, to the good of all in society: laws must represent a vision of the good of all. Thus, Ely speaks of the duty of winners of legislative battles to "virtually represent" the losers in making law for all.[70] Rousseau himself tried a variety of ways of specifying what he meant by the "general will," without much success. For example,

> every act of sovereignty (that is, every authentic act of the general will) obligates or favors all citizens equally, so that the sovereign knows only the nation as a body and does not draw distinctions between any of those members that make it up.[71]

Taken literally, Rousseau here seems to require the impossible: that every citizen must always be treated equally, or the same way, by a law. But surely it must sometimes be legitimate to draw distinctions among citizens: the old and the young, those who have paid their taxes and those who have not. Rousseau must mean that all citizens must be treated as equals, each having his or her good taken equally seriously by lawmakers.[72] It seems to me that the Rousseauian requirement of generality makes sense as the claim that it is not enough for all to play a role in the legislative process, but that the good of each and all must also be represented in the substance of the end product—and that occurs when the end product can be publicly justified by reasons speaking to the good of all. Groups must not be allowed to use politics merely for their own ends, while respecting the formal rights of everyone to a voice in the lawmaking process.

Now I do not want to claim that Epstein is a closet "Rousseauian." There is, however, in both Rousseau and Epstein, a rigid insistence that proper laws must not reflect "particular perspectives" or partial interests.[73] Of course, whereas Rousseau wanted to create the relevant generality of perspective by requiring each to give up all of his property without reservation to the whole,[74] Epstein insists that the whole has no right to take property without compensation or to distribute surpluses non-proportionately.[75]

There is a more profound difference between Rousseau and Epstein. According to what I have called the Rousseauian ideal, legitimate laws should have public justifications that could conscientiously be judged to be good for all. Public justifications are inclusive, and inclusiveness might be tested by looking at the reasons that have been offered in support of the law, and asking whether those reasons could be seen as part of a reasonable, constitutional interpretation of the good of all. Rousseauians would hold that the right form of justification is one that refers to the good of society as a whole, leaving no one out (again, not only of input into the process but of being represented in the product).

Epstein tests the inclusiveness of the legislative process not by examining the reasons offered for a legislative package, but rather by seeing whether everyone has in fact benefited in proportionate monetary terms (looking not for abstract reasons but proportionate dividends). Epstein, distinctively, monetizes the relevant generality requirement, and builds it into the incentive structure of political actors from the outset so that they never have an incentive to behave factiously, or to promote policies which advance their own good disproportionately—they know from the start that they will not be allowed to benefit disproportionately from any measure that passes. The disproportionate impact test monetizes Rousseau's general will and constitutionalizes it via the takings clauses.

Epstein is profoundly distrustful of political discretion unstructured by constitutional rules assuming thoroughgoing self-interest. And here we can recall another well-known republican theorist, Kant, who denied that a "republican constitution" required "a state of angels." It should, rather, make use of "those self-seeking inclinations. . . . to create a good organization for the state," and so, "As hard as it may sound, the problem of setting up a state can be solved even by a nation of devils (so long as they possess understanding)."[76]

Epstein believes that not only virtuous behavior but virtuous attitudes themselves have the best chance of flourishing in the regime he describes:

> Civic virtue does not prosper in a world in which courts refuse to protect either personal autonomy or property rights. The eminent domain clause thus improves the soil from which civic virtue can grow. It controls abuse by demanding that losers in the legislative process retain rights that leave them as well off as they were before.[77]

Part of the output of his system, Epstein claims, is civic virtue.[78] Virtue should be fostered by reducing "the opportunities for illicit gains from legislative intrigue."[79] And civic virtue can be positively exercised in the provision of charity, and in "responsible participation in the provision of public goods."[80]

Is it farfetched to expect that an Epsteinian regime would produce not only greater wealth, but also a more virtuous citizenry? Courts are, on the liberal view that Epstein shares, among the proper fora for the rigorous justification of government acts to individuals who feel aggrieved. Heightened judicial scrutiny means that the reasons and motives for economic regulations are more likely to become publicized. Requiring the open acknowledgment of reasons and purposes may itself help to filter out unjust laws.

Kant put the matter abstractly when he asserted the "transcendental formula of public right: 'All actions affecting the rights of other human beings are wrong if their maxim is not compatible with their being made public.' "[81] And in defending the "extended republic," Madison seems to assert that here political groups can form only through open and public communications, a fact that helps filter out groups with pernicious motives: "where there is a consciousness of unjust or dishonorable purposes, communication is always checked by distrust in proportion to the number whose concurrence is necessary."[82] And perhaps it was in part the public nature of the repudiation which the Court gives to unjust measures which led Hamilton to suggest that judicial review

> operates as a check upon the legislative body in passing them [unjust and partial laws]; who, perceiving that obstacles to the success of iniquitous intention are to be expected from the scruples of the courts, are in a manner compelled, by the very motives of the injustice they mediate, to qualify their attempts. This is a circumstance calculated to have more influence upon the character of our governments than but few may be aware of.[83]

In addition to the fact that virtue is more likely to flourish in the absence of opportunities for corruption, it is also the case that the more open and reasonable political process that Epstein would help fashion might itself exercise an elevating influence, which could eventually shape people's attitudes and character and not only their behavior.

Perhaps somewhat surprisingly, then, Epstein's political regime has something to be said for it from the point of view of a concern with reasonable self-government and civic virtue. His polity would be an economist's dream, but Epstein also offers a formula (if we accept his defense of property rights and his hopes for widespread prosperity) for public policy without injustice. The disproportionate impact test attempts to ascertain whether people have been treated as equals. Epstein gives cash value to the requirement of "equal concern and respect," advancing a morality of legislation and a system of judicially enforced takings rules to enforce it.

V. How Far Can We Go with Epstein?

The political process of Epstein's ideal regime would be reviewed by judges to insure that power is exercised only for securing stringently-defined public goods. But, clearly, a related issue needs to be faced: what counts, under our Constitution, as a representation of the common good? How do we go about deciding what counts as a sufficiently reasonable legislative version of the common good? Here, Epstein is very strict: only proportionately bigger pies, with no redistribution among sliceholders. The question is whether the Constitution itself requires a strict proportionate impact test, or whether a more complex and flexible test of reasonable legislation better accords with the founding document.

We cannot swallow Epstein's argument whole, because too much of it is only vaguely derived from the Constitution. Before considering which aspects of the argument we should accept, let me offer three sets of reasons why we cannot accept Epstein's analysis wholesale. Those reasons, already alluded to, can be grouped under the labels constitutional, representational, and political.

First, Epstein's analysis is too heavily rooted in an abstract economic theory to be convincing as an interpretation of the Constitution. Economic theory and a libertarian interpretation of rights, common law, and the proper ends of government are the sources from which Epstein draws his analysis of the takings clause.

Consider, for example, Epstein's theory of the legitimate ends of government. This he derives from a theory of property rights and rules designed to minimize transaction costs and deter rent-seeking while allowing the curtailment of nuisances, the provision of public goods, and the settlement of common pool problems. Perhaps this is what government should be for, but does the Constitution itself announce such a theory? Not really. The Constitution does talk about rights, but natural rights theory really does no work in Epstein's argument. His total renunciation of transfers (from which the proportional impact test springs) rests on the assertion that, once any transfers are allowed, a political dynamic is generated which is bound to take them too far in generating "negative wealth effects," so "no transfers" is the best constitutional rule.

Personally, I might be persuaded to accept Epstein's assertion that, given the realities of human nature and the political process, pretty much everyone would be better off with a constitutional rule of "no transfers." But we would still be a long way from establishing such a claim in constitutional terms. It can be argued that transfer programs promote commercial prosperity and the nation's economic health, broad ends that underlie some of the specific grants of power to Congress. Transfer programs, that is, might be seen as means toward the promotion of a reasonable conception of constitutional purposes.[84] And it simply is not clear that any particular clause of the Constitution disallows transfers.

Epstein pays little attention to how particular constitutional provisions might be interpreted in light of the larger values and ends implicit in the document. He refers, at one point, to the Bill of Rights as a statement of the ends of government.[85] But the Constitution also states its ends in places like the Preamble and in Congress's enumeration of powers. Instead of looking to these sources, Epstein tends to think about the purposes of government in terms of his libertarian theory of the police power ("an inherent attribute of sovereignty at all levels of government"), a theory largely divorced from the text of the Constitution itself.[86]

Before conceding a general police power to the federal government, or establishing the contours of the national government's ends, one would certainly want to look at Congress's enumeration of powers in Article 1, Section 8 of the Constitution. The first eight powers concern commerce broadly: the power to tax, to borrow money on credit, to regulate commerce, to establish uniform rules of naturalization and bankruptcy, to "coin money," to punish counterfeiting, to establish post offices, and to grant exclusive patents and copyrights. Congress's other powers are to provide for lower courts, for governing the District of Columbia, and for national defense. Section 8 closes with the elastic clause: Congress may "make all laws which shall be necessary and proper for carrying into execution for foregoing Powers, and all other powers vested by this Constitution in the Government of the United States."

How broadly we should read the elastic (or "necessary and proper") clause is a hard question. One plausible approach to the elastic clause was articulated by Chief Justice John Marshall. In the famous case of *McCulloch v. Maryland* (1819), Marshall held that the specific grants of Section 8 are the "great outlines" of Congress's powers, which do not exhaust the means by which Congress may pursue its great ends. The very "nature" of the Constitution, said Marshall, requires that it avoid "the prolixity of a legal code," its "great outlines should be marked, its important objects designated, and the main ingredients which compose those objects deduced from the nature of the objects themselves."[87] And so Marshall held that while the Constitution does not specifically grant Congress the power to establish a national bank, that power is a legitimate means that facilitates the achievement of ends that are granted: to lay and collect taxes, coin money, regulate commerce, and support armies and navies. Even on Marshall's expansive reading, the ends and purposes of the national government remain limited. Congress may not use its powers as "pretexts" for purposes unrelated to commerce and national security.[88]

There certainly are problems with Marshall's manner of reading Congress's powers, as I have argued elsewhere.[89] But while Marshall's method stretches the logic of a government of enumerated powers and limited purposes, it does not overturn it. And Marshall's method has the virtue of interpreting one of the Constitution's open-ended phrases (the necessary and proper clause) in light of the apparent purposes implicit in other parts of the document and the Constitution as a whole. This seems to me to be a fundamentally proper method for making sense of the constitutional text and respecting its integrity.

Epstein, by contrast, looks at the takings clause in veritable isolation from the rest of the document: he says it is best to treat the eminent domain clause "as a self-contained intellectual proposition."[90] As a consequence of his interpretative strictures, Epstein never really comes to grips with the Constitution as a whole; indeed, he simply does not believe in the usefulness of arguments about purposes, ends, and values. And so he rejects the notion that the First Amendment should be interpreted in light of the "ends or social values that it is intended to serve," because "the great question is, who picks the values? . . . If all terms can be understood only with reference to their purposes, then explication quickly turns into an infinite regress."[91]

Epstein claims to support the authority of "ordinary usage" when interpreting the meanings of constitutional terms.[92] But while ordinary usage may sometimes be helpful in ascertaining the meaning of constitutional phrases, it will rarely be sufficient to determine either what a constitutional provision means or how it should be applied. (The Framers certainly disagreed about what the Constitution would require in particular cases, and to call them all "Lockeans" in some loose sense hardly settles the problem. It is doubtful that any of the framers adhered strictly to Locke; Epstein, in any case, certainly does not.) By the authoritative "ordinary usage," Epstein seems to have in mind his libertarian interpretation of the common law, but the defense of that understanding of law surely gets us back not to the analysis of ordinary usage, but to the defensibility of competing theories of the Constitution's ends and purposes. We simply cannot avoid the question: can Epstein's theory be read as the best interpretation of the Constitution as a whole, including its apparent implicit ends and purposes?

The Constitution speaks in broad language, and the Preamble sets out the document's ends:

> in Order to form a more perfect Union, establish Justice, insure domestic Tranquility, provide for the common defence, promote the general Welfare, and secure the Blessings of Liberty to ourselves and our Posterity. . . .

The Constitution's expansive terms are hard to define. Indeed, the preamble identifies the ends of the document with concepts about which people *ordinarily* disagree. The Constitution's invocation of "contested" concepts does not end with the Preamble, but is pervasive. There is the Ninth Amendment, for example: "The enumeration in the Constitution, of certain rights, shall not be construed to deny or disparage others retained by the people." But what other rights do we have? Surely, a Constitution of bright lines and clear rules would not leave that question unanswered. And, of course, there are the majestic generalities of the Fourteenth Amendment:

> No State shall make or enforce any law which shall abridge the privileges
> and immunities of citizens of the United States; nor shall any State deprive
> any person of life, liberty, or property, without due process of law; nor
> deny to any person within its jurisdiction the equal protection of the laws.

These phrases did not establish bright lines and clear rules. They changed the
Constitution significantly, or so many argued, but how they did so (and even
whether they did so) has been a source of tremendous controversy. How
could it have been otherwise?

The document, I would suggest, reads as though it was intended to
structure an ongoing argument about subjects on which either the Framers did
not—in specific terms—agree, or they did not want to close off further
debate and progress (or both). Indeed, debate and deliberation about (and,
perhaps, progressively improving understanding of) general requirements
(like "the equal protection of the laws") seem positively invited by the
decision to write broadly-worded requirements into the fundamental law.
Should we—can we—really try to eliminate such controversies? Or are
public debates and controversies about the meaning of "equal protection of
the laws" part of the Constitution's plan for us, and a source of moral
growth?

Epstein's exasperation with talk about values, ends, and purposes stems
in part, I think, from his desire to get on with what is for him the important
task of law: settling disputes about property claims so as to facilitate trade
and productivity, generate wealth, and maximize welfare. But is Epstein's
vision of politics the Constitution's vision of politics? Is Epstein's vision of
what is important the one implied in the Constitution?

The language of the Constitution itself encourages us to stop and pause
over matters that Epstein wants to dismiss. The very language of the
Constitution encourages us to engage in political arguments about things that
Epstein wants to settle with bright lines and clear rules. Epstein's argument
turns on regarding political deliberation as merely a cost. But political
argument is a cost only from a certain perspective, one that always asks
whether time spent arguing about politics could be spent more profitably.
And Epstein's extreme distrust of legislative discretion does not square with
the Constitution itself. Indeed, it was the Antifederalists who opposed the
Constitution precisely because

> They wanted detailed explicitness which would confine the discretion of
> Congressional majorities within narrow boundaries. . . . These men wanted
> everything down in black and white, with no latitude of discretion or
> interpretation left to their representatives in Congress.[93]

But, again, the Constitution's choice of broad, eminently arguable language
may itself imply that political deliberation is intrinsically valuable. It may

also imply that compromise in search of a consensus in a large and disparate republic is salutary and, in any case, necessary. Too many bright lines and clear rules might, apart from choking off political argument, leave the Constitution too inflexible and therefore incapable of continuing to attract allegiance over the course of centuries.

The problem for Epstein is, of course, that once one begins interpreting parts of the Constitution in terms of the whole, including its broad language and implicit ends and purposes, it becomes harder to find bright lines and clear rules. And it becomes difficult to justify the blanket judgment, never stated or implied in the Constitution, that all transfers are, in principle, unconstitutional. As soon as one provides a constitutional place for political deliberation and compromise, one opens a Pandora's box of rent-seeking opportunities.

It would be wrong to think that Epstein opts for simplicity out of an impolitic concern with theoretical elegance. He is convinced that the history of our regime and the teachings of economic theory show that, once opportunities for rent-seeking are available, rampant and ever-expanding abuses are inevitable:

> There's no stable, satisfactory, political equilibrium that can redress income inequality through coercive means, once we start to convert the rhetoric of risk aversion into the language of rights. The political system is such that you will get wild overproduction of transfers. My argument is that given the disastrous political equilibrium, the zero point of coerced transfers is the appropriate point.[94]

The political equilibrium is so degenerative that it is better to cut off the whole process before it can start. And so he reads the Constitution as embodying a simple set of ends, he adopts a simple conception of representation, and he tries to whittle political discretion down to a bare minimum. The question is whether we can, as Epstein would like, interpret the Constitution as precluding so much scope for political deliberation and judgment, as well as the opportunities for rent-seeking that inevitably accompany discretion.

Epstein rightly sees the notion of representation as central to any conception of the liberal state. His theory would, in a subtle way, represent us politically just as property owners and wealth-seekers. That, I would argue, is a much simpler conception of representation than the one embodied in our Constitution.

Epstein wants, as I said above, everyone's good to be represented in the legislative product: all property holders, at least, must share proportionately in the surplus generated by state activity. But each is, for Epstein, represented *only as* a property owner—there are no other grounds on which one can make a political claim. And, as in a joint stock company, each is represented in the product, as it were, in proportion to his or her original holdings. There can be no redistribution because people are present politically, for Epstein, only as wealth holders. Citizens cannot claim a share as equal citizens, or as equal persons.

Given Epstein's conception of how we are represented by government, political equality becomes paradoxical. If the appropriate model for politics is a private holding company, why should there be equal *political* power? Why not make political power proportionate to economic shares, as among stockholders in a company? Our equality as property owners is captured in the requirement of the proportionate impact test, so why should the poor be equally (disproportionately) represented in the legislature? Political equality inevitably contributes to an imbalance between political and economic incentives.

If we accept political equality as part of the Constitution's scheme of values, then the Constitution must represent us as more than wealth holders. We must be represented by the Constitution as equals, in some important way, and not only as holders of various amounts of wealth.[95] But, again, to admit a more complex conception of representation than Epstein allows opens the door to the kinds of political judgments Epstein wants to avoid: how else should we be treated as equals? What claims can we make based on our moral equality? What transfer programs might our equality help to justify?

Epstein would not deny that his conception of representation is simple, and would claim, indeed, that the political simplicity of the regime he advocates (its avoidance of "irreconcilable dualities") is one of its chief virtues.[96] The abandonment of simplicity creates opportunities for negative-sum games by making boundary lines fuzzy.[97] Complexity creates opportunities for debate and argument that can be exploited and manipulated for personal advantage by rent-seekers. The preference for simplicity is part and parcel of Epstein's suspicion of political deliberation about values and purposes.

Epstein's preference for simple and clear rules raises many questions. Much of political judgment is a matter of complex weighing of competing values, and much of political activity is inevitably a matter of give-and-take and compromise, providing scope for arguable judgments and many opportunities for self-interested political action. But Epstein wants to banish "irreconcilable dualities" from politics, and so it often seems that he wants to banish the pith and marrow of politics itself. The problem is, as I have argued, that it is hard to read the Constitution as having no room for politics.

Although Epstein's overall approach to constitutional interpretation is unacceptable, I would like to argue, in very general terms, that we should follow Epstein in two broad areas: first, in his insistence on a heightened level of review in economic liberty cases, and second, in his refusal to allow uncompensated takings under the guise of a regulation that leaves "reasonable value" with the property owner. Let me comment briefly on these two planks.

First, as I argued above, real critical bite must be put into the Court's analysis of the "reasonableness" of state infringements on economic liberty under the due process clause. Granted the existence of some nuisance that the state may legitimately regulate, or the existence of some aspect of the general welfare (understood in constitutional terms) that governments may legitimately pursue, the Court must still ask whether the means chosen are too broad or too narrow.[98] That is, does the police power regulation either burden some who are innocent of, or excuse some who are implicated in, the claimed evil? Either case would be a *prima facie* example of legislative unfairness, a failure to treat like cases alike, and a signal of the possible presence of some ulterior and illegitimate legislative motive. "Differential treatment," for Epstein, "is always a telltale sign that the police power has become a cloak of illegitimate ends whose influence overwhelms the stated reasons."[99]

Besides the issues of underinclusiveness and overinclusiveness, the Court should (since economic liberty has a legitimate place in the Constitution's scheme of values) also ask whether less intrusive means are available to achieve the purpose in question. These, Epstein rightly asserts, are the sorts of questions that the Court should but typically does not ask in cases where property rights and economic liberties are at stake. They are the sorts of questions that the Court does ask, however, under the guise of applying an "intermediate" standard of review in equal protection cases.[100] By beefing up the standard of review in cases involving economic liberty, the Court can help insure that the process of self-government is reasonable and is seen to be so.

Second, my sense is that when takings are allowed, we should join Epstein in requiring full compensation, including compensation for any impairment of value based on future earnings potential (thus overturning *Penn Central*). When value is taken from a few in order to provide a general benefit, full compensation should be paid. There is no good reason why an arbitrarily-selected group (the owners, say, of particular buildings) should be saddled with the costs of general benefits. A judicially-enforced principle of strict compensation would help avoid at least some gross forms of exploitation and unfairness.

I do not, however, see how we could go further with Epstein, holding either that general taxation is governed by takings principles or that all transfers are unconstitutional. I do not agree, in other words, that the Constitution can be read as requiring that all benefits be distributed in proportion to wealth holdings. Progressive taxation may be pernicious as a policy choice, but it is a policy choice that seems well within the Sixteenth Amendment's broad language: "Congress shall have power to lay and collect taxes on incomes, from whatever source derived, without apportionment among the several States, and without regard to any census or enumeration." My sense is that while it is unreasonable (and a violation of the takings clause) to single out the owners of buildings that are designated landmarks to bear the cost of their preservation, it is not constitutionally unreasonable to require higher-income groups to pay higher marginal income tax rates.[101] Different orders of unfairness are involved in these two cases, and the takings clause speaks clearly only to the first case.

If transfers are not, in principle, unconstitutional, then it may also often be within the bounds of constitutional reasonableness for the benefits of regulations to include some forms of redistribution. That is, assuming that a particular regulation generates in-kind benefits sufficient to compensate for all takings, the surplus generated (by a zoning regulation, for example) might be focused onto relatively poor segments of the populace. Epstein's pervasively-applied proportionate impact requirement, despite its many attractions, is simply not, so far as I can see, a recognizably constitutional limitation on government activity.

I have suggested that we go part of the way with Epstein, but not all of the way. We cannot, in other words, swallow his "tale of the two pies," or the implacable application of the proportionate impact rule to every act of government. Requiring a heightened standard of reasonableness and full compensation when property is taken leaves us far short of the "bright lines" and "clear rules" that Epstein seeks. Many opportunities for rent-seeking will remain, and the Pandora's box that Epstein wants firmly shut remains open—if less widely than at present.

VI. Conclusion

We can learn from Epstein's distrust of electoral politics, but we should not adopt his theory wholesale. In order to plan for a future in which economic liberties and property rights are more secure, we will need a more complete theory of the ends and purposes of the Constitution than Epstein offers, as well as a more complex conception of representation. We will need, as well, to place more trust in the political process, and to place economics within a larger political understanding of the Constitution, rather than allowing economic theory to overshadow the Constitution. In closing, let me recommend four broad kinds of departures from Epstein's defense of economic liberty.

1) On the Constitution's Ends and Purposes

I have argued that the Constitution in fact embodies many of the kind of "irreconcilable dualities" that Epstein wants to avoid. The Constitution's goals are complex, its purposes expressed in broad language. It seems to invite just the sort of argument and discussion that constitutes our tradition of constitutional interpretation; in that respect, the Constitution has been a success, not a failure. If we consider structured, partially institutionalized political argument to be conducive to moral progress, then we should be glad that the Constitution is more than a collection of bright lines and clear rules.

The broad, moral language written into the Constitution is best understood as a delegation to future generations directing them to continue both pondering questions of justice and struggling to complete the task of liberal construction. That is basically how Lincoln, for one, understood the conflict between the basic principle of human equality, enshrined in the Declaration, and the practice of slavery, explicitly (but not ringingly) protected for a time by the Constitution. The Framers, Lincoln held, saw no way to get rid of slavery at the time, but intended to set it on the course of ultimate extinction, in part by endorsing human equality as a fundamental principle:

> They meant to set up a standard maxim for free society which should be familiar to all: constantly looked to, constantly labored for, and even, though never perfectly attained, constantly approximated, and thereby constantly spreading and deepening its influence and augmenting the happiness and value to life to all people, of all colors, every where.[102]

With Sotirios A. Barber and Gary J. Jacobsohn, I would argue that the Constitution is essentially aspirational, and must be interpreted in light of the broad moral aspirations announced by the text.[103] Interpretation, both in the courts and in our politics more broadly, should, on this view, be about precisely the sorts of values and purposes about which Epstein is skeptical and dismissive.

2) On Representation and Moderation

The Constitution is not just about moral aspirations: it is also about political moderation and compromise, virtues that are captured in the complexity of the Constitution's scheme of representation. Epstein puts little weight on political moderation, and none on the complex goals of representation. As I have stressed, his government would represent us from a single perspective only: as wealth-holders and welfare maximizers.

The Constitution does not tie down elected officials with strict and rigid rules; it calls, rather, upon public officials to exercise judgment and discretion. Madison and the other founders, while realistic about and largely accepting of human self-interest, also placed no small measure of confidence in the elevating potential of the Constitution's scheme of representation. Representation, as Madison put it, filters popular views through

> the medium of a choosen body of citizens, whose wisdom may best discern the true interest of their country and whose patriotism and love of justice will be least likely to sacrifice it to temporary or partial considerations.[104]

This is not to say that elected representatives were meant to be simple "trustees" of the public good. With their relatively short terms, Members of the House of Representatives, in particular, are encouraged to bring the felt interests and local concerns of constituents to bear on policymaking.

That representatives often represent the particular interests of their constituents is unarguable. A certain amount of interest-group representation may be justified as a way of helping to attract the voluntary allegiance and support of a wide range of people. It may be, that is, that any simple conception of representation would alienate elements within a disparate polity. Commentators as different as Aristotle and the Antifederalist Melancton Smith have argued, for example, that for actual polities to be stable, they must try to represent more than virtue.[105]

Cass Sunstein rightly refers to the Constitution's scheme of representative government as a "hybrid conception."[106] Constitutional representation seeks both to elicit serious deliberation about the public good from elected representatives presumed to be more virtuous than the citizenry and to keep the representatives close enough to the felt interests and local concerns of their constituents to forestall the popular alienation that might result from a too high-minded and remote national government. Paradoxical as it sounds, truly good government might not be government that attracts the voluntary allegiance of all the people.[107] It may also be helpful to have representatives who cultivate, more directly and personally, the sympathy and support of constituents.[108]

Epstein assumes that his plan to represent people simply as wealth pursuers would not give rise to serious problems of alienation and disaffection. I am not so sure. As it is, our complex (even messy) representative system affords numerous points of access for people to exert influence and express grievances. And while the open and responsive nature of our system may mean that it has a hard time filtering out rent-seekers and implementing coherent and sustained public policies, it may also help to impart unity and moderation to a large, diverse country like ours.[109]

3) On Citizenship and Political Participation

If we regard the Constitution as aspirational, and if we regard fulfilling and furthering those aspirations as of independent importance, then we are unlikely to regard political participation as a mere cost. We will, more likely, consider a certain amount of deliberation about the Constitution and its broad goals of justice, welfare, and freedom as built into the ideal of citizenship implicit in the founding document. If we regard the Constitution as adumbrating an intrinsically valuable form of political association, then we should not resist assigning citizens some measure of duty to reflect on the founding document's meaning and to carry forward the tradition of its interpretation.

Aside from a moral concern with duty, it may also be worth considering how economic liberty and democratic citizenship tend to be mutually supportive in practice. In describing how economic freedom and a more democratic political order emerged together, Adam Smith emphasized the tendency of commerce to undermine the "servile dependency" of the old feudal order.[110] Economic independence seems to lead naturally, for Smith, to an insistence on political independence, as among the rebellious American colonies.[111] Economic and political liberty converge in an ideal of a self-governing liberal character.

From a constitutional perspective, it is important that commercial liberty is indirectly and gently educative and character-shaping: it attracts the natural passion for gain and advancement and shapes men into self-controlled, independent citizens. And so Publius argued that commerce was conducive to an industrious, prudent, and sober citizenry.[112] Smith and Tocqueville argued that commerce can help encourage energy and independence, rather than passivity and servility.[113]

Economic liberty deserves a more prominent place within the Constitution, but not only as a means of producing wealth. The political defense of a commercial republic rests, in part, on its capacity to encourage a certain sort of character suited to self-government in a liberal society. We need to understand economic liberty and property rights, then, as part of a larger plan for constitutional self-government, in the manner of Publius, Smith, and Tocqueville.

4) A Constitutional Case for Economic Liberty

I have suggested that the case for economic liberty must be more complex than Epstein allows; it must include a broader sense of the Constitution's ends and purposes, an acceptance of the value of some measure of political participation, a more complex conception of representation, and an account of the ways in which economic liberty promotes the sort of character needed for free self-government. We should avoid building the case for economic liberty on a narrow economic base. Though it may be overstated, there is something to Tocqueville's warning against linking the case for freedom too closely to economic rewards,

> Nor do I think that a genuine love of freedom is ever quickened by the prospect of material rewards; indeed, that prospect is often dubious, anyhow as regards the immediate future. True, in the long run freedom always brings to those who know how to retain it comfort and well-being, and often great prosperity. Nevertheless, for the moment it sometimes tells against amenities of this nature, and there are times, indeed, when despotism can best ensure a brief enjoyment of them. In fact, those who prize freedom only for the material benefits it offers have never kept it long.
>
> What has made so many men, since untold ages, stake their all on liberty is its intrinsic glamour, a fascination it has in itself, apart from all "practical" considerations. For only in countries where it reigns can a man speak, live, and breathe freely, owing obedience to no authority save God and the laws of the land. The man who asks of freedom anything other than itself is born to be a slave.[114]

Much as many of us might resist the phrase, a constitution is inevitably a political *plan* for the future.[115] Our Constitution establishes a comprehensive set of arrangements for a political order, capable of achieving certain valued goals and of preserving itself over time. But the Constitution also constitutes a society more broadly and, indeed, shapes a certain kind of personality: one fulfilled by and supportive of a liberal political order. The future of economic liberty will, I think, be best promoted and secured from a full-blown constitutionalist perspective, one capable of comprehending the Constitution as a comprehensive (if not detailed) plan for the future of constitutional self-government.

Notes

1. I am indebted to the editors of this volume and the other contributors to it for helpful comments on an earlier draft of this article.

2. For a critical discussion of the double standard, *see* G. GUNTHER, CONSTITUTIONAL LAW 472–75 (11th ed. 1985).

3. The phrase "discrete and insular minorities" is from the famous footnote four in U.S. v. Carolene Products Co., 304 U.S. 144 n. 4 (1938).

4. U.S. CONST. Art. I, §10, prohibits any state "Law impairing the Obligation of Contracts." The Third Amendment protects the sanctity of the home against the quartering of troops, and the Fourth Amendment protects "The right of the people to be secure in their persons, houses, papers, and effects, against unreasonable searchers and seizures." Personal security and privacy are thus clearly linked with property ownership. The Fifth Amendment brings life, liberty, and property under the protection of "due process of law," and the Fourteenth Amendment. The Fifth Amendment also requires that private property may be taken only for public use and with "just compensation."

5. I will focus on R. A. EPSTEIN, TAKINGS: PRIVATE PROPERTY AND THE POWER OF EMINENT DOMAIN (1985).

6. 198 U.S. 45 (1905).

7. Allgeyer v. Louisiana, 165 U.S. 578, 589 (1897). I have drawn this quote, and benefited generally, from B. H. Siegan, *Economic Liberties and the Constitution: Protection at the State Level,* in ECONOMIC LIBERTIES AND THE JUDICIARY 149 (J. A. Dorn & H. G. Manne eds. 1987). *See* Meyer v. Nebraska, 262 U.S. 390 (1923) and Pierce v. Society of Sisters, 268 U.S. 510 (1925) for two cases in which the old Court gave a broad reading to the liberty protected by the Fourteenth Amendment—a reading that included personal as well as economic freedoms.

8. *See* U.S. v. E.C. Knight, 156 U.S. 1 (1895); U.S. CONST. Art. I, §8.

9. Wickard v. Filburn, 317 U.S. 111 (1942).

10. *Id.*

11. Epstein, *The Proper Scope of the Commerce Power,* 73 VA. L. REV. 1387, 1393–95 (1987).

12. Northern Securities Co. v. U.S., 193 U.S. 197 (1904).

13. 22 U.S. (9 Wheat.) 1 (1824).

14. Wickard v. Filburn, 317 U.S. 111 at 120.

15. Gibbons v. Ogden, 22 U.S. 1 at 195.

16. Epstein carries this analysis much further in Epstein, *supra* note 11.

17. Williamson v. Lee Optical, 348 U.S. 343 (1955); Ferguson v. Skrupka, 372 U.S. 726 (1963).

18. In haste, I here pass over many things reviewed at greater length in S. MACEDO, THE NEW RIGHT V. THE CONSTITUTION (2nd ed. 1987).

19. City of Cleburne v. Cleburne Living Center, 473 U.S. 432, 452 (1985). *See also* Justice Stevens's concurring opinion in Craig v. Boren, 429 U.S. 190 (1976).

20. Macedo, *Liberal Virtues, Constitutional Community,* 50 REV. POL. 215 (1988).

21. McCulloch v. Maryland, 4 Wheaton 316, 407 (1819).

22. Such as the regulation of morals: *see* Champion v. Ames, 199 U.S. 321 (1903). And *see* the excellent discussion in S. A. BARBER, ON WHAT THE CONSTITUTION MEANS, ch. 4 (1984).

23. Before 1937, the Court sought to limit the commerce power by a variety of means, based partly on the supposition that the power to regulate commerce internal to a state belongs to the state itself; the language of the clause suggests the relevance of such a distinction, but it is, nevertheless, not easy to draw. *See* U.S. v. E.C. Knight, 156 U.S. 1 (1895), which sought to distinguish the *direct* from the *indirect* effects of local commerce on interstate commerce; *compare* Houston E. & W. Texas Ry. Co. v. United States (The Shreveport Rate Case), 234 U.S. 342 (1914), which sustained Congress's power to reach those intrastate activities with *substantial* economic effects on interstate commerce. As Gerald Gunther argues, these cases represent two distinct standards for allowing Congress to reach arguably local commerce as a means to some national policy: under *Knight,* the Court required a logical nexus between the regulated activity and interstate commerce, whereas under the Shreveport Rate Case rule, the Court required a showing that local commerce has a substantial economic effect on interstate commerce; see GUNTHER, *supra* note 2, at 105–12. *Shreveport's* liberal construction is hard to dismiss, and that mode was operative in *Wickard.* The vice of *Wickard* may simply be that inadequate weight is given to liberty interests that directly compete with Congress's interest in setting national commercial policy.

24. Consider Justice McReynolds's description of the liberty protected by the Fourteenth Amendment:

> Without doubt, it denotes not merely freedom from bodily restraint, but also the right of the individual to contract, to engage in any of the common occupations of life, to acquire useful knowledge, to marry, establish a home and bring up children, to worship God according to the dictates of his conscience, and generally to enjoy those privileges long recognized at common law as essential to the orderly pursuit of happiness by free men.

Meyer v. Nebraska, 262 U.S. 390, 399 (1923). I expand on this discussion in Macedo, *supra* note 18, at 54–57, 82–85.

25. ROBERT NOZICK, ANARCHY, STATE AND UTOPIA, ix (1974).

26. Epstein, *supra* note 5, at 337–38.

27. *Id.* at 335–38.

28. *Proceedings of the Conference on Takings and the Constitution,* 41 MIAMI L. REV. 49, 109 (1986).

29. Epstein, *supra* note 5, at ix.

30. T. HOBBES, LEVIATHAN 209 (C.B. Macpherson ed. 1980), italics in original. Epstein's approach is, admittedly, far gentler than that of Hobbes, but that may not save him from the ire of some rights-oriented liberals; *see also* his remarks on prostitution, 41 MIAMI L. REV. 82–83 (1986).

31. Epstein, *supra* note 5, at 95; emphasis in original.

32. *Id.* at 166–69, 202–3, 216–28.

33. *Id.* at 5, and *see* 3–6, 163–64, 197–99.

34. *Id.* at 200, 331–32, 337.

35. *Id.* at 3–6, 11; I have drawn here on Rogers M. Smith's characteristically insightful discussion of *Takings* in *'Don't Look Back, Something Might Be Gaining on You': The Dilemmas of Constitutional Neoconservatives,* 1987 AMERICAN BAR FOUNDATION RESEARCH JOURNAL 281–309 (1987, no. 1).

36. Epstein, *supra* note 5, at 5.

37. Economic rent is payment to a factor in excess of what is necessary to keep it on the market. My sense is that "rent-seeking" is an elastic term with a fairly broad political connotation. In its rather broad and loose political usages, then, rent-seeking behavior is non-productive, transfer-seeking behavior. Rent-seeking is costly, most obviously, because it represents a choice to expend resources for non-productive purposes (hiring a lobbyist, say, rather than making a productive investment in plant or equipment). But rent-seeking also has numerous secondary effects: others may be encouraged to engage in similar expenditures, either defensively or by positive example, and as rent-seeking becomes rampant, the productive activities of those who are the victims (or potential victims) of rent-seeking are discouraged.

38. Epstein, *supra* note 5, at 172.

39. *Id.* at 172–73.

40. *Id., see* ch. 13.

41. *Id.* at 174.

42. Rent control laws, by contrast, fail to pass constitutional muster, both because there is no natural monopoly arising from necessity and the surplus is not divided; *id.* at 177. Urban renewal does not provide a pure public good since there is no right of access. Comprehensive urban renewal plans might claim to be ridding a city of a nuisance, but no surplus is paid to the property owners. When the aim is to provide public housing, eligibility conditions render the programs discriminatory and redistributive. Urban renewal, according to Epstein, also fails to pass muster; *id.* at 178–80.

43. *Id.* at 190.

44. *See* Justice Brennan's opinion for the Court in Penn Central Transportation Co. v. New York City, 438 U.S. 104 124–25, 127, 130 n. 27 (1978). I have benefited here, and in this section generally, from P. H. Aranson, *Judicial Control of the Political Branches: Public Purpose and Public Law*, in Dorn and Manne, *supra* note 7, at 47–110.

45. Aranson, *supra* note 44, at 67. See also Agins v. City of Tiburon, 447 U.S. 255 (1980), in which the Court rejected an attack on a zoning ordinance limiting construction on a five-acre tract to single family dwellings at low density on the grounds that the owners continued to enjoy an "economically viable use" of their property; *id.* at 260.

46. Epstein, *supra* note 5, at 107–8.

47. *Id.* at 111.

48. *Id.* at 110.

49. *Id.* at 112.

50. *Id.* at 123, and *see generally* ch. 9.

51. *Id.* at 164–65.

52. *Id.* at 196.

53. *Id.* at 197.

54. *Id.* at 167; user fees could be another way of spreading costs fairly: *see id.* at 168.

55. THE FEDERALIST No. 10, at 78 (A. Hamilton, Mentor ed. (1961)).

56. Epstein, *supra* note 5, at 105.

57. *Id.* at 210.

58. ARISTOTLE, NICHOMACHEAN ETHICS bk. 5, at 111–45 (M. Ostwald trans. 1962). Of course, Aristotle would not have agreed with Epstein's method for determining proper shares or with his conception of the ends of political association.

59. Epstein, *supra* note 5, at 207.

60. *Id.* at 209.

61. *Id.* at 324.

62. *Id.* at 327.

63. *Id.* at 327.

64. *Id.* at 211.

65. *Id.*

66. *Id.* at 214, and *see* J. H. ELY, DEMOCRACY AND DISTRUST (1980).

67. *Id., see* ch. 5.

68. *Id., see* ch. 6.

69. J.J. ROUSSEAU, THE SOCIAL CONTRACT bk. 2, i–iv, at 29–35 (D.A. Cress trans. 1983).

70. Ely, *supra* note 66, at 82–87.

71. Rousseau, *supra* note 69, at 34.

72. For a more recent interpretation of equality in the spirit of Rousseau, see the discussion of "equal concern and respect" in R. DWORKIN, TAKING RIGHTS SERIOUSLY, 180–83, 272–78 (1977).

73. Rousseau, *supra* note 69, at 55.

74. *Id.* at 24, 32.

75. Of course, the differences do not end there, and the comparison may be simply too ludicrous.

76. I. Kant, *Perpetual Peace,* in KANT'S POLITICAL WRITINGS 93, 112–13 (H. Reiss ed. 1977).

77. Epstein, *supra* note 5, at 346.

78. Epstein, *Beyond the Rule of Law: Civic Virtue and Constitutional Structure,* 56 GEO WASH. L. REV. 149 (1987).

79. Epstein, *supra* note 5, at 345.

80. *Id.* at 345–46.

81. Kant, *supra* note 76, at 126.

82. THE FEDERALIST No. 10, *supra* note 55, at 83.

83. THE FEDERALIST No. 78, *id.* at 470.

84. *See* Barber, *supra* note 22, at 88–91.

85. Epstein, *supra* note 5, at 18.

86. *Id.* at 107.

87. *McCulloch v. Maryland,* 4 Wheaton 316, 407.

88. For his discussion of the ends of the national government, and the importance of the pretextual limitation implicit in *McCulloch,* I am indebted to Barber, *supra* note 22, at 97–104.

89. *See* Macedo, *supra* note 18, at 33–37.

90. Epstein, *supra* note 5, at 28.

91. *Id.* at 25–26.

92. *Id.* at 23.

93. C. M. Kenyon, *Men of Little Faith: The Anti-Federalists on the Nature of Representative Government,* 12 WM. & MARY Q. 3–40, 21–22 (1955).

94. MIAMI L. REV., *supra* note 28, at 82, and *see* Epstein, *supra* note 5, at 314–24.

95. Recall the Tenth Federalist's remark that the "first object of government" is not the protection of property rights, but "the protection of different and unequal faculties of acquiring property," THE FEDERALIST 10, *supra* note 55, at 78.

96. MIAMI L. REV., *supra* note 28, at 67.

97. *See* Epstein's comment on Nozick, *supra* note 5, at 336.

98. *Id.* at 132–33.

99. *Id.* at 133.

100. *See* Craig v. Boren, 429 U.S. 190 (1976), especially the concurring opinion by Justice Stevens at 211–14. It is encouraging to see a more substantial rationality test, one that approaches the intermediate standard of review of *Craig,* in cases such as Plyler v. Doe, 457 U.S. 202 (1982), and City of Cleburne v. Cleburne Living Center, 473 U.S. 432 (1985). Justice Brennan's opinion in *Plyler* reads *Craig* as requiring "the assurance that the [legislative] classification reflects a reasoned judgment consistent with the ideal of equal protection by inquiring whether it may fairly be viewed as furthering a substantial interest of the State." (at 217–18)

101. Perhaps some forms or degrees of progressivity would be constitutionally unreasonable. With regard to the unfairness of placing special burdens on the owners of buildings designated landmarks, it is, obviously, reasonable to adjust compensation to take into account the benefits provided by designation, in the form of higher rents and property values and perhaps the value to the owners as citizens (if that is significant).

102. A. Lincoln, *Debate with Stephen Douglas at Alton, Ill., October 15, 1858,* THE LINCOLN-DOUGLAS DEBATES 304 (R. W. Johannsen ed. 1978).

103. On the Constitution as an aspirational document, *see* Barber, *supra* note 22, and G.J. Jacobsohn, *Abraham Lincoln 'On this Question of Judicial Authority': The Theory of Constitutional Aspiration*, 36 W. POL. Q. 52 (1983).

104. THE FEDERALIST No. 10, *supra* note 55.

105. *See* ARISTOTLE, POLITICS, book 3 at 86–117 (C. Lord trans. 1984); and the excerpts of Melancton Smith's remarks in the New York State ratifying convention, in THE ANTI-FEDERALIST at 338–49, nn. 13–23 at 357–58 (H. J. Storing ed. 1985), pp. 338–49 and the accompanying footnotes at pp. 357–58.

106. C. Sunstein, *Interest Groups in American Public Law*, 38 STAN L. REV. 29, 46 (1985). I have learned much from this excellent article.

107. *See* Melancton Smith's exchange with Chancellor Livingston, *supra* n. 104, at 343–45, and n. 23 at 358.

108. *See* R. F. FENNO, JR.'S discussion in HOMESTYLE (1978), warning against the imposition of any simple model on the representative activities of House members.

109. For a lucid defense of America's open, ideologically flexible political system—a system that promotes the compromise of sectional and class interests—*see* PENDLETON HERRING, THE POLITICS OF DEMOCRACY (1940).

110. A. SMITH, WEALTH OF NATIONS vol. 1, bk. III.iv, at 413–21 (Campbell and Skinner eds. 1979).

111. *Id.*, bk. III.i.5, at 379.

112. *See* THE FEDERALIST No. 44, *supra* note 55, and the interesting discussions in M. F. Plattner, *American Democracy and the Acquisitive Spirit*, and S. Miller, *The Constitution and the Spirit of Commerce*, both in HOW CAPITALISTIC IS THE CONSTITUTION? (R.A. Goldwin and W.A. Schambra eds. 1982).

113. *See* A. DE TOCQUEVILLE, DEMOCRACY IN AMERICA vol. 1, pt. 1, chs. 3–5 (S. Gilbert trans. 1969); and Smith, *supra* note 110, book 3, chs. 3–4.

114. Tocqueville, THE OLD REGIME AND THE FRENCH REVOLUTION 168 (S. Gilbert trans. 1955).

115. The idea of the Constitution as a "planning document" is being developed by Professors Sotirios A. Barber and Jeffrey K. Tulis.

Tutelary Jurisprudence
and Constitutional Property

FRANK MICHELMAN

I. Introduction

Uneasy lies the state of property rights in American constitutional law. Uncertain is the course of constitutional-legal argument about them. I think we can explain much of the unease and the uncertainty by examining the interplay of two tensions in the American political-moral vision: one between classical liberal (hereafter liberal) and republican notions of constitutional rights in general and of property in particular, and a second between negative and affirmative property claims. More tentatively, I will suggest the possible bearing of a third distinction—that between academic and judicial discourse—when we come to projecting the future of constitutional property.

Liberal vs. Republican Constitutionalism

Much recent scholarship has portrayed the ideological milieu of American constitutionalism's formative era as organized by a tension or struggle between nascent liberal and ancient republican understandings of the state and its relation to the citizen.[1] According to some, this formative tension has persisted throughout the entire subsequent history of American constitutional debate as a central, organizing dialectic.[2] Scholars writing in this dualistic, ideological-historical vein tend to agree that the drafting and ratification of the Constitution, and the subsequent (if slightly delayed) resolution and consolidation of its underlying program by the judiciary led by John Marshall, reflected the subordination of such Revolutionary Era republican leanings as there may have been to a prevailingly liberal outlook.[3] What many still regard as an open and interesting question is how far the republican strain survived as a recessive but still detectable influence on the subsequent history of American constitutional-legal thought and doctrine.[4]

There is no standard version of the historical republican/liberal opposition to which we can refer. But for present purposes, painting in broad strokes, let us say that in the republican constitutional vision, individual rights are reflexes of laws consequent upon the determinations of a popularly-based political will; the state is the forum of the public deliberations and debates by which the lawmaking political will is determined; and the central problem of the state is that of maintaining diversity and public-spiritedness in those deliberations, so that they do not ossify into self-serving, factional division. In the liberal constitutional vision, by contrast, individuals have rights pre-politically; the state is the appointed guarantor of the rights; and the central problem of the state is to keep it from preying on the rights it is established to protect.[5]

Negative vs. Affirmative Property

We usually think of property as a ground of "negative" claims to be let alone to hold, keep, and enjoy what you lawfully acquire on your own, as opposed to "affirmative" claims to others' active assistance in obtaining or enjoying the use of wealth. Putative rights of the latter kind include what are often called welfare rights. The relation between negative property and welfare rights is obviously problematic. Abstractly, it appears that in any system where negative property broadly and strongly prevails, welfare rights are logically excluded.[6] But in actual constitutional-legal experience, the relation has been much more interestingly dialectical — *within* the liberal vision and *within* the republican vision, as well as across the two.

Plan of the Essay

By gathering into a single treatment the two oppositions between liberal and republican constitutionalism and between affirmative and negative property, I hope to explain and clarify some major features of American constitutional-legal disputation over property rights. But the point is to explain and clarify by denying, not affirming, what might seem an obvious term-for-term correlation between the two oppositions — liberal yoked with negative, republican yoked with affirmative. My thesis is that one simply can't, at least not while thinking or talking as an insider to American constitutionalism, quite abandon either pole of the liberal/republican axis[7] — and that even if one could, the trick would leave unresolved the problem of negative-vs.-affirmative rights.

Our trail sets out from an historical account of early American constitutional practice respecting property rights, cast in terms of the opposition between liberal and republican constitutional visions that has preoccupied recent American constitutional-historical scholarship. We trace that opposition into two contrasting models of constitutional jurisprudence, reflecting in two contrasting argumentative and judicial styles. We then use the jurisprudential models to describe and analyze recent essays by two exceptionally able and prominent participants—one academic (Richard Epstein) and one judicial (Antonin Scalia)—in contemporary constitutional-legal debate over property.

Both Professor Epstein and Justice Scalia have been widely identified as contributors to an incipient revival within constitutional law of the cause of classical liberal, negative property. In using the two jurisprudential models to analyze their respective contributions to the debate, we shall find the claims of affirmative property raising difficulties for both the professor and the judge. We shall also find the two responding in quite different ways to the dilemmas thus arising. In trying to describe and explain the difference, we shall use the jurisprudential models. We shall also consider the possible explanatory bearing of our two exemplars' different offices and situations. That consideration will lead, finally, to a brief, concluding speculation about the likely future course of American constitutional-legal protection for property.

II. Liberal vs. Republican Constitutional
Jurisprudence: Historical and Ideal Types

Liberal vs. Republican Property in Early American
Constitutional Thought

Historian William Treanor has used the republican/liberal oppositional framework to describe and, in some measure, explain a certain movement in early American thought about the constitutional-legal status of property.[8] Treanor begins with the period before and just after the Revolution, during which "the principle that the state necessarily owes compensation when it takes private property was not generally accepted."[9] In colonial and early state practice, there was, reports Treanor, no sense of a strict requirement of payment by governments to private landholders for occupation of their erstwhile holdings by standard public projects such as roads.[10] Treanor contrasts this relatively lax, old-fashioned attitude with our more commanding, modern sense of negative constitutional-legal property rights. The modern sense, he says, was in the process of overtaking the older in time to find sponsorship in the federal Bill of Rights.[11]

In Treanor's account, an essential difference between the earlier republican and later liberal positions lay in the former's communitarianism as compared with the latter's individualism.[12] Treanor contrasts a republican sense of the moral primacy of the community's general interest over the particular interests of individuals with a liberal sense of the individual's moral primacy. Republican thought accordingly regards the land as belonging, *au fond,* to the community and its nominal owner as the community's tenant or functionary, as opposed to a liberal sense of the land as belonging simply to its innocent appropriator or the latter's voluntary transferee.[13] It is to this underlying difference in social-moral vision that Treanor traces the difference he reports in pre- and post-Constitutional ideals about the appropriate rigor and breadth of higher-legal protection for negative property. Treanor sees the republican communitarian vision finding constitutional expression (at the pole) in a notion of legally unbounded state power, and similarly for the connection between the vision of libertarian individualism and strict constitutional-legal limitations on state power.[14]

The next thing to notice about Treanor's account is how it already begins to suggest cross-imitation between our two supposedly polar visions. Treanor relates that colonial and early state practice often omitted compensation in certain circumstances, where later generations would automatically expect it. Treanor does not, however, make refusal the republican rule. To the contrary, he reports that in certain other circumstances, the regular practice was to pay. Thus, while the early practice would characteristically omit compensation in cases of public roads built across unimproved land, it would pay when the land was improved.[15] Treanor suggests no motivation for payment other than prevailing precepts of good governmental practice or political morality. We are left to imagine the republican citizenry deliberating its way to the judgment that the common good, or common justice, requires some degree of respect for private property. And that is an eminently plausible scenario, since we know that republican thought has reasons for such a judgment—reasons that are not, after all, completely foreign to liberal ideas. In republican thought, property supports the citizen's independent-minded, public-spirited, resistance against hegemonic extensions of power through might and patronage.[16] In moderation, it enables and encourages the domestic virtues of industry and thrift, without endangering public-spiritedness.[17] It preserves to individuals and groups—of family members, co-workers, religious societies, neighbors— their spheres of socially unsupervised relationship and self-formation, thereby sustaining diversity within the political community, on which the value of republican politics depends.[18] When all is said, Treanor's account of a compensation practice shaped by dominantly republican influence could without much strain be described not as an antithesis of the liberal understanding that overtook it, but rather as a politicized or compromised version of that understanding.

Jurisprudences of Democratic Containment: Two Abstract Models

In liberal constitutionalism, a constitutional right is the institutionally positivized form of a natural right rooted in trans-political reason or revelation. It is true that insomuch as a constitutional right is a *legal* right, legal positivists (which means the huge preponderance of contemporary American thinkers about law) must find for every such right some basis in the politically enacted Constitution, rather than derive it directly from moral-theoretical reason or natural law. But in the liberal understanding, the Constitution does not so much create rights as recognize, endorse, and positivize pre-political claims of right.[19] It is on that quasi-naturalistic understanding of their origin and point that the scopes and applications of the rights are judicially construed.

In republican constitutionalism, a right is nothing but a matter of political determination. It has no grounding beyond actual human deliberation; it exerts no claim over or against the political resolutions that alone give it existence. In the republican vision, if there are constitutional rights, that is only because the people politically engaged have so resolved.

It does not follow that republican constitutional thought is careless of rights or of their importance. To those who perceive the highest human interests to depend upon the maintenance of good politics, the practice of politics becomes a matter of utmost concern. That concern provides a basis for constitutionalizing rights that may be as various as freedom of speech, personal privacy, negative property, and material welfare.[20] Still, the underlying republican understanding imparts a different spin than a liberal one does to judicial review of the actions of ordinary (sub-constitutional) representative assemblies where due regard for the rights is in question.

We can illustrate the difference in "spins" with a doctrine of American constitutional law that will play a major role in what is to follow. The Supreme Court has repeatedly affirmed the principle that " 'all property in this country is held under the implied obligation that the owner's use of it shall not be injurious to [others or to] the community.' "[21] Let us call this the *proviso principle*. From the proviso principle, it easily follows that governments violate no constitutional prohibition against taking or deprivation of property when they forbid socially harmful deployments of things in private ownership.[22]

Consider, now, the following three pairs of cases:

Case 1a: A state forbids owners of beachfront land to build anything on their lands, including ordinary houses, that would even partially obstruct people's view of the sea from any public street or highway.

Case 1b: A state forbids beachfront landowners to bar or hinder members of the public from walking across their sandy back yards in the course of traveling from one public beach site to another.

Case 2a: a state forbids landlords to charge any tenant a higher rental than the market would bear in the absence of a rental-housing "shortage."

Case 2b: A state forbids landlords to charge any tenant who is poor (according to an official definition) a rental so high that it would (in the judgment of an administrator) cause that tenant "severe financial distress."

Case 3a: A state forbids people to use things they own to kill each other.

Case 3b: Through tax-financed public assistance programs, a state overrides the refusals of many people to contribute from private wealth to the financial support of others.

In which of these cases does the state commit an unconstitutional violation of property rights?

Certainly no American judge or legal commentator would find a constitutional violation in case 3a. Justice Scalia has found violations in cases 1b and 2b; he has virtually declared that he would find none in case 3b; and he has publicly and hospitably entertained, although not quite adopted, the possibility of finding no violations in cases 1a and 2a.[23] Professor Epstein, by contrast, would easily find violations in all the cases except 3a.[24] How do we explain these distinctions and disagreements?

From the Supreme Court's unwavering commitment to the proviso principle, we know that in order to decide whether any instance of state coercion violates property rights, a judge must first answer the question of whether whatever it is that the state thereby makes owners stop doing with their property (including just keeping it out of reach of others) is socially harmful. According to our models, a classical liberal judge would think that the answer to the question of harmful deployment must be rigorously derivable (although the task might be intellectually arduous, and fallible judges might, therefore, disagree about the answer) from a naturalistic, pre-political notion of property.[25] The judge would take the judicial task to be that of working out the answer without regard to popular judgments expressed or implied by political enactment of the laws whose validity she is appraising.

To a republican judge, by contrast, when the people approve—by the distinctively deliberative and consensual processes we know as constitution-making[26]—a precept of political morality or prudence such as that of securing property against uncompensated taking, they are publicly committing themselves to the recognition that important values or interests are jeopardized or infringed by uncompensated expropriations, and announcing their determination to restrain their future actions and those of their governmental agents accordingly. The function of the republican judge engaged in review of ordinary legislation is, then, to support the people in this determination.[27]

Such a conception of the judicial office is less receptive than might first appear to the idea of judges ascertaining limits upon political action by rigorous derivation from uncontested premises. Whether a given instance of political action ought to be rejected as unconstitutional expropriation always depends on how gravely that action impairs public values and interests motivating constitutional protection for property, considered in light of any tendency in that same action to advance other such values and interests, and possibly also the values and interests underlying other constitutional provisions. If the relevant values are plural and not necessarily consonant, the constitutional question itself may become deeply political. A republican judge may then find that the best she can do is to intervene if, and only if, either (i) it appears that the electorally accountable authors of the challenged action did not themselves give focused or sincere consideration to all the constitutional commitments at stake, or (ii) it appears that, even if they did, their action carries such a strong public suggestion of disregard for constitutionally recognized values and interests as to erode the people's continuing confidence in each others' commitment to maintaining them.[28]

Jurisprudences of Democratic Containment: Two Historical Strategies

Abstract as they are, our models of contrasting styles of constitutional adjudication are not—at any rate, not solely—inventions of my imagination.

Jennifer Nedelsky is one of those scholars in whose view the Constitution represents an incomplete triumph of liberalism over republicanism.[29] For our purposes, Nedelsky's depiction is especially interesting because of its focus on the central, symbolic significance of property in the historical sweep of American constitutionalist ideology.

In Nedelsky's account of the Constitution's adoption and judicial consolidation, the liberal principle of pre-political right and limited government dominates over the republican principle of popular self-determination. The Founders succeeded, she argues, in bequeathing to American posterity a strong and healthy sense of the importance of

effectively bounding off state power from social and private domains, but at
the cost of also leaving Americans with weak and shallow commitments to
the values of democratic political engagement and the concomitant
importance of sustaining, by action of the state as necessary, the social and
economic conditions of effectively democratic popular self-rule.

The Founders, Nedelsky says (and here John Marshall joins James
Madison as the Constitution's co-father), wrought these effects by adapting,
refining, and securely instilling in the American consciousness the idea of the
Constitution as a compendium of broad and strict higher-law precepts of
political morality. For precepts to be thus "higher" means, of course, for
them to be regarded as beyond partisan political resolution in majoritarian
assemblies. But since it does no good to substitute the partisanship of judges
for that of assemblies, judicial determinations of the applications of higher
law to contested cases must themselves be credibly derived through a method
not itself tainted by partisan considerations. The judicial method must
observably be one of law as opposed to politics. It follows that serviceable
higher law precepts must be not only sufficiently abstract to be accepted as
nonpartisan, but also sufficiently decisive (stable, well-defined, mutually
consistent) to serve as premises from which specific applications can be
derived by courses of reasoning so compellingly transparent as to free them,
too, from suspicion of personal bias.

Exemplary, it seems, would be a broad and strong principle of negative
property right securing owners in the full retention and enjoyment of lawfully
obtained wealth. Nedelsky argues that from the Founding onwards, the
symbolic epitome of the higher-law idea, from which that idea drew its
continuing inspiration and credibility, was property in its negative-right
sense. Landed property, with its long history of successful judicial
elucidation as the core of the common law, and with its naturalistic imagery
of clearly-demarcated private domains effectively closed against the
unwanted entry even of the Crown itself, was Atlantic legal culture's model
of a private sphere effectively and rightfully guarded by trans-political law
against social encroachment.

Nedelsky is of course fully aware that, in modern legal culture,
"property" connotes not just legally secure possession of tangible things, but
all legally warranted expectations of continuing advantageous disposition
over assets—no matter how abstractly conceived or non-possessory in
character. The spread of sophisticated, dephysicalized notions of property
greatly intensifies Nedelsky's worry about the corrosive effects on the
ideological girders of constitutionalism of strenuous regulatory and
welfare-state legislation. For from the sophisticated there is no hiding the
truth that the interventions of the regulatory and the welfare state profoundly
attack the very notion of negative property on which, Nedelsky argues, has

primarily rested the belief, hence the confidence, of Americans in the principle of limited government. Which is why John Marshall—Nedelsky is clearly intimating—could not have allowed these interventions to survive a properly framed constitutional attack.

Accepting this as Marshall's view, his is not the uncontested Founders' view of these matters. The figure who, more than any other, has come to represent in his own person the confluence of liberal and republican themes in American constitutional thought is James Madison. The historical evidence strongly confirms that Madison did indeed understand the Fifth Amendment's requirement of just compensation for property taken to speak for a broadly applicable principle of anti-redistributive, negative property that popular politics ought ideally to respect.[30] The evidence further suggests that a chief means by which he hoped to achieve that effect was the traditionally republican means of a continuing reinculcation in citizens and lawmakers of civic virtue, in part through emulation of honored founders.[31]

For Madison, it appears, may not have relied upon or expected the judiciary to enforce a strict anti-redistributive principle broadly against a contrary government. It may be that insofar as he anticipated judicial enforcement at all, it was only in the narrow core of cases most obviously called to mind by the words of the clause: physical dispossession of tangible property (by agents other than the tax collector). By what may have been Madison's understanding, the main value of the clause would be tutelary. Its presence in the honored text, and the occasions of judicial enforcement (presumably rare but correspondingly dramatic), would teach a lesson of respect for negative property broader than either the ordinary signification of the text itself or the specific occasions of enforcement. That lesson would, Madison hoped, carry over into a spirit of popular and legislative moderation when it came to the exercise of regulatory and taxing powers over which the judiciary would exercise no direct control.[32]

So far as I am acquainted with the historiography, we have to fill in for ourselves the reasons why Madison would have relied so tangentially on the compulsion of law for the total disciplinary effect at which he aimed. Madison was a famously pragmatic statesman. He understood the dangers posed to popularly-based government by both excessive concentrations and excessive shortages of wealth,[33] and he knew there would be myriad other occasions when governmental regulation could have redistributive ramifications. Perhaps he appreciated, therefore, that an anti-redistributive principle could not be too broadly and strongly enforced by judges without their seeming to stray into politics and thus compromise the country's confidence in the integrity of law, upon which his hopes for government popular, limited, and enduring also depended.[34]

III. Two Samples of Contemporary Discourse

Professor Epstein

Richard Epstein takes the position that judges ought to have read and applied constitutional protections for property so sweepingly as to have invalidated the welfare state, although obviously they have not done so.[35] To the defense of that position, Epstein has summoned Marshallian constitutional jurisprudence.[36]

Epstein's methodological argument is straightforward and time-honored: if a court effectively abdicates to democratic politics the protection of property—either intentionally and candidly, or by allowing protection to be whittled away by "balancing" property rights against asserted governmental objectives and social needs—that court gives away limited government. If, on the other hand, a court intervenes protectively, but does so on the basis of what appear to be *ad hoc,* instrumental (that is "political") judgments not rigorously derivable from some very high-order premise of political morality or prudence, that court usurps democracy and we fall under unbridled (or, at any rate, undisciplinable) judicial power.[37] We seek safe passage between the whirlpool and the rocks, between democratic and judicial politics. That passage can be secured only by a judicial posture of readiness to act protectively against democratic excess—more specifically, to act on the basis of straightforward derivations from a set of highly general (but also implicitly decisive) constitutional-legal premises. It follows that constitutional interpretation is properly a process of exegetical rationalization of the sometimes-cryptic text. It is a process of looking behind the words for the large principles of political morality that animate, integrate, and justify the text—principles of which the text is intensionally indicative but is also, inevitably, an extensionally imperfect expression—principles that, once articulated, impart to the text the Cartesian clarity demanded by the Marshallian ideal of higher law.[38]

Epstein contends that the Cartesian principle animating the textual stricture against uncompensated public takings of private property is simply that of anti-redistribution, of protecting the extant proportional distribution of wealth against disturbance by government action. He marshals in support a set of considerations pertaining to the specific text itself, to that text's structural relations (as keystone, he thinks) to the rest of the Constitution, and to the intellectual-historical setting in which the Constitution was drafted and adopted.

This anti-redistribution principle Epstein further defends by noticing how it serves the demand of liberal constitutional jurisprudence for a Cartesian major premise from which courts can rigorously derive specific applications, effectively limiting government power. True, the principle thus serves only when broadly read as covering all redistributive actions, including many that do not usually spring to mind when someone speaks of a "taking of property." That locution plainly signifies an express expropriation of legal title by the government in a formal condemnation proceeding. It further irresistibly signifies (lest form ridiculously triumph over substance) physical ouster of former rightful occupants by government agents other than tax collectors. It does not, pre-exegetically, signify the sundry government actions we conventionally know and name as taxes, tariffs, regulations, monetary and fiscal policies, and so on. Yet if the Cartesian principle of political morality for which "taking of property" speaks *is* the anti-redistribution principle, then the phrase *does,* as thus exegetically rationalized, apply to all those other kinds of action, because they all obviously threaten to disturb the extant proportional distribution of wealth. Hence Epstein concludes that they all are challengeable as unconstitutional uncompensated takings.[39]

What of the ever-present question of whether the apparent taking is not a real taking because the advantage of which it deprives the complaining owner, being bound up with a socially harmful deployment of the property, is not one to which she was ever legally entitled?[40] Consistently with the Marshallian jurisprudential strategy of democratic containment, Epstein denies that the issues thus posed[41] are so indeterminate—that the notion of harm is so essentially contested—as to negate the possibility of nonpartisan resolution. He does not doubt that these issues will sometimes confront courts with difficult problems giving rise to disagreement. But he does insist that they can be formulated as inquiries into the implicit logic of a universal system of property rights (as basically contoured by the common law) that have, in principle, right answers. If so, then judges, by honestly seeking those answers, can always rise above politics, partisanship, or judicial personal whim or preference.[42]

So far our account of Epsteinian constitutional jurisprudence accords perfectly with the widespread expectation of finding in Epstein's work a contemporary expression of the classical-liberal pole in constitutional-legal discourse with specific reference to property.[43] All the more striking, then, is Epstein's recent commendation of his position as sound republican constitutional doctrine.[44]

To the republican constitutional artificer, seeking to institutionalize civic virtue as the foundation of popular government disposed to serve the common good, Epstein commends adoption of an uncompromising constitutional rule against all governmental actions having redistributive impacts. Such a rule, Epstein explains, has the consequence of driving all governmental actions toward the Paretian virtue of benefiting everyone. (Measures satisfying the rule of distributive proportionality must be either universally enriching or universally impoverishing, and actions of the latter type are an unlikely outcome of popular politics.) The rule thus constrains legislative deliberations toward the common good, because particularistically exploitative ("rent-seeking") actions would be destined by the rule for judicial invalidation. Public knowledge of the rule and its happy Paretian consequence sustains among the citizens exactly that spirit of mutual trust and confidence in the quality and motivation of public deliberations that republicanism associates with civic virtue. Liberal policy, loyally enforced, paves the road to republican bliss. The twain have met. Eureka.

It is, I think, a remarkable fact that in thus turning to a republican justification for a sweeping doctrine of constitutional protection for negative property, Epstein's argument pushes negative property from its natural-right status of a primary objective to which the state and its workings are instrumentally secondary. The republican argument inverts the liberal conception of the proper instrumental relationship between the negative-property principle and the good state; it places the principle at the service of the state, rather than the state at the service of the principle. One can hardly overstate the liberal objection to this inversion. It apparently leaves the principle of negative property exposed to whatever qualification or modification may be persuasively recommended by instrumental argument conducted under all its usual contingencies, cognitive and empirical.[45]

To be sure, Epstein joins good classical liberal company in highlighting the dangers to prosperity, stability, and freedom posed by the susceptibility of welfare-statist, majoritarian politics to strategic exploitation of some citizens by others.[46] Perhaps the whole company might fly republican colors. For when it comes to concern about majoritarian exploitation, the republican tradition of constitutional thought has stolen a march on the liberal one. Republicanism traditionally identified the problem as that of the "corruption" of a citizen's judgment regarding the common good—or of the citizen's will to express that judgment honestly in public deliberations and votes—by the pressure of particular interest or need. The problem was, indeed, understood in the republican tradition as a systemic one: one of maintaining the bonds of civic mutuality against corrosion by the privatization—"corruption"—of politics.[47] A traditional republican solution to the problem was restriction of the franchised citizenry to persons whose material and social circumstances were such as to guarantee the "independence" of their inputs to public deliberations and decisions. High on the lists of those excluded by this principle were public clients of all descriptions—not just "pensioners," but "placemen" too.[48]

Modern democracy having ruled out that solution, a higher law rule against redistributive political action recommends itself as a substitute. But for democratic republicans, there is a rub: historically, republican political discourse has been distinguished by awareness that the general economic and social circumstances of citizens—their individual well-being and their social relations of status and power—are no less crucial to the quality of popular politics than are the specific ties of citizens to the government.[49] These circumstances are crucial, moreover, in ways that militate powerfully against constitutional foreclosure of state-mandated provision for people's biological, environmental, and developmental needs, or of even broader state control of the distribution and deployment of wealth so as to prevent plutocratic domination—itself a form of corruption—of nominally popular political deliberations.[50] Similar perceptions have, of course, made their way deeply into latter-day liberal political argument as well.[51]

The result is a profound republican (and a parallel liberal-democratic) tension—the seed of a dialectic—of negative and affirmative property. If the quality and independence of many citizens' contributions to public life and legislation are compromised—as Hayek, Epstein, and others understandably fear—by the temptations of public clientage and majoritarian machination, so are they also compromised by the material deprivation and private clientage into which many must fall without the state's active and calculated protection and assistance: concentrations of private power secured by negative property themselves become sources of dependency, manipulation, and insecurity.[52] If "independence" bespeaks negative property, it also bespeaks its negation.

Epstein's "civic virtue" argument just flattens the republican dialectic into a one-sided case for absolute negative property. It thus belongs to Marshallian constitutional jurisprudence. Obviously, Epstein cannot be oblivious to the force of arguments calling for an active, even redistributive, state role in supporting the material and social conditions of effective and reliable democratic citizenship. His "civic virtue" argument *deliberately,* not negligently, subordinates that role—and subordinates it totally—to the protection of civic virtue by an uncompromising constitutional rule against politically engineered redistributions. The strategy is evidently rule-utilitarian, proceeding from a very high-order empirical best guess that the relentless discipline of the Cartesian rule will, over the long pull, be less costly and painful than the uncontainable, creeping chaos invited by relaxation in the direction of more particularistic judicial assessments of the good judgment or good faith of legislative assemblies.[53]

Insofar as it rests upon such a utilitarian and empirical—as opposed to naturalistic and moral—base, Epstein's argument may seem to deviate from our model of liberal or Marshallian constitutional jurisprudence.[54] But in raising empirical best-guessing to a level of abstraction, and thus of quasi-certainty, so high as to produce a constitutional-legal doctrine that practically replicates a natural-right jurisprudence, and in doing so for the sake of imposing a double-edged curb on the political excesses of both courts and democratic assemblies, Epstein's argument fits neatly within the Marshallian mold.

Let no one suppose, however, that Epstein's anti-welfare state result is forced or preordained by the discourse terms or conceptual resources of classical liberal constitutional jurisprudence. The dialectic of negative and affirmative property is preserved, not resolved, by the deep structure of liberal jurisprudence—specifically, in the proviso principle. Perhaps property owners perpetrate social harms by denying access to their "surplus" holdings to others whose competent citizenship (or natural rights) depend upon such access; if so, then the state commits no "taking" by using its power of taxation to overcome such illicit denial. Epstein, in effect, treats that question as answering itself, in the negative. Not so (as we'll see) Justice Scalia.

Justice Scalia

Among Supreme Court justices of recent memory, it is the next-to-newest justice, Antonin Scalia, whose work has most excited the hopeful attention of those who favor greatly increased firmness in constitutional-legal protection of negative property.[55] Two of Scalia's opinions, in particular, have attracted such notice: his opinion for the Court (actually, a bare majority of the justices) in *Nollan v. California Coastal Commission,*[56] and his dissenting opinion in *Pennell v. San Jose.*[57] *Nollan* is one of the precious few occasions since the famous *Mahon* case in 1922[58] on which the Court has found a compensable taking of property by government action in the form of a regulatory restriction on use, as opposed to a direct governmental trespass on possession.[59] *Pennell* set Scalia to explaining why he would have had the Court invalidate a rent control law—albeit a rather unusual one—as an uncompensated taking of property.[60]

We first examine these opinions of Justice Scalia's on the assumption that they are grounded in the kind of constitutional property theory and associated jurisprudence that I have modelled as liberal and Marshallian. We are going to find that, thus regarded, the justice's arguments end inconclusively. Major issues of principle seem to dangle in irresolution, or even looming contradiction. Arguments seem to be left gapingly incomplete, without directions for completing them. But Antonin Scalia is an exceptionally clear-thinking and clear-spoken person who understands well the art of constructing a compelling argument. That fact is evident from examination of his writings in general, and not disconfirmed by examination, at a micro-level, of any randomly-selected passage from either of the opinions we're about to dissect. How, then, does the justice come to land in such macro-ambiguity as—if I am right—he seems to have done? I ask the reader to suspend disbelief and consider, as we proceed, the possible correspondence of Scalia's performance of his judicial role in these cases to Madison's apparent understanding of how constitutional adjudication might best contribute to maintaining the essential tensions among individual liberty, popular authority, and governmental effectiveness.

Let us first examine the liberal strain of Scalia's thought in the *Nollan* case. The California Coastal Commission administers a system of building controls in pursuance of its charge from the legislature to protect public access to the California seacoast. Owners of coastal lots are required by law to obtain permits from the Commission for any construction on such lots of new or enlarged buildings. In order to facilitate public pedestrian travel between two public beach areas separated by a certain stretch of privately-owned lots, the Commission, in return for permission to build, decided to condition its issuance of building permits for lots falling within that stretch on the applicant lot-owners' willingness to dedicate an easement of public foot passage across their lot. The required easement would run laterally to the shore, across the sandy backyard of the parcel undergoing improvement. It was this practice of conditioning building permits on dedication of lateral-passage easements that the Supreme Court majority, speaking through Justice Scalia, invalidated in the *Nollan* case as an uncompensated public taking of private property.

Scalia's argument began with an assumed premise so plausible that few who have had anything to say about the case have seemed prepared to question it.[61] That premise is that had the State attempted to gain its end (that is, lateral passage for the public) by forbidding the Nollans to bar or hinder public pedestrian passage across their lands on the prescribed paths outright—imposing that prohibition not as a condition on building, but irrespective of anything the Nollans had ever done or proposed to do on their land—the State would thereby have effectively taken from the Nollans property (consisting of an easement) for which compensation would be constitutionally required. This premise the Justice drew directly from *Loretto v. Teleprompter Corp.*[62] In *Loretto,* the Court invalidated a New York regulation requiring landlords to allow CATV carriers to run cables across the roofs of their buildings free of charge. In so doing, the Court laid down the rule that where a regulation imposes a "permanent physical occupation" upon the property of an unwilling owner, a taking results *ipso facto.*

With the *Loretto* rule for a premise, Scalia plausibly reasoned that the conditional form of the Coastal Commission's dedication requirement ought not make any difference, except insofar as the owner's proposed action that brings the condition into play would (but for the condition) be the cause of some public harm that the condition is aptly designed to ameliorate or requite. Without such a "nexus" between the dedication condition and the prevention or correction of social harms stemming from the activity of the owner to which that condition is attached, Scalia argued, the conditional form of the dedication demand is just a ruse for evading compensation that would otherwise obviously be due. (In case you're having trouble seeing Scalia's point, just imagine California enacting a law requiring all owners of California littoral to stop polluting the atmosphere by breathing until they dedicate the demanded easements.)

Scalia's *Nollan* opinion thus held that when the state seeks to encroach by regulatory means upon the exclusive possessory rights of private owners, the requirement of some instrumental connection between the state's regulatory encroachment and the avoidance of some social harm sets a constitutional-legal limit on this sort of possession-infringing state action. But to hold *that* is already, it seems, to retrench quite a distance from anything like absolute protection for negative property. Quite strikingly, Scalia seems to have gone out of his way in *Nollan* to make this very point. Without purporting to decide the question, he introduced the possibility that the state's police power—its authority to prevent infliction of social harms by property owners without incurring obligations to compensate the restricted owners for property taken—might extend as far as prohibiting improvement of privately-owned land in such a way as to impair views of the sea from the public road. On the hypothesis that the police power does extend that far, Scalia further suggested that the Commission might quite properly have conditioned coastal-lot building permits on dedication by the improvers of public viewpoint easements on their improved parcels (i.e., assigned spots to which members of the public might freely stroll from the street whence to regard the sea), by way of offsetting any net loss of publicly visible seascape that would otherwise result from the improving. Conditioning new or enlarged construction on dedication of the hypothetical viewpoint easement, Scalia is saying, would satisfy the nexus requirement.

The nexus requirement, then, is a specific application of the proviso principle—the principle that, in our constitutional system, all legal titles are encumbered and qualified by the proviso that the property will not be used in a socially harmful fashion.[63] Scalia's "nexus" analysis in the *Nollan* case thus implicitly affirms this seemingly elastic qualification on constitutional protection for negative property. Indeed, as we're about to see, the question is how the qualification can be anything short of total.

According to Scalia, the actual lateral-passage easement condition in the *Nollan* case, unlike the hypothetical viewpoint easement condition, fails beyond argument to satisfy the nexus requirement. The reason is that putting more stuff on the front of your land in no way causes or aggravates the social disutility consisting of inability on the part of members of the public (who desire to do so) to walk along the sandy back; so there's no special reason to burden owners with lateral-passage easement just because they build in front.

But of course there is something else that *any* owner may do that *does* contribute to that social disutility, and that is simply to withhold permission from would-be lateral passers-through, thereby interposing against them the barrier of the law of trespass with its risk of legal penalty. So now let us suppose that California does the very thing that Scalia begins by treating as axiomatically unconstitutional: it simply and directly regulates every private littoral title in California by prohibiting owners from excluding or hindering lateral pedestrian passage along the beach—in effect, a *pro tanto* repeal of the law of trespass. Suppose, further, that the State, now duly educated by Scalia's *Nollan* opinion, argues as follows in defense of its prohibition:

> No one denies that California may regard the hindrance of public pedestrian passage along the Pacific shore as a public evil or social cost, against which the State may take apt counter-measures. Nor does anyone deny that regulating these public easements into effect is a precisely apt counter-measure. The only issue is whether we must compensate landowners whose interests in exclusive possession are adversely affected by our apt counter-measure. That depends, we are advised, on whether there is a clear 'nexus' between the need for the counter-measure and something those landowners do. But nothing could be more obvious than the tight-as-possible 'nexus' between specific increments of the social evil we are countering and specific choices by the landowners to refuse or prevent passage across their lands. Each such refusal—each such exercise of unregulated owner-power—aggravates the evil. *Nollan* establishes that the State, therefore, is within its rights in conditioning title to littoral land—that is, conditioning access to the legal status of rightful possessor of littoral with all its attendant powers for good and evil—on submission to the lateral-passage easement.

What, after *Nollan,* might the Court—remaining within the discourse of Marshallian liberal constitutional jurisprudence—possibly say is wrong with that argument?

There can be no doubt about the general form that the Court's answer would have to take. The Court would have to say that the general proviso concededly encumbering all titles—that the property is not to be deployed in a socially harmful fashion—does not extend to *every* category of property use that a political majority disprefer because that use disappoints some people, inconveniences them, or perhaps even leaves them gravely worse off than their preferred use would have done.

"Some use choices," the Court would, in effect, be saying, "just belong to the owner by right, regardless of the wishes, interests, or even needs of anyone (or everyone) else. Arguably (we can resolve the issue when and if we are ever called upon to do so), a state may determine that it is a harm to the public to restrict the public's sight of the sea by putting buildings in the way. But it incontrovertibly is not—whatever any state may say—a harm to the public to keep it from using your land as a shore route or, in general, to keep unwanted intruders off your land. That can't count as harming, because keeping unwanted others off your land is something that owners as such just have a right to do."

It seems that the Court would have to assert that (i) it has a way of telling where the line falls between deploying your property (subject to the state's sufferance) beyond your strict rights and deploying it (with immunity against the state) within those rights; and that (ii) quite conceivably the line falls somewhere between deploying your property so as to block people's view of the sea across it and deploying it so as to block people's bodies from entering it. It seems further as though the Court would have to say that both the general principle of the line's location and the Court's promised ability to resolve this particular question about its location are implicit in the notion of "property" itself, as that notion has been enacted into higher law by the ratifiers of the Constitution.[64] Only insofar as these are tenable assertions, it seems, can there remain a semblance of firm and dependable constitutional-legal (judicial) protection for negative property against democratic politics, once the Court admits the general qualification of all property that underlies Justice Scalia's "nexus" analysis in *Nollan*.

At least, that is how it all seems in what I am calling a liberal constitutional-jurisprudential vision. If Justice Scalia really means to commit himself to all this by his distinction of the viewpoint easement from the actual *Nollan* facts and (*a fortiori*) from my hypothetical case, then his *Nollan* opinion really is a very bold instance of what I have modeled as liberal constitutional jurisprudence.

There are, however, grave reasons for doubt that Scalia could have meant in *Nollan* to commit himself implicitly to this strong, classical liberal jurisprudential line. Nothing could better disclose those reasons than the Justice's own essay in *Pennell*.

Perhaps our discussion of the hypothetical case of direct, unconditional regulatory imposition of lateral-passage easement on all littoral titles confirms at least to this extent the possibility of liberal constitutional jurisprudence: it shows that in order to resolve a case like *Nollan* decisively against the state, no very strenuous divination of the higher-law signification of "property" (as positivized by the ratifiers of the takings clause) is required of the classical liberal judge. It suffices for the judge to read out of (or into) the higher law the weak message that to have property is, at the barest conceivable minimum, to have the unqualified right in general to decide for yourself who does and who does not physically enter what is, after all, supposed to be *your* land. The judge need only read the Constitution as conceding absolutely to negative property that much of a minimal core of a "right to exclude."[65] If that core postulate holds, then *Nollan* provides at least one showcase for liberal constitutional jurisprudence.

It turns out to be very difficult for American judges to allow the core postulate to hold. However minimal the core postulate may seem, it has, if taken seriously (just ask Richard Epstein), the immense consequence of ruling out the welfare state—which operates, after all, by seizing assets from the lawfully obtained possessions of some people just in order to translate those assets into benefits for others. If you are not prepared to support the owner's right of exclusive possession in that obvious and straightforward application, how can you profess to be honoring it as a reliable *rule* fit for service in a Marshallian, higher-law constitutional jurisprudence?[66] That is Epstein's question. The *Pennell* case squarely presents it. Those determined to do so can find in Justice Scalia's treatment of the case a libertarian response, of sorts; indeed, I mean to help them do so. But that exercise contains a surprise: to read Justice Scalia's *Pennell* dissent as an essay in liberal jurisprudence is to commit its author to the sponsorship of constitutional welfare rights.

On behalf of the city's landlords, Pennell complained against the constitutionality of a San Jose rent-control ordinance. As a general matter, the ordinance followed the usual pattern of permitting annual rent increases sufficient to provide landlords with returns deemed fair and reasonable. The ordinance, however, further provided for the possibility of administrative reduction of the normally allowable annual increase for a given unit, if the unit in question was occupied by a "particular tenant" for whom the unreduced, standardly allowable increase would "constitute . . . an unreasonably severe financial or economic hardship."[67] The complaining landlords characterized this "tenant hardship" provision as, in effect, a device for making guiltless, individual landlords fund (out of the fair and reasonable rental-income stream that would otherwise be theirs by right) a program of public assistance for poor people. The landlords contended that this arbitrary assignment to them of social costs that belong by rights to the public at large amounted to (i) an unconstitutional taking of their property without just compensation, (ii) an irrational (and therefore unconstitutional) interference with their property, and (iii) an arbitrary (and therefore unconstitutional) discrimination against landlords who lease to poor tenants.[68]

Chief Justice Rehnquist wrote for the Supreme Court majority. For reasons unrelated to our concerns here, the majority declined to pass on the uncompensated-taking claim.[69] The majority denied the irrational interference claim, because the tenant-hardship feature of the San Jose ordinance was a rationally chosen means toward the legitimate governmental aim of relief for financially distressed tenants. The majority further denied the arbitrary discrimination claim. The Chief Justice reasoned that San Jose had a straightforwardly obvious, commonsensical reason for letting the hardship tenant's landlord be the one to bear the burden of the rent-restriction by which the state's objective was rationally achieved: the landlord, as the person to whom the hardship tenant pays rent, just happens to be in harm's way. Whether or in what sense the landlord can be held causally responsible for the tenant's hardship was, according to the Chief Justice's thinking, "beside the point."[70]

To Justice Scalia, by contrast, that question was crucial. Although Scalia chose to rest his dissent on the taking-of-property rather than the arbitrary-discrimination claim, his reasoning brings the two claims together.[71] The justice based his argument on a reading of the takings clause as inspired by a constitutional norm opposed to political exploitation by arbitrarily discriminatory laws. "*The* purpose" of the constitutional proscription against uncompensated public takings of private property, Scalia wrote (recalling an oft-quoted passage from the Court's 1960 decision in *Armstrong v. United States*[72]), is " 'to bar Government from forcing some people alone to bear public burdens which, in all fairness and justice, should be borne by the public as a whole.' "[73]

The *Armstrong* antidiscrimination principle upon which Scalia relied in *Pennell* is interestingly reminiscent of Epstein's "civic virtue" argument against the welfare state, of which there is, indeed (as we'll soon see), a clear echo in Scalia's opinion.[74] Scalia, however, also finds in that principle the makings of an answer quite different from Epstein's strategic, rule-utilitarian response[75] to the question of the relation between the liberal proviso on negative property and the constitutional legitimacy of the welfare state.[76]

As it arises in *Pennell,* that question is whether it lies within the competence of the political community to treat as a form of overreaching by property owners the ordinary market behavior of selling what they own at the competitive, market-clearing price, when the effect is to charge poor people, for things they badly need (by prevailing social standards), more than they can pay without forgoing other necessities. Scalia takes the question seriously enough to grant *arguendo* that the answer is yes.[77] That answer, he reasons, cannot save the San Jose ordinance, because even if we thus grant the legitimacy of treating a landlord's ordinary market behavior as perpetrating harms upon poor tenants, it would still be obvious that any given poor person's plight is no more thus "caused or exploited" by his landlord charging him rent in a market than by the purveyors of his food, clothing, and medicine; by those who either refuse to employ him or do so only at a stingy wage; and—Scalia might well have added—by you and me who don't step forward to share enough of our own wealth with him to make him comfortable. Accordingly, Scalia observes,

> the traditional manner in which American government has met the problem of those who cannot pay reasonable prices for privately sold necessities—a problem caused by society at large—has been the distribution to such persons of funds raised from the public at large through taxes. . . . Unless we are to abandon the guiding principle of the Taking Clause that 'public burdens . . . should be borne by the public as a whole,' . . . this is the only manner that our Constitution permits.[78]

Thus would Scalia draw the line between the constitutionally improper San Jose tenant hardship regulation and the constitutionally proper fiscal transfer operations of the welfare state.

For a judge supposedly operating within a Marshallian or liberal constitutional jurisprudence, this way of legitimizing the welfare state would have remarkable implications. Among its crucial liberal premises seems to be our old friend, the no-harming proviso: those who would so deploy their holdings as to cause harm to others have no complaint when their holdings are imposed upon in order to avoid or requite the harm.[79] What's required to set that premise to work in liberal defense of the constitutional legitimacy of the welfare state is just to perceive the poverty of the poor (the existence in our midst of "those who cannot pay reasonable prices for privately sold necessities") as an objectionable state of affairs (a "problem") that we all ("society at large") jointly "cause," presumably by politically maintaining and personally participating in the capitalist economy and keeping our resultant incomes (insofar as we do) for ourselves. Being thus joint contributors to causing the harm consisting of the distress of the poor, we are all jointly ("the public as a whole") responsible—not just those of us who happen to rent housing to poor people—for the costs of repairing that harm.

In short, to understand Scalia's judicial blessing upon tax-financed poverty relief as containable within the program of liberal-Marshallian constitutional jurisprudence is to understand Scalia as claiming the ability to derive from some higher-law notion of property (although he does not exhibit the derivation) the conclusion that contributing to the causation of poor people's distress by participating in capitalism (including just by hanging on to your own earnings) is tantamount to harmful use of property. It is further to understand the Justice as claiming the accomplishment of this derivation by some method (not yet exhibited) supposed to be proof against infiltration by political bias.[80] It is to understand Justice Scalia, then, as treading dangerously close to the judicial affirmation of constitutional welfare rights. But for that last point, we are not yet quite ready.

We first have to deal with the alternative possibility that Scalia's line-drawing in the *Pennell* dissent is completely explainable by the *Armstrong* anti-discrimination principle, beefed up with some Epsteinian civic-virtue argument, without need for resort to any higher-law based theory of harmful use. It is certainly true that the justice explicitly draws the connection between the *Armstrong* principle and the goal of protecting San Jose landlords against political exploitation by fellow citizens using the trick of regulation to enrich themselves at the landlords' expense, by extracting from them more than their proper share of the costs of a public benefit—poor relief—in which the exploiters fully share.[81] Scalia presents this as a case of the same sort of danger to the democratic political process as that on which Epstein's civic virtue argument is trained.[82]

What Scalia does not explain, however, is why the argument applies with less force—a reduction in force enough to make a constitutional difference—to welfare-state redistributions operating through the treasury. He does not explain why—again, this is Epstein's question—we should exclude those who stand to gain from state-imposed "welfare" redistributions from the population of potential political exploiters.[83] Ancient and early modern republicans dealt with this concern by disfranchising "pensioners," but modern American liberal-democratic universalists constitutionally deny themselves that solution.[84] We do not exclude from our electorates beneficiaries, actual and potential, of state "welfare" programs; and as Epstein, Hayek, and others would be quick to point out, they too can learn the tricks of political exploitation—by strategic coalition-building, or just by pegging the level of need or eligibility for receipt of transfers at a point where an effective political majority will be on the receiving end.[85]

As preparation for the final assault on the liberal implications of the *Pennell* dissent, let us revert for a moment to our hypothetical variant of the *Nollan* case, in which the state by unconditional regulation injects a lateral-passage public easement into every possessory title to California littoral. This regulation applies without exception to every person positioned by property ownership to impede public passage along the seashore. Would Justice Scalia, then, uphold it against a "taking" attack because it conforms to the *Armstrong* rule against forcing "some people" to bear burdens that rightly ought to be shared by "the public as a whole"? Of course not. No such conclusion would be possible without overruling the *Loretto* decision, on which Scalia relied heavily for the first premise of his own reasoning in *Nollan*.[86]

But how are these cases of politically-engineered, selective, redistributive imposition on owners of apartment houses and littoral supposed to differ from state-imposed transfers of wealth from those who pay net taxes to those who are net recipients of program benefits? How can Justice Scalia accept the latter but not the former as constitutional? How can he think that the former case does, while the latter does not, involve the illicit exploitation of "some people" by "the public as a whole" through the exercise of majoritarian power?[87] If Scalia is to be understood from within the frame of Marshallian-liberal jurisprudence, then, in the final analysis, his line-drawings in *Nollan* and *Pennell* are not sufficiently explained by either the *Armstrong* antidiscrimination principle or an Epsteinian civic virtue argument; they must depend upon some unspoken, higher law-based theory of harmful use. Construed as a Marshallian-liberal judge, Scalia must be regarded as having deduced from higher-law premises that while owners of littoral do not overreach their rights by refusing entry to strangers, and owners of rental housing do not overreach by refusing entry to those who will not pay the market price, owners of surplus generic wealth do overreach—do engage in a harmful deployment of their property wealth—by withholding their surpluses from persons in conditions of need.

But Scalia cannot really think *that*. Whoever thinks *that* thinks, in effect, that there are constitutional welfare rights; and this is, on the evidence, something that Justice Scalia (along with a majority of his colleagues) decidedly does not think.[88]

Were he working from within a liberal jurisprudential frame of mind, only welfare rights could reconcile Justice Scalia's insistence that, in general, the costs of public goods be shared across "the public as a whole" with his acceptance that state-coerced redistribution of wealth *from* the (relatively) affluent *to* the needy is a legitimate object of state coercion. Insofar—but only insofar—as democratically enacted transfer programs are responsive to the *rights* of recipients, such enactments are beyond libertarian reproach as exploitative abuses of majority rule. To just that same extent, such enactments cannot be regarded as violations of the negative property rights of taxpayers (assuming fair distribution of the tax burden), because in executing them the state's minions must rather be viewed as marching up to, but not across, the borders that separate any such negative rights from the welfare rights they vindicate.[89] In other words, the liberal way to deny that tax-financed poverty relief violates property rights is the way of the proviso: there just is no redistribution taking place, because in these circumstances for you to withhold your wealth from the tax-collector is to perpetrate a current, or aggravate a past, harmful deployment of your holdings, insomuch as in these circumstances the withholding results in others suffering a current violation of their welfare rights, or going without a remedy for a past one.

But there is arguably a republican face to Justice Scalia's thought. Imagine a republican judge: aware of the multiplicity of values associated in

American constitutional thought with the idea of property rights—and, in a given context, the possible conflicts among them—falling under the general heads of privacy, security, and independence;[90] aware that these values always involve concerns about the distribution as well as the retention of wealth;[91] and aware, too, of a general qualification of these property-right values by constitutional commitments to popular self-government and to a legal regime that duly provides for the general welfare. Imbued with a Madisonian caution about getting too deeply involved, as a judge, in specific resolutions of conflicts of constitutional values, but also with a Madisonian determination to act on behalf of constitutional morale when the case is sufficiently suggestive of disrespect by elected representatives for one or another of those values,[92] our judge confronts cases like *Nollan* and *Pennell*.

In *Nollan*, the judge might well begin with the observation that an unconditional imposition by the state on the privacy of residential landowners, by making them put up with strangers passing at will across their backyards for the sake of no object more urgent than the recreational convenience of those who pass, is too gross and direct an insult to ordinary understandings of what property rights mean, and thus too heavy a public disparagement of the values of property in general, to be tolerated. The republican judge, in other words, might well start where Justice Scalia did when he adopted as the first premise of his argument in *Nollan* the rule-of-thumb proposition that state regulatory laws directly subjecting property to unwanted "permanent physical occupations" are presumptively violations of the takings clause. The leading authority for that proposition is *Loretto*, and the reasoning in *Loretto* depends heavily on the perceived centrality of "the right to exclude others" to the ordinary conception of ownership.[93] If it may be said that the Court's actual application of the presumptive proposition to the circumstances of the *Loretto* case itself was too formalistic and wooden for our republican jurisprudential model,[94] that would hardly be true for the circumstances of *Nollan*. Gross insult to the "ordinary observer's" understanding of what property is all about at the core[95] is just what it takes to raise the republican judicial hackles. The republican judge has no further need to undertake—as Justice Scalia in *Nollan* indeed did not—to defend and deploy a complete, naturalistic theory of property by way of logical demonstration that an owner's insistence on excluding others cannot be a wrongful, or "harmful," overreaching of the constitutionally intended prerogatives and benefits of ownership.

How would a republican judge, then, appraise a *conditional* regulatory invasion of privacy, such as the actual *Nollan* case involved? Perhaps by inquiring whether the activity of the owner upon which the condition is imposed, even if it cannot quite be said to have *no* adverse effect on the interests that the condition would further, has a bearing on those interests so palpably tenuous as to impart to the whole regulatory venture the kind of manipulative (or "extortionary") feel that suggests a failure of true respect for the constitutional values of property. That seems to be approximately what Justice Scalia's demand for intensified—not desultory—judicial scrutiny of the "nexus" question amounts to.[96]

Upon examination, we may also detect latent republicanism in Justice Scalia's *Pennell* opinion. Consider, first, a curious passage in his dissent that has so far escaped out attention. Evidently not wishing to confront in *Pennell* the broadest questions about the constitutionality of rent control, but rather to confine his determination of unconstitutionality to the peculiar tenant-hardship feature of the San Jose ordinance, the Justice took pains in his opinion to suggest how the tenant-hardship feature might be distinguished from "rent regulation in general":

> [When] the owner's use of the property is (or, but for the regulation, would be) the source of the social problem, it cannot be said that he has been singled out unfairly. . . . [Such a] cause-and-effect relationship is popularly thought to justify emergency price regulation: When commodities have been priced at a level that produces exorbitant returns, the owners of those commodities can be viewed as responsible for the economic hardship that occurs. Whether or not that is an accurate perception of the way a free-market operates, it is at least true that the owners reap unique benefits from the situation that produces the economic hardship, and in that respect singling them out to relieve it may not be regarded as "unfair." That justification might apply to the rent regulation in the present case, apart from the single feature [i.e., the tenant-hardship provision] under attack here.[97]

Justice Scalia thus introduces into the constitutional-legal analysis of rent control a supposed normative distinction between a landlord's innocuously withholding property from use by others, however grave their needs, except on condition of receiving in exchange a normal return[98] (whatever *that* is), as opposed to a landlord's trespassorily (as it were) demanding from anyone, rich or poor, as much rental as the market will bear in a "shortage"[99] (whatever *that* is). From the standpoint of Marshallian-liberal constitutional jurisprudence, the justice would have to be suggesting the possibility that such a normative distinction has been enacted into law by a constitutional text's reference to "property." But the distinction seems obviously too controversial—too political—an inference from that simple constitutional locution to work as Marshallian higher law.[100]

Also at odds with a Marshallian reading of this passage is the way its judicial author expressly doubts his own distinction's validity as economic science ("whether or not that is an accurate perception of the way a free market operates . . ."), and otherwise rhetorically distances himself from the "popular" perceptions by which ordinary rent laws are "regarded" as fair responses to acts by landlords that are "viewed" as causing harm to others. A Marshallian judge would feel compelled to decide whether *it is morally and legally true*—whether it is a correct derivation from the morally and legally correct theory of property—that landlords who charge what their market will bear are guiltily responsible for the resulting hardship. This Justice, by contrast, will apparently be satisfied by people's generally perceiving this to be so, whether their perception is "accurate" or not.

But how can this be? Insomuch as law—and especially constitutional law—is supposed to curb, limit, and discipline raw popular impulse, how can any constitutional adjudicator take popular perception as itself defining the legal premises? Only, it would seem, by understanding the judicial role in republican fashion as that of helping the people keep faith with *their own* most strongly professed principles of political morality—the ones that they have seen fit to constitutionalize—in part by interposing against legislative acts that smack of disparagement of those principles and threaten their consequent loss, by erosion, of serious public respect.[101] On that understanding, what Justice Scalia would have determined by his observations about the popular attribution of fault (in the pertinent sense) to those who receive so-called exorbitant profits is that a law forbidding such receipts does not flout any principle of property right that contains—as the American constitutional principle does—the proviso against harmful deployment. His point would be that, speaking from the constitutional adjudicator's standpoint, the worst that can be said of ordinary rent control is that it proceeds from an erroneous understanding of economic science, and that (shades of Holmes!) a commitment to getting our economic science right is not one of our constitutional values.

Let us now return to another nettlesome feature of Scalia's opinion: its complaint against the $32,400 income-eligibility ceiling for tenant-hardship treatment. Scalia suggests that the ceiling seems too high, especially considering that is was legislated "off-budget."[102] Who, after all, is Scalia, a judge, to be second-guessing such a quintessentially political determination as the income-eligibility standard in a poverty-relief law?[103] And why should he suppose that any member of the popularly accountable San Jose City Council, or any interested constituent, would fail to notice the number, or miss its meaning, just because it appears in a rent regulation rather than in a fiscal-transfer program?

Consider, as it might be perceived by a republican judge, a conflict among two clusters of constitutional values, *V1* and *V2*. *V1* encompasses whatever values—independence, autonomy, security, productivity—the judge's readings of history, precedent, and contemporary popular understanding lead him to associate with constitutional valorization of negative property. $V2$—similarly derived with reference to constitutional texts adverting to property, equality, and citizenship, not to mention general welfare and even republican government—encompasses constitutional values served by affirmative property (*alias* welfare rights or redistribution). These might include any or all of the polity's interests in a competent, public-spirited, industrious, frugal, independent-minded, and diverse citizenry;[104] the interests of individuals in (i.e., their putative rights to) the material prerequisites of effective citizenry; or even (in a republicanism more strongly cross-bred with the natural-rights tradition[105]) the claims of natural justice exerted by individuals who, without assistance, will suffer severe privation and the polity's corresponding interest in doing justice by performing its reciprocal obligation.

When, as in *Pennell*, a legislative body acts in apparent derogation of any given constitutional value or value cluster ($V1$), a republican judge wants assurance that it does so deliberately in the good-faith pursuit of another constitutional value ($V2$) that cannot, in the circumstances, be adequately served without some compromise or curtailment of $V1$. For such a judge, it would be entirely in order to observe that the eligibility limit in the rent ordinance looks suspiciously high, in the context of the additional observation that the issue of political justice thus posed has never been placed at the focus of a public deliberation. On that basis, the republican judge might intervene with no profession of a method for discovering with anything like certainty or precision where the line belongs between the conflicting claims of negative and affirmative property. The judge would be professing, rather, an acculturated sense of when a quite different line has been breached—the line of credibility separating those legislative acts that smack unacceptably of contempt of constitutional values from those in which the presumption of good-faith deliberation stands firm. The republican judge acts in dialogic relation with the people, exercising a kind of suspensive veto. In the face of a combination of circumstances raising suspicion of corrosive contempt for negative property, the judge demands the additional assurance of a remand of the question to the citizens (mediately through their elected representatives) for their more focal consideration.[106]

The unspoken but indispensable premise of this sort of judicial performance is that the citizens (or the representatives) will respond to the question, once properly framed and focused, not only as a question of self-interest but also, and in good faith, as one of constitutional value. Of course, this may be on the judge's part more a leap of faith, or a dictate of role, than an empirical conviction; but still it would be a distinctively republican leap or sense of role.

IV. Conclusion

Some say that the takings clause enacts negative property as a constitutional principle *simpliciter*—as a constitutional rule, so to speak, in its own right, entitled, as such, to unqualified respect. Some say that the clause gives constitutional expression to a cluster of values—independence, privacy, security—that, in practice, imply a due (meaning a circumspect) regard for negative property as an important way of realizing those values, among other (sometimes conflicting) ways. The first version belongs to a Cartesian constitutional jurisprudence of rules. The second version belongs to a pragmatic constitutional jurisprudence of values. Without question, Professor Epstein's work described here belongs to the Cartesian constitutional-legal style. Perhaps more debatably—quite conceivably to the justice's own amazement[107]—I have here claimed Justice Scalia's work in *Nollan* and *Pennell,* at least, for the pragmatic style.

There might be any number of imaginable explanations for such a difference in legal-argumentative styles. Some might look first for underlying differences in politics or temperament. Here such explanations are idle. We know that Justice Scalia's constitutional jurisprudence would admit poor relief to the class of "moral values of society" that governments may enforce without constitutional transgression, whereas Professor Epstein's would not.[108] But we know not whether Scalia's personal leanings are any less libertarian (or whatever) than Epstein's. Nor, on the available evidence, is Scalia temperamentally less inclined than is Epstein towards adjudicative Cartesianism. To the contrary, there is plenty of indication on the written record of Scalian Cartesianism; the Justice sometimes seems just the man to rewrite the book of constitutional law as a Euclid of transparent inferences among clear and distinct ideas.[109]

Yet the contrast in our two exemplars' respective approaches to specific issues of constitutional protection for property is striking and undeniable. That much, I have documented. So perhaps we ought to consider, with due caution, whether that contrast might have anything to do with differences in their respective social and professional positions, offices, or roles.[110] In introducing here the idea of constraints of judicial role, I don't primarily mean considerations of institutional capacity classically explored by Professors Hart and Sacks,[111] and more recently invoked by Judge Frank Coffin to explain the typically atheoretical character of judicial work.[112] Rather, I mean something more like the judicial incumbent's existential sense of power—his or her sense of care and caution in the face of awareness of his or her own potency for the perpetration of evil or good, wrong or right, injustice or justice.[113] In this regard, the judge's problem is to self-govern his or her exercises of power in ways that he or she can comfortably respect as neither excessive nor abdicative. Especially when doing constitutional adjudication, judges want self-discipline in their very acts of disciplining the democracy.

Professor Epstein would have judges erect such a double-edged discipline by rigorizing the Constitution. At least in the realm of constitutional law, he urges that judicial judgment should strive to reduce itself to ratiocination. Only by cultivating a judicial discourse of rational inference from and among constitutional postulates of Cartesian simplicity and clarity, Epstein suggests, can judges manage to restrain the despotic tendencies of democratic majorities without lapsing into their own. It follows that each constitutional postulate ideally ought to be internally unitary, and that the whole set ought to form an unproblematically consistent whole. Intuitions, no matter how compelling, of irreducible plurality and conflict among constitutional values ought to be squeezed out of the postulates, even when that can be done only through a highly muscular leap of empirical speculation.[114] Epstein's own most profound, motivating intuition is to mistrust the levels of competence and good faith to be expected of openly deliberated (as opposed to logically closed) resolutions of public issues, whether in democratic popular assemblies or among judges engaged in contextually informed construals and "balancings" of constitutional values. In Epstein's final analysis, there would *be* no constitutional *values* worth mentioning. Judges and lawyers would argumentatively invoke only the constitutional *rules* that would have once-and-for-all regimented the candidate values into a Euclidean system.

What we have noticed is that Justice Scalia's judicial work on constitutional property rights shatters the Cartesian—we may now say, reverting to our initial categories, the Marshallian-liberal—model. Conceivably (I surely am in no position to assert it confidently), we observe here the effect of the judicial office, including the reflections and dialogues incited by confrontation with specific cases and with the case-focused arguments of advocates and colleagues.

One imagines that American judges typically approach constitutional adjudication with the sense that among the ultimate judicial abuses is that of enforcing upon the country, in the name of law, a rule that simply is not the country's law. The most activist constitutional adjudicators represent themselves, presumably in good faith, as ministers of an unfolding political morality to which the country is committed by its constitutional history to date.[115] My claim is that no set of Cartesian postulates can plausibly pretend to be the country's law, least of all in that sense of unfolding political morality, because any Cartesian set must suppress the complexities, the intersections and conflicts, of historic American constitutional values.

Insofar as there is truth in that observation, those among us whose works are least likely to escape its influence are judges, the ones who actually *do* constitutional adjudication.

The lesson for the constitutional-legal future of negative property must be obvious. The "bad" news is that its future will be vexed. The good news is that its vexed future seems assured.

Notes

1. The historical literature has long been committed to "liberal" as the standard counter to "republican." I here use "liberal" (and occasionally "classical liberal") specifically to mean the nascent classical liberalism contemplated by founding-era histories. I do not intend by it to refer to the full range of positions commonly known as "liberal" in contemporary American politics. There is no well-defined opposition between our contemporary liberalisms and republicanism. *See, e.g.,* Michelman, *Law's Republic,* 97 YALE L.J. 1493 (1988); Sunstein, *Beyond the Republican Revival,* 97 YALE L.J. 1539 (1988).

Locke is standardly identified as the major historical antecedent of the liberal understanding. *See, e.g.,* L. HARTZ, THE LIBERAL TRADITION IN AMERICA (1955); Kramnick, *Republican Revisionism Revisited,* 88 AM. HIST. REV. 629 (1982). On the republican side, some scholars have been intent on detecting the influences of French political sociology, especially Rousseau and Montesquieu. *See* Horwitz, *Republicanism and Liberalism in American Constitutional Thought,* 29 WM. & MARY L. REV. 57, 71–73 (1987). Others have linked American formative-era republicanism with the moral sense philosophers of the Scottish Enlightenment. *See* G. WILLS, INVENTING AMERICA: JEFFERSON'S DECLARATION OF INDEPENDENCE 193–206 & *passim* (1978). *But see* Hamowy, *Jefferson and the Scottish Enlightenment: A Critique of Gary Wills'* Inventing America: Jefferson's Declaration of Independence, 36 WM. & MARY Q. 503, 514 (1979). The most influential recent scholarship has traced the republican strain in a path running from the ancients, to Machiavelli, to Harrington, to the "commonwealthmen" and "country party" of the English 18th century, to colonial and revolutionary America. *E.g.,* B. BAILYN, IDEOLOGICAL ORIGINS OF THE AMERICAN REVOLUTION (1967); J. POCOCK, THE MACHIAVELLIAN MOMENT: FLORENTINE POLITICAL THOUGHT AND THE ATLANTIC REPUBLICAN TRADITION (1975).

Some writers have regarded the Antifederalists of the American founding era as republicans and the Federalists as liberals. *See* Michelman, *The Supreme Court, 1985 Term—Foreword: Traces of Self-Government,* 100 HARV. L. REV. 4, 20 & nn. 88–90 (1986) (citing examples but questioning this correlation). Others have found republicanism rampant in revolutionary America but, by the time of the constitutional

debates, widely in the process of being overtaken by liberalism. *See* G. WOOD, THE
CREATION OF THE AMERICAN REPUBLIC 1776–1787 (1969). Among the principal
founders, Jefferson, Madison, and Wilson have all been claimed for both camps. On
Jefferson, *compare* G. WILLS, *supra* note 1 *with* Appleby, *What Is Still American in
the Political Philosophy of Thomas Jefferson,* 39 WM. & MARY Q. 287 (1982). On
Madison and Wilson, *see, e.g.,* J. NEDELSKY, PRIVATE PROPERTY AND THE LIMITS OF
AMERICAN CONSTITUTIONALISM: A VIEW FROM THE FORMATION chs. 2, 4 (1989).

2. *See, e.g.,* Horwitz, *supra* note 1, at 64.

3. *See, e.g.,* J. NEDELSKY, *supra* note 1; G. WOOD, *supra* note 1; Note, *The
Origins and Original Significance of the Just Compensation Clause of the Fifth
Amendment,* 94 YALE L.J. 694 (1985) (by William Treanor) (hereinafter cited as
Treanor).

4. *See* Michelman, *supra* note 1, at 17–18.

5. Obviously, any attempt to limn two such polar positions must oversimplify
what Americans have actually thought at any historical moment. This must be so if
for no reason than that there has always been, as we'll see, a powerful tendency for
each polar position to incorporate and replicate aspects of the other. But I agree, too,
with those who find oversimplification in the very idea of representing American
normative political argument of the founding era and beyond as a structurally
contained, bipolar dialectic. I agree that a more numerous and nuanced typology is
required to get us anywhere near the historical truth of these matters. *See, e.g.* Fisher,
*Ideology, Religion, and the Constitutional Protection of Private Property:
1760–1860,* 68 N. C. L. REV. (forthcoming 1989). Despite all such concessions,
however, the bipolar dialectical framework remains a useful device for presenting
some major preoccupations and movements in American constitutional disputation
over property rights negative and affirmative, and in that spirit I am going to use it.

6. Logical incompatibility can be defeated by imagining a duly constituted
"property-owning democracy" in which the *ab initio* restrictions on wealth-
engrossment—whether through inheritance, industrial concentration, capital accumu-
lation, or otherwise—are so strong, the public-education and related economic-
empowerment systems so effective, and voluntary assistance to the residually needy
so generous and discreet that the economy under this basic structure generates in
ordinary course a welfare-right satisfying distribution without resort to explicit,
post-earnings "transfers." *See, e.g.,* Krause & McPherson, *Capitalism, "Property-
Owning Democracy," and the Welfare State* in DEMOCRACY AND THE WELFARE STATE
79 (A. Gutmann ed. 1988). I have framed this essay on the alternative assumption:
that the constitutional-legal basis of political economy in the United States continues
to be such that maintaining everyone at a plausible welfare-rights standard requires an
interminable series of explicit governmental "interventions" in the form of
post-earnings ("redistributive") taxes and wealth transfers; and that there continues,
therefore, to be live controversy—some of which takes constitutional-legal
form—over how far our state system shall be that of a welfare (as opposed, say, to a
night-watchman) state.

7. *See* Michelman, *Law's Republic, supra* note 1.

8. *See* Treanor, *supra* note 3. On terminology, *see supra* note 1.

9. *Id.*

10. *See id.* at 695.

11. *See* U.S. CONST. amend. V ("nor shall private property be taken for public use, without just compensation"); Treanor, *supra* note 3, at 714–15.

12. Another, and related, essential difference lay in the degree of confidence with which republican and liberal thought expected legislatures spontaneously to act with a due regard for individual rights. *See id.* at 700–701, 704–5.

13.. *See id.* at 694 nn. 1–2, 695, 696 n.6, 697.

14. *See id.* at 699–701. Treanor thus perceives in republican thought an identification of community with state. It is worth noting my doubt that such a conceptual tie between community and state underlies the best of republican thought about the conditions of self-government in and through association with others. *See* Michelman, *supra* note 1, at 1531–32. But this is not to gainsay that just this tie has been deeply characteristic of American constitutional disputation about negative property. *See, e.g., infra* p. 131 & nn. 21–22. If there is heuristic value in talking about a "republican" influence on this thought and disputation, it must be a statist version of republicanism that we have in mind (although this may not be the quintessential stuff).

15. *See id.* at 695–96 & n.6.

16. The civic republican tradition in political thought is, of course, famous for its preoccupations not only with the general dependence of a country's constitutional fate—its political freedom and stability—on its pattern of wealth distribution, but also with the specific tie between the "independent" quality of the citizen's contribution to public deliberations regarding the common good and the citizen's legally secure command over material resources sufficient to ward off the "corruption" threatened by pressing material need or beholdenness to patrons. For brief reviews, *see* Michelman, *Possession vs. Distribution in the Constitutional Idea of Property,* 72 IOWA L. REV. 1319, 1329 (1987); Treanor, *supra* note 3, at 699. For a recent, famous libertarian analogue, *see* Reich, *The New Property,* 73 YALE L.J. 733 (1963).

17. *See, e.g.,* T. JEFFERSON, NOTES ON THE STATE OF VIRGINIA; J. POCOCK, *supra* note 1, at 463–64; D. MCCOY, THE ELUSIVE REPUBLIC: POLITICAL ECONOMY IN JEFFERSONIAN AMERICA (1980).

18. *See* Michelman, *supra* note 1, at 1504–5, 1526–37.

19. *See* Kahn, *Reason and Will in the Origins of American Constitutionalism,* 98 YALE L.J. 449, 478, 480–81, 483, 486 (1989). For variant examples of this libertarian way of naturalizing legal-positivist constitutional thought, see *Proceedings*

of the Conference on Takings of Property and the Constitution, 41 MIAMI L. REV. 49, 133–34 (1986) (remarks of Ellen Paul); *id.* at 203 (remarks of Richard Epstein).

20. *See supra* p. 130 & nn. 16–18. In republican constitutional thought there is, then, a circular relation between politics and rights—good rights depend on good politics, good politics depend on good rights. *See* Michelman, *supra* note 1, at 1501, 1505.

21. Keystone Bituminous Coal Ass'n v. DeBenedictis, 107 S. Ct. 1232, 1245 (1987), quoting from Mugler v. Kansas, 123 U.S. 623, 665 (1887).

22. Although, as the *Keystone/Mugler* dictum illustrates, the Supreme Court's renditions of the proviso often have a communitarian flavor, recognition of the proviso does not in itself import any concession to a communitarian (as opposed to a strictly individualistic) strain in the underlying moral theory of property. The proviso is an entailment of classical liberal universalization of individual rights. Each individual's right must be defined so as not to contradict the similarly defined rights of others: "*sic utero tuo ut alienum non laedas.*"

23. *See infra* pp.141–45; *infra* note 77; *infra* pp. 146–48.

24. *See* Epstein, *The Supreme Court 1987 Term—Foreword: Unconstitutional Conditions, State Power, and the Limits of Consent*, 107 HARV. L. REV. 5, 61, 63–64 (1988); Epstein, *Rent Control and the Theory of Efficient Regulation* 54 BROOKLYN L. REV. 741 (1988); *infra* pp. 136–37.

25. Here I must note a certain oversimplification or omission in our jurisprudential typology. Some readers may wonder whether my account of a naturalistic liberal constitutional-legal theory of property—and particularly my repeated attribution to this theory of a claimed ability to derive *from the notion of property itself* a line separating privileged (innocuous) from trespassory (harmful) deployments of property—covers the variant form of legal-property naturalism known as "vested rights." Vested rights theory looks to standing law for the answers to all questions about which *de facto* advantageous situations respecting material goods count as property entitlements *de jure*. To this extent, vested rights theory belongs to legal positivism. Its naturalistic element lies in its insistence that a positivistically grounded entitlement, once duly established according to extant law, shall suffer no retroactive disturbance without appropriate remedy. *See, e.g.*, United States v. Willow River Power Co., 324 U.S. 499 (1945).

Historically, it seems that vested rights theory has tended to regard its positivistically grounded entitlements (*de jure* property) as always implicitly qualified by the usual, general proviso of no harmful use. *See, e.g.*, Coates v. Mayor of New York City, 7 Cow. 585, 605 (N.Y. Sup. Ct. 1827); Commonwealth v. Chapin, 5 Pick. 199, 202–03 (Mass. 1827). On that understanding, resort to vested rights can do nothing to relieve libertarian property jurisprudence of its commitment to naturalistic derivation of the line separating harmful from benign deployments of property. But what if the positivistic entitlement itself consists of a specifically recognized privilege of "harmful" use? Consider, for example, a line of judicial decisions plainly establishing the rule that you don't commit a legal wrong by building skyward within your own lot lines, no matter how severe the resulting interference with your neighbor's light or prospect. Under a vested rights approach, it would obviously be possible for a court to hold unconstitutional the retrospective application of a new rule defining as tortious the construction or maintenance of a building that blocks a neighbor's light or view without that court's having to make or defend any naturalistically based determination that blocking lights is not "harming."

What I have done, in effect, for the purposes of this essay, is to posit that a constitutional regime affording no protection to property beyond such a formal rule against regulatory retrospectivity allocates too great a share of decisive authority to politics, reserving too little to trans-political morality or reason, to qualify as "liberal" under my stipulative definition.

26. *See* Ackerman, *The Storrs Lectures: Discovering the Constitution*, 93 YALE L.J. 1013 (1984).

27. Here we may note a second oversimplification or omission in our jurisprudential typology. The typology assumes—not unrealistically—that courts (although not commentators, *see, e.g., Symposium on the Constitution as an Economic Document*, 56 GEO. WASH. L. REV. 1 (1987)) virtually always treat constitutional enactments (although not other legislation, *see, e.g.*, Kassel v. Consolidated Freightways Corp., 450 U.S. 662 (1981)) on the unquestioned assumption that they are sincere attempts to give expression to public values or interests, not just outcomes of privately self-serving strategic behavior. For thoughts about possible reasons for this phenomenon, *see* Michelman, *supra* note 1; Michelman, *Conceptions of Democracy in American Constitutional Argument: The Case of Pornography Regulation*, 56 TENN. L. REV. (forthcoming 1989).

28. Here is the place to note a third and last omission or oversimplification in our jurisprudential models. The republican model treats the values and interests associated with a given constitutional text as known and fixed as of the moment of enactment. It ignores the question—one that I have elsewhere regarded as crucial for a complete republican theory of constitutional law—of intertemporal change in those values. *See* Michelman, *supra* note 1.

29. J. NEDELSKY, *supra* note 1; Nedelsky, *Confining Democratic Politics: Anti-Federalists, Federalists, and the Constitution*, 96 HARV. L. REV. 340 (1982).

30. The perception of Madison as proto-liberal devotee of higher-law rights, centrally including negative property rights, is of course familiar in American constitutional historiography. For recent documentation, *see, e.g.*, J. NEDELSKY, *supra* note 1, chs. 3, 5; Treanor, *supra* note 3, at 709–10. A spate of other recent writings on American constitutional foundations has turned the spotlight on Madison's republican side, particularly his recognition of the dependence in practice of respect for "rights of others" and "rules of justice" on a well-contrived political

system resting on a well-disposed base. *See, e.g.*, D. MCCOY, *supra* note 17; G. WILLS, EXPLAINING AMERICA: THE FEDERALIST (1981); Sunstein, *supra* note 1, at 1558–64.

31. For the reading of Madison's thought that follows, *see* J. NEDELSKY, *supra* note 1; Fisher, *The Significance of Public Perceptions of the Takings Doctrine*, 88 COLUM. L. REV. 774, 1782–83 (1988); Treanor, *supra* note 3, at 710–11, 712 n. 99. Nedelsky states that "although Madison (who introduced the [bill of rights] in Congress) had little faith in paper values, he thought [the amendments] might have the salutary effect of instilling basic values in the population." In support, Nedelsky cites a letter from Madison to Thomas Jefferson and notices Madison's general lack of attention to judicial review. Treanor's reading is an inference drawn from a combination of (i) the weight placed by Madison, when introducing the Bill of Rights in Congress, on its educative function, (ii) Madison's proposed text for the takings clause, (iii) early interpretations of the clause, and (iv) passages in Madison's essay on *Property* written not long after ratification of the Bill of Rights. Fisher relies on Treanor, citing in further support Madison's correspondence with Jefferson confirming Madison's emphasis on the educative function of constitutional law emanating from venerated framers, and recalling Madison's general inclination to rely on artfully-conceived political mechanisms for due restraint of officialdom.

32. For other historical evocations of the tutelary style of republican judgecraft, *see* Presser, *Saving God's Republic: The Jurisprudence of Samuel Chase*, 1984 U. ILL. L. REV. 1102; Lerner, *The Supreme Court as Republican Schoolmaster*, 1967 SUP. CT. REV. 127. Daniel Webster described "adjudged cases, well reported," as "so many land-marks, to guide erratick opinion." 1 THE PAPERS OF DANIEL WEBSTER: LEGAL PAPERS 172 (A. Konefsky & A. King eds. 1982), quoted in Konefsky, *Law and Culture in Antebellum Boston*, 40 STAN. L. REV. 1119, 1132 (1988).

In presenting as "republican" the idea of a tutelary judiciary, I recognize that history also offers a quite different picture—perhaps most vividly in Newmyer's account of Joseph Story—of the republican constitutional jurist as very close, in all respects relevant to my purposes here, to what I have presented as the Marshallian view. *See* R. NEWMYER, SUPREME COURT JUSTICE JOSEPH STORY: STATESMAN OF THE OLD REPUBLIC 191 (1985); Konefsky, *supra* note 32 at 1142–43. *But see*, for an account of Story's constitutional jurisprudence fitting closely to the Madisonian model as I develop it here, Powell, *Joseph Story's Commentaries on the Constitution: A Belated Review*, 94 YALE L.J. 1282, 1309–13 (1985).

33. *See* 14 PAPERS OF JAMES MADISON 197–98 (R. A. Rutland *et al.* eds. 1962), article in *National Gazette* by "j. m."; D. MCCOY, *supra* note 17, at 121–27, 131, 134–36, 143–45 (1980).

34. *See* J. NEDELSKY, *supra* note 1.

35. *See* R. Epstein, TAKINGS: PRIVATE PROPERTY AND THE LAW OF EMINENT DOMAIN 306–24 (1985).

36. *See* R. EPSTEIN, *supra* note 35 at 19–31; Epstein, *Not Deference But Doctrine: The Eminent Domain Clause*, 1982 SUP. CT. REV. 351. One might speculate that it is the appeal of Epstein's argument at the jurisprudential level that gains it a respectful hearing despite its evident implausibility as contemporary constitutional interpretation or as explanatory theorization of historic or prevailing judicial doctrine. *Cf.* Ross, *Taking* Takings *Seriously*, 80 NW. I. L. REV. 1591, 1603 (1986):

> *Takings* offers a coherent view of the legal world and a simple solution to the takings issue. Most legal academics see the law as inherently more complex and the takings issue as more intractable than Epstein projects. The popular audience, alternatively, is more likely to accept, even welcome, Epstein's simplifications.

37. *See* R. EPSTEIN, *supra* note 35, at 19–20.

38. *Cf.* Epstein, *The Classical Legal Tradition*, 73 CORNELL L. REV. 292, 293–95 (admiring Roman law for projecting "the image . . . of a kind of timeless, Cartesian stability . . . stand[ing] outside the forces of history and circumstance," for its practitioners' "ability to deduce in a formal way particular conclusions from accepted principle," and for "always looking for the core, and not the penumbra"; but faulting its practitioners for "skirt[ing] the problem of finding ways to justify the first principles in which they so strongly believed."

39. Epstein would, however, leave all measures so challenged open to the defense that the takee's share of the social benefits generated by the public project or program in which the taking occurs provides enough compensation to reduce resultant net redistribution to zero. *See* R. EPSTEIN, *supra* note 35, at 195–215.

40. *See* R. EPSTEIN, *supra* note 35, at 107–8; *supra* p. 132.

41. Recall the exemplary cases *supra* p. 132.

42. *See id.* at 107–45. It is consistent with this insistence on right answers in principle for Epstein's judges to defer to legislative judgments about applications in the face of empirical uncertainty, when the judges have reason—considering both "legislative competence and legislative bias"—to believe that "a legislative decision is likely to be more accurate than their own." *Id.* at 128–29.

43. *See, e.g.,* Fisher, *supra* note 31, at 1781–82 & n. 35; Radin, *The Liberal Conception of Property: Cross-Currents in the Jurisprudence of Takings*, 88 COLUM. L. REV. 1667, 1668 (1988).

44. *See* R. EPSTEIN, *supra* note 35, at 344–46; Epstein, *Beyond the Rule of Law: Civic Virtue and Constitutional Structure*, 56 GEO. WASH. L. REV. 149 (1987).

45. *See, e.g.,* J. Shearmur, *From Dialogue Rights to Property Rights: Foundations for Hayek's Legal Theory*, paper presented at the annual meeting of the American Political Science Association, Chicago, September 1987.

46. *See, e.g.,* F. HAYEK, THE ROAD TO SERFDOM (1944); F. HAYEK, THE CONSTITUTION OF LIBERTY (1960); G. STIGLER, THE CITIZEN AND THE STATE (1975).

47. *See, e.g.,* Pocock, *Civic Humanism and Its Role in Anglo-American Thought,* in J. POCOCK, POLITICS, LANGUAGE AND TIME: ESSAYS ON POLITICAL THOUGHT AND HISTORY 86–90 (1973); Skinner, *The Idea of Negative Liberty,* in R. RORTY, J. SCHNEEWIND & Q. SKINNER, PHILOSOPHY IN HISTORY 193, 218 (1984).

48. *See, e.g.,* Michelman, *supra* note 16, at 1329; Michelman, *supra* note 1, at 49–50 & n. 256.

49. *See* Horwitz, *supra* note 1, at 72; Michelman, *supra* note 16, at 1329–34.

50. *See, e.g.,* Fiss, *Why the State,* 100 HARV L. REV. 781 (1987).

51. *See, e.g.,* B. ACKERMAN, SOCIAL JUSTICE IN THE LIBERAL STATE (1980); GUTMANN, DEMOCRATIC EDUCATION 134–37 (1987); Holmes, *Liberal Guilt,* in RESPONSIBILITY, RIGHTS, AND WELFARE (J. Moon ed. 1988).

52. For a classic discussion, *see* Cohen, *Property and Sovereignty,* 13 CORNELL L. Q. 8, 11, 14 (1927). One might wonder how such dependence and resultant "corruption" of citizens could ever be a concern if the state were effectively limited, as libertarians ideally would limit it, to the effectuation of pre-political rights, so that all governance questions became, accordingly, strictly decidable by technical criteria. In return, it may be asked why libertarians accept, when they do, the forms of political democracy. To that question, the most cogent answer seems to be the Schumpeterian one: that in some historical and cultural circumstances, at least, constitutional arrangements featuring a periodic, plebiscitory opportunity to turn the rascals out provides the best hope of constraining the state to its proper functions. See J. SCHUMPETER, CAPITALISM, SOCIALISM, AND DEMOCRACY 271–72 (3d ed. 1950). But then libertarians would have good reason for deploring the corruption of citizens by dependency. *See id.* at 294–96, 301. Be all that as it may, Epstein's republican argument presupposes, for whatever reasons, a broad scope in practice for democratic policymaking authority.

53. This interpretation of Epstein's position is supported by colloquies in the conference discussions transcribed in *Proceedings, supra* note 19. *See also* Epstein, *supra* note 38, at 298–99: "I think that the new accounts of property and contract, at bottom, will have to be functional and utilitarian."

54. *See supra* pp. 131–35.

55. As all are forced to concede, such protection at its strongest is deeply qualified by eminent domain—the government's conceded authority to expropriate any item of property for public use on condition of paying fair value in exchange. Under the broadly permissive reading of the "public use" condition in Hawaii Housing Auth. v. Midkiff, 104 S. Ct. 2321 (1984) (*see also* Berman v. Parker, 348 U.S. 26 (1954)), constitutional protection for negative property does not, in practice, yield protection of specific holdings but of generic wealth.

56. 107 Sup. Ct. 3141 (1987). *See* Fisher, *supra* note 31, at 1774 & n.3

(compiling journalistic appraisals of the *Nollan* decision as portending "much greater" protection for property rights).

57. 108 Sup. Ct. 849, 859 (1988) (joined by O'Connor, J.)

58. *See* Pennsylvania Coal Co. v. Mahon, 260 U.S. 393 (1922).

59. *See* Michelman, *Takings, 1987,* 88 COLUM. L. REV. 1600, 1621–22 & nn. 104–5.

60. I focus here on selected aspects of these opinions—not necessarily the most interesting from either a practical or a theoretical standpoint, but the ones germane to this paper. I have discussed other aspects of *Nollan* in Michelman, *supra* note 59.

61. *But see Nollan,* 107 S. Ct. 3150, 3156–57 (Brennan, J., dissenting).

62. 458 U.S. 419 (1982).

63. *See supra* p. 131. Douglas Kmiec suggests the possibility of explaining the nexus requirement as a manifestation of a different general principle: that of antidiscrimination, or (as the Court put it in Armstrong v. United States, 364 U.S. 40, 49 (1960)) of "bar[ring] Government from forcing some people to bear public burdens which, in all fairness and justice, should be borne by the public as a whole." *See* Kmiec, *The Original Understanding of the Taking Clause is Neither Weak nor Obtuse,* 88 COLUM. L. REV. 1630, 160–552 (1988). As we shall see below in connection with *Pennell,* Justice Scalia does indeed, just as Kmiec suggests, finally repair to this antidiscrimination principle as foundational for constitutional "takings" analysis. There is, however, no inconsistency between this observation and my tracing Scalia's demand for nexus in *Nollan* to the proviso principle, because, as we shall also see below, in this context the antidiscrimination principle is parasitic upon—it is idle without input from—the proviso principle. Asked to explain why the exaction of viewpoint easements from beachfront *improvers* but not beachfront owners at large would not violate antidiscrimination, Scalia's response would have to be that it is only fair to exact requital specifically from improvers whose improvements overreach the proviso (i.e., by harmfully blocking views of the sea from public ways). This relation of dependency between antidiscrimination analysis and the court's ability—as required by the proviso principle—to sort deployments of property into the categories of the noxious (hence trespassory) and the innocuous (hence privileged) is involved in much of the following discussion of Scalia's *Nollan* and *Pennell* opinions.

64. *See supra* pp. 131–32. *See also supra* note 25 for brief discussion of a "vested rights" alternative.

65. *See, e.g.,* Kaiser Aetna v. United States, 444 U.S. 164, 179–80 (1979) (per Rehnquist, J.) (referring to the "'right to exclude,' so universally held to be a fundamental element of the property right").

66. Perhaps you intuitively feel that taxes, the instrument *a la mode* of the welfare state, are categorically different from regulations and cannot be takings. But

from the standpoint of anyone inclined toward a naturalistically inspired, abstractly principled, liberal jurisprudence of constitutional property rights (as positivized by the takings clause), the distinction is elusive.

One defense of it might start by recasting the takings clause as just an emphatic antidiscrimination doctrine directed to government actions redistributing wealth, and then say that a tax—being scaled to wealth or income by a general rule—cannot violate antidiscrimination. But that seems unpersuasive, to put it mildly, as applied to a tax that has, in effect, net-positive rates for some people and net-negative rates for others. *See, e.g.,* F. HAYEK, THE CONSTITUTION OF LIBERTY ch. 20 (1960). This matter is pursued further at pp. 148–49 below.

A more interesting possibility for categorically exempting taxes from a naturalistic-liberal anti-taking doctrine is the appeal to the idea that people have morally stronger claims to retain control over specific items of property than they have to retain control over generic wealth in the form of money. (This approach is a non-starter under the Supreme Court's current lax construal of the public-use requirement for eminent domain, because, under the lax interpretation, constitutional property rights are not, in practical effect, anything other than rights against redistribution of generic wealth. *See supra* note 55. But Justice Scalia is not bound to the lax construal of "public use," and it is his thought that we are here trying to reconstruct.) Margaret Jane Radin has convincingly deployed a body of moral theory capable of supporting a constitutional-legal distinction between rights respecting "personal" property and those respecting "fungible" property, according to which "personal" property merits much the stronger protection. *See* Radin, *Property and Personhood,* 34 STAN. L. REV. 957 (1981–82); Radin, *Residential Rent Control,* 15 PHIL. & PUB. AFF. 350 (1986). It is certainly worth considering whether most or all of Scalia's results—both express and implied—in both his *Nollan* and *Pennell* opinions are not reconcilable with Radin's proposed distinction. The difficulty I run into in the attempt is that Scalia complains of unconstitutional, *because uncompensated,* takings in *Nollan* and *Pennell;* he hasn't suggested that the regulations in those cases lack a legitimate public purpose or would, on other grounds, be unconstitutional if accompanied by compensation to disproportionately burdened owners. Straightfor-wardly, it doesn't seem that a stronger constitutional demand for *monetary compensation* for takings of personal property than of the fungible kind (as distinguished from a stronger demand for *injunctions against* personal-property takings, or a stronger application of the public-use requirement against them) is an apt form of legal-remedial recognition of the personal/fungible distinction. This question must await further discussion from Professor Radin. In the meanwhile, nothing Scalia has said by way of explanation of his holdings particularly suggests that he has anything like Radin's distinction in mind.

I offer below what strikes me as a more plausible explanation of Scalia's opinions in these cases, but readers conversant with Radin's theory will certainly want to bear it in mind as we proceed.

67. *Pennell,* 108 S. Ct. at 854.

68. The taking claim was based on the Fourteenth Amendment's command that "No State shall . . . deprive any person of . . . property, without due process of law," which the Supreme Court construes as containing the sense of the Fifth Amendment's prohibition against uncompensated takings of private property for public use. U.S. CONST. amend. V; *id*. amend. XIV, §1; *see* Chicago, B. & Q. R.R. v. Chicago, 166 U.S. 226, 235–41 (1897). The irrational interference claim was also based on the Fourteenth Amendment's due process clause. *Cf*. Nectow v. Cambridge, 277 U.S. 183 (1928). The arbitrary discrimination claim was based on the Fourteenth Amendment's prohibition against denials by states of "the equal protection of the laws." U.S. CONST. amend. XIV, §1.

69. The majority held that the claim was premature because the tenant hardship provision had never been applied, and there was no proof of the magnitude of the financial burden it would actually impose on landlords in practice; *see Pennell*, 108 S. Ct. at 856–57, a holding for which they were excoriated by Scalia, *see id*. at 859–61 (Scalia, J., dissenting).

70. *See id*. at 859.

71. *See supra* note 63.

72. 364 U.S. 40, 49.

73. 108 S. Ct. at 861–62 (emphasis supplied).

74. *See id*. at 864 (Scalia, J., dissenting) ("[The] fostering of an intelligent democratic process is one of the happy effects of the constitutional prescription— perhaps accidental, perhaps not."); *infra* p. 138; *supra* p. 148.

75. *See supra* p. 139.

76. *See supra* pp. 128, 131.

77. Scalia was prepared, at least *arguendo,* to equate the controlled rental prior to any tenant-hardship reduction with the competitive price. He allowed for the possibility of upholding "rent regulation in general," insofar as it was designed to deny to landlords "exorbitant" returns due to a housing "shortage," on the ground that, in such circumstances, one might find a "cause-and-effect relationship" between overreaching on the landlord's part and the hardship (i.e., harm) suffered by the poor tenant: "When commodities have been priced at a level that produce exorbitant returns, the owners of those commodities can be viewed as responsible for the economic hardship that occurs." 108 Sup. Ct. at 862. But the San Jose tenant-hardship clause is, Scalia believes, beyond any such possible justification, because it subsidizes the poor tenant at the expense of a landlord who is merely, innocuously, demanding a fair, reasonable, ordinarily competitive return on investment. But, as the text following this note explains, Scalia was willing to hold even this conclusion in abeyance for the sake of argument.

78. 108 S. Ct. at 862–63.

79. *See supra* p. 131; *supra* note 22.

80. *See supra* pp. 133–34.

81. *See* 108 S. Ct. at 863–64.

82. *See id.* 863 ("There is no end to the social transformations that can be accomplished by so-called 'regulation,' at great expense to the democratic process.")

83. Tax-financed "welfare" programs are, in this regard, just an extreme case of the exploitation Epstein fears from tax-financed, compensated expropriations of private property: "Left unregulated, a majority could use a system of taxation and transfers to secure systematic expropriation of property. Taxes could be used to purchase property, which could then be conveyed to some preferred groups via 'bargain sales,' at a fraction of its true value." Epstein, *supra* note 39, at 23; *see id.* at 62: "The protection . . . afforded [by a compensation requirement] is imperfect . . . because there is always the risk that one group . . . will be able to purchase [property that benefits them specially] with money raised by taxes imposed upon the public generally."

84. *See supra* p. 138 & note 48.

85. This consideration seems to cut the ground from under a remark of Justice Scalia's that if the redistribution designed by the San Jose rent regulation had been frontally presented to the electorate "on budget," rather than tucked away "off-budget" in a regulatory ordinance, it would probably have suffered political defeat because "the citizens of San Jose" would have balked at providing—as the rental ordinance does—"hardship" relief for families of four receiving annually as much as $32,400 of income. *See* 108 S. Ct. at 863. The Justice seems thus to reason as if the franchised "citizens of San Jose" are always defined so as to exclude those who will benefit directly from the relief. Precisely because the opposite is true, there is no telling how high an eligibility ceiling may be called for by a political strategy aimed at forming an effective-majority coalition of self-interested supporters of the ordinance; the higher the ceiling, after all, the more self-serving allies you have. This is not to say that the sky is the limit. You may have all kinds of reasons for restraint: keeping alive the golden goose, for example, or holding down the number of allies among whom spoils must be shared. For sophisticated discussion, *see, e.g.,* W. RIKER, THE THEORY OF POLITICAL COALITIONS (1961).

86. *See supra* p. 141. The regulation in *Loretto* similarly applied without exception to all landlords.

87. We have already considered the possibility of distinguishing on the ground that the easement case involves specific land parcels while the tax-transfer case involves possession of mere money. *See supra* note 66.

88. *See, e.g.,* Bowen v. Gilliard, 107 S. Ct. 3008 (1987); Scalia, *Morality, Pragmatism, and the Legal Order,* 9 HARV. J. L. & PUB. POL'Y. 123 (1986).

89. Despite the unlikeliness of Justice Scalia's meaning to be endorsing or

even intimating any such idea, it may be worthwhile to exhibit the substantial case for classical liberal constitutional welfare rights having this kind of argumentative force. Liberal constitutional thought about property is committed to universal rights to both freedom of active enjoyment and security against invasive harm. The most obvious legal confrontation with this dual commitment (encapsulated in private-law doctrines of trespass, nuisance, and waste) occurs in so-called border conflicts between owners whose preferred modes of use and enjoyment of their holdings are functionally interdependent. One of these owners may appear to us as engaged in an "active" project whose pursuit "disturbs" the other parcel in a way destructive to what *its* owner wants it for. The latter's project thus appears (relatively to the former's) passive—save, on reflection, in this sense: that if we set the legal rule (locate the border) so as to subordinate the "active" owner's preferred mode of enjoyment to that of the "passive" owner, the latter by insisting on her rights will now be in the position of aggressor upon the other's enjoyment. Relative to each other, one owner demands freedom to enjoy, the other, security from intrusion. Which owner is in which posture is said by many to be either a matter of perspective or a mere reflex of the applicable legal rule. *See, e.g.,* Coase, *The Problem of Social Cost,* 3 J.L. & ECON. 1 (1960). By those committed to libertarian jurisprudence, however (as we have noticed several times by now: *see supra* pp. 132, 144), the assignment to the disputants of the respective postures of active perpetrator and passive victim (and the inference from this assignment of the correct legal rule) must be—and is—said to be derivable by reason from the correct notion of property.

   This problematic structural feature of liberal property theory is, by now, familiar fare. *See, e.g.,* Singer, *The Legal Rights Debate in Analytical Jurisprudence from Bentham to Hohfeld,* 1982 WIS L. REV. 975. Also familiar is its application to borders demarcating conflicting entitlements in non-physical dimensions—for example, in the temporal dimension, where the problem appears in legal form as the doctrine of waste. So it is just a matter of course that if there are any welfare rights, the application extends to the conceptual border described by the confrontation of such rights with the putative antiredistributive, negative property rights that are their logical converses. *See supra* p. 128.

   It is well within the natural-right tradition to regard state-of-nature liberty and property as encompassing entitlement, enforceable by self-help, to relief against severe economic privation; and as also, therefore, encompassing the corresponding liabilities. *See, e.g.,* J. LOCKE, THE FIRST TREATISE OF GOVERNMENT §42; J. LOCKE, THE SECOND TREATISE OF GOVERNMENT §6; S. PUFENDORF, DE JURE NATURAE ET GENTIUM, bk. II, ch. VI, §6. According to these authorities, the necessitous person who takes from another's excess acts according to natural justice; the affluent person who bars such a taking acts against natural justice. (To be sure, there is the question of where to locate the border—of what conditions amount to "necessity" and "excess." That question is, for the moment, beside the point.) If, as in liberal constitutional thought as I have modeled it, the reciprocal entitlements and obligations of natural justice are deemed to pass to the agencies of civil order when instituted—as we receive civil rights in exchange for relinquishing natural self-help—it follows that a government, in failing to tax the affluent as required to assist the necessitous, is thereby depriving the latter of their property: an affirmative property right, in the nature of a welfare right.

It is true that the government has no way of avoiding this deprivation without intrusion on negative property. That is just another outcropping of the problematically reciprocating structure of libertarian entitlement theory. The necessary—if credulity-testing—inference is that liberal theory has sufficient substantive content to enable a judge (in principle) to locate, with precision enough to cool down hot political dispute, the border between the rights of taxpayers and the rights of the needy.

90. *See supra* pp. 130–31 & nn. 16–18.

91. *See supra* p. 139.

92. *See supra* p. 135.

93.. *See Loretto,* 458 U.S. at 436, citing Michelman, *Property, Utility, and Fairness: Comments on the Ethical Foundations of "Just Compensation" Law,* 80 HARV. L. REV. 1165, 1228 & n. 110 (1980). *See also* Hodel v. Irving, 107 S. Ct. 2076, 2083 (1987), where the Court ruled that laws totally abrogating "the right to pass on property" after death are, like laws imposing permanent physical occupations, presumptively unconstitutional, reasoning that the said right is, like the right to exclude, among "the most essential sticks in the bundle of rights that are commonly characterized as property."

94. *See, e.g.,* Radin, *supra* note 43, at 1689.

95. *See* B. ACKERMAN, PRIVATE PROPERTY AND THE CONSTITUTION (1975).

96. Justice Scalia's *Nollan* opinion does not in the end assert, and certainly it does not sustain, any claim that there is *no* rationally identifiable connection between the Coastal Commission's conditional exaction of a lateral-passage easement and the amelioration of social costs occasioned by the Nollans' improvement of their land. *See Nollan,* 107 S. Ct. at 3150; *id.* at 3151–56, 3161 (Brennan, J., dissenting); Lawrence, *Means, Motives, and Takings: The Nexus Test of* Nollan v. California Coastal Commission, 12 HARV. ENVTL. L. REV. 213, 242–48 (1988); Michelman, *supra* note 59, at 1608 n. 42.

97. *Pennell,* 108 Sup. Ct. at 852 (Scalia, J., dissenting).

98. *See id.* at 862 (Scalia, J., dissenting) (complaining that the tenant hardship provision is not restricted to landlords who "reap . . . distinctively high profits").

99. *Id.* at 862 (Scalia, J., dissenting).

100. The distinction seems to involve a regression from modern, individualistic natural-right theory towards an earlier "just price" tradition. Perhaps an example can be found in H. GROTIUS, DE JURE BELLI AC PACIS, bk. II, ch. III, sec. 1. *See* E. PAUL, PROPERTY RIGHTS AND EMINENT DOMAIN 198 (1987).

101. *See supra* p. 132–33.

102. *See supra* note 85.

103. *See* M. WALZER, SPHERES OF JUSTICE 66–67, 79 (1983); Walzer, *Philosophy and Democracy,* 9 POL. THEORY 379 (1981).

104. *See supra* pp. 7–8.

105. *See supra* note 89.

106. *Compare* A. BICKEL, THE LEAST DANGEROUS BRANCH: THE SUPREME COURT AT THE BAR OF POLITICS 24–28 (1962).

107. As I write, Justice Scalia is billed to deliver a major lecture at Harvard Law School entitled "The Rule of Law As a Law of Rules."

108. *See* Scalia, *supra* note 88, at 124–25.

109. *See, e.g.,* Morrison v. Olson, 56 U.S.L. Week 4835, 4847 (1988) (Scalia, J., dissenting) (the special-prosecutor case); Mistretta v. United States, 57 U.S.L. Week 4102, 4116 (1989) (Scalia, J., dissenting).

110. I was prompted to consider the matter from this angle by Mark Tushnet's recent proposal to explain the gaping difference between judicial and academic treatments of "state action" doctrine in terms of the different situations and responsibilities of judges and professors. *See* Tushnet, *Shelley v. Kraemer and Theories of Equality,* 33 N.Y.L. SCH. L. REV. 383, 405–8 (1988). *See also* Kennedy, *Freedom and Constraint in Adjudication: A Critical Phenomenology,* 36 J. LEG. EDUC. 518 (1986).

111. *See* H. HART & A. SACKS, THE LEGAL PROCESS (1958).

112. *See* Coffin, *Judicial Balancing: The Protean Scales of Justice,* 63 N.Y.U.L. REV. 16, 18:

> When a judge is granted temporary access to academia, he or she is tempted to take on the coloration of the academic and substitute creative theorizing for plodding craftwork, the general for the specific, and the absolutist for the eclectic. . . . But we really are not at home in jurispruding, and few of us are good at it. . . . We don't have, or have not made, enough time to read what all the relevant and respectable scholars are saying on any given subject. We don't have the faintest idea of who or what is "in" or "out"—and if we do, we don't really know why. We don't have research assistants; our law clerks have quite enough to do assisting us with our own and our colleagues' opinions. And our "data base" is simply the cases we have helped decide.

113. I am not here asserting as a matter of sociological fact that judicial decisions "matter" awfully much (although I think they sometimes do). I am merely assuming that to a justice of the Supreme Court, it must feel as if they do.

114. *See supra* pp. 139–40.

115. That a judge's own political-moral vision enters consciously into the work of adjudication does not, in my view, belie the good faith of judicial professions to be effectuating the country's law. *See, e.g.,* R. DWORKIN, LAW'S EMPIRE (1986); Michelman, *supra* note 1, at 1514–15.

Takings: Of Maginot Lines and Constitutional Compromises

RICHARD A. EPSTEIN

The central task of constitutional law is to demarcate the scope of individual freedom within a system of government power. The very existence of an articulated constitution suggests that some form of social control, coercive and unwanted by some, is permissible. But any showing that some government power is permissible is only a prelude to determining its permissible extent. One important element in a system of social control is the doctrine of enumerated powers, which has been effectively eviscerated by the expansive interpretations of the commerce clause.[1] The second is the specific protection of certain liberties against the state. In my book *Takings,*[2] I argued that given these limitations in our Constitution, the scope of government power, both at the state and the federal level, is far narrower than has been traditionally believed. I also insisted that this restrictive conception of government also follows from the first principles of political theory. In making these dual claims, I have been rightly understood as having asserted that the Constitution forbids the common forms of legislation, regulation, and taxation which comprehensively have come to be known as the New Deal.[3] Notwithstanding the bitter denunciations that the book has received, both for its constitutional and political theory,[4] I continue to believe that the proper set of social relations are essentially as they were described in *Takings.*

It seems evident, however, that my position has not carried the day. Indeed it may be a minority position held by one person—me. Nonetheless, it continues to attract a fair share of attention, and I hope that it has caused serious scholars to reexamine old verities in search of newer and better understandings. The three essays by Professors Lino A. Graglia,[5] Stephen Macedo,[6] and Frank Michelman[7] are part of the ongoing commentary that *Takings* has generated. My task here is not to restate anew my basic position; Macedo and Michelman have provided the reader with a careful road map of my theory in their contributions to this volume. Instead, I shall content myself with answering their major criticisms of my position. First, I shall address Graglia's roundhouse attack on my book; Graglia erects a Maginot line against political theory, which, once overrun, excludes him from any important debate over the structure and meaning of our Constitution. Thereafter, I shall turn to the more restrained criticisms of Macedo and Michelman, both of whom insist that my position on the takings clause is flawed because it unnecessarily downgrades the republican commitment to citizen participation in the search for the common good. I shall first try to establish that my own constitutional position preserves what is good about republican institutions. I shall then offer to Michelman, and for that matter to Macedo, a constitutional compromise, which (for all I know) they might accept. But first I must respond to Graglia.

I. Professor Graglia's Maginot Line

Professor Graglia gives me no quarter when he accuses me of making the same intellectual mistakes as the judicial activists in the liberal camp, most notably Justice Brennan and Professor Dworkin, about whom I shall have more to say later.[8] But Graglia's attacks might be more persuasive if he had supplied us with his own theory of constitutional interpretation in general, or of the eminent domain clause in particular. But that positive program is no part of his mission here, or indeed elsewhere in his published work. Rather, he is quintessentially negative, someone who—like the classical counterpuncher—will always be a challenger but never a champion. In his view, the Constitution is a minimalist doctrine, both because it is "short" and because its primary function was to establish the organizational structure of government, not to provide any protection for individual rights. It is almost as if the Bill of Rights did not exist, or was set in small type. Graglia is therefore no scholar of original intent, but must be understood as an unalloyed defender of majority rule and popular democracy: his constant complaint is that unelected judges have imposed their will upon the democratic process, without any real warrant from the constitutional text. In his view, the Constitution was "adopted primarily for the very mundane purposes of commerce and trade: basically, to create a national common market by empowering Congress to remove state-imposed impediments to interstate trade."[9]

The first question, of course, is how Graglia comes up with his account of the primary purpose of the Constitution. At most, he has given one (apparently quite narrow) account of the scope of the commerce clause. But he has surely not given a complete account of the Constitution itself, once we take into account its complex jurisdictional limitations and the catalogue of substantive protections, found both in the original constitution and in its subsequent amendments. Thus the contracts clause[10] surely has some direct relationship to trade, even if it is only confined to the protection of contracts formed prior to state legislation.[11]

The commerce clause, therefore, is not the only clause that impinges on commerce. It is just not possible to duck the demands of political theory. Even Professor Graglia acknowledges that there are some limitations on state power, for he condemns *Home Building & Loan Ass'n v. Blaisdell Corporation*[12] as one of the rare erroneous decisions upholding an unconstitutional state statute. But why is it erroneous? To answer that question, we have to have some sense as to why retroactive statutes are more dangerous than prospective ones; this drives us back towards the treacherous shoals of political theory. Again, the Court in *Blaisdell* justified its statute under the police power. Why shouldn't Graglia read the police power into the contracts clause if his faith in majority rule is as great as he claims? Surely his argument cannot be that it is improper to read *any* exceptions into any substantive limitation on government powers. Even with the contracts clause, it has long been settled that the state can condemn property that private parties have received by state grant so long as it is prepared to pay just compensation.[13] That decision seems to make perfectly good sense, even if it allows the government to violate the categorical nature of its own promise; otherwise, property once sold by the government under a warranty deed could never be reacquired. Yet allowing the condemnation is only possible if "just compensation" limitation is read into the contracts clause, even though it is not included in the text.

Graglia is thus faced with a dilemma. Does he refuse to read any implied exception into the contracts clause, in which case he has imposed a major limitation on the power of democratically elected state legislatures? Or does he open the door ever so narrowly, and then develop some substantive theory to explain why the just compensation exception to the contracts clause is acceptable when the police power limitation is not? Either way, he needs some kind of legal theory.

The same problem applies to the takings clause. Professor Graglia, as ever, does not offer any substantive theory of his own. Instead, he takes the position that there are two powerful objections to my theory which make any further account of the clause unnecessary and, indeed, redundant. First, he notes that the clause applies only against the federal government, and therefore does not limit the power of the several states because the doctrine of "incorporation," whereby the specific guarantees of the Bill of Rights are applied to the states via the Fourteenth Amendment, is wholly illegitimate. He then insists that words are but means to communicate the intentions of speakers. So long as we know that the Framers had limited visions as to what the takings clause was designed to do—prevent the confiscation of private property—then we can dismiss out of hand the idea that the clause applies to the various forms of regulation and taxation to which it has sometimes been directed, even by the present Court. On his narrow construction, if the state does not occupy the land in fee simple at the end of the day, there is no taking at all.

Graglia is wrong on both counts. I will begin with incorporation. Initially, it is wrong to assume that we need not worry about the scope of the takings clause at all because it does not reach any form of state regulation. There are major and important forms of federal regulation that can be, and have been, challenged under the takings clause. Here are a few important examples.

First, the National Labor Relations Act and the Railway Labor Act each in their own way impose extensive restrictions on the ability of employers to use their own property and to choose their own employees. I take it as tolerably clear that the Railway Labor Act falls within the scope of the commerce clause, and assume that Graglia would agree with me that the National Labor Relations Act does not[14]—although it would force him to override democratic institutions in order to show fidelity to the doctrine of enumerated powers. But if they are valid under the commerce power, does either of these statutes effect a taking? Note that the labor statute, at the very least, requires the employer to admit onto his premises persons whom he would rather exclude. Yet, for its part, the ordinary accounts of property, known to and accepted by the Framers, include within the owner's bundle of rights the right of exclusive possession, protected by an ordinary action for trespass, and qualified only by a narrow doctrine of privilege (e.g., to save one's own life from imminent peril) that is not remotely applicable here. Graglia should strike down these statutes on takings grounds, even though such an action would place a powerful crimp in democratic institutions at the national level. If he does not, then he should tell us just how he construes the takings clause, or why the labor statutes promote free trade.

The problem does not stop with the labor statutes. Take another small piece of congressional handiwork, the Civil Rights Act of 1964. Again we have a federal statute, and again Graglia has to decide between his fidelity to the original commerce clause and his deference to congressional control. Assume (for the sake of argument) that he swallows his pride on the commerce clause. How, then, can he justify the statute, which again calls into question the storekeeper's and manufacturer's right to exclude? The Supreme Court took refuge in the tattered distinction between takings and mere regulations, and in the familiar broad account of the police power.[15] We still need to have a theory of constitutional adjudication to decide who is right and who is wrong. Unless, therefore, Graglia wants to spin out a very clever account of the ubiquitous police power, which he has rejected for *Blaisdell*, he will be forced to strike this statute down as well. What goes for the

National Labor Relations Act and the Civil Rights Act also applies to the misnamed "Fair Labor Standards Act," which covers such important issues as the minimum wage, the federal mandatory retirement rules, and the like. The expansion of the federal commerce power beyond all recognition has placed enormous stress on the takings clause as it applies to Congress.

Nor would our problems be at an end if we could turn back the clock to the sound jurisprudence of *E.C. Knight v. United States,*[16] when interstate commerce did not include local manufacture. *Gibbons v. Ogden*[17] held that the commerce power "comprehended navigation" which allowed Congress to control what happens on navigable waters. Nonetheless, it hardly follows that Congress has an all-powerful "navigation servitude" that allows it to swallow up ordinary riparian rights in navigable waters (including access from the shore) without any compensation.[18] And when private parties create navigable waterways at their own expense on their own land, it does not follow (and here the Supreme Court agrees) that the United States can open them up to the general public without paying compensation to the owner.[19] Water rights are hard to understand, but not that hard. The takings clause requires that we say something intelligent about water rights. But Graglia gives us no clue as to how to proceed or why.

Similarly, Congress has a clear power to regulate bankruptcy, but when it discharges debtors from preexisting obligations, or reduces the protection that secured creditors receive below the protection that they have enjoyed under state law, someone has to answer the takings questions that its exercise of power raises.[20] Even foreign affairs is not the exclusive province of Congress and the President. Could the Congress and the President acting together waive all claims that American creditors had against Iranian firms, without providing them rights of action of equal value?[21]

Unhappily for Graglia, we can't stop the further analysis even if *Barron v. Baltimore* were right.[22] It would be appropriate for him to furnish some explanation as to where I have gone wrong in my analysis of what counts as taking of private property, as compensation for that taking, as a public use, or as a proper exercise of the police power. Surely the answer cannot be that property covers only bare possession, given that the standard ordinary language and common law accounts always included rights of use and disposition as well. Are we to believe that the state can permanently prohibit the sale or lease of all real property tomorrow without compensation? Graglia's rhetoric forms an intellectual Maginot line, impregnable to substantive discourse about constitutional principles, but totally useless once overrun.

So far I have shown that Graglia's view of the Constitution is impoverished, even if his view of incorporation is correct. But is he correct? There are, in essence, two ways to go on incorporation. By the first, we can assume that the only way in which the takings clause (along with all others) can be applied to the states is through the due process clause of the Fourteenth Amendment: "Nor shall any person be deprived of life, liberty or property, without due process of law." On Graglia's view, it follows that the doctrine must be a textual absurdity, because the takings clause deals with substance and the due process clause has to deal with procedure and nothing else. But is it that clear? It is worth noting here that the original application of the takings principle (I cannot say clause) to the states did not come through the doctrine of incorporation, but preceded it by some thirty years—in *Chicago, Burlington & Quincy Railroad v. Chicago,* when Justice Harlan read the words "without due process" to *mean* "without just compensation."[23]

Obviously there is some difference between the two expressions, but there are some similarities as well. The state of Texas imposes a tax on me, a resident of Illinois, and brings suit against me in Illinois to collect. It gives me notice and an opportunity to defend. Procedures notwithstanding, that tax will be struck down on due process grounds because I have no contact with Texas. Now the want of due process looks a lot like a taking (via the tax) without just compensation: the state of Texas has not provided me with any services. So the takings clause and the due process clause are closer together than they initially appear.

Take another example: the due process clause generally provides a person with protection against a biased tribunal. But why should a litigant care whether the tribunal is composed of family members of his opponent? Because if he is a defendant, then the court will order a taking of his property which the evidence does not justify. Or because if he is a plaintiff, his cause of action, while valid, will be rendered worthless—or at least less valuable. Litigation provides a road map that directs the state in its use of coercive power to take property. To care about bias is to care about process and substance at the same time. The broad gulf between them is simply not there.

Suppose, however, I am wrong on this point as well, and that the due process clause is ill-fitted for incorporation, notwithstanding the Supreme Court's continued use of it. Other avenues of incorporation still remain. After all, the Fourteenth Amendment *was* designed to force a massive shift in federal/state relations. Even though the federal government received no new direct powers of subject-matter regulation, it did obtain powers to limit the scope and power of state laws. There is, for example, the privileges and immunities clause of the Fourteenth Amendment: "No state shall make or enforce any law which shall abridge the privileges and immunities of citizens of the United States." Surely it was generally understood that privileges and immunities under Article IV, Section 2 encompassed individual economic liberties; note, for example, the broad declaration in *Corfield v. Coryell,*[24] which included the right "to take, hold, and dispose of property,"—rights of which citizens could be deprived only with just compensation. In the *Slaughterhouse Cases*,[25] the privileges and immunities clause was given the narrowest possible construction. All persons were protected, but only insofar as they had rights in their capacities as citizens of the United States. So the clause protected the rights of ordinary people to go to Washington to petition Congress for their grievances. Is that really all that the Civil War was about? What Gettysburg was about? Do we want to read out the protection for all those persons who fall into the class of United States citizens? A better reading is that all persons born in the United States are citizens, and that (a) these people enjoy privileges and immunities that state governments cannot infringe and (b) these privileges and immunities include the right to hold property which can be taken only if just compensation is provided. The Fourteenth Amendment *shrunk* the size of state governments, and then gave Congress power only to enforce that shrinkage. There should have been less total government after the Civil Rights Amendments than before. We cannot presuppose the soundness of the *Slaughterhouse Cases* for all deliberation that follows.

Graglia's second point can be answered more briefly. It is often the case that the implications of a general proposition are not fully understood by those who support it. My colleague Professor McConnell has given one illustration with the religion clause.[26] The case is *Marsh v. Chambers*,[27] which upheld the right of the states to hire legislative chaplains. The historical understanding seems clear, because the Congress had voted to hire chaplains just three days before it approved the clauses having to do with religion in the First Amendment. But the manifest tension between the establishment clause and the statute calls for some principled explanation as to why Congress's failure to recognize the implicit conflict should be dispositive on the meaning of the establishment clause. In the end, some argument from text, structure, and (yes) theory is required—precisely what Graglia refuses to provide.

Much the same can be said about the takings clause. Here, however, there was very little substantive debate in the Congress, and there was no effort to line up the constitutional provision against the various forms of legislation that Congress had passed or might pass. To a great extent, hewing to generalities is the natural pattern of many debates. In part, this came about because there were few instances of federal legislation in 1791 against which to test the principle. Nonetheless the strong philosophical tradition behind the eminent domain principle is evident in such writers as Locke and Blackstone,[28] and the clause cannot be dismissed from active consideration simply because it is short. It is comprehensive as well: it does not say, "Some private property may be taken for public use, without just compensation."

But Graglia has one more trump card: beware, he says, or you will suffer the fate of Ronald Dworkin. Now no one could mistake Dworkin for me or vice versa. By linking us together, Professor Graglia has perhaps succeeded in a rare double: offending both Dworkin and me at the same time. However, there are differences in the way in which Dworkin and I do our work. In *Takings,* I carefully tried to analyze each of the constituent elements of the eminent domain clause and to show how it fits into a general theory that governs all relations between persons over property. At various points, my approach does tie into both political and economic theory: indeed, I fail to see how the task of interpretation could go on without them. But the theories of politics that I use are heavily dependent upon the Framers' orientation to their own work. We *do* know that the Framers did not operate in the pure libertarian tradition that said that private property rights could only be sacrificed by voluntary agreement or the commission of the tort. We know this because the Constitution provided for the imposition and collection of taxes that staunch libertarians condemn. The eminent domain clause, moreover, accepts forced exchanges in the general case, so long as they are for some public use. Any explication of the Constitution that embraced without qualification Robert Nozick's principles of justice—limited acquisition, protection, and transfer[29]—would be inappropriate for interpreting constitutional text, even if it were the soundest political theory known to man.

My interpretation of the eminent domain clause is faithful to this acceptance of forced exchanges initiated by the state. It is also consistent with the other concerns expressed by the Framers. As a group, they were very concerned about the dangers that self-interest and faction could pose to political organization. They regarded private property as an essential element of any constitutional system—as a bulwark of liberty against the power of the state. They thought that redistribution of income and wealth was fraught with the dangers of class struggle. So what if they did not know the definition of an economic rent, and could not show the degenerative outcome of a prisoner's dilemma?

We know a couple of other things about the Framers as well. They were not egalitarians or levelers, and they were certainly not proto– or closet Marxists. They did not even address the question of whether private discrimination on grounds of race or sex was an evil, and would have been astonished at the suggestion that all voluntary contracts are suspect. The differences between myself and Dworkin arise at two levels. First, which political philosophy is that of the Framers? Second, why should we import our political philosophy to the construction of the constitution that they drafted? I regard my political philosophy as relevant to a defense of the eminent domain clause, because it is a philosophy that tries to make sense of the clause as written. It is not an effort to bore at the Constitution from within. I would urge its retention if Dworkin, or anyone else, moved that it be excised from the Constitution at the next (shudder) constitutional convention. I regard my account of the takings clause as an explication of a desirable first premise, not as a flight of moral fancy at the expense of constitutional text.

In order to show where I have gone wrong, Graglia should give us a hint as to how he would set me right. But that task requires him to abandon his critical posture, and to assume a constructive position on matters of technical interpretation. He can't do that by giving a crabbed interpretation to the Bill of Rights, or by crouching low behind a constitutional Maginot line of his own making.

II. Professors Macedo and Michelman:
Politics, Participation, and Compromise

My disagreements with Professors Macedo and Michelman are not as great as those with Professor Graglia. Unlike Graglia, both Macedo and Michelman assume that the takings clause properly applies to the states, and that some form of political discourse may (indeed, must) be brought to the interpretive task. In addition, Macedo—and perhaps even Michelman— endorses more extensive property protection than the Court now provides. But they do not travel with me the entire way. The question that each in his own way asks is whether I have tried to take so much from the political process that it would result in making it a pale shadow of what it should be in a healthy democratic state. Macedo reaches this conclusion by using ordinary interpretative devices to make sense of the takings clause within our larger constitutional and institutional structure. Michelman, for his part, uses the takings clause as a convenient tool to examine the tension between the liberal tradition (not in the sense of the "L-word," but, broadly construed, the Lockean tradition) and the republican tradition, in both my work and that of Justice Scalia.

In this section, I shall try to square the circle, and to show how my reading of the takings clause both meets the interpretive strictures of Macedo and comports (with only a little tugging and hauling) with the best of the republican tradition championed by Michelman. As there is a fair bit in common between their views, much of what I say in response to Macedo applies to Michelman and vice versa.

Professor Macedo. Macedo attacks me on several fronts. He first argues that I have not read the takings clause in context because I have falsely assumed the existence of a federal police power, even though none is found in the grants of congressional power contained in Article I, Section 8 of the Constitution.[30] Thereafter, he switches gears and assumes that the Founders, by virtue of having given extensive powers to Congress, did not want their exercise to be as tightly circumscribed as my reading of the takings clause would require. They attached some currency to the belief that "political deliberation is intrinsically valuable."[31] For Macedo, my vision of representative government is quite impoverished because I see Congress (and, by implication, the state legislatures as well) only as a process that gives voice to the interests of "property owners and wealth-seekers,"[32] as opposed to the full range of interests that a more complex theory of representation would require. Although he does not quite say it, he is obviously much influenced by the expanded notions of citizenship and participation that animate Michelman's vision of the well-functioning republican government.

I think that Macedo is wrong on these counts. First, the police power is used in two senses in constitutional discourse. One is as a direct source of power, which is an inherent attribute of the sovereignty possessed by the several states. That general police power is not possessed by the federal government, whose own powers are enumerated. These jurisdictional limitations were thought to be an effective way to preserve the independent domains of the states and to prevent the creation of a national colossus capable of threatening the liberties of individual citizens. I quite agree with Macedo's assessment of the constitutional design, and think that the enormous expansion of the commerce power culminating in the New Deal cases is a major structural blunder.[33]

The second sense of the police power refers to an implicit limitation of the individual substantive protections contained in the Bill of Rights. This limitation holds true not only for the takings clause but also for the other substantive protections found in the Bill of Rights, such as those having to do with speech and religion. Now the police power question arises at the third stage of a three-stage process. The first step is the jurisdictional inquiry: does Congress's power reach the task? In 1789, it seemed clear that the Congress could not have regulated local agriculture and manufacture. Since its jurisdiction was at an end, the Bill of Rights had no work to do on this issue. But Congress could in 1789 regulate interstate trade by road or by sea. Suppose it then passed a rule which said that no one could ship newspapers critical of the United States in interstate commerce: no problem for Article I, Section 8. Nonetheless, the First Amendment's guarantee of freedom of the press is presumptively violated. The police power inquiry would then ask whether this restriction was justified in order to protect the health, morals, and welfare of the nation. This ban on speech would fail, but one restricted only to newspapers offering a financial reward for the immediate assassination of the President would not. The scope of the police power exception to the speech clause raises issues clearly distinguishable from the underlying scope of Congress's power under Article I.

In my view, the eminent domain clause functions in exactly the same way. When the scope of the federal power is constrained, then the occasions for invoking the takings clause are few. Nonetheless, Congress cannot condemn the bricks and mortar to build a public road without just compensation. When the scope of the federal power expands, then the occasions for invoking the takings clause are numerous, as the illustrations in my response to Graglia indicate. There is therefore no reason to fold the takings clause into the commerce power. The same interpretation of the takings clause works whether we read the commerce clause as narrowly as Justice Marshall did in *Gibbons v. Ogden,*[34] or as broadly as it has been read in *National Labor Relations Board v. Jones & Laughlin Steel Corp.*[35]

Second, nothing in my theory of the takings clause commits me to one theory of representative government or another. Thus the original constitution called for the election of senators by state legislatures. Today the Seventeenth Amendment calls for the direct election of senators. Surely there is some change in the theory of representation (not to mention the distribution of state and federal power), but why should this affect our reading of the takings clause or any other provision in the Bill of Rights? These individual guarantees don't attach to the process as such, but to the outcomes it generates.

The same argument applies to other electoral rules. Should the interpretation of the takings clause change if we abolish the electoral college tomorrow? Did it change when the Nineteenth Amendment extended the right to vote to women? I fail to see how our views of representation influence the analysis of the takings question. Legislatures, in 1789 or today, may consist of rich and powerful wealth holders. The attacks that I make on rent-seeking within legislative situations are not limited by race, color, religion, national origin, or sex. The rich and the powerful can be every bit as corrupt and self-centered as the poor, and my view of the takings clause is designed to curb the one set of excesses as much as the others. In a world with sharp restrictions on the franchise, the takings clause will have to work overtime against the rich and powerful: they control the legislative machinery, and hence the legislative outcomes. Where the franchise is made universal, the dangers may well come from another quarter—or, given the vagaries of political coalitions, from all quarters at the same time. But so long as the same standards are applied to the manifold forms of legislative abuse, then the courts have done their job.

Finally, I agree with Macedo that deliberation is an important vehicle for getting the right collective result. Indeed, I cannot think of a single private body, whether business, charitable, or religious, that makes its collective decisions without any collective deliberations. Oscar Wilde had it only partly right: voluntary charitable work can ruin your evenings just as much as socialism. Surely, no one can believe that the right construction of the takings clause can dispense with all deliberation, any more than it can dispense of all legislation. But Macedo then misses the critical question: what preconditions tend to make deliberation successful? Within the private area, one critical point is the range of issues that can be placed on the table. Shareholders of the corporation can debate the corporate budget, but not the rearing of the children of minority shareholders. Educational institutions can discuss appointments and fundraising, but collectively they should (and usually do) stay out of national politics. A limited set of functions thus focuses the debate and makes it possible for individuals to join collective organizations for particular purposes without having to sacrifice their autonomy on a host of unrelated issues.

The need to remove certain items from the table is even more important with political organizations than with private ones. Private organizations are voluntary associations, so they can count on a certain preselection of members that helps promote a commonality of opinion. A Jewish organization does not have to debate Christian theology, and vice versa. With politics, however, no one gets to select his fellow citizens; people often vote against their own elected representatives. The range of potential differences of opinion is therefore greater, and so too the likelihood of a protracted struggle in which debate functions both as a weapon and (occasionally) a source of deliberation. Removing issues from the collective plate has the desirable feature of reducing the stresses that fundamental political differences create.

In this regard, the short list of enumerated powers in the original constitutional design was a great advantage over the sprawling mass of issues over which Congress can now deliberate at leisure. The takings clause reinforces the constraints on deliberation in the same way. By reducing the odds that group A will be able to take property from group B, each side can go into collective deliberations with some modest confidence that it will not be left worse off after the vote is taken than it was before. The size of the bargaining range is narrowed, and the resources that will be expended in pursuit of partisan ends will be reduced. The quality of deliberation should accordingly improve because people will know that the only way they can advance their own self-interest is to find a way to help their rivals.

One example might help. In *Takings,* I argued that while Congress had the power to tax income, it was bound to impose only flat taxes in order to minimize the likelihood of redistribution through government.[36] In essence, the position left Congress free to set whatever tax budget it liked, so long as everyone paid pro rata amounts on income. In my view, this structural constraint is relatively easy to enforce: there is one tax bracket, period. What is more is that it can only improve the nature of deliberation, as the endless wrangling over differential tax burdens will be eliminated, and greater attention will be directed toward the critical issue of whether the project has a social value that exceeds its total cost.

Professor Macedo recognizes that some intermediate level of scrutiny is required to ensure that persons are not net losers through new government programs.[37] I am at a loss to think of why he wants to leave political actors the luxury to dissipate the cooperative surplus from government programs by the usual forms of political intrigue. The beauty of the disproportionate impact test is that it necessarily protects each person's share of the cooperative surplus, just as it protects their share of original entitlements. The cost of protecting that surplus is relatively low, and the benefit is high. The half measure adopted by Macedo may appear to be a benevolent recognition of the multiple values that any system of constitutional government may serve. In practice, however, his complex structure forces us to settle for less than is achievable by a scrupulous enforcement of the public use requirement of the eminent domain clause.[38] So long as there are any public goods—defense, courts, roads, air quality—there will have to be deliberation. The trick of constitutional structure is to provide the institutional setting that increases the chances that the deliberation will be conducive to the public good. We don't want, or need, to have "a complex weighing of competing values"[39] to get the right result on the takings question. We need rules strong enough to resist the "Chicago" style (the city, not the university) of deliberation, taken nationwide.

Professor Michelman. The last remarks about deliberation provide a convenient transition to Michelman's latest article on the interaction between liberal and republican traditions.[40] As Michelman himself observes, my defense of the takings clause as a bulwark of political deliberation[41] may seem ironic, but it is nonetheless part of the essential program. In order to see why this is so, it is necessary to address the relationship between government control and private property. I shall do this in several stages. First, I shall turn my attention more directly to the foundational questions of property itself, and argue that traditional Lockean notions of property are desirable even if we assume that property rights are communitarian and not individualistic. The same theme, I argue in the second section, applies even if we consider property rights to be political and not "prepolitical" in nature. The system of liberal (i.e., Lockean) property rights subject to the takings power can and should be desired for the instrumental values that it, and only it, can serve. Properly executed, sound deliberative processes should generate a strong private and a small public sector. Finally, I shall address the status of redistribution in both property-based and republican systems in an effort to propose a compromise that I hope would be acceptable to Professor Michelman. In making these arguments, I hope to narrow the gap between the liberal and republican tradition in ways, I hope, that are congenial to the best in both—for I do think that the convergence between these two political outlooks, while far from complete, may be greater than has often been supposed. Historically, these two traditions shared a common origin, as both were born out of an opposition to Hobbesian claims of absolute royal power.[42] There is some sense in which they can be cautiously reunited.

III. The "Liberal" Vision of Property

In the course of his paper, Michelman relies heavily upon the contrast between classical liberal and republican property that is set out by William Treanor.[43] The difference between these two orientations is critical in thinking about property rights. Michelman, for example, relies heavily on Treanor's account of early eminent domain practices:

> Treanor relates that colonial and early state practice often omitted compensation in certain circumstances, where later generations would automatically expect it. Treanor does not, however, make refusal the republican rule. To the contrary he reports that in certain other circumstances, the regular practice was to pay. Thus while the early practice would characteristically omit compensation in case of public roads built across unimproved land, it would pay when the land was improved. Treanor suggests no motivation for payment other than prevailing precepts of good governmental practice or political morality.[44]

Michelman (and Treanor) use these early condemnation practices to show that there was an uneasy accommodation between the liberal vision and its republican opposite. Michelman himself prefaces his summary of Treanor's historical account as one that "begins to suggest cross-imitation between our two supposedly polar visions"[45]—liberal and republican. For Michelman, the difference between improved and unimproved land deftly undercuts the hard, systematic quality of liberal thought, so that the diversity of practices becomes testimony to the indispensable persistence of republican tendencies, even in a period of supposed liberal dominance. Indeed, the irony is that the condemnation practices in the early period of limited government were, if anything, more lax than they are today.

Yet the historical evidence is susceptible to a very different interpretation. More concretely, the practices described in the colonies and early states are entirely consistent with the just compensation principle as articulated in the eminent domain clause. The key point here, as with so many other cases, is to ask about both benefits and burdens of government actions simultaneously. Where the state takes land for a highway, the burden on landowners is explicit. They have lost the exclusive possession of their own property: a taking has surely occurred. But the benefit side includes not only the cash that is paid by the government, but also what I have called the "implicit in-kind compensation" that is provided by the government by the same action that worked the taking.[46] Here, the owner of unimproved land typically retains large portions of his original land with direct and immediate access to the public highway in question: the colonial period, after all, did not specialize in the limited access freeways of modern America. The road itself had enormous value for its immediate neighbors. It meant access to markets for crops, access to towns for supplies, and access to military protection when needed. It seems highly probable that the retained portion of the land, while somewhat smaller, was worth far more to the owner than the original, larger tract without access to highways, markets, and protection. After all, would you rather have 100 acres worth $1.00 per acre or 98 acres worth $1.50 per acre? Why pay compensation in the ordinary case when the landowner comes out, on these modest assumptions, nearly 50 percent ahead? It is more likely that landowners should pay the state to build the road on their property instead of some distance away. The practice of no compensation doubtless reflected the implicit bidding structure across regions to get state roads. Landowners would gladly chip in the land if the state funded the costs of internal improvements.

The situation changes radically once the improvements are ripped down to make way for the road. Improvements cost money, and had value in excess of raw land. By demanding explicit compensation here, the rule had two desirable consequences. It first induced road builders to construct their highways elsewhere, where this particular cost could be avoided. Second, it overcame the great likelihood, when improved property was taken, that the original landowner would come out worse from the deal: even though the remaining value of his land might have been increased, there is a huge private burden that makes it probable that he suffered a large net loss, or in the alternative obtained a far smaller share of the gain than other landowners who had to contribute only unimproved land to the public. It follows, therefore, that it was far less likely to find implicit in-kind compensation where the land was improved than where it was not. There is therefore a coherent inner structure to the "precepts of good governmental practice or political morality" that goes beyond just being comfortable with practices that we don't quite understand. It is the precept of the just compensation clause as a classical liberal would have it.

IV. Individual or Communitarian Conceptions of Property

What, then, of the origins of property? Again, Michelman follows Treanor's work in stating the position between the republican and his liberal adversary.

> In Treanor's account, an essential difference between the earlier republican and later liberal positions lay in the former's communitarianism as compared with the latter's individualism. Treanor contrasts a republican sense of the community's general interest over the particular interests of individuals with a liberal sense of the individual's moral primacy. Republican thought accordingly regards the land as belonging, *au fond,* to the community and its nominal owner as the community's tenant or functionary, as opposed to a liberal sense of the land belonging simply to its innocent appropriator or the latter's voluntary transferee.[47]

In essence, Michelman paints here a contrast between the individualistic and the communitarian visions of property rights. In one sense, however, it is important to recognize that there is a Lockean origin to both sides of the debate. Thus Locke did not think, as did the common lawyers, that property in the state of nature was unowned and hence subject to appropriation by its first taker. He thought that it was "held in common," itself some form of nascent communitarianism, which required the first taker to respect certain conditions when he took the land for his own use, at least before the time when trade became possible. Thus, the famous proviso of "leaving as much again and as good" and the prohibition against waste. It is hard to resist the conclusion that these were important precisely because taking from the commons did, or at least could, impose important costs upon other individuals. Locke was therefore torn between the two positions, and it is, I think, important to state what a liberal Lockean means by individualistic property. In essence, property is individualistic because there are well-defined holdings over which single persons can make binding decisions without the concurrence of other individuals; that cannot be done under a collective or communitarian regime. Nonetheless, the system of property rights is not individualistic if that phrase is meant to entail that there are no correlative duties that are placed upon other citizens by an assignment of property rights. Within the tradition of negative rights, these duties are essentially those of non-interference, but their defense rests not on some simple proposition that it is good for individuals who have property to keep it, but from some comparative calculus which asks about the level of human satisfaction achievable under alternative property arrangements. To the earlier Lockean thinkers, the gulf between the consequential or utilitarian arguments and the natural rights arguments did not seem nearly as broad as it does to us today, and I concur.[48]

The liberal justification for property does not defend private ownership out of sympathy for the narrow interest of the property owner and stony indifference toward the welfare of outsiders. Rather, it defends it as a good republican would want, as part of a larger social system that works for the long-term social advantage. The justifications are social. Private property facilitates the responsible use of resources and makes possible regimes of active and beneficial trade. Communitarian systems of collective ownership fare badly in comparison on both these points, and are prone to the ravages of the guild mentality. A considered social judgment about the right form of property rights thus leads to the defense of the older natural law systems.

Prepolitical and Political Property. The consequentialist arguments briefly sketched out above help place the next difference between liberal and republican regimes in context: are property rights determined politically as the republican indicates, or are they determined *"pre*politically" as Michelman's liberal, or libertarian, would have it? In Michelman's words, the contrast between the two visions is as follows:

> for present purposes, painting in broad strokes, let us say that in the republican constitutional vision, individual rights are reflexes of laws consequent upon the determinations of a popularly-based political will; the state is the forum of the public deliberations and debates by which the lawmaking political will is determined; and the central problem of the state is that of maintaining diversity and public-spiritedness in those deliberations, so that they do not ossify into self-serving, factional division. In the liberal constitutional vision, by contrast, individuals have rights prepolitically; the state is the appointed guarantor of the rights; and the central problem of the state is to keep it from preying on the rights it is established to protect.[49]

But here it is too easy to fall into conceptual traps because of the easy and seductive use of the word "prepolitical." On one reading, the term could be regarded as a fatal concession that the Lockean liberal can offer no political justification for the system of property rights he wishes to defend, and so is therefore reduced to say that this system of rights is intuitively

correct, historically natural, or socially inevitable. The want of any
normative underpinning for private property thus makes it fair game for
sophisticated attacks from those who insist that private property is the
consequence of collective political deliberations and not its uncontrovertible
presupposition.

The Lockean, or Michelman's libertarian, can do better by private
property once the ambiguities in the charge of "prepolitical" are exposed.
Historically, it seems quite clear that the evolution of property rights was
roughly coterminous with the evolution of the larger society itself. It would
be very hard to identify two spheres of time, one prepolitical time where
property rights were just defined, and one postpolitical time where they were
enforced by sovereign power. Rather, the historical process reveals that the
conventional definitions of property rights as understood at common law had
commendable durability that made them good for the long haul. In some
contexts, these rights called for individual owners, but in other cases
ownership in common made more sense. The English system of riparian
water rights was a system of ownership in common made sensible by water's
physical nature and the many important but conflicting uses of its underlying
asset: water for transportation, water for drink, and water to power mills. To
the extent that a natural lawyer relies upon a gradual evolution of property
rights into some stable equilibrium, it is not clear which side of the pre- or
postpolitical battle he is on—or why he should care.

Liberals and republicans are, I believe, not divided over the origin of
property rights. Rather, they are divided over the question of whether
property rights are a fit object for entrenched constitutional protection. If one
thought that common law property rights were not robust—thought that they
did not serve well in widely different types of social contexts—then there
would be little to gain by "freezing" them into a constitutional mode. Rapid
changes in technology would overwhelm the usefulness of any prior, fixed
system of rights. Hard-pressed legislatures would have to cope both with the
problems of the new technology and the antiquated laws. In this context, the
key argument in favor of eminent domain protection is that the optimal
configuration of property rights *is* sufficiently stable over time and across
economic, social, and technical settings so that it should be memorialized in
a constitution. Changes in property rights can still be accommodated, but
only with, as it were, a showing of cause.

I believe that these conditions are satisfied. The key feature of common
law property rights is that they create valuable bundles of rights both for use
and for trade. So long as trade is a viable option, most change in desired
resource use can be achieved not by a redesign of the underlying rights
structure but by swapping rights between persons under that structure, in
accordance with the minimal requirements of exchange, such as writing and

recordation. The key liberal argument for a takings provision is the sense of the relative *permanence* of the desirable rights configuration of the common law and customary bundles of rights. So long as property rights can be taken upon paying just compensation, the dangers of holdout in the individual case (e.g., blocking the needed highway) or outmoded rights structures (i.e., conveyancing without recordation) can generally be overcome without undue stress on the system. For major social changes, moreover, cash need not be paid since the rules of "implicit in-kind" compensation require us to count as part of a just compensation package all the indirect benefits that any holder of property rights receives from any government program.[50]

Sometimes it is asserted that the difference between Lockean and republican property is that the former is said to represent a primacy of private interests and judgments over collective ones. But again, I think that the point oversimplifies what is going on. Initially, there can be no system of private rights that depends solely on the will of the owner. Property rights must be good against the rest of the world. Locke himself understood that the individual who took property on his own initiative did so because the alternative of unanimous consent promised only starvation for all.[51] He understood, therefore, the holdout problem that blocked any explicit collective definition of property. But, in so doing, he implicitly acknowledged that private property afforded the best answer to the collective action problem. He did not understand or assume that the gains to the first possessor were all that mattered. The losses imposed mattered as well. In this limited sense, the collective is always prior to the individual.

The risks of collective action are, if anything, increased by the momentous nature of the one fundamental choice. Therefore finding some way to parcel out individual claims with a minimum of collective fuss and bother is critical to the success of the basic mission. The common law rule of acquiring property by taking initial possession of it is one convenient way to make the separation without having any explicit collective determination of who will get what. To repeat, the point is that the fewest collective decisions are best, not that no collective decisions are necessary for the system to run.

The ultimate standard of property rights, then, is in some sense collective, but in ways that show a vitally important difference between the liberal and republican conceptions of property. The liberal conception of property does not rest upon any vision of the common good which is independent of the welfare of the individuals within the society. There is no emergence of collective group rights which are not a direct summation of individual rights. It is just for this reason, as Michelman recognizes,[52] that liberal thinkers are frequently drawn to the Paretian and Kaldor-Hicks criteria of social welfare whenever they think about their system in the round, for both these measures of welfare do not try to go behind the subjective utilities (or preferences) that individuals attach to given things.

For its part, the republican theory tries to find some collective good which is not the mere sum of the individual goods, and so runs the risk of being mired in hopeless abstractions or falling prey to authoritarian impulses that require everyone to adhere to *my* (if there is to be one, let it be mine) conception of the public good. Republican theorists are aware of the problem, and constantly fret over the "corruption" of political life, and its antidote in collective deliberation.

But there is a genuine irony here. While Michelman and other republicans tell us the importance of deliberation, they never tell us the substantive principles that make it possible to reach collective decisions through deliberation.[53] Thus, Michelman is quite right to note that my own preferred justifications for private property are very far removed from those which are offered by traditional natural law theorists—a point which has not escaped more orthodox libertarian thinkers, who have voiced unhappiness about my defection from their philosophical ranks.[54] Michelman then observes that this inversion of the traditional mode of thought "apparently leaves the principle of negative property exposed to whatever qualification or modification may be persuasively recommended by instrumental argument conduct under all its usual contingencies, cognitive and empirical."[55] So it does, for there are no deductive victories to be had on ultimate questions of political theory. Indeed, it is just that awareness of the counterarguments that can be made which explains huge portions of the traditional common law doctrines which are wholly unintelligible if the libertarian principle of negative property is regarded as an ultimate absolute that neither needs nor can receive any further justification. But are we really to reject all the doctrines of live and let live in the law of nuisance, of private and public necessity, and of restitution, eminent domain, and taxation because they do not conform to the negative property principle? Quite the opposite: each of these bodies of law can be shaped and understood in ways that conform to the expanded takings principle, as with the practices of condemnation of lands for highways during the founding era of this country.

One can go one step further. Michelman's point about empirical and contingent judgments is a two-edged sword. The basic change in orientation also allows the defender of limited government to make empirical and contingent arguments on behalf of the regime he supports. There is no reason to hide inside of the language of necessary truth to justify institutions which have powerful functional justifications. It now becomes possible to mass a good deal of support in favor of the substantive positions that I have advanced. But Michelman has not done the necessary legwork to organize an alternative conception that allows us to both control the "corruption" problem while still allowing the state sufficient discretion to achieve the more ambitious ends that he sets for it. Very often, the result of sensible and informed deliberation is that political harmony is best assured if people are allowed to go their separate ways.[56] The convergence therefore between the republican and liberal conceptions is not complete, especially on this last point. Where they diverge, I think that the liberal conception is preferable, because it offers us greater protections against the very real risks of political tyranny arising from a well-intentioned or self-righteous government gone astray.

Redistribution. The last difference between liberal and republican government goes to the legitimacy of redistribution of income and wealth by coercive means. As Michelman notes, liberal property tends to bring forth negative obligations, and republican property tends to generate affirmative, welfare rights.[57] The difference between these two conceptions is not merely verbal. A negative system of property describes individual obligations in terms of the forbearance of force and fraud. The republican system of affirmative rights finds the liberal conception of property severely wanting at just this point. If people are in need, then we have an obligation to help them with a share of what we own. At root, I believe that the impulse for this position rests on the belief that interpersonal comparisons of utility (the kind precluded both by Pareto and Kaldor-Hicks standards of social welfare) are both possible and indispensable. People know abject need when they see it, even if they cannot demonstrate that need formally.

I share a lot of the republican intuitions on this point, and indeed think that the whole regime of "imperfect" obligations for voluntary charity, supported by most natural rights thinkers, are wholly incomprehensible if *no* interpersonal comparisons of utility could be made. But, at this point, the question arises (as Macedo accurately stated) as to whether coercive transactions offer a better promise to aid those in need than voluntary ones. Anyone who shares my grim assessment of the dangers of legislative misbehavior will shrink back from systems that authorize wholesale redistribution by state power. All too often, those who receive are not those who are in need but those who are in possession of political clout or bureaucratic office.[58] The distortion of incentives and the increase in administrative costs don't make this a game worth playing. So the categorical rule of no forced redistribution of wealth is, again, not an argument for greed and selfish conduct, but a cautious appreciation of enormous dangers inherent in any system of coercive redistribution.

My categorical opposition to all forms of redistribution has, quite simply, lost politically. We have, and will continue to have (as both Michelman and Macedo insist) a mixed system. But does it follow that there is no way to make sense out of the practices of redistribution? It is there that Michelman rightly sees the struggle evident in the writing of Justice Scalia,[59] who has labored to reconcile, at least in part, the modern practice of forced redistribution with his general preference for a system of negative property, which itself has a powerful constitutional pedigree.

There are two ways for the argument to run. First, it is possible to argue that the plight of the poor is not of their own making, but is "caused" by the misconduct of those who control political power.[60] Ironically, this position has great weight today because the heavy hand of state regulation and taxation takes an enormous toll on the poor—who is hurt most by state minimum prices on milk? The welfare system thus becomes a way to compensate for the hurt thus caused by collective action. If pushed to its limit, then this line of argument is really quite radical, for it suggests that the right to (some) welfare is constitutionally protected, lest the people who cause harm escape its loss.

The weakness in this argument is that it points not to a welfare state, but to removing root and branch the regulatory mess created by the modern welfare state. Once that is done, then we have undercut any argument of the social causation of private harm. Nonetheless, even if we had a government that regulated as little as I would have it do, the impulse for redistribution through political means still would remain irresistible. The question is: can we find any way to tame it? Here Scalia and I (independently, I think) reached the same conclusion of how best to proceed. If the public at large wants to have a welfare system for some portion of the population, then let it pay for that indulgence out of general revenues funded by the tax-paying public.[61] This modest constraint is designed to prevent the politics of redistribution from taking the form of "let's you and him fight."

The immediate problem that brought Scalia to this solution was the system of rent control in San Jose which denied the landlord the power to make rent increases that would otherwise have been allowable because of the weak financial condition of the tenant. In *Pennell v. San Jose*,[62] Scalia used just this insight to say (albeit in dissent) that the San Jose financing scheme was improper because it cast the burdens of caring for the poor upon a few landlords when a system of rent supplements paid by general revenues can do the trick. In writing about Scalia's dissent in *Pennell*, I have urged that the decision is sound not only as a matter of equity, but also because it creates powerful political pressures to reduce the level of welfare programs to that which the majority is prepared to fund. People are less willing to give their own money to charity than they are willing to vote to make others pay. If we are to have welfare, then let us use the right decision rules.

Ironically, Scalia does not seem to appreciate the extent to which this principle revolutionizes takings jurisprudence, and with the political economy of the United States. There is no way to limit the application of this principle to the special system of rental determinations used by San Jose. The same argument strikes down all systems of rent control unless the state is prepared to pay the landlord, in cold cash, the difference between market value and the amount that it receives under regulation for as long as the regulation lasts. I doubt that any political coalition could extract these benefits from the public treasury. Scalia tries to resist this argument by saying that rent control is a response to some old-fashioned gouging by landlords.[63] But, in so doing, he falsely assumes that landlords can earn a supra-competitive rate of return when entry into the market is unrestricted. Landlords can't get "exorbitant returns" unless they can lock out their rivals, typically by illicit zoning restrictions. So his gouging argument will not work to limit the scope of his demand to tax–funded redistributions. If ordinary rental contracts are gouging, so is every other contract.

Justice Scalia's prohibition against "off-budget" financing, moreover, is of course not limited to rent control. Zoning is one obvious extension. If the state wants to stop me from building on my land, then it should fund the loss of development rights out of general revenues. We can go further. By this no off-budget standard, the antidiscrimination statutes run into rough constitutional waters as well. In a recent article, for example, I urged the repeal of any antidiscrimination legislation which requires employers to purchase health or life insurance for AIDS victims, and fashioned the modest proposal that the state could fund the additional premiums for AIDS patients out of, of course, general revenues.[64]

Professor Michelman sees in Scalia's approach an obvious tension between liberal and republican thinking in responding to the claims of redistribution. I certainly agree that this fallback position is not as clean or intellectually compelling as the hard-line prohibition of all redistribution. But in a world of second-best solutions, this compromise strikes me as pretty good. It controls the greatest abuses in redistribution and leaves some faint hope that the most needy will get the greatest share of the benefits from the surviving programs. Politics is, of course, a messy compromise between the desirable and the possible, and Justice Scalia, as a sitting Justice, is right not to ignore the powerful institutional constraints that hem in his every action. He doesn't quite have the freedom of restless academics like myself.

Still, there may be light at the end of the tunnel, for there might be a political solution to a constitutional dilemma that could satisfy both the liberal and the republican impulses simultaneously. The old-style liberal will drop the conception of negative property to the extent that makes permissible the targeting of redistribution, perhaps any amount of redistribution, to the poor. The republican will then insist categorically that all forms of redistribution be funded by the public at large. A simple treaty; my signature is herewith on the bottom line. I wonder whether Professor Michelman, or for that matter Professors Macedo and Graglia, will sign too. Tough question.

Notes

1. *See, e.g.,* NLRB v. Jones & Laughlin Steel Co., 301 U.S. 1 (1937). I have criticized the development in Epstein, *The Proper Scope of the Commerce Power,* 73 VA. L. REV. 1387 (1987).

2. RICHARD A. EPSTEIN, TAKINGS: PRIVATE PROPERTY AND THE POWER OF EMINENT DOMAIN (1985) [hereinafter TAKINGS].

3. *Id.* at 281.

4. *See, e.g.,* Thomas Grey, The Malthusian Constitution, 41 U. MIAMI L. REV. 21–48 (1986); *see especially* Kelman, *Taking Takings Seriously: An Essay for Centrists,* 74 CALIF. L. REV. 1829 (1986); *Symposium on Richard Epstein's Takings: Private Property and the Power of Eminent Domain,* 41 U. MIAMI L. REV. 1–275 (1986).

5. *See* Lino A. Graglia, *Judicial Activism of the Right: A Mistaken and Futile Hope* [hereinafter Graglia], in this volume.

6. *See* Stephen Macedo, *Economic Liberty and the Future of Constitutional Self-Government* [hereinafter Macedo], in this volume.

7. *See* Frank Michelman, *Tutelary Jurisprudence and Constitutional Property* [hereinafter Michelman], in this volume.

8. *See infra* at pp. 180–81.

9. Graglia at 66.

10. Art. I, § 10. "No State . . . shall . . . pass any Law impairing the Obligation of Contracts."

11. *See generally* Richard A. Epstein, *Toward a Revitalization of the Contract Clause,* 51 U. CHI. L. REV. 703 (1984).

12. 290 U.S. 398 (1934).

13. West River Bridge Co. v. Dix, 47 U.S. 507 (1848).

14. For my views, *see* Richard A. Epstein, *The Proper Scope of the Commerce Power,* 73 VA. L. REV. 1387–1455 (1987).

15. *See, e.g.,* Katzenbach v. McClung, 379 U.S. 294 (1964).

16. 156 U.S. 1 (1985), which I have defended, 73 VA. L. REV. 1433–37.

17. 22 U.S. 1 (1824).

18. *See, e.g.,* United States v. Rands, 389 U.S. 121 (2967), criticized in TAKINGS 67–73.

19. *See* Kaiser Aetna v. United States, 444 U.S. 164 (1979) (requiring compensation).

20. TAKINGS, at 226–27.

21. Dames & Moore v. Regan, 453 U.S. 654 (1981), discussed in *Takings* at 226–27. Note that equal value is not face value, so a sharp discount is required to avoid overcompensation to the creditors.

22. 32 U.S. 243 (1833).

23. 166 U.S. 226 (1897).

24. 6 Fed Cases. 546, 551–52 (CC.E.D. Pa. 1823).

25. 83 U.S. 36 (1872).

26. Michael W. McConnell, *On Reading the Constitution*, 73 CORNELL L. REV. 359–63 (1988).

27. 463 U.S. 783 (1983).

28. *See, e.g.*, 1 W. BLACKSTONE, COMMENTARIES ON THE LAW OF ENGLAND *139 (1765).

29. *See* ROBERT NOZICK, ANARCHY, STATE, AND UTOPIA 151–53 (1974).

30. Macedo at 108–9.

31. Macedo at 111.

32. Macedo at 112.

33. *See* Epstein, *The Proper Scope of the Commerce Power*, 73 VA. L. REV. 1387 (1987).

34. 22 U.S. 1 (1824).

35. 301 U.S. 1 (1937).

36. TAKINGS at 297–303.

37. Macedo at 113–114.

38. I address some of these issues at great length in Epstein, *Foreword: Unconstitutional Conditions, State Action, and the Limits of Consent*, 102 HARV. L. REV. 4 (1988).

39. Macedo at 113.

40. For earlier views, see Michelman, *Law's Republic*, 97 YALE L.J. 1493 (1988); Michelman, Foreword: Traces of Self-Government, 100 HARV. L. REV. 4 (1985).

41. Michelman at 140–41, n. 44.

42. *See* Epstein, *Modern Republicanism—The Flight From Substance*, 97 YALE L. J. 1633 (1988).

43. Note, *The Origins and Original Significance of the Just Compensation Clause of the Fifth Amendment*, 9 YALE L. J. 694 (1985).

44. Michelman at 130.

45. *Id.*

46. *See* TAKINGS ch. 14.

47. Michelman at 130.

48. *See* Richard A. Epstein, *The Utilitarian Foundations of Natural Law,* HARV. J. L. PUB. POL'Y (forthcoming).

49. Michelman at 127–28.

50. See TAKINGS, ch. 14.

51. J. LOCKE, SECOND TREATISE OF GOVERNMENT, ch. 5, § 28 (1690).

52. Michelman at 137–38.

53. *See* Epstein, *Modern Republicanism—or the Flight From Substance,* 97 YALE L.J. 1633 (1988).

54. *See* Ellen Paul, *A Reflection on Epstein and His Critics,* 41 U. MIAMI L. REV. 235 (1986); Eric Mack, *The Costly Road to Natural Law,* HARV. J. L. PUB. POL'Y (forthcoming) written in response to my paper, The Utilitarian Foundations of Natural Law.

55. Michelman at 138.

56. *See supra* the discussion of Macedo at 184.

57. Michelman at 128.

58. *See, e.g.,* Gwartney & McCaleb, *Have Antipoverty Programs Increased Poverty?,* 5 CATO J. 1–16 (1985). Roberts, *A Positive Model of Private Charity and Public Transfers,* 92 J. POL. ECON. 136–48 (1984).

59. Pennell v. City of San Jose, 108 Sup. Ct. 849 (1988). *See* Michelman, 151–53. For my comments on the case *see* Epstein, *Rent Control and the Theory of Efficient Regulation,* 54 BROOKLYN L. REV. 741, 750–55 (1988).

60. Michelman at 149.

61. *See* Epstein, *Rent Control and the Theory of Efficient Regulation,* 54 BROOKLYN L. REV. 755 (1988); *AIDS, Testing, and the Workplace,* 1988 U. CHI. L. F. 33.

62. 485 U.S. 1, 108 Sup. Ct. 849 (1988).

63. *Pennell* at 862.

64. *See* Epstein, *AIDS, Testing, and the Workplace,* 1988 U. CHI. L. F. 33.

The Politics of the New Property:
Welfare Rights in Congress and the Courts

R. SHEP MELNICK

Since 1932 the federal judiciary's attitudes toward social welfare programs have undergone several transformations. The Supreme Court's conservative opposition to many of Franklin Roosevelt's initiatives created a constitutional crisis and, in 1937, a precipitous judicial retreat. From 1937 until the mid-1960s, acquiescence to legislative enactments and deference to administrative expertise characterized court decisions on welfare issues. Then, in the last few years of the Warren Court, the judiciary reentered the picture, ushering in the "due process revolution," declaring a number of restrictions on government benefits unconstitutional, and promising (or threatening) to find a fundamental constitutional right to minimum levels of income and education. Within a few years, though, the tide had turned once again. The Burger Court dashed the hopes of those favoring substantive judicial definition of welfare rights, and began to retreat on procedural issues as well. To those who focus on constitutional law, the New Deal pattern of judicial abstention seemed to have returned.[1]

Yet for those who study particular welfare programs, it has become nearly impossible to understand policymaking without examining court decisions. In the late 1960s and early 1970s, scores of federal court decisions enlarged and transformed Aid to Families with Dependent Children (AFDC), turning a highly discretionary, state-run program into one which is far more rule–bound and nationally uniform. A smaller number of carefully managed and well-timed food stamp cases helped make that program one of the largest income maintenance programs run by the federal government. The battle between the executive branch and the courts over disability insurance—a conflict which reached the newspaper headlines in the early 1980s—has played a crucial role in shaping that multi-billion-dollar program. Hundreds of court decisions under the Education for All Handicapped Children Act have altered state and local education practices. Public housing, Medicaid, and unemployment compensation have likewise been the subject of important litigation.[2]

The apparent contradiction between the courts' constitutional restraint

199

and their policy activism is easy to resolve: most court decisions on entitlements fall into the category of statutory interpretation rather than constitutional adjudication. Instead of confronting Congress and the executive branch with unconditional constitutional demands, the courts claim to insist merely that state and federal administrators comply with congressional enactments. Indeed, Congress has encouraged such court action by adding broad judicial review provisions to authorizing statutes, by lowering general jurisdictional requirements, and by offering attorneys' fees to successful plaintiffs.[3] This does not mean that Congress always agrees with the courts' rulings. On occasion it has overturned judicial decisions and even precluded the courts from hearing certain controversies. The institutional picture is a complex one, with alliances shifting from issue to issue and from time to time.

This complexity, though, should not divert attention from two important facts. The first is that the courts now play a key role in defining entitlements. Under the New Deal model of policymaking, defining entitlements was the job of Congress, federal administrators, and state governments. The federal court played little or no role. Today federal judges are quite willing to overturn administrators' interpretations of statutory entitlements, particularly when these administrators are in the employ of state governments. The courts have not only increased their own power at the expense of the executive, but have increased the power of the federal government as a whole at the expense of the states.

The second fact is that these institutional changes have almost always resulted in an expansion of benefits. For several reasons (examined later in this paper), the courts have been less cost-conscious and more sympathetic to recipients than have the other branches of government. Once the courts expand benefits, it is politically difficult for Congress and the president to agree on retrenchment. In short, changing patterns of statutory interpretation have brought about a redistribution of governmental power with important consequences for policy.

I. The "Rights-Privileges" Canard

For all that has been written about "welfare rights," the courts' role in entitlement politics is surprisingly poorly understood. In part, the failure to recognize the importance of the judiciary's non-constitutional decisions results from academic division of labor. On the one hand, those who study "policymaking"—which generally means the activities of Congress, the president, agencies, and interest groups—usually treat court decisions as random or even bizarre occurrences. On the other hand, those who study the courts tend to be preoccupied with constitutional law and procedural issues. They are more interested in such abstract themes as "structural due process" and "dignitary values" than in how much money recipients get from the government. They favor judicial expansion of entitlements, but want far more than the courts have delivered. To them, the enlargement of the welfare state achieved by the courts is hardly worthy of mention.

Just as importantly, conventional nostrums about the "demise of the right-privilege distinction" have hidden from view the most important changes in the courts' role since 1965. "The demise of the right-privilege distinction" is without doubt the most common explanation for heightened judicial scrutiny of welfare policy.[4] Before the mid-1960s (so the story goes), common law property received extensive judicial protection, but government "largess" such as drivers' licenses, public employment, Social Security checks, and public housing were treated as "privileges" which could be granted or withheld as legislators and administrators saw fit. As citizens became more dependent on government benefits, arbitrary denial of these "privileges" threatened to undermine personal autonomy and security. Consequently, the courts expanded their conception of property to include government benefits, requiring agencies to conduct "due process" hearings before depriving citizens of this "new property" and carefully scrutinizing the rationales put forth by administrators. In the latter half of the 1960s, courts and commentators alike announced the "demise of the right-privilege distinction," and all danced on its grave.[5]

The frequency with which this story is told is matched only by the amount of evidence showing that it is an inadequate explanation of the transformation of judicial treatment of welfare statutes.[6] The most glaring problem is that the federal courts, in fact, had always been willing to hear cases involving alleged denial of statutory entitlements. Throughout the nineteenth century, the federal courts heard cases on veterans' pensions and land grants, occasionally ordering administrators to provide plaintiffs with contested benefits. After World War I court intervention expanded benefits paid under the War Risk Insurance program, which provided life and disability insurance to veterans. Most importantly, the courts heard hundreds of Social Security cases during the 1940s and 1950s. Seldom did the courts ask whether the benefit in question was a right or a privilege. Rather, the central question was whether the administrator had followed the congressional mandate.[7]

Consider the old age insurance program, which has formed the keystone of the American welfare state since 1935. The Social Security Act hardly left disappointed claimants without procedural or judicial recourse. Claimants could first demand a hearing before the Social Security Board, and then challenge the administrative ruling in federal district court if they were still dissatisfied. The Act waived the usual $10,000 jurisdictional threshold, allowing access to the courts "irrespective of the amount in controversy." That Social Security benefits should be paid as a matter of right was a guiding tenet of the system. In the words of Arthur Altmeyer, long-time Commissioner of Social Security and one of the program's founding fathers: "Because of contributions there were certain rights, statutory rights, that had to be recognized and achieved, and we had an obligation."[8]

To be sure, most Social Security cases heard by the courts were not very exciting. The claimant would argue that the Board's reading of "covered employment," "widow," or "fully insured individual" was too narrow. With monotonous frequency, the courts upheld the Board.[9] The Act made the Board's "findings" conclusive if they were supported by "substantial evidence." The courts, in effect, applied the extremely lenient "substantial evidence" test not just to "findings of fact," but to "interpretations of law" as well. In the words of the Sixth Circuit, "The court should be hesitant to set aside the Board's interpretation of an Act under which it functions unless the Act itself or the *unambiguous* legislative intent thereof is *obviously* misapplied."[10] What is most striking about these cases is not the deference to agency expertise—this was a staple of New Deal jurisprudence—but the total absence of reference to the "right-privilege distinction." No one doubted that a citizen denied a Social Security check could take his claim to court.[11]

Between 1935 and 1965, the nature of judicial review varied according to the nature of the program involved. Soon after the institution of federal disability insurance (and before the "demise of the right-privilege distinction") the courts were overturning the disability determinations of the Social Security Administration with some frequency. Although the House Ways and Means Committee complained about the "growing body of court interpretations of the statute which . . . could result in substantial further increases in cost in the future" and passed legislation designed to reduce court intervention, the courts persisted.[12] Federal judicial review of AFDC, in contrast, was virtually nonexistent before 1965. This is because the states ran AFDC; they were subject to only a few basic federal requirements. The federal government's role was limited to approving state plans, offering advice, and matching state expenditures. The paucity of federal court cases reflected the fact that the federal AFDC statute created a program of grants to the states rather than payments to individuals.

Even when statutes creating individual entitlements (as opposed to those establishing grant-in-aid programs) failed to include explicit provisions for judicial review, plaintiffs could rely on the generic Administrative Procedures Act (APA) of 1946 to gain admission to the courtroom. Section 706(1) of the APA requires reviewing courts to "compel agency action unlawfully withheld or unreasonably delayed," and the courts applied this to various forms of statutory benefits. This was one of several parts of the APA which merely codified existing practices. The fact that in the 1930s Congress explicitly insulated from judicial review one set of entitlements—those distributed by the Veterans Administration—is further evidence that the courts were normally open to those who alleged they had been denied benefits promised by statute.[13] In short, attributing the explosion of entitlement litigation to the courts' sudden refusal to treat statutory benefits as "privileges" which could arbitrarily be revoked by willful administrators not only distorts thirty years of litigation history, but, more importantly, ends the search for more significant changes in judicial thinking and in the political system as a whole far too prematurely.

II. Judicial Review and Administrative Discretion

Conventional arguments about the right-privilege distinction also distort the reality of contemporary welfare litigation. Virtually all federal court decisions on entitlements are based on the premise that the courts must prevent the executive branch and the states from withholding benefits offered by statutes that have been passed by Congress. In other words, judges deciding statutory interpretation cases claim not to *define* entitlements, but merely to *defend* the entitlements already defined by legislators. Obviously, the argument that the courts should prevent the executive branch and the states from emasculating programs mandated by Congress has some appeal. Nowhere is this rationale for judicial review stated more clearly than in Judge Miles Lord's opinion in a 1974 food stamp case:

> The Court is compelled in such circumstances to order the Secretary to use these funds already appropriated by the Congress for the purpose intended—to provide for expansion through effective outreach efforts of a program designed to alleviate hunger . . . To do less would be to allow the Secretary to disregard the rule of law. The elected representatives of the people have established the law. It is the Secretary's responsibility and duty to implement that law. When it is demonstrated that he has failed to do so, it is the responsibility of the Court to require compliance with the standards set by Congress.[14]

The flaw in this stirring rhetoric (and the key problem in almost every entitlement case) is that the meaning of key legal phrases is usually unclear. Neither the canons of statutory interpretations frequently cited by the courts nor extensive judicial examinations of legislative history provide cut-and-dried answers to the questions raised in most cases.[15] Even in the 1972–75 period, when legislative-executive relations were at an all-time low and administrative malfeasance was unusually widespread, it is hard to find an example of a clearly mistaken administrative interpretation of an entitlement law.

If the courts were, as they maintain, merely protecting congressional mandates from executive lawlessness, then one would expect judicial activity to be proportional to the specificity of statutes. But the opposite is true: judicial involvement tends to be greater when statutes are more ambiguous. For example, the courts played a significant role in shaping the food stamps program before 1977, when the Act spoke in broad generalities, but not after the passage of the detailed 1977 Amendments. In fact, the House Agriculture Committee explained that "more specific provisions explicitly defining in the statute for the first time" both eligibility standards and benefit levels "should also prevent frequent judicial invalidation of the Department's income regulations . . . and/or the even broader judicially-developed interpretation of the Act's purpose as guaranteeing households the right to obtain a nutritionally adequate diet."[16]

Other contrasts testify to the link between statutory ambiguity and judicial activism. While the brief AFDC section of the Social Security Act has generated enormous amounts of litigation, judicial decisions have had little effect on implementation of the detailed old age insurance title of that act. The most remarkable proliferation of court decisions has come under the Education for All Handicapped Children Act, which creates a right to a "free appropriate public education"—as open-ended an entitlement as was ever established. In general, the less Congress says, the more the courts do.

At the heart of judicial review of statutory entitlements lies this paradox: to the extent that the courts limit themselves to striking down executive actions clearly contrary to statute, judicial review will be little in demand and have little practical effect; to the extent it has effect and is in demand, it is almost always based on something other than the "clear meaning" of the statute in question. Judicial review is easiest to defend when statutes are specific, leaving little discretion to administrators. But here the task of distributing benefits is readily routinized and controlled administratively. Unless one assumes that administrators are frequently either incompetent or malevolent, the courts will have little to do other than correct an occasional mistake. This does not mean that judicial review serves no purpose; it may help keep administrators on their toes. But so do congressional oversight, media attention, and a variety of management techniques.

In practice, almost all appeals to the courts in entitlement cases involve challenges to the exercise of one of two types of executive discretion. The first form of discretion is exercised when program administrators or other "gatekeepers" (such as physicians who determine whether an applicant is "disabled," or special education teachers who evaluate the extent of children's disabilities) must make individualized determinations of eligibility.[17] In these cases legislative guidance is generally thin—speaking only in such general terms as "permanently and totally disabled" or "appropriate education"—and the argument for deference to professional judgment is particularly strong. Physicians presumably know more about physical impairment than do judges; special education teachers know what techniques are available for educating the handicapped and how likely they are to work.

The second form of executive discretion frequently challenged in court is the use of general rulemaking authority to establish specific eligibility standards and benefit levels. No statute passed by a legislature has ever been sufficient in itself to answer all questions about who can receive benefits and how much each will get. Who is a "widow"? Who is a "parent"? Is a step-father a "parent"? What constitutes "resources," a "family," a "household," or "unemployment"? Do federal housing subsidies constitute "income"? What happens to applicants previously found guilty of fraud? These are the types of detailed but highly significant issues which administrators inevitably must address. Most federal entitlement laws acknowledge the incompleteness of statutory provisions by granting general rulemaking authority either to a federal agency or to the states. Judges reviewing these administrative rules are placed in the paradoxical position of having to decide whether the administratively-announced details are consistent with a statute which does not pretend to descend to this level of specificity.

As a result, the key questions asked by judges in almost all entitlement cases is not "What is the *letter* of the law?" or "What did Congress *say*?" but rather "Is this administrative determination consistent with the *spirit* of the law?" and "What did Congress *mean*?" To ascertain legislative intent, judges frequently look to legislative histories.[18] Yet legislative histories usually raise more questions than they answer, and judges have been notoriously promiscuous in using legislative material. Judge Harold Leventhal once remarked (borrowing a phrase from Santayana) that citing legislative histories is like "looking over a crowd and picking out your friends."[19] Another technique of statutory construction employed with increasing frequency in recent years is reading an act's preamble to establish its purpose, and then asking whether the challenged policy furthers or retards this purpose. As reasonable as this may seem at first, it is hard to deny that in passing most statutes Congress has many purposes in mind. Legislators want to help the needy but not spend too much money, to encourage employment yet provide subsistence to those who cannot work, and to promote family stability while protecting families' privacy. Judges' use of legislative purpose tends to be as selective as their use of legislative history. In short, behind the sharp upswing of welfare litigation in the post-1965 period lies highly "creative" statutory interpretation which gives judges a high degree of discretion.

III. The Two Meanings of "Entitlement"

To understand how the courts have used this discretion to shape welfare policy, it is important to recognize that judges (and many other participants and commentators) have oscillated between two very different meanings of the term "entitlement." On the one hand, "entitlement" can simply mean a benefit to an individual established by an open-ended authorization. This is how the term is usually used by students of Congress and the budgetary process. Such entitlements are distinguished from other forms of government spending by the fact that they are not subject to annual appropriations. Total spending is determined by the number of people who apply and qualify for benefits, rather than by a predetermined appropriations ceiling.[20] On the other hand, "entitlement" can mean a right to benefits which are fully adequate to meet individual needs. In the words of the man who gave the "new property" its name, former Yale Law School professor Charles Reich, "The idea of entitlement is simply that when individuals have insufficient resources to live under conditions of health and decency, society has obligations to provide support, and the individual is entitled to that support as of right."[21]

According to the first view—described as "formalistic" and "positivist" by its critics—entitlements are entirely the creation of the legislative process. This means that they can be revoked, reduced, limited, or redefined in almost any way by subsequent legislation. A 1970 Senate Finance Committee report highly critical of the Supreme Court's AFDC rulings pointedly explained this understanding of the term:

> Welfare is a statutory right, and like any other statutory right, is subject to the establishment by Congress of specific conditions and limitations which may be altered or repealed by subsequent congressional action. . . . The 'right to welfare' implies no vested, inherent or inalienable right to benefits. It confers no constitutionally protected benefits on the recipient. To the contrary, the right to welfare is no more substantial and has no more legal effect, than any other benefit conferred by a generous legislature. . . . It is the ability to change the nature of a statutory right which distinguishes it

from a property right or any right considered inviolable under the Constitution.

Essentially, this is also the view taken by Justice Rehnquist in his famous and controversial assertion that those who receive benefits from the government must take "the bitter"—all statutory restrictions, procedural as well as substantive—with "the sweet"—the enjoyment of government largess.[23] But even Justice Brennan has at times endorsed this understanding. In a 1985 food stamp case he wrote:

> Where 'new' property interests—that is, statutory entitlements—are involved, however, claimants have an interest only in their benefit level as correctly determined under the law, rather than in any particular preordained amount. Thus, while *any* deprivation of tangible property by the State implicates the Due Process Clause, only an *erroneous* governmental reduction of benefits, one resulting in less than the statutorily specified amount, effects a deprivation subject to constitutional constraint. It is the error, and not the reduction per se, that is the deprivation.[24]

This apparently straightforward view has some surprising implications. Consider, for example, what is called the "Foley amendment" to the Food Stamp Act and its effect on the Supreme Court's best known decision on welfare rights, *Goldberg v. Kelly*.[25] In 1970 *Goldberg* marked the official end of the "right-privilege distinction" by announcing: "It may be realistic today to regard welfare entitlements as more like 'property' than a 'gratuity' " and "public assistance, then, is not mere charity."[26] The Supreme Court ruled that recipients facing "brutal need" cannot have their AFDC or general assistance benefits terminated before receiving a "due process" hearing. This requirement came not from the statute (the Social Security Act provided for a hearing, but did not specify when it must be held), but from the due process clauses of the Fifth and Fourteenth Amendments.

The "Foley amendment," a little-noted section of the Food Stamp Amendments of 1977, states that eligibility for food stamps lasts for a maximum of three months. Recipients must reapply at the end of each three-month "certification period." The House Agriculture Committee explained that it refused "to view food stamps as a continuing entitlement," and recommended instead "a program of distinct and separate entitlements known as certification periods."[27] A recipient dropped from the food stamps rolls at the end of three months has no right to a pretermination hearing, since the "property" originally granted incorporated a specific expiration date. Thus, as some legal commentators have noted, this narrow reading of "entitlement" has the potential for knocking the legs out from under much of the entitlement jurisprudence of the late 1960s and early 1970s.[28] So far, though, this provision has withstood legal attack.[29]

The second, broader view is more difficult to describe, since it is so rarely fully and explicitly defended. Perhaps the best place to start is with a revealing quotation from the influential law review article written by Charles Reich and cited approvingly in *Goldberg v. Kelly*:

> Today we see poverty as the consequence of large impersonal forces in a complex industrial society . . . It is closer to the truth to say that the poor are affirmative contributors to today's society, for we are so organized as virtually to compel this sacrifice by a segment of the population. Since the enactment of the Social Security Act, we have recognized that they have a right—not a mere privilege—to a minimal share in the commonwealth. . . . To the greatest degree possible, public welfare should rest upon a comprehensive concept of actual need spelled out in objectively defined eligibility [sic] that assure a maximum degree of security and independence.[30]

This "actual need" view of entitlements has a number of controversial corollaries. Most obviously, benefits should never be based on such extraneous factors as the color of one's skin, the state in which one resides, or the circumstances of one's birth (and, more particularly, whether one is born in or out of wedlock). Moreover, requiring that benefits should be based on "actual need" means that they should *not* be affected by the behavior of recipients—by whether, for example, a mother observes the sexual norms of the community, whether parents accept work, or whether beneficiaries cooperate with caseworkers. Nor should benefits be offered to certain "categories" of the poor—the elderly, the disabled, and broken families— but denied to others with similar needs—especially poor intact families or unemployed able-bodied individuals of working age. If put into effect, this understanding of "entitlement" would reshape the entire American welfare system, which is not only highly decentralized, but also is based on the assumption that only certain "categories" of the poor—those not able to work—deserve benefits.

Some of those who championed this broad view of "entitlement" tried to convince the Supreme Court to read a "right to welfare" into the Fourteenth Amendment. Edward Sparer, chief strategist for the Legal Services attorneys who mounted an important litigation campaign in the late 1960s and early 1970s, described the effort as a "struggle to establish a legal right to an adequate welfare grant, without onerous conditions and with fair administration, for all persons in need of financial assistance."[31] For reasons Samuel Krislov laid out some years ago, this effort to "constitutionalize a right to welfare" achieved a few early successes but ultimately collapsed.[32] What has generally gone unrecognized is the extent to which the courts relied on the same understanding of entitlement when interpreting the "intent" of such federal welfare statutes as the Food Stamp Act and the AFDC section of the Social Security Act.

If belief in legislative supremacy is the foundation of the narrower understanding of entitlements, then a particular view of the causes of poverty—and the judiciary's superior understanding of them—underlies the second. Henry Aaron's description catches the essential elements of the world view which informed many court decisions:

> If poverty is believed to be the resultant of forces exogenous to the poor, then the attachment of unpleasant conditions to assistance is a gratuitous cruelty inflicted upon the already victimized. Indeed, this conception of poverty suggests that welfare should be regarded as a right—as a form of just compensation for a kind of casualty loss, the accident of poverty. This view, or something very much like it, lay behind the drive in the early 1970s, to deliver welfare payments in dignified settings, with rights of appeal and the assurance of due process, and without any coercion or requirements that the recipients of aid do anything in return for it. . . . [T]hese contentions all came to the same thing: Cash should be provided on the basis of economic need and without strings.[33]

It should be noted that Aaron is referring not primarily to the opinions of judges, but to the opinions of welfare reform advocates in the executive branch, Congress, interest groups, and academia. In 1970 and 1972, President Nixon proposed and Congress came close to passing a welfare proposal which would have created a non-categorical, nationally uniform welfare system similar in many respects to that sought by "welfare rights" advocates.[34] A similar proposal molded by the Carter Administration passed the House in 1979. More importantly, the Nixon Administration and Congress created a food stamp program during the 1970s which made need virtually its only eligibility requirement.[35] Thus, while the term "guaranteed income" raised the hackles of many elected officials, non-categorical, need-based welfare programs garnered significant support outside as well as inside the courtroom.

At the same time, such a need-only approach to welfare conflicts with much of the existing welfare structure and with strong elements of American political culture. Among advanced industrial democracies, the United States is unusual in the amount of authority it delegates to sub-national government. Moreover, the American welfare system establishes one set of rules for those expected to work (all able-bodied people under 65 who have no young children at home) and another set for those who are not expected to. Indeed, the primary purpose of our "categorical" welfare system is to distinguish between those who cannot work (because they are too old, or disabled, or must provide care for young children) and those who can.[36] In their study of congressional opinions about welfare, Bill Cavala and Aaron Wildavsky found that

> Policies that provide unearned income run counter to widely held and deeply felt American values, such as achievement, work, and equality of opportunity. . . . Although we had anticipated that Congressmen would be concerned about work incentives, we did not realize how persistent and deep these feelings would be. . . . [Congressmen] believe that people have to work for their own salvation. . . . The Congressmen we interviewed did not believe that their middle-class and working class constituents and their union leaders would support a guaranteed income.[37]

A number of other studies have found strong public opposition to government programs which seem to excuse refusal to work.[38] To advocates of a need-based welfare system, equality means "equal benefits for equal need." But to most congressmen and their constituents, equality means "equal rewards for equal work"—which, in turn, means that those on welfare should always receive less than those who work. This is the rock upon which all recent welfare reform efforts have foundered.[39]

Another societal norm running counter to a need-only approach is the belief that parents bear primary responsibility for taking care of their children. To the extent that welfare reform decreases family stability (as experiments show is probably true of a guaranteed income[40]) or reduces the financial obligations of parents (for example, by making it less painful for fathers to leave their families), it will receive a hostile response from politicians and the public. In addition, all efforts to replace the present categorical system with some form of a guaranteed income cost a great deal of money. This ensures opposition from guardians of the treasury at both the state and federal level. In short, a need-based approach to welfare is bound to run into concerted political opposition.

Judges, of course, did not make a habit of announcing that they were superimposing this broader conception of entitlements onto statutes passed by Congress. The closest they came to this was to argue that reading a statute in any other way would raise constitutional issues that it would be prudent to avoid. Typically, the argument of the court follows this pattern: since the purpose of the statute is to aid the needy (perhaps citing the act's preamble), eligibility should be interpreted broadly and non-financial restrictions read narrowly. Despite the fact that the canons of statutory interpretation frown on heavy reliance on prefatory language, use of this indicator of legislative purpose is ubiquitous in welfare litigation. The *sub rosa* nature of the courts' basic argument about entitlements, though, created extensive disagreement among the lower courts, as well as variations over time as judicial moods shifted.

IV. The Political Context

In scholarly work it is sometimes useful to state the obvious. Here, the obvious fact is that changes in judicial behavior in welfare cases coincided with the second major expansion of the American welfare state in the twentieth century. In 1964 and 1965, Lyndon Johnson launched the Great Society and the War on Poverty. Changes in court rulings were most pronounced in the period of 1966–70. It is hard to believe that this sequence of events was accidental.

There are many links between the War on Poverty and changes in judicial behavior. The lawyers who instituted almost all major welfare cases were funded by the Office of Economic Opportunity (OEO), the command post of the War on Poverty. Moreover, both the War on Poverty and the judicial expansion of welfare rights were seen by participants and observers as the second phase of the struggle for civil rights. The long, intense battle over civil rights legislation eventually discredited arguments about "states' rights" and made almost all interstate variations suspect. Not surprisingly, Lyndon Johnson tended to appoint and promote judges who shared his administration's views on civil rights and an activist federal government. To say that the courts were, in the words of Mr. Dooley, "following the illiction returns" is an overstatement—on civil rights, after all, they were roughly a decade ahead of the electorate. Clearly, however, judges were influenced by the tremendous political and intellectual changes of that turbulent decade.

The politics of this second great expansion of the welfare state were vastly different from the politics of the first—the New Deal—and these differences had important consequences for the role of the judiciary in policymaking. In the 1930s Franklin Roosevelt did much more than oversee the passage of such legislation as the Social Security Act, the National Labor Relations Act, and the Agricultural Adjustment Act. He also helped to create a long-lasting electoral coalition, a powerful executive establishment, a more deferential, restrained judiciary, and (for a while, at least) a pliant Congress. Together these institutions sustained, protected, and expanded the programmatic initiatives of the Roosevelt administration. In short, FDR reshaped central political institutions to make them compatible with New Deal programs.

This was not true of LBJ and his Great Society. In the words of Hugh Heclo,

> If the historiography of the 1960s suggests anything, it is the extremely
> fragile political bases on which new antipoverty policy commitments were
> built. . . . In general there appears to have been little public demand for

launching a major attack on poverty and a great deal of skepticism about eliminating poverty in the United States. Likewise histories of the period show that the political parties did little to prepare the intellectual or political groundwork for putting poverty on the national agenda; in a sense antipoverty policy adopted the Democratic Party rather than the other way around. Interest groups did not appear to have been clamoring for a war on poverty, although as always many groups were zealous in protecting and advancing their piece of the action once President Johnson declared such a war.[41]

Indeed, by 1967 the War on Poverty had run out of political steam. The Congress that convened in that year had significantly more Republican members than the 89th Congress, and began to reduce funding for Great Society programs. President Johnson himself was devoting more of his time and his budget to the war in Vietnam.

The initiatives of the mid-1960s produced more contentiousness than consensus. From this conflict new institutional patterns emerged. For New Dealers the presidency and the bureaucracy were the chief engines of reform; Congress and the courts were essentially conservative and parochial forces to be restrained whenever possible. In the post-1967 period these expectations were reversed. Reformers pinned their hopes on Congress and the courts rather than on the executive branch, which for sixteen of the next twenty-two years would be (at least nominally) in the hands of Republicans. Not only did judicial activism become a regular and accepted part of the political landscape, but increasing hostility between Republican presidents and a Democratic Congress gave federal judges many opportunities to address (and, at times, resolve) important policy issues.

Since welfare cases centered on judicial interpretation of the intent of Congress, and since Congress remained free to revise statutes in response to such decisions, it is important to understand how Congress changed in the late 1960s and early 1970s. As many writers have pointed out, the legislative branch underwent a remarkable transformation during those years. It became more liberal, more activist, more decentralized, and more distrustful of the executive branch.[42]

Entitlements played a central role in this reconstruction of Congress. Liberals within Congress sought to expand domestic programs—and, at the same time, increase their own power—by strengthening authorizing committees (which tend to be dominated by program advocates) while weakening the more conservative appropriations committees, by reducing the influence of conservative southern Democratic committee chairmen, and by limiting the ability of the president (particularly one president, Richard Nixon) to set budget priorities. No longer would authorizing committees rest content to pass broad, ambiguous legislation, trusting the president and his subordinates to fill in the details and allowing the economy-minded appropriations committees to set budget ceilings. In the "New Congress," authorizing committees insisted on writing legislation which would not just *permit* new expenditures, but *mandate* payments to all eligible individuals and subnational governments. The appropriations committees, the Office of Management and Budget (OMB), and presidents called this "uncontrollable spending." Authorizing committees and other program advocates preferred a less ominous term: entitlements.[43] Once an entitlement statute is enacted, administrators cannot refuse to spend the specified funds. Nor can appropriations bills set spending ceilings which reduce the obligations of the government. Spending totals, in fact, are never chosen, but result from millions of individual eligibility determinations.

Whether called "entitlements" or"uncontrollable spending," this form of expenditure increased dramatically in the 1970s. In 1970 entitlement payments to individuals amounted to $61 billion ($151 billion in 1982 dollars, or 31% of the federal budget). By 1980 this had risen to $255.7 billion ($299.5 billion in 1982 dollars, or 43.3% of the federal budget). Growing deficits fueled what Allen Schick has called the "Seven Years Budget War" (1967–74), pitting appropriations committees against authorizing committees, spending committees against taxing committees, and, above all, president against Congress. Presidents Nixon and Ford vetoed unprecedented numbers of spending bills and repeatedly accused Congress of fiscal irresponsibility. Congress overrode many of these vetoes, limited the president's ability to impound appropriated funds, and established a new budget process in 1974 designed to establish *congressional* budget priorities. Budgetary conflict between president and Congress abated during the first two years of the Carter Administration, but reemerged when the economy took a downturn. Since 1981 budgetary disputes have dominated national politics. With the president and Congress fighting over entitlement programs, it is hardly surprising that a third party, the courts, frequently intervened to resolve heated disputes.[44]

Congressional reform not only reinforced general public distrust of the executive branch, but also encouraged judicial activism in several more specific ways. Most obviously, it created a huge body of entitlement law for the courts to interpret. Just as importantly, Congress promoted litigation by protecting the budget and the independence of the Legal Services Corporation, by expanding the circumstances in which courts can award attorneys fees, and by making it easier for plaintiffs to get into court.[45] The subcommittees which dominate policymaking in the reformed Congress often wrote lengthy committee reports (and at times even constructed elaborate *post hoc* legislative "histories") which provided extensive ammunition to enterprising plaintiffs and energetic judges.[46]

Just as importantly, Congress was reluctant to pass legislation
overturning judicial expansions of welfare benefits. Program advocates held
many key positions within Congress, and could usually muster enough votes
in at least one house to block such proposals. Moreover, during the 1970s
hostility to the executive was often so strong that the mere assertion that
administrators had violated "congressional intent" was sufficient to
immunize judicially developed policies from revision.

That the courts have had their defenders in Congress, though, does not
mean that they were always following congressional "intent." For reasons
explained above, the issues which come to court are almost always those on
which clear majorities have not spoken—controversial issues not resolved or
unanticipated problems never squarely faced. The subcommittee chairs,
committee staffers, and other program advocates who defend the courts'
reading of "legislative intent" had usually failed to make this intent explicit
in the legislation originally passed by Congress and presented to the president
for his signature. While the courts' use of legislative history and of statutory
purpose undoubtedly increases the influence of congressional subcommittees,
it is far less clear that these court decisions reflect the intent of Congress as
a whole—to say nothing of the intent of the president, who is made part of
the legislative process by the Constitution.

For all these reasons, the interplay among the courts, Congress, and the
executive were much more subtle and varied than is generally appreciated.
To understand the process more clearly it will be useful to examine one
program in greater detail.

V. AFDC: Judicial Reform, Reagan Retrenchment

Aid to Families with Dependent Children (AFDC) is the most important
and the most controversial of the federal government's means-tested income
maintenance programs. It not only constitutes the major source of support for
over 10 million women and children, but also establishes eligibility for other
programs, including Medicaid. No other welfare program has been the
subject of so much litigation. Before 1966 there were only two reported
federal court opinions on AFDC. Since then, hundreds of decisions have
been issued by the federal courts, changing the program in fundamental
ways. Almost all of these cases were brought by the federal Legal Services
Corporation as part of a skillfully orchestrated litigational campaign. For
many years, they represented the cutting edge of welfare reform litigation.

AFDC was established in Title IV of the Social Security Act of 1935. It received very little attention at that time, riding the legislative coattails of two much more popular programs, old age assistance (a means-tested program for the elderly poor) and old age and survivors insurance (what we now commonly call "social security"). Title IV was presented by its supporters on the President's Committee on Economic Security and in Congress as a way to expand and help finance the "mothers' pension" programs already established by many states to help widows care for their children. When FDR's proposal came before Congress, the only issue debated was the extent of federal control over state programs. The Senate was particularly adamant about removing all vestiges of federal dictation. Both the House and Senate Reports explained that a state could "impose such other eligibility requirements—as to means, moral character, etc.—as it sees fit." The Senate Report added, "Less Federal control is provided than in any recent Federal aid law."[47]

Title IV clearly established AFDC as a grant-in-aid program which would reimburse participating states for payments made for the care of children (and later "caretaker relatives")—provided that these children were "needy" according to state standards and had been "deprived of parental support or care by reason of the death, continued absence from the home, or physical or mental incapacity of a parent." Federal administrators were never happy with their lack of control over the states, but soon resigned themselves to the fact that they could do little but offer professional advice and encouragement to induce state administrators to change state rules.[48]

AFDC rolls began to grow rapidly in the 1960s, calling public attention to a program which had previously escaped the limelight. No longer were recipients primarily widows and their children, but rather families deserted by the father and mothers with illegitimate children.[49] It was hard to find anyone who liked AFDC. Liberals decried the low benefits (especially in southern states), the punitive and often discriminatory administration of the program in many states (again, especially in southern states), the failure to provide benefits to intact poor families, and the lack of aid to the working poor. Conservatives criticized what they saw as the encouraging of illegitimacy and dependency, the growing cost of welfare, and the lack of a work requirement in the federal statute. Radicals described the entire welfare system as oppressive, and claimed that its purpose was to "regulate" rather than help the poor. This discontent spurred a number of reform efforts, most notably Nixon's Family Assistance Plan and Carter's Program for Better Income and Jobs. While the former came close to passing, none of these reform packages emerged from the legislative process.[50]

AFDC in the Supreme Court. While Congress was debating these proposals, a second reform effort was underway in the courts. The first, constitutional phase of the "welfare rights" campaign produced two notable decisions, *Goldberg v. Kelly,* which required pre-termination hearings, and *Shapiro v. Thompson,*[51] which struck down durational residency requirements. In two subsequent AFDC cases, *Dandridge v. Williams* and *Jefferson v. Hackney,*[52] a majority on the Burger Court refused to find a right to welfare in the Constitution. At that point statutory interpretation became the chief tool of judicial reformers.

To describe all the court decisions which affected the development of state AFDC programs would be a huge task. Not only have there been hundreds of decisions on the many detailed rules of the fifty states, but the Supreme Court has sent conflicting messages to the lower courts, first demanding strict scrutiny of state rules and then suggesting that judges show more deference to state and federal administrators. As a result, many of the decisions of the courts have an *ad hoc* quality that defies easy description.[53]

Despite the doubts occasionally expressed by temporary majorities on the Supreme Court, the core of AFDC jurisprudence remains three Court decisions—known as the "King-Townsend-Remillard trilogy"—decided between 1968 and 1972. These decisions reversed the presumption about AFDC eligibility which had guided policymaking for the preceding thirty years. States, the Supreme Court ruled, could impose no restrictions on eligibility unless these restrictions had been clearly authorized in the federal statute. Since the statute was silent on almost all matters (a result, ironically, of Congress's dedication to state control), the Court cast doubt on the validity of all state rules denying benefits to "needy, dependent children." By standing the statute on its head the Court moved AFDC closer to the broad, need-based understanding of "entitlement" described above.

In *King v. Smith,*[54] the first leg of the "trilogy" and the most important of the Supreme Court's AFDC decisions, the Court was looking for a way to strike down Alabama's harsh (and probably racially motivated) "substitute parent" rule, long a target of reformers. According to Alabama's law, a man with whom a welfare mother has even the most casual sexual relations constitutes a "substitute parent." Children with such "substitute parents" are ineligible for AFDC.[55] Finding no explicit prohibition of this practice in the federal law and recognizing that Congress had tolerated such restrictions in 1935, Chief Justice Warren nevertheless claimed that the "mood of the Congress" was different in the 1960s than in the 1930s, and that "federal welfare policy now rests on a basis considerably more sophisticated and enlightened than the 'worthy person' concept of earlier times." Paying little attention to statutory language, Warren asserted that "Congress has determined that immorality and illegitimacy should be dealt with through rehabilitative measures rather than measures that punish dependent children, and that protection of such children is the paramount goal of AFDC."[56]

While readily defensible in policy terms, Warren's reading of legislative intent not only twisted the 1935 Act beyond recognition, but also ignored the fact that in 1967, just months before the *King* decision was announced, Congress had passed welfare amendments which most liberal reformers considered drastic and punitive. Far from endorsing the Supreme Court's "sophisticated and enlightened" view, Congress voted to impose new work requirements on recipients and to reduce federal funds to states failing to control the number of illegitimate children on AFDC. The *Washington Post* described the 1967 Amendments as going "Back to Barbarism."[57] With equally characteristic hyperbole, Daniel Patrick Moynihan called them "the first purposively punitive welfare legislation in the history of American national government."[58] Senator Robert Kennedy complained that "the man-in-the-house rule emerged from the conference strengthened rather than weakened," and joined with other liberals in an unsuccessful attempt to kill the conference report.[59] At the very least, the 1967 Amendments provide convincing evidence that Congress did not fully subscribe to Warren's "sophisticated and enlightened" view.

The Supreme Court, nonetheless, grew more adamant in its attack on state restrictions on eligibility, even those involving neither race nor sexual behavior. In *Townsend v. Swank*[60] Legal Services attorneys challenged an Illinois law which allowed children between 18 and 20 to receive AFDC only if they attended high school or vocational school. Federal legislation gave states the option of covering those over 18 who are in school, and Illinois had picked up one sector of this optional population. The Supreme Court ordered Illinois to extend benefits to those attending all types of schools.[61] More important than the ruling on this particular issue was the sweeping language of Justice Brennan's opinion:

> *King v. Smith* establishes that, at least in the absence of congressional authorization for the exclusion clearly evidenced from the Social Security Act or its legislative history, a state eligibility standard that excluded persons eligible for assistance under federal AFDC standards violates the Social Security Act and is therefore invalid under the Supremacy Clause. (at 286)

Lurking behind this interpretation of the statute, Brennan indicated, were important constitutional issues: "We doubt the rationality of the classification" excluding those attending colleges and universities. The implication was that need, not the type of institution attended, was the only rational basis for distributing benefits.

In *Carleson v. Remillard* the Court again repeated that the Social Security Act does not permit states "to vary eligibility requirements from the federal standards without express or clearly implied congressional authorization."[62] California could not deny benefits to the family of a man serving in the military, since the family's income was below the state's "standard of need" and the father was physically "absent from the home" (he was stationed overseas). Conveniently overlooking the *categorical* nature of AFDC, Justice Douglas asserted that Congress "intended to provide a program for the economic security and protection of *all* children." He expressed confidence that "Congress could not have designed an Act leaving uncared for an entire class who become 'needy children' because their fathers were in the Armed Services defending their country." The counter-argument—that Congress meant to limit AFDC to children without a father capable of providing any support—was ignored. In the hands of the Supreme Court, welfare "categories" were slowly crumbling.

In a few subsequent cases, the Court departed from this strict presumption of eligibility. In an arbitrary fashion it allowed states to revoke the eligibility of mothers who fail to permit "home visits" by social workers (a conventional requirement, but not one mentioned in the Social Security Act) or who fail to register for state-run work incentive programs (which supplement federal work programs but are not recognized in the statute).[63] The Court continued, however, to take a hard line against state rules which seemed to enforce middle-class morality. It struck down a California law which attributed to the AFDC family part of the income of a "man assuming the role of spouse," that is, a man living with a woman receiving AFDC. The Court ruled that the state could not reduce the family's AFDC grant in this way, even if the "man assuming the role of spouse" married the mother without legally adopting her children.[64] Several years later New York attempted to reduce grants to families with "lodgers"—unrelated persons living in the home of a welfare family—on the ground that such "lodgers" should contribute a pro-rated share of the rent. The Supreme Court prohibited the practice. According to Justice Brennan's majority opinion, under the Social Security Act "States may not seek to accomplish policies aimed at lodgers by depriving needy children of benefits."[65] Any goal other than providing benefits to needy children—especially the purpose of regulating the lifestyle of recipients—faced tough sledding in the Court.

Activism in the Lower Courts. For an appellate body that devotes most of its attention to constitutional issues, the Supreme Court has decided a surprisingly large number of statutory AFDC cases. Even so, when dealing with complex statutes, the Supreme Court can only announce general themes. The lower courts have the job of applying these themes to the details of program operations. The lower courts were more than willing to follow the Supreme Court's lead. In the words of one legal commentator, "recipient attacks on state-created eligibility standards have met with striking success" in the lower courts.[66] Even before the Supreme Court had announced *Townsend* or *Remillard,* one district court judge asserted:

> It is the opinion of the Court that the Act creates the right to a grant of
> assistance and aid to a needy and dependent child, once such need and
> dependency have been established, and a participating agency may not
> withhold the granting of such aid by the promulgation of an additional
> eligibility requirement.[67]

This encapsulates the general view of the lower courts.

Among the state welfare rules struck down by federal district court and
circuit court judges are the following:

- laws passed by most states requiring mothers receiving AFDC to identify
the father of their children,[68]
- state laws requiring recipients to accept various types of work,[69]
- state laws requiring a parent to be absent for at least 30 days before the
family becomes eligible for AFDC,[70]
- rules disqualifying those previously found guilty of fraud and reducing
AFDC grants in order to recoup past overpayments by the state,[71]
- state laws disqualifying strikers,[72]
- and state rules requiring stepparents of AFDC children to disclose their
income.[73]

Building on the Supreme Court's rulings on "lodgers" and "men assuming
the role of spouse," the lower courts prohibited states from automatically
counting as income such sources of revenue as the following: Social Security
benefits or support payments paid to one child, tax refunds and insurance
payments, or the income of a grandparent or stepparent living in the same
household as an AFDC family.[74] In two controversial decisions with
nationwide applicability, federal courts in the District of Columbia struck
down HEW rules limiting the resources which can be held by AFDC
recipients and rules instituting "quality control" sanctions designed to reduce
state error rates.[75]

The clearest instance of the lower courts interpreting the Social Security
Act to broaden welfare categories and to meet what they considered to be the
individual needs of welfare recipients came in a series of cases on benefits for
pregnant women. The only mention of pregnancy benefits in the 1935 Act
came not in Title IV, but in Title V, which provided federal matching funds
for pre- and postnatal health services. For many years HEW had allowed
states the option of considering a fetus a "dependent child," thus making
pregnant women eligible for AFDC and increasing the grants of those already
eligible. In the early 1970s Legal Services mounted an extensive legal
campaign to force all states to exercise this option. Of the fourteen district
courts to decide the issue, ten ruled that Congress had intended to include the
unborn in the Act's definition of "dependent children." Five of the six circuit
courts reviewing these decisions agreed. The Supreme Court, however, was
not prepared to go this far.[76]

That the courts would read "child" to include a fetus is, to say the least, somewhat odd. Not only does the statute require the child to be "living with" a particular relative and base residency on the child's place of birth, but, shortly before this controversy heated up, the Supreme Court announced in *Roe v. Wade* that a fetus is *not* a person. If a fetus is a child, after all, then abortion is murder. Reduced to its essence, the argument advanced by the lower courts was that the term "child" is at least somewhat ambiguous and that all ambiguity should be resolved in a way which furthers the Act's goal of helping the needy. The First Circuit stated,

> We think that a finding of eligibility for the unborn is consistent with the purposes and policies of the Social Security Act. The Supreme Court has declared the 'paramount goal' of the AFDC program to be the protection of needy children. Payments to the unborn are an appropriate, if not essential, measure to that end.[77]

The Fifth Circuit added,

> Payments to expectant mothers are consistent with the purposes of the Act . . . It cannot be doubted that proper prenatal care is vital to the physical and mental health of the child, and an unborn child deprived of said care may reasonably be said to be as 'needy' and 'dependent' as a child in similar circumstances.[78]

To the Seventh Circuit the argument for covering pregnancy was even stronger: "[It is] difficult to discern a rational basis for denying pregnant women the same assistance during pregnancy [when] . . . the need may be greater."[79]

In 1975 the Supreme Court reversed these lower court decisions and announced that "this departure from ordinary principles of statutory interpretation is not supported by the Court's prior decisions." The King-Townsend-Remillard trilogy, Justice Powell claimed, did not establish the principle applied by the lower courts, namely that

> persons who are arguably included in the federal eligibility standard must be deemed eligible unless the Act or its legislative history clearly exhibits an intent to exclude them from coverage, in effect creating a presumption of coverage when the statute is ambiguous.[80]

The Court accepted HEW's interpretation that pregnancy benefits are optional but not mandatory.

Despite the Supreme Court's denial that special rules of interpretation apply to AFDC, most lower courts have continued to insist upon the presumption of eligibility. A year later one district court judge called attention to the policy of the Social Security Act and regulations to assure that the minimal needs of each child will be satisfied. The state cannot, consistent with the Act and regulations, reduce payments without a guarantee that those minimal needs will in fact be satisfied.[81]

In 1982 another district court opinion demonstrated that the *Burns* decision had little effect on the thinking of the lower courts:

If anything, congressional failure to specify that states should deny benefits for a specific reason under the AFDC program is evidence of its intent not to allow states to deny benefits for that reason. . . . *King v. Smith* and its progeny have erected a fundamental principle of AFDC jurisprudence: that the Social Security Act will not countenance depriving needy children of benefits because of factors beyond their control, and unrelated to need.[82]

Of course, having two parents at home is "beyond the control" of children and "unrelated to need." So far, however, no court has claimed that the statute requires states to make intact families eligible for AFDC.

Even the Supreme Court has periodically reverted to its previous habit of using the Act's alleged purpose to create a presumption of eligibility. In a 1979 case involving "caretaker relatives" who met eligibility requirements for both regular AFDC and the higher paying "AFDC-Foster Care" program, Justice Marshall found the Act to require states to make the higher payments:

A participating State may not deny assistance to persons who meet eligibility standards defined in the Social Security Act unless Congress clearly has indicated that the standards are permissive. . . . Neither the legislative history nor the structure of the Act indicates that Congress intended to differentiate among neglected children based on their relationship to their foster parents. Indeed, such a distinction would conflict in several respects with the overriding goal of providing the best available care for all dependent children removed from their homes.[83]

Given the Supreme Court's failure to follow a consistent line of argument, it is not surprising that the lower courts have gone off on their own.

Statutory interpretation of Title IV of the Social Security Act did not by any stretch of the imagination constitute a conscientious effort by the courts to determine the intent of those who passed the Act of 1935 or its many amendments. Rather, it was an on-again, off-again attempt to bring federal policy into line with the "sophisticated and enlightened" social welfare positions endorsed by the courts. In the absence of clear congressional directives to the contrary, the courts insisted that states base eligibility solely on the "actual," "individual"[84] need of the family requesting assistance. Many judges no doubt expected that Congress would eventually follow their lead. For a brief time (1969–72), it appeared that Congress indeed might reject both categorical welfare programs and the state control which kept benefits so low in some parts of the country. But eventually reform stalled, and Congress slowly undid much of the courts' work.

The Congressional Response. Given the extent to which the courts reversed settled expectations about the operation of AFDC, it is not surprising that some Congressmen familiar with the program were upset with their decisions. Opposition to the courts centered in the Senate Finance Committee. In 1970 and 1972, the Committee issued two blistering critiques of judicial activity, and launched an unsuccessful effort to reverse the major decisions of the preceding five years. Throughout the 1970s Congress remained deadlocked on virtually all welfare issues, rejecting the proposals of Presidents Nixon and Carter as well as those of the Senate Finance Committee. It was not until the early 1980s that the logjam broke and Congress began to overturn the policies established by the courts.

Much of the credit (or blame, depending on one's perspective) for the congressional enactments of the 1980s must go to two persistent foes of the courts, Senator Russell Long (D-La.), chairman of the Senate Finance Committee, and President Ronald Reagan. A forceful advocate of states' rights, workfare, and programs to force fathers to pay for the upbringing of their children, Long was outraged by the Supreme Court's revision of Title IV of the Social Security Act. He could usually count on the support of a majority on his committee, but he had a much harder time steering his perennial proposals through the Senate floor and conferences with the House.

Reagan, too, began battling with the courts in the early 1970s, after they struck down many key provisions of the welfare reform package he championed in California.[85] When he came to Washington, Reagan brought with him several of the advisors who had designed his California welfare plan. Their agenda was similar to that of Russell Long: to give the states more control over AFDC, to force most recipients to work, and to require relatives—especially fathers—to assume financial responsibility for needy children. The Omnibus Budget and Reconciliation Act of 1981, the Tax Equity and Fiscal Responsibility Act of 1982, and the Deficit Reduction Act of 1984 all contain pieces of the Long-Reagan welfare program.

Gathering enough support in Congress to pass this welfare legislation was not easy. The House was particularly reluctant to reduce benefits to AFDC recipients. The Democratic majority on the House Ways and Means Committee—and especially its subcommittee on Public Assistance—generally favored expansion of benefits, not retrenchment. Not until the prospect of major expansion had finally flickered out and the authority of the House committee had weakened did the attack on the courts begin to succeed.[86]

The conservative counterattack first took shape in 1970, when the Senate Finance Committee report noted that "Court decisions have played a major role in the phenomenal growth of the welfare rolls in the last three years."[87] Two years later the Committee added,

> These decisions have used the very broadness of the Federal statute (intended to allow States more latitude) against the States by saying sometimes that anything the Congress did not expressly prohibit it must have intended to require—and sometimes that what Congress did not expressly permit it must have intended not to permit.[88]

The Committee sought to reestablish AFDC as "a federally shared program under which States can provide assistance to needy families," to reject a long list of judicial interpretations of the statute, and even to limit the application of the two major constitutional rulings on AFDC, *Shapiro v. Thompson* and *Goldberg v. Kelly*.

Among the court decisions criticized by the Senate Finance Committee were the following:

- *King v. Smith* and a variety of other decisions striking down state rules on the financial responsibilities of "men in the house," stepparents, and "men assuming the role of spouse";
- lower court decisions prohibiting states from requiring recipients to allow home visits by caseworkers and to cooperate in determining the paternity of their children;
- the pre-*Burns* decisions on pregnancy benefits;
- the *Townsend* ruling on eligibility of college students;
- a number of decisions expanding the AFDC-U program, which makes families eligible for benefits when the father is unemployed;
- and lower court decisions limiting the states' ability to recoup overpayments and to exclude aliens.

As other court decisions were handed down, they too were added to the Committee's "hit list." The Finance Committee subsequently recommended reversal of the Supreme Court's decisions on servicemen, "lodgers," individualized (as opposed to standardized) work expense deductions, and eligibility of those receiving unemployment compensation, as well as lower court decisions on strikers, resource limitations, and quality control.

The Senate Committee also attacked what it saw as a principal cause of this extensive litigation—Legal Services. Senator Long was fond of repeating that "Only an idiot would hire someone to sue himself." Claiming that Legal Service's litigation campaign on welfare "aims at undermining established institutions that were consciously created through acts of Congress," the Committee sought to block funding for this form of litigation, and a majority of those Senators casting their votes during the 1972 welfare debate agreed.[89]

A few liberals rose to the defense of the courts and Legal Services. Senator Fred Harris (D-Oklahoma), for example, argued that Legal Services had "com-

piled a remarkable record of service to poor people" and that litigation in the
federal courts had "begun to nudge the welfare system toward a more equitable
and enlightened program." His 1970 floor amendment to delete the Committee's recommendations on residency requirements and "men in the house" was
defeated by a vote of 27–42.[90] But on these issues—and almost all others
related to AFDC litigation—the House refused to go along with the Senate. The
judicially created *status quo* remained intact.

A few of the proposals put forth by Senator Long and his allies did
manage to survive the "obstacle course on Capitol Hill" during the 1970s. In
1971 the "Talmadge amendment" strengthened federal work requirements
for parents with children over six years of age. In 1973–74 liberals finally
joined Long in supporting a bill to step up federal efforts to force fathers to
make support payments to their children and former wives.[91] These,
however, were exceptions; stalemate remained the rule.

This changed markedly in the 1980s. Two factors helped conservatives
enact a variety of changes in AFDC. Most obvious was the budget-cutting,
anti-government mood which gripped Congress after the election of Ronald
Reagan and a Republican Senate. Just as important was the Reagan
Administration's skillful use of "reconciliation," a procedural device which
allowed a huge list of budget cuts to be grouped together and voted on as a
whole. Reconciliation, as Allen Schick has noted, constitutes a large,
omnibus "discharge petition" which allowed a determined president to stage
an end-run around hostile House committees. With the "conservative
coalition" stronger than it had been in many years, the reconciliation
procedure allowed Reagan, Long, and their allies to push through Congress
many of the proposals which had languished in the House for years.

The list of legislative changes aimed at policies established in whole or
part by the courts is impressive. In 1981, 1982, and 1985, Congress made the
following changes in the Social Security Act:

- required states to count the income of stepparents, overturning *Lewis v.
Martin*;
- removed the open-ended work expense deduction mandated by the
Supreme Court in *Shea v. Vialpando*;
- modified the Supreme Court's expansion of AFDC-U in *Califano v.
Westcott* by limiting eligibility to families in which the principal wage
earner is unemployed;
- required the Department of Health and Human Services to establish
resource limits and quality control guidelines similar to those struck down
by the lower courts;
- overturned the *Townsend* decision on benefits for college students;
- reversed the *Carleson* decision on benefits to families of servicemen;
- overturned the *Hurley* decision on "lodgers";

- overturned the decisions of two circuit courts which defined "income" so as to increase benefits to recipients with jobs;
- and established a "standard filing unit" which effectively reversed scores of court decisions on "available income."

Although these provisions were all attached to deficit reduction bills, they did not produce large budgetary savings. The only major reduction in AFDC cost was achieved by ending the so-called "thirty and one third" rule, which allowed recipients to exclude part of their monthly earnings from the calculation of "available income." This rule, though, had been the product of legislative and executive action, not court decisions. Budget bills provided the Reagan Administration with vehicles for passing AFDC legislation it favored for other reasons.

In fact, the AFDC package included in the 1981 Reconciliation bill was not constructed by the Office of Management and Budget, but almost entirely by Robert Carleson, who had helped develop Reagan's California welfare reform proposals during the late 1960s and early 1970s. In January of 1981 President Reagan approved a package of changes which Carleson expected to submit to Congress as a separate piece of legislation. Shortly thereafter, Carleson seized the opportunity to push this legislation through Congress by attaching it to the Administration's reconciliation bill. He reportedly told OMB Director David Stockman: "Here is something that has already been approved. All you have to do is plug it in. It's like a cassette." Carleson later stated, "The purpose of welfare reform was policy, not to save money but to reduce dependency and redirect funds to the truly needy."[92]

The major purpose of these changes in AFDC law, as Nathan Glazer has pointed out, was not so much to lower the *cost* of welfare programs as much as to alter their *character*. Underlying these amendments was a view of welfare far removed from the conception of entitlements tacitly accepted by the federal courts:

> The approach was not to encourage family stability by means of an incentive; it was to promote stability by imposing a norm—i.e., that a man living with a mother and her children had an obligation to support the woman with whom he lived as husband, the children with whom he lived as father. . . . Welfare's hitherto non-judgmental, supportive role was now modified. . . . The traditional incentives, to work and family support, were now assumed rather than paid for.[93]

Without attacking the courts directly—as the Senate Finance Committee had done a decade before—Congress whittled away at two decades of court decisions, which were based on a view of welfare Congress had never endorsed but had never rejected either.

As important as these changes were, it is also worth noting two things that did *not* happen in the early 1980s. First, liberal Democrats did not put up much of a fight to protect these judicially initiated policies. Liberals correctly sensed that cuts in welfare spending were inevitable, and looked for the least painful places to cut. Court decisions had created a number of quirks in the system: welfare families with relatively well-off stepfathers, with parents serving in the military, and with high work expenses. Such policies may have affected only a small percentage of welfare recipients, but they diverted scarce funds to less needy families and increased public indignation about welfare "abuse." Rather than defend such practices, liberals chose (when they had any choice) to trade off concessions in these areas for minor changes elsewhere. For example, they accepted the "standard filing unit" in return for a $50 per month deduction for child support payments.

Second, conservatives made no concerted effort to remove the courts from AFDC policymaking, to increase state control over AFDC substantially, or to reimpose such punitive rules as Alabama's "substitute parent" regulation. All the major legislative controversies involved particular eligibility rules; standards of judicial review were hardly mentioned in congressional debates. Ironically, many of these rules reduced rather than increased the discretion of the states. During the brief period they controlled the legislative process in Washington, conservatives tried to impose their policies on the states rather than to increase state autonomy. While there was a great deal of talk (but far less action) about increasing penalties for those who fail to work, there was little congressional interest in imposing penalties on those who violated community norms of sexual behavior. To this extent *King v. Smith* had won broad acceptance.

By 1988 Ronald Reagan was an exceedingly lame duck, the Democrats controlled the Senate as well as the House, and Congress passed welfare reform legislation costing an additional three and a half billion dollars over five years. What characterized the "newfound if tenuous consensus"[94] behind this bill was an emphasis on family responsibility and work. The new law requires the states to step up efforts to identify the fathers of AFDC children and to force them to pay child support. It provides more money for education and training programs, but requires more recipients to enroll in them. It offers transitional Medicaid and childcare benefits for those leaving AFDC for jobs. It requires states to provide AFDC benefits to intact families when the principal wage-earner is unemployed, but requires this wage-earner to enroll in a "workfare" program. Perhaps the best summary of this legislation was written a year before its passage in a report by the American Enterprise Institute's "Working Seminar on Welfare":

> The new strategy is a blend of conservative and liberal themes. It includes
> a new emphasis on training and other services for poor persons, and it is
> also job-focused, taking as its premise the idea that all able-bodied persons

ought to work. It is obligational, requiring aid recipients to meet certain responsibilities in return for their benefits.[95]

Thus, at the very time Congress was voting more money for AFDC and expanding eligibility, it was distancing itself from the "need-only" understanding of entitlements which underlay the activism of the federal courts.

VI. Conclusion

In this brief examination of AFDC, we can see several characteristics of welfare litigation in general. First, the courts had their greatest effect on policy not by insisting on new procedures or by insisting that the states and the executive branch follow statutory requirements, but by grafting onto Title IV of the Social Security Act a need-only understanding of entitlements. This was done through "creative" statutory interpretation which most likely would have shocked those who wrote and voted for the Act in 1935.

Second, all three branches of government were internally divided on the question of how far to go in this direction. This was particularly evident in Congress, which for years was unable to pass any coherent welfare package. Administrators in the Department of Health, Education, and Welfare at first cheered on the courts, but reversed direction after 1972.[96] The Supreme Court also reversed direction in the early 1970s. In recent years, it has instructed the lower courts to show more deference to administrators and even to ignore the interpretive approach it developed in the "King-Townsend-Remillard trilogy." Some lower courts have followed this advice; others have not. One consequence of these internal divisions is that AFDC policy is a hodgepodge of often-inconsistent court decisions, statutory provisions, and administrative regulations. Another is that only on rare occasions is Congress capable of acting decisively to accept, reject, expand, or contract court rulings. This gives the courts a great deal of influence over welfare policy.

Finally, underlying court decisions on AFDC was the belief that the judiciary is uniquely suited to divine the direction of progress. Court rulings on welfare programs are perhaps best described by a phrase coined by Yale Law School Dean Guido Calabresi: "a common law for the age of statutes." Calabresi argues that, in interpreting statutes, courts should consciously and explicitly revise laws passed by legislators whenever such laws become "out of date, out of phase, or ill adapted to the legal topography." Such judicial

amendment of "anachronistic" legislation is necessary to keep the law
"consistent with current thinking."[97] Underlying this approach to statutory
interpretation—an approach, as Calabresi points out, which describes what
the courts do, not what they admit to doing—is a belief in progress and in the
courts' special ability to detect the direction of history. What Alexander
Bickel said of the constitutional jurisprudence of the Warren Court applies
equally well to the more mundane welfare decisions of the federal judiciary:
"Belief in man-made progress was the new faith, and the supremacy of
judges as its carrier and executor was not denied."[98]

To many judges and to most legal commentators who wrote about
welfare policy, progress meant jettisoning the heritage of the Elizabethan
poor laws, the ultimate source of the localistic, moralistic, stigmatizing, and
categorical American welfare system. Progress also meant moving toward
some form of guaranteed income paid in cash without strings and without any
indication that the poor are "undeserving." A progressive welfare system
does not impose societal norms on recipients, but provides each with "a
minimal share of the commonwealth." This was the catechism of the
"enlightened and sophisticated" view to which Chief Justice Warren refers in
King v. Smith.

Subsequent events in the welfare area have cast a shadow on this view
of history-as-progress. The legislative changes of the Reagan era—even
those pushed by liberal Democrats—have strengthened rather than weakened
the categorical nature of the American welfare system. As John Palmer and
Elizabeth Sawhill of the Urban Institute note in their description of the
legislative changes of 1981–82: "At a programmatic level, these shifts
express a New Deal concept of 'the deserving poor' and reject the expanded
objectives of the 1960s War on Poverty."[99] Ronald Reagan espoused
unabashedly moralistic and localistic views on welfare for years. While he
has not been entirely successful in his attempts to revise the welfare system,
in recent years the opinions of Reagan and his advisors have been more
influential than any others. Not even today's liberal Democrats are willing to
go as far in the direction of a nationally uniform, noncategorical guaranteed
income as Richard Nixon was nearly two decades ago. The negative income
tax, as Martin Levin and Barbara Ferman have pointed out, is "a good idea
whose time has come and gone."[100]

That the view of entitlements embraced by the courts in the 1960s and
1970s is currently out of favor with the Congress and president may convince
some people that the courts should strive all the harder to purge welfare
policy of the prejudiced and punitive attitudes of elected officials. More
disturbing to advocates of judicial activism should be the fact that, in recent
years, intellectuals—those most consistently critical of existing welfare
policies and supposedly best able to chart the course of progress—have

themselves begun to question the viability and desirability of a "non-judgmental" guaranteed income. During the 1970s economists and policy analysts struggled to produce a non-categorical income maintenance program which combined adequate initial benefits with work incentives at a reasonable cost. They failed. Meanwhile, the results of income maintenance experiments indicated that cash assistance without strings can, in some cases, diminish rather than increase family stability. In the words of Henry Aaron, "Advocates of noncategorical cash assistance had reached an intellectual and political *cul de sac*."[101]

The current intellectual debate on welfare reform focuses not on *whether* government programs should impose "middle class morality," but rather on *how* the government can instill norms about work and family responsibility.[102] Academics and other "opinion leaders," it seems, are moving closer and closer to the position of the average member of Congress, who over the past two decades has been willing to spend significant sums on social welfare programs, but only if they promise to increase work effort and family stability. It is unclear whether this shift in intellectual currents will shake judges' faith in their ability to"anticipate the future" (to use Bickel's phrase). If not, one can expect years of skirmishes between courts and elected lawmakers on the meaning of "welfare rights."

Notes

1. Martin Shapiro explains these changes in *The Supreme Court and Economic Rights,* in ESSAYS ON THE CONSTITUTION OF THE UNITED STATES (M. Judd Harmon ed. 1978). Many of the key cases will be discussed later in this paper.

2. On AFDC see Doolittle, *State-Imposed Nonfinancial Eligibility Conditions on AFDC: Confusion in Supreme Court Decisions and a Need for Congressional Clarification* 19 HARV. J. ON LEGIS. 1 (1982) and Block, *Cooperative Federalism and the Role of Litigation in the Development of Federal AFDC Policy,* 1979 WIS. L. REV. 1. On food stamps, see J. BERRY, FEEDING HUNGRY PEOPLE (1986); on disability insurance, STONE, THE DISABLED STATE, (1984) and S. G. MEZEY, NO LONGER DISABLED: THE FEDERAL COURTS AND THE POLITICS OF SOCIAL SECURITY DISABILITY (1988); on education of the handicapped, *Symposium: Children with Special Needs,* LAW & CONTEMP. PROBS. (Winter and Spring 1985). Also see R. Rosenblatt, *Health Care Reform and Administrative Law: A Structural Approach,* 88 YALE L. J. 243 (1978) and F. Michelman, "The Right to Housing," in THE RIGHTS OF AMERICANS (N. Dorsen, ed. 1971).

3. In 1980, for example, Congress eliminated the $10,000 "amount in

controversy" requirement of federal jurisdiction. (Public Law 96–486). There was little opposition to this legislation. In 1986 Congress passed legislation providing attorneys' fees for plaintiffs bringing successful cases under the EAHCA (Education for All Handicapped Children Act). The Supreme Court had previously ruled that the original legislation did not authorize attorneys' fees. *See* CONGRESSIONAL QUARTERLY WEEKLY REPORT, July 26, 1986, at 1690.

In 1988, after many years of dispute, Congress finally authorized judicial review of eligibility decisions made by the Veterans Administration (VA). It also authorized judges to award "reasonable" attorneys' fees. For decades, the statute establishing veterans' benefits had precluded judicial review and set a ten dollar limit on attorneys' fees. CONGRESSIONAL QUARTERLY WEEKLY REPORT, October 22, 1988, at 3058–59.

4. There is a huge literature on this subject. Among the best known and most useful law review articles are the following: Reich, *The New Property*, 73 YALE L. J. 733 (1964) and *Individual Rights and Social Welfare: The Emerging Legal Issues*, 74 YALE L.J. 1245 (1965); Van Alstyne, *The Demise of the Right-Privilege Distinction in Constitutional Law*, 81 HARVARD L. REV. 1439 (1968) and *Cracks in the 'New Property': Adjudicative Due Process and the Administrative State*, CORNELL L. REV. 445 (1977); and Smolla, *The Reemergence of the Right-Privilege Distinction in Constitutional Law*, 35 STAN L. REV. 69 (1982).

5. See, for example, LAFRANCE, WELFARE LAW: STRUCTURE AND ENTITLEMENT 82–94 (1979); Rosenblatt, *Legal Entitlements and Welfare Benefits*, THE POLITICS OF LAW: A PROGRESSIVE CRITIQUE (D. Kairys ed. 1982); and Barrett, *The New Role of the Courts in Developing Public Welfare Law*, 1970 DUKE L. REV. 1 at 7–8.

6. The "demise of the right-privilege distinction," it should be noted, did have an important impact on public employment and licensing practices.

7. The best description of court action in benefit cases is JAFFE, JUDICIAL CONTROL OF ADMINISTRATIVE ACTION 176–92 (1965). WEST'S FEDERAL DIGEST for 1940–60 contains descriptions of scores of old age insurance and disability insurance cases decided before the alleged "demise of the right-privilege distinction," 39–61. STONE'S THE DISABLED STATE 72–76 (*supra* note 2) provides a discussion of War Risk Insurance. For an early view of court review of old age insurance, see Wollenberg, *Vested Rights in Social Security Benefits*, 37 OR. L. REV. 299 (1958).

8. Quoted in M. DERTHICK, POLICYMAKING FOR SOCIAL SECURITY (1979).

9. See, for example, the following cases: Walker v. Altmeyer, 137 F.2d 531 (2nd Cir., 1943); O'Leary v. Social Security Board, 153 F.2d 704 (3rd Cir., 1946); U.S. v. LaLone, 152 F.2d 43 (9th Cir., 1945); Social Security Board v. Warren, 142 F.2d 974 (8th Cir., 1944); and Schroeder v. Hobby 222 F.2d 713 (10th Cir., 1955). It should be noted that the client-serving ethos of the Social Security Board helps explain why so few of its decisions were overturned. In close cases, the Board usually sided with alleged beneficiaries.

10. Lietz v. Flemming 264 F.2d 311 (1959), emphasis added.

11. One famous Social Security case, Flemming v. Nestor, 363 U.S. 603 (1960), is frequently cited as evidence of the vitality of the right-privilege distinction. The issue in this case, though, was not whether Nestor had been deprived of a benefit conferred by statute, but whether Congress could by statute deny him a benefit which he claimed he had earned by contributing payroll taxes to the Social Security trust fund. Ironically, if Nestor and the liberal dissenters on the Court had prevailed in their argument that benefits should be based on contribution, then the redistributive aspects of Social Security would have been threatened.

12. The House Report language is quoted in Stone, *supra* note 2, at 85. See p. 153 for a discussion of congressional reaction to court decisions. Jerry Mashaw's discussion of the conflicting demands placed on the disability insurance program helps explain why litigation has been so prevalent in it. *See* BUREAUCRATIC JUSTICE: MANAGING SOCIAL SECURITY DISABILITY CLAIMS chs. 2 and 3 (1983).

13. This was not the first time Congress had passed legislation to reduce litigation over veterans' benefits. After the Civil War, Congress passed a law limiting attorneys' fees to $10 per case. Despite the fact that the VA distributes billions of dollars in benefits annually, this arrangement generated little criticism until the 1970s. Ironically, the veterans' cases the courts eventually chose to hear were not those relating to particular individuals denied benefits, but rather were challenges to general policies established by the VA. This is but one indication that the courts were more interested in broad policy issues than in protecting the statutory rights of isolated individuals mistreated by lower level bureaucrats. See Merged Area X (Ed) v. Cleland 604 F.2nd 1075 (1979); Evergreen State College v. Cleland 621 F.2d 1002 (1980); Wayne State University v. Cleland 590 F.2nd 627 (1978); Comment, *Congressional Preclusion of Judicial Review of Federal Benefit Disbursement: Reasserting the Separation of Powers,* 97 HARV L. REV. 778 (1984); and MASHAW, DUE PROCESS IN THE ADMINISTRATIVE STATE 267 (1985). As noted above, these statutory limits on judicial review and attorneys fees were finally lifted in 1988.

14. Bennett v. Butz 386 F.Supp. 1059 (D. Minn., 1974). In fact, no one in Congress (or elsewhere) had any idea what constituted an "effective outreach effort." Congress eventually removed this provision from the Act.

15. Legal scholars have long noted that these canons not only are too general to produce answers in most cases, but that some canons are in conflict with others. The classic statement to this effect is Llewellyn, *Remarks on the Theory of Appellate Decision and the Rules or Canons About How Statutes Are To Be Construed,* 3 VAND. L. REV. 395 (1950). Felix Frankfurter noted, "Difficulties emerge when canons compete in soliciting judgement, because they conflict rather than converge" in *Some Reflections on the Reading of Statutes,* 47 COLUM. L. REV. 527 (1947).

16. House Report 95–464, p. 19. See also the statement of Rep. Thomas Foley, the floor manager of the bill, 123 CONGRESSIONAL RECORD 29568 (September 16, 1977), which provides a more detailed explanation of the link between statutory detail and reduced judicial intervention.

17. I have borrowed the term "gatekeeper" from DEBORAH STONE. Her book on disability insurance, THE DISABLED STATE, *supra* note 2, provides the best description of this sort of high-discretion entitlement program.

18. Use of legislative histories has increased rapidly in recent years. See Carro and Brann, *The U.S. Supreme Court and the Use of Legislative History: A Statistical Analysis,* 22 JURIMETRICS J. 294 (1982); and Wald, *Some Observations on the Use of Legislative History in the 1981 Supreme Court Term,* 68 IOWA L. REV. 195 (1983).

R. DICKENSON'S INTERPRETATION AND APPLICATION OF STATUTES (1975) contains an extensive review of legal doctrine on the use of legislative histories. He claims, "The courts' current widespread use of federal legislative material is professionally shocking" (p. 163). In recent years Justice Scalia has taken up this theme, arguing that "routine deference to the details of committee reports . . . [is] converting a system of judicial construction into a system of committee-staff prescription." Hirschey v. Federal Energy Regulatory Commission 777 F.2d 1 at 7–8 (D.C. Cir., 1985). Scalia has also complained that judges will "pick the sections that they like. They'll leave out the section they don't like." Quoted in JUDGES AND LEGISLATORS: TOWARD INSTITUTIONAL COMITY 172 (R. Katzmann, ed. 1988).

19. Quoted in Wald, *ibid.* Judge Wald's article shows that even during one term of one court, judges' use of legislative history was highly selective.

20. According to the Congressional Budget Act of 1974, entitlement authority is

> legislation that requires the payment of benefits . . . to any person or unit of government that meets the eligibility requirements established by such law. Authorizations for entitlement constitute a binding obligation on the part of the Federal Government, and eligible recipients have legal recourse if the obligation is not fulfilled.

Quoted in Weaver, *Controlling Entitlements,* in THE NEW DIRECTION IN AMERICAN POLITICS 308 J. Chubb & P. Peterson eds. 1985). The significance of this meaning of "entitlements" for congressional politics is best described in SCHICK, CONGRESS AND MONEY: BUDGETING, SPENDING, AND TAXING (1980) and A. WILDAVSKY, THE POLITICS OF THE BUDGETARY PROCESS (1984, 4th ed.).

21. Reich, *Individual Rights, supra* note 4, at 1256. Consider also the following statement of Justice Marshall in his dissenting opinion in Board of Regents v. Roth, 408 U.S. 564 (1972):

> In my view, every citizen who applies for a government job is entitled to it unless the government can establish some reason for denying the employment. This is the 'property' right that I believe is protected by the Fourteenth Amendment and that cannot be denied without due process of law. And it is also liberty—liberty to work—which is the 'very essence of the personal freedom and opportunity' secured by the Fourteenth Amendment.

This statement is made all the more striking by the fact that the case involved a university's failure to renew the contract of a non-tenured faculty member.

22. Senate Report #91-1431 (1970), 357.

23. Arnett v. Kennedy, 416 U.S. 134 (1974) at 154. The significance of Rehnquist's opinion is discussed in Van Alstyne, *Cracks in the 'New Property,' supra* note 4, at 460–66.

24. Atkins v. Parker, 86 L.Ed.2 81 at 104.

25. 397 U.S. 254 (1970). The Foley amendment was enacted in 1977 and is contained in sections 11(e)(4) and (10) of the Act.

26. At 262 n.8 and 265.

27. House Report #95–464 (1977), p. 282.

28. Smolla, *The Reemergence of the Right-Privilege Distinction, supra* note 4, at 90–94. This narrow view of entitlements rather than the "right-privilege distinction" is essentially the position adopted by the courts before the mid-1960s. The courts looked at statutes to see if administrators had failed to deliver benefits clearly promised by statute—nothing more and nothing less. The legal attack on the "right-privilege distinction" was really an attack on this limited definition of entitlements.

29. Banks v. Block, 700 F.2d 292 (6th Cir., 1983). The Supreme Court denied cert.

30. *The New Property, supra* note 4, cited in Goldberg at 1225–56.

31. *The Right to Welfare*, in THE RIGHTS OF AMERICANS, *supra* note 2, at 65. In his many writings, Sparer candidly explained that the goal of this litigation was not to provide procedural safeguards or to give effect to congressional mandates, but to remake a welfare system he and his colleagues considered woefully inadequate.

32. *The OEO Lawyers Fail to Constitutionalize a Right to Welfare: A Study in the Uses and Limits of the Judicial Process*, 58 MINN. L. REV. 211 (1973). The two major constitutional victories of the OEO lawyers were *Goldberg v. Kelly* and *Shapiro v. Thompson*, 394 U.S. 618 (1969), which declared state residency requirements unconstitutional. The Krislov and Sparer articles both describe the broader conception of entitlements advocated by Legal Services attorneys and often accepted by the courts.

33. *Six Welfare Questions Still Searching for Answers*, THE BROOKINGS REV. 13–14 (Fall 1984). Although Aaron considers this view naive, he is hardly an enemy of welfare reform. He served as Assistant Secretary of HEW in the Carter administration and played a major role in the development of the Carter welfare reform proposal.

34. This is not to say that "welfare rights" advocates threw their support behind Nixon's Family Assistance Plan (FAP). Most wanted to "Zap FAP," primarily because its initial support levels were too low. FAP also included a mild penalty for those who refused to accept work; however, as several commentators have pointed

out, this was primarily a sop thrown to discontented conservatives, and would most likely have been ineffective in practice. D. MOYNIHAN, THE POLITICS OF A GUARANTEED INCOME 141–42, 220 (1973). VINCENT & V. BURKE, NIXON'S GOOD DEED: WELFARE REFORM 84–85 (1974); K. BOWLER, THE NIXON GUARANTEED INCOME PROPOSAL 29 (1974).

35. Richard Nathan points this out in *Food Stamps and Welfare Reform*, POL'Y ANALYSIS (Winter, 1976).

36. This is explained in detail in Stone, *supra* note 2, at chs. 1 and 2.

37. *The Political Feasibility of Income by Right*, PUB. POL'Y 321–26 (Spring 1970).

38. H. MCCLOSKY & J. ZALLER, THE AMERICAN ETHOS: PUBLIC ATTITUDES TOWARD CAPITALISM AND DEMOCRACY 84, 109, 226 (1984). See also S. VERBA & G. ORREN, EQUALITY IN AMERICA: THE VIEW FROM THE TOP (1985).

39. It is instructive to note that one of the general principles guiding the Carter Administration's welfare reform effort was "No non-working family will have higher income than a comparable working family." Quoted in L. LYNN & D. WHITMAN, THE PRESIDENT AS POLICYMAKER: JIMMY CARTER AND WELFARE REFORM 106 (1981). As Deborah Stone explains, in any system, socialist as well as capitalist, a need-based reward system is always in conflict with the predominant work-based reward system. THE DISABLED STATE, *supra* note 2, at 15–25.

40. The results of the New Jersey and Seattle-Denver studies are discussed in G. STEINER, THE FUTILITY OF FAMILY POLICY 96–111 (1981).

41. *The Political Foundations of Antipoverty Policy*, in FIGHTING POVERTY: WHAT WORKS AND WHAT DOESN'T 319 (S. Danziger and D. Weinberg eds. 1986).

42. A large literature describes these changes in Congress. Most helpful are the following: CONGRESS RECONSIDERED, 3rd ed. (L. Dodd and B. Oppenheimer eds. 1985); THE NEW CONGRESS (T. Mann and N. Ornstein eds. 1981); J. SUNDQUIST, THE DECLINE AND RESURGENCE OF CONGRESS (1981); A. MAASS, CONGRESS AND THE COMMON GOOD (1983); G. ORFIELD, CONGRESSIONAL POWER: CONGRESS AND SOCIAL CHANGE (1974); and M. FOLEY, THE NEW SENATE (1980).

43. The most thorough discussion of the politics of the congressional budget process during these years is ALLEN SCHICK'S CONGRESS AND MONEY: BUDGETING, SPENDING, AND TAXING (1980). Kent Weaver provides a concise and perceptive analysis of the entitlement politics of the 1980s in *Controlling Entitlements, supra* note 20.

44. For a more detailed description of court action in terms of legislative-executive conflict, see Melnick, *The Politics of Partnership*, 45 PUB. ADM. REV. 653 (1985).

45. For a review of congressional action on Legal Services, see George,

Development of the Legal Services Corporation, 61 CORN. L. REV. 681 (1976). Jurisdictional and attorneys' fees issues are discussed in J. Malmberg, *Note: 1976 Developments in Welfare Law—AFDC, ibid.* Much of this legislation, it should be noted, originated not in committees with jurisdiction over entitlement programs, but in the House and Senate Judiciary Committees. These committees tended to be more hospitable to judicial activism than other committees during the 1970s. Surprisingly little has been written about how the Judiciary Committees have encouraged judicial resolution of policy disputes.

46. On the use of *post hoc* legislative histories, see R. KATZMANN, INSTITUTIONAL DISABILITY: THE SAGE OF TRANSPORTATION POLICY FOR THE DISABLED 52–54, 75–76 (1986). On the manipulation of legislative histories by congressional staffers, see B. ACKERMAN and W. HASSLER, CLEAN COAL/DIRTY AIR (1981), M. MALBIN, UNELECTED REPRESENTATIVES (1979), and R. S. MELNICK, REGULATION AND THE COURTS: THE CASE OF THE CLEAN AIR ACT 77–78, 130–32, 252–55, 340–42, and 373–79 (1983).

47. Senate Report #74–628 (1935), pp. 4, 36; House Report #74–615 (1935), p. 24. The President's bill required that AFDC benefits be adequate to allow recipients to live "in decency and health." Several Senators complained about this provision in hearings on the bill. The bill which finally emerged from Congress required only that a participating state provide aid "as far as practicable under the conditions in such State." See M. DERTHICK, THE INFLUENCE OF FEDERAL GRANTS: PUBLIC ASSISTANCE IN MASSACHUSETTS 43ff. (1970), and Doolittle, *State-Imposed Non-financial Eligibility Conditions,* pp. 29–33. Winifred Bell, an outspoken opponent of non-financial eligibility requirements and an author cited frequently by the Supreme Court, stated in 1965, "These provisions reflect the intent of Congress to leave the control over the nature and size of the program essentially to the states." AID TO DEPENDENT CHILDREN (1965). She and other reformers tried to amend the statute the old-fashioned way—by having Congress pass a law. The states-rights orientation of the 1935 Act is also emphasized by G. STEINER in SOCIAL INSECURITY: THE POLITICS OF WELFARE (1966) and THE STATE OF WELFARE (1971).

48. This is explained in detail in DERTHICK, THE INFLUENCE OF FEDERAL GRANTS.

49. The percentage of AFDC children made eligible by the death of their father dropped from 88% in 1937 to 21% in 1951 to 7.7% in 1961 and 5.5% in 1967. The number of people receiving AFDC rose from 3.5 million in 1961 to over 5 million in 1967 and nearly 8 million in 1970. STEINER, *supra* note 47, SOCIAL INSECURITY, 114 and STATE OF WELFARE, pp. 32 and 42. D. P. Moynihan described the political consequences of these changes in *The Crisis in Welfare,* first published in 1967 and reprinted in COPING: ON THE PRACTICE OF GOVERNMENT (1973).

50. Although different in many of their details, the Nixon and Carter proposals shared the following features: a nationally uniform minimum benefit level, eligibility for two-parent families, greater federal control over program administration, and reduction of the benefit reduction rate (or marginal tax rate) for earned income. The

huge literature on this phase of welfare reform includes the works by Moynihan, the Burkes, and Bowler cited *supra* note 34, Lynn and Whitman (*supra* note 40), Steiner, *The State of Welfare* (*supra* note 47) C. LEMANN, THE COLLAPSE OF WELFARE REFORM 1980), and Marmor and Rien, *Reforming the 'Welfare Mess': The Fate of the Family Assistance Plan, 1969–72*, in POLICY AND POLITICS IN AMERICA (A. Sindler ed. 1973).

51. 394 U.S. 618 (1969).

52. 397 U.S. 471 (1970) and 406 U.S. 535 (1971).

53. The hundreds of decisions summarized in WEST'S FEDERAL DIGEST are only one part of the corpus of federal AFDC jurisprudence. Many lower court opinions are never published. Most of these are summarized in the CLEARINGHOUSE REVIEW, published by Legal Services. The most useful discussions of AFDC litigation are the Doolittle and Block articles cited *supra* note 2; Lupu, *Welfare and Federalism: AFDC Eligibility Policies and the Scope of State Discretion*, 57 B.U.L. REV. 1 (1977), A. LAFRANCE, WELFARE LAW: STRUCTURES AND ENTITLEMENTS (1979); Block, *The Role of Litigation in the Development of Federal Welfare Policy*, Ph.D. diss., Politics Department, Brandeis University, 1978.

54. 392 U.S. 309 (1968).

55. This common practice and its close relation, the "suitable home provision," are described in BELL, AID TO DEPENDENT CHILDREN chs. 5–8.

56. At 324–25. The Court's strongest argument was that, by approving in 1962 the "Flemming Ruling" issued by HEW in 1960, Congress had expressed its disapproval not just of the "suitable home" provisions declared contrary to the Social Security Act by HEW, but of the similar "substitute parent" rules as well. In the 1962 legislation, though, Congress watered down the "Flemming Ruling," giving no indication that it intended to expand it even further. This is made clear in STEINER, SOCIAL INSECURITY, *supra* note 47, 99–101 and Lupu, *supra* note 53, at 3–11. No advocates of welfare reform claimed to have won in 1962.

57. August 18, 1967, p. A20.

58. *The Crisis in Welfare, supra* note 49, at 134.

59. CONGRESSIONAL RECORD, December 14, 1967, p. 36785.

60. 404 U.S. 282 (1971).

61. It is important to note that the Court ordered the state to expand its program, and did not (as one might expect) order the federal government to withhold funding from the offending state. This was a most important choice of remedy, but one which was never justified by the Supreme Court or any other federal court.

62. 406 U.S. 598 (1972) at 601, 604.

63. Wyman v. James, 400 U.S. 309 (1971) and New York State Department of

Social Welfare v. Dublino, 413 U.S. 405 (1973). These anomalies are discussed in Doolittle, *supra* note 2, at 15–20. He suggests that when the Court decided these cases, non-welfare issues—specifically, search and seizure as well as preemption—were foremost in the mind of the majority. In Batterton v. Francis, 432 U.S. 416 (1977); Bacon v. Blum, 457 U.S. 132 (1982); and Heckler v. Turner, 84 L Ed. 138 (1985); the Supreme Court showed greater willingness to defer to federal (but not state) administrators.

64. Lewis v. Martin, 397 U.S. 552 (1970). The Court required the state to prove that the income of the "man assuming the role of spouse" was "actually available" for use by the welfare family. Since this is nearly impossible to prove in practice, the ruling had the effect described in the text.

65. Van Lare v. Hurley, 421 U.S. 338 (1975) at 348. Judge Oakes, who dissented in the Second Circuit and whose views were vindicated by the Supreme Court, argued that *King* prohibited AFDC from being used as "a lever in the hands of state legislators to compel compliance with local standards of moral conduct." Federal statutes and case law "forbid the State from enforcing its predilections *which are irrelevant to the welfare of the child* by depriving the eligible child of its need." Taylor v. Lavine, 497 F.2d 1208 (1974) at 1218 and 1221 (emphasis in the original).

66. Lupu, *Welfare and Federalism*, *supra* note 53, at 20. In fact the lower courts moved to "constitutionalize a right to welfare" before the Warren Court did. Despite the novelty of Goldberg v. Kelly and Shapiro v. Thompson, almost all the lower courts which decided the case sided with recipients rather than state governments. For details, see Block, *The Role of Litigation*, *supra* note 53, at 56–66, 90–97.

67. Saddler v. Winstead, 332 F. Supp. 139 (1971).

68. Doe v. Shapiro, 302 F. Supp. 761 (D. Conn, 1969); Doe v. Harder, 310 F. Supp. 302 (D. Conn, 1970); Meyer v. Juras, 327 F. Supp. 759 (D. Ore., 1971); Taylor v. Martin, 330 F. Supp. 85 (N.D. Cal., 1971); Doe v. Schmidt, 330 F. Supp. 159 (E.D. Wisc., 1971); Doe v. Swank, 332 F. Supp. 61 (N.D. Ill., 1971); and others.

69. Anderson v. Burson, 300 F. Supp. 401 (N.D. Ga., 1968); Woolfork v. Brown, 325 F. Supp. 1162 (E.D. Va., 1971), 358 F. Supp. 524 (1973), and 393 F. Supp. 263 (1975); Bueno v. Juras, 349 F. Supp. 1255 (D. Ore., 1972); Davis v. Reagan, 485 F. Supp. 1255 (S.D. Iowa, 1980); and McLean v. Mathews, 458 F. Supp. 285 (1977).

70. Doe v. Hursh, 337 F. Supp. 614 (D. Minn., 1970); Linnane v. Betit, 331 F. Supp. 868 (D. Vt., 1971); and Arizona v. HEW, 449 F.2d 456 (9th Cir., 1971).

71. J.A. V. Ritti, 377 F. Supp. 1046 (D.N.J., 1974); Cooper v. Laupheim, 316 F. Supp. 264 (E.D. Pa., 1970); Bradford v. Juras, 331 F. Supp. 167 (D. Ore., 1971); and NWRO v. Weinberger, 377 F. Supp. 861 (D.D.C., 1974).

72. Francis v. Davidson, 340 F. Supp. 351 (D. Mar., 1972). This decision was later modified by the Supreme Court in Batterton v. Francis.

73. Rosen v. Hursh, 464 F.2d 731 (8th Cir., 1972).

74. There has been an enormous amount of litigation on the issue of the income and resources a state can consider "available" to the AFDC family. See the cases cited in LAFRANCE, WELFARE LAW, *supra* note 53, at 326–34; T. JOE & C. ROGERS, BY THE FEW, FOR THE FEW: THE REAGAN WELFARE LEGACY 69–73 (1985); and Block, *The Role of Litigation, supra* note 53, at 81–90, 204–9.

75. NWRO v. Mathews, 553 F.2d 637 (D.C.C., 1976) and Maryland v. Mathews 415 F. Supp. 1206 (D.D.C., 1976). There has also been an enormous amount of litigation on how the states define their "standard of need" and calculate benefit levels. This highly controversial litigation proved a major disappointment for Legal Services attorneys. The major Supreme Court case was Rosado v. Wyman 397 U.S. 397 (1970). The complex issues addressed by the lower courts and the political context of this subset of AFDC cases are discussed in LAFANCE, WELFARE LAW, *supra* note 53, at 351–70 and Rabin, *Implementation of Cost of Living Adjustments for AFDC Recipients: A Case in Welfare Administration,* 118 U. PA. L. REV. 1143.

76. Burns v. Alcala, 420 U.S. 575 (1975). The lower court decisions are cited in Parks v. Hardin, 504 F.2d 861 (5th Cir., 1974) at 863 n. 4.

77. Carver v. Hooker, 501 F.2d 1244 (1st Cir., 1974) at 1247.

78. Parks v. Hardin, 504 F.2d 861 (5th Cir., 1974) at 872.

79. Wilson v. Weaver, 449 F.2d 155 (7th Cir., 1974) at 158.

80. Burns v. Alcala, *supra* note 76, 88.

81. Gurley v. Wohlgemuth, 421 F. Supp. 1337 at 1347 (1976).

82. Simpson v. Miller, 535 F. Supp. 1041 at 1048, 1050 (1982).

83. Miller v. Youakim, 440 U.S. 125 at 133, 138–39 (1979).

84. The Supreme Court stressed the theme of individual treatment of recipients in Shea v. Vialpando, 416 U.S. 251 (1974). In this case the Court struck down state ceilings on work expense deductions for AFDC, insisting that these deductions be tailored to individual circumstances. The *Shea* decision was eventually overturned by Congress, but has been used by the lower courts to invalidate a large number of state rules attributing various types of income and resources to welfare recipients.

85. The lengthy battle between Ronald Reagan and the courts is documented in Doolittle and Wiseman, *The California Welfare Reform Act: A Litigational History,* Working Paper #71, Institute of Business and Economic Research, University of California, Berkeley (August, 1976).

86. The passage of the budget reconciliation bill in 1981 represented a clear and dramatic attack on the authority of all House committees. But the control of the Ways and Means Committee over welfare policy had been challenged several times in the preceding years. In 1979 the Republican substitute for the Committee's welfare

reform proposal lost by a mere five votes, 200–205. Conservatives pushing "quality control" sanctions used appropriations riders to bypass the Ways and Means Committee. Led by Minority Leader Robert Michel (R.-Ill.), "quality control" advocates consistently won on the floor. 1979 CQ ALMANAC, 242, 509.

87. Senate Report #91–1431, p. 357.

88. Senate Report #92–1605, p. 452.

89. 1970 Report, p. 364 and 1972 Report, pp. 488–90. The Committee never explained how one could distinguish "welfare reform" litigation from ordinary litigation. In 1972 Senator Cranston's amendment to remove the restrictions on Legal Services from the Committee's bill was defeated by a vote of 35–38. CONGRESSIONAL RECORD, October 5, 1972, pp. 33974–80.

90. 1970 CQ ALMANAC, p. 1041.

91. Gilbert Steiner describes the controversy over child support in THE FUTILITY OF FAMILY POLICY, *supra* note 40, at 111–28. On the Talmadge Amendment, see MEAD, BEYOND ENTITLEMENT 121–26 (1986).

92. The quotations are taken from F. Doolittle, "Ronald Reagan and Conservative Welfare Reform" (unpublished manuscript, July 1986). Doolittle's manuscript traces in detail the link between Reagan's California experience and congressional actions of the 1980s.

93. *The Social Policy of the Reagan Administration: A Review,* PUB. INTEREST (Spring 1984), 87–88.

94. The phrase comes from CONGRESSIONAL QUARTERLY WEEKLY REPORT October 1, 1988, p. 2699.

95. THE NEW CONSENSUS ON FAMILIES AND WELFARE 82 (1987).

96. In 1968 HEW Secretary Wilbur Cohen stated, "Today there is a growing recognition of the legal right to the receipt of public assistance, a legal right to insist that it be fairly designed and fairly administered—and a legal right to invoke the Constitution to assure the fairness of the system." Quoted in STEINER, THE STATE OF WELFARE, *supra* note 47, at 90. Cohen backed up his words by announcing, prior to Goldberg v. Kelly, hearing requirements even more stringent than those later required by the Supreme Court.

The Deputy General Counsel at HEW during this period described relations between the courts and HEW as cooperative rather than adversarial:

> If for any reason the federal administrators were inhibited in the development of new rules—perhaps because of the disapproving views of members of an appropriation committee—the courts could assume the lead in developing new legal requirements. Once the courts had spoken, the federal administrators could then respond by framing a rule embodying the judicially-enunciated principle, perhaps even embellishing it a bit. . . . Development of the law could thus proceed in an ever-ascending spiral with

no single participant in the process having the capacity to block progressive development.

Barrett, *The New Role of the Courts in Developing Public Welfare Law*, 1970 DUKE L. J. 1 at 8. Soon after the 1972 elections, the Nixon Administration mounted a successful effort to put conservatives in charge of policymaking at HEW. R. Randall, *Presidential Power versus Bureaucratic Instransigence: The Influence of the Nixon Administration on Welfare Policy* 73 AM. POL. SCI. REV. 795; and M. DERTHICK, UNCONTROLLABLE SPENDING FOR SOCIAL SERVICES GRANTS (1975).

97. A COMMON LAW FOR THE AGE OF STATUTES (1982). The first phrase comes from p. 18, the last from p. 37. Calabresi frequently refers to "anachronistic" laws.

98. THE SUPREME COURT AND THE IDEA OF PROGRESS 19 (1970).

99. THE REAGAN EXPERIMENT 26 (1982). At least for AFDC, the claim that the Reagan administration has attempted to undo the New Deal is clearly wrong. Rather, the courts rejected the legacy of the New Deal, and the Reagan Administration partially revived it.

100. THE POLITICAL HAND: POLICY IMPLEMENTATION AND YOUTH EMPLOYMENT PROGRAMS 136–37 (1985).

101. *Six Welfare Questions, supra* note 33, at 14. Policy analysts' growing disenchantment with "noncategorical" assistance is described in LYNN & WHITMAN, THE PRESIDENT AS POLICYMAKER, *supra* note 39. See also Friedman and Hausman, *Welfare in Retreat: A Dilemma for the Federal System*," 25 PUB. POL'Y 24 (Winter 1977).

102. THE NEW CONSENSUS ON FAMILIES AND WELFARE, *supra* note 94; Wilson, *The Rediscovery of Character: Private Virtue and Public Policy*, PUB. INTEREST (Fall 1985); M. Kaus, *The Work Ethic State*, NEW REPUBLIC, July 7, 1986; and Ellwood and Summers, *Poverty in America: Is Welfare the Answer or the Problem?*, in FIGHTING POVERTY, *supra* note 41.

Work, Government, and the Constitution: Determining the Proper Allocation of Rights and Powers

THOMAS R. HAGGARD

As hunter/gatherers, homesteaders, artisans, manufacturers, mechanics, entrepreneurs. independent contractors, employees, or managers of capital resources,[1] we all work in one fashion or another. Work is the predicate of all our other activities. It makes possible the exercise of the cherished freedoms of religion, press, speech, travel, association, and privacy. Indeed, since it is essential to our survival, work may be the most fundamental of all human activities.

The importance of work in the hierarchy of human activities is not in dispute. What is in dispute is the proper role of government in regulating this activity.[2] There are two radically divergent views of government's proper role here.

One view is that work, because of its fundamental nature, is also a "natural" or "inalienable" right, second only to the right to life and equally inviolate. Thus, unless we earn our subsistence by violating the rights of others through force or fraud, the sovereign should leave us alone, to work or contract for work as our desires and abilities permit. By thus protecting the *right* of the individual to be productive, the law also incidentally promotes the wealth and well-being of society as well.

The other view begins with the proposition that the *power* of the sovereign necessarily extends to all great matters of concern to the individual and the society in which he lives. Given its importance, the activity of work therefore simply cannot be left to the vagaries of the marketplace and private decision-making. Rather, government regulation is necessary to ensure "economic justice" and to serve the "public interest."

Under the influence of these two competing viewpoints, the line between the individual's *right* to work and society's *power* to regulate the activity has shifted over the years. Indeed, the matter has been in constant dispute, from the Founding of the Republic to the present.

The immediate arbiter of this dispute has been the United States

241

Supreme Court, with the Constitution serving as the Court's benchmark for judgment. The Court and Constitution, however, are the ultimate authority only in a sense. On work– and employment-related issues, the operative words of the Constitution are enormously open-textured. Whether the Court is operating in a strict or liberal constructionist mode, the application of these words to specific facts and situations is by no means a mechanical process.

Moreover, the members of a constantly-changing Court do not exist in an intellectual vacuum. The ideas, experiences, perceptions, and aspirations of the society around them inevitably have an influence on the judges and their decisions. Indeed, no matter how historically accurate or philosophically sound a particular approach may be, the record shows that the Supreme Court will not hold out long against a "national consensus" to the contrary[3]—even if it takes a Civil War to accomplish it.

In a real sense, that intangible anthropomorphic entity we call "society," its values, and its perception of reality at any given point in time are thus the ultimate arbiters of this constitutional dispute. However one yearns for a more abstract and principled approach to constitutional litigation, one must take into account the fact that the application of law to facts is an enormously subjective endeavor and that few decision-makers can, or should, ignore totally the immediate practical consequences of their theories. Rightly or wrongly, this has had an enormous influence on constitutional litigation over work-related legislation.

This paper will therefore focus not only on finely-spun legal and constitutional theories but also (albeit in abbreviated fashion) on underlying social concerns and values.

I. The First Manifestations of the Debate: the Criminal Conspiracy Doctrine and Its place in Post-Revolutionary American Jurisprudence[4]

Anglo-American political sovereigns, be they King or Congress, have long had a penchant for regulating the work relationship—to the advantage of whoever was in favor.

When the Black Death of 1348 reduced the number of available workers and correspondingly increased the demanded wage rate, Parliament responded with the command that workers "shall be bound to serve him that doth require him" and that "the old wages, and no more, shall be given."[5]

The thirteenth, fourteenth, and fifteenth centuries saw numerous other statutes which fixed wages, bound servants to serve their masters, created closed-shop guilds, regulated apprenticeships, and prohibited workmen's associations.[6] In particular, The Bill of Conspiracies of Victualers and Craftsmen of 1548[7] provided punishment for workers who "do conspire, covenant or promise together" not to work "but at a certain price or rate," or to "do but a certain work in a day," or "not work but at certain hours and times."

In addition to the express criminal conspiracy statutes, one can find in the dicta of 17th Century English decisions the suggestion that a conspiracy to commit an act not otherwise illegal might also be illegal under the common law.[8] However, the common law criminal conspiracy doctrine came into being primarily as a result of an offhand comment by Hawkins in his *Pleas of the Crown,* published in 1716, where he stated: "There can be no doubt, but that all confederacies whatsoever, wrongfully to prejudice a third person, are highly criminal at common law."[9]

Subsequently, in *The King v. Journeymen-Taylors of Cambridge,*[10] the defendants were charged with a common law conspiracy to raise their wages. In the course of its opinion, the court stated that "a conspiracy of any kind is illegal, although the matter about which they conspired might have been lawful for them, or any of them, to do, if they had not conspired to do it, as appears in the case of *The Tubwomen v. The Brewers of London.*"[11] The *Journeymen-Taylors* case, and others like it, thus set the stage for the first American labor law case.

Following the American revolution, Pennsylvania, like most other states, adopted the English common law.[12] As defined by English courts, the common law was, however, merely the point of departure for American jurisprudence. By necessity and design, it was to evolve into a common law that reflected some uniquely American concepts of liberty, justice, and social order. But the evolution was not without its points of conflict, and the controversy over the criminal conspiracy doctrine is an early instance of this.

In the early 1800s, journeymen bootmakers (or "cordwainers") in Philadelphia organized themselves into a society. Members of the society, with some degree of success, imposed a "closed shop" on the industry by refusing to work or live in the same boarding house with journeymen who did not join the society and thereby promise to be bound by the society's work rules. In 1805, the society called a "turn out" or strike to force the masters to raise the piecework rate on work done for export to the South. The masters, faced with stiff English competition in this market, refused. After several weeks, eight leaders of the strike were arrested and indicted under the common law criminal conspiracy doctrine. The case is known as *Commonwealth v. Pullis.*[13]

The strike itself was not particularly significant, and the case was tried in a minor Philadelphia municipal court. Yet the legal issues were novel and the case soon became a *cause célèbre,* drawing the attention of the two major political parties, with the prosecution and defense being conducted by leading members of the Pennsylvania and Delaware bars. Although the narrow legal question was over the meaning of the English criminal conspiracy doctrine and whether the English precedent on this issue survived the American Revolution, the broader and truer issue was one of public policy and the proper functions of law in a free society.

Supporting the prosecution were the Hamiltonian Federalists, who saw the strike as a threat to manufacturing interests and thus inimical to the good of the community. The prosecution summarized its case in these terms.

> It is not intended to take away the right of any man to put his own price upon his own labour; they may ask what they please, individually. But when they associate, combine, and conspire, to prevent others from taking what they deem a sufficient compensation for their labour . . . and where they undertake to regulate the trade of the city, they undertake to regulate what interferes with your rights and mine . . . This is a large, increasing, manufacturing city. Those best acquainted with our situation, believe that manufactures will, bye and by, become one of its chief means of support. . . . It is then proper to support this manufacture. Will you permit men to destroy it, who have no permanent stake in the city; men who can pack up their all in a knapsack, or carry them in their pockets to New-York or Baltimore?. . .
>
> If the court and jury shall decide, that journeymen may associate together, and determine that none shall work under certain prices; then, when orders arrive for considerable quantities of any article, the association may determine to raise the wages, and reduce the contractors to diminish their profit; to sustain a loss, or to abandon the execution of the orders. . . .
>
> It must be plain to you, that the master employers have no particular interest in the thing . . . if they pay higher wages, you must pay higher for the articles. They, in truth, are protecting the community.[14]

In somewhat more contemporary jurisprudential terms, the prosecution gave broad meaning to the concepts of "coercion" and "jural harm" (an injury that the law can properly remedy and prevent). Journeymen who were willing to work at less than union wages were "coerced" into not doing so by the society's economic and social boycott. The employers for whom they worked were similarly "coerced" by the journeymen's refusal to work in a shop that employed a nonmember. But, more importantly, the community as a whole was being "coerced" and injured by the defendants' conduct. And for such "coercion," the law should provide redress by outlawing the activity. The prosecution was thus essentially utilitarian in its approach to labor associations. Since they did not serve to maximize utility either individually or socially, no one had a "right" to form them and the proper function of law was to prohibit them.

On the other hand, vigorously supporting the defense were the Jeffersonian Republicans, who saw the criminal conspiracy doctrine as a threat to the ideals of the Revolution and inconsistent with constitutional liberty. Nelles summarized it in these terms:

> That the prosecution was subversive of American freedom was the main contention of the defense. Even if it were conceded (as of course it was not) that at English common law the cordwainers' society would be a criminal conspiracy, that common law was not American common law. In support of this, counsel argued, relying upon Tucker's Blackstone, that if a doctrine of labor conspiracy had been used in this country during the colonial period—which it had not—it could not survive as law in one of the United States, even under a constitution or statute which continued "the common law" in general terms. For it would be in derogation of the natural and unalienable rights of man, and inconsistent with democracy.[15]

The basic premise of the defense was a notion of self-ownership. Speaking of the journeymen, counsel said:

> They conceived that every man being the sole owner, and master of his own goods and labour, had a right to affix the price of them; leaving to those who were to employ or purchase, the right to accept or reject as they might think proper. These appeared to them, and doubtless they will to you, to be principles founded on the plainest grounds of equity and justice.[16]

More specifically, the defense contended that "[o]ur constitution says that 'the citizens have a right in a peaceable manner to assemble together for 'the common good.' "[17] Thus, the defense stated:

> There is no crime in my refusing to work with a man who is not of the same association with myself. Supposing the ground of my refusal to be ever so unreasonble [sic] or ridiculous . . . to be in reality, mere caprice or whim . . . Still it is no crime . . . The motive for my refusal may be liberal, but it furnishes no legal foundation for a prosecution: I cannot be indicted for it. Every man may chuse his company, or refuse to associate with any one whose company may be disagreeable to him, without being obliged to give a reason for it: and without violating the laws of the land.[18]

The defense conceded that the society's actions caused economic harm or inconvenience to masters and non-member journeymen alike, but dismissed this as mere "damnum absque injuria,"[19] which refers to a "loss, hurt, or harm without injury in the legal sense, that is, without such breach of duty as is redressable by an action."[20] On the other hand, the defense admitted that "if any journeyman who chose to work at the rates or prices offered by the employers, contrary to the wish of other journeymen, were threatened by them, or any of them, with injury to his person or property, he has a complete and ample remedy provided for him by law without resorting to the measures which have been adopted."[21] Finally, the defense simply rejected the central thesis of the criminal conspiracy doctrine, asserting that "a purpose innocent or lawful in one man, cannot be otherwise in a society or body of men."[22]

The jurisprudential posture of the defense can be summarized as follows. It obviously proceeds from the Lockean notion of the natural law right of self-ownership. From it was derived the right of the journeyman defendants to conditionally withhold their labor and to refuse to work or associate with journeymen who were not of the society. While this may have caused economic injury to nonmembers and employers alike, especially because it was done in concert, this represented an exercise rather than the violation of anyone's rights, and the activity was thus beyond the reach of government prohibition.

The arguments in *Commonwealth v. Pullis* provide an unusually clear example of two competing philosophies—utilitarianism and natural rights. In one guise or another, these two philosophies underlie a good bit of the debate over the constitutionality of work-related legislation.

After a three-day trial, the jury in *Commonwealth v. Pullis* found the defendants guilty of "a combination to raise their wages"[23]—thus establishing in this country the existence of a government *power* to prohibit a certain kind of work-related activity, claims of inalienable *rights* to the contrary notwithstanding.

The Jeffersonian position, however, was to find ultimate vindication in the 1842 case of *Commonwealth v. Hunt.*[24] This case was decided by the prestigious Massachusetts Supreme Court in an opinion written by the highly respected Chief Justice Shaw, and is thus frequently regarded as "a landmark of American law."[25] The defendants had been indicted for criminally conspiring to refuse to work for any employer who hired journeymen who were not members of the society, and for attempting to impoverish the bootmaker with whom they would not work and his would-be employers.

The court began by narrowly defining a criminal conspiracy as "a combination of two or more persons, by some concerted action, to accomplish some criminal or unlawful purpose, or to accomplish some purpose, not in itself criminal or unlawful, by criminal or unlawful means."[26] The court then found that the purpose here, inducing persons to join the society, was not itself unlawful. Turning to the means used, the court observed that "every free man, whether skilled laborer, mechanic, farmer or domestic servant, may work or not work, or work or refuse to work with any company or individual, at his own option, except so far as he is bound by contract."[27] Thus, "in this state of things, we cannot perceive that it is criminal for men to agree together to exercise their own acknowledged rights, in such a manner as best to subserve their own interests."[28] The court also noted that in a competitive economy many concerted acts have a tendency to reduce the income or profits of another, but that this was not illegal as long as no force or fraud was involved.[29]

Commonwealth v. Hunt has been called "the Magna Charta of American trade unionism,"[30] and, to the extent it freed workers from the constraints of the criminal conspiracy doctrine, there may be some truth to that. But the case is significant for more than its narrow holding. The underlying thesis was that refusing to work or contract for work except upon terms satisfactory to both parties represents an exercise of rights rather than a violation of rights, regardless of the consequent economic disadvantage to other workers, the employer, or the community at large.

While labor unionists thus liked the holding of the case, they soon discovered that the underlying thesis had disturbing implications — particularly when translated into constitutional doctrine. For if a union member can refuse to work unless the employer also hires only other union members, then by the same token an employer should have the equivalent liberty to refuse to hire workers unless they agree not to join the union. And, indeed, such a liberty was soon to be recognized.

II. Compulsory Labor: The Constitutional Status of Slavery

While white skilled craftsmen in the northeastern states began to enjoy some degree of liberty to associate and refuse to work except on terms mutually agreeable, black agricultural workers in the South suffered from an almost total deprivation of liberty in this regard. This was because of the state-sanctioned institution of slavery.

As originally written, the United States Constitution did not outlaw slavery. To the contrary, it implicitly and even explicitly allowed it. Section 2, Article IV provided that "No Person held to Service or Labour in one State, under the Laws thereof, escaping into another, shall, in Consequence of any Law or Regulation therein, be discharged from such Service or Labour, but shall be delivered up on Claim of the Party to whom such Service or Labour may be due." In other words, fugitive slaves must be sent back to their masters.

On the other hand, that same section of the Constitution said that "the Citizens of each State shall be entitled to all Privileges and Immunities of Citizens of the Several States." Some read that as saying that if an individual enjoyed "free man" status under New York law, then he or she also enjoyed that status in South Carolina, regardless of local law. That seemed to provide an enormous opportunity for local law to control the emancipation of slaves.

Thus, while slavery could not be attacked directly under the Constitution, it could be attacked indirectly by exploiting the conflict between those two provisions. For the most part, the litigation was enormously technical, involving complex questions of state comity and conflict of law.[31] The status of fugitive slaves was the issue most commonly litigated. And in this regard, *Dred Scott v. Sandford*[32] was the most famous case.[33] The case itself is a monument to the technical complexity of the fugitive slave issue. The case was argued twice before the Court, and the decision consists of nine separate opinions, covering 248 pages in the United States Reports. The facts and results have been summarized as follows:

> Scott, held as a slave by Sandford in Missouri, brought a diversity suit in federal court claiming that he was entitled freedom because a previous owner had taken him to Illinois, a free state, and from there to parts of the Louisiana Territory made free under the Missouri Compromise. Chief Justice Taney's opinion announcing the Supreme Court's decision held that no federal jurisdiction existed to hear Scott's claim since no Negro, free or slave, could be a "citizen" of a state or of the United States in the required constitutional sense, and thus no Negro could take advantage of the federal courts' "diversity of citizenship" jurisdiction. . . . After finding no federal jurisdiction, the Court nonetheless proceeded gratuitously and irresponsibly to reach the merits, concluding that the Missouri Compromise was unconstitutional.[34]

The *Dred Scott* decision is a good example of how the Supreme Court, when it wants to, can avoid fundamental questions of human rights by deciding a case on technical grounds. The specific issues involved in that case were, of course, mooted by the Union Army and the Thirteenth, Fourteenth, and Fifteenth Amendments to the Constitution. However, as we shall see, the philosophical underpinnings of the antislavery movement were later to play an important role in defining the additional rights of free persons, white or black, to pursue lawful callings without the coercive interference of the state.

III. The Establishment of a Constitutional Liberty to Contract for Work: The Economic Due Process Era

Most of the major battles over the constitutionality of work-related legislation were fought over a period of roughly 75 years, from the close of the Civil War to the early 1930s. This is a much–misunderstood era of American constitutional law. Liberal commentators and justices have promoted the notion that during the heyday of economic due process, the Supreme Court was manned by conservative ideologues, apologists for powerful business and industrial interests, who acted as a "super–legislature" and consistently struck down all attempts at economic regulation merely because they disagreed with the idea of it and without any significant constitutional justification for doing so.[35]

The conventional view, by and large, is wrong. True, the justices were generally "conservative," as was much of the country.[36] And although many of them had a business-law background and orientation, one is hard–pressed to find any tangible evidence of actual bias. During this era, the Court upheld more legislation than it struck down.[37] Indeed, throughout the period in question, the Court seemed to vacillate enormously on questions of economic regulation. And while the Court often appeared to be impinging on the prerogative of the legislature to find facts and make policy judgments based on those facts, this could also be viewed more favorably in terms of a proper refusal to defer to the legislature when important constitutional interests are at issue. The Court *did* have a theory of constitutional law. One may disagree with it, and certain members of that court did at the time, but it was hardly irrational or aberrational.

Before looking at the specific cases and constitutional theories involved, it will be helpful first to identify some of the economic, political, ideological, philosophical, and social influences that were at work and which, as we shall see, clearly manifest themselves in the Court's decisions.

The Influences

During this period of time, the Court was subjected to two large sets of overlapping and conflicting influences. The first set predominated from the end of the war up to the turn of the century, and provided the impetus for the whole economic due process theory. These influences included a healthy respect for the natural right of the individual to order economic relationships without interference by the state, the industrial revolution (which emphasized the public benefits of such a liberty), and the lingering effects of the antislavery movement. But by the time these influences were beginning to be felt at the Supreme Court level, another set of influences was already in ascendancy.

This second set of influences included a growing sense of humanitarianism, a belief in the primacy of community over selfish individualism, a repudiation of natural rights, an expanded conception of the kinds of private "coercion" that should be made against the law, a conviction that government was responsible for creating the "good society," and the notion that the "Great Depression" itself was proof positive of the need for government regulation.

From the late 1880s to the early 1930s, the two forces battled it out—in the community at large, in the political arena, and in the courts in the guise of constitutional litigation. The details of the underlying dispute are as follows:

In Support of Economic Due Process. During the second half of the nineteenth century, the law's generally negative attitude toward the power of government over work was heavily influenced by three things, as indicated above—a concept of natural rights, the industrial revolution, and the antislavery movement.

Under what is generally regarded as the Lockean view of natural rights, such rights were regarded as inalienable, absolute by definition, and essentially negative in character; rights were in the realm of philosophy, not pragmatics.

That is, rights flowed from God or from "the nature of things," thus rendering them inalienable and not subject to abridgment by majority vote or social policy. Indeed, limiting democratic excesses in this regard was thought to be a primary purpose of the Constitution.

Rights were also thought of as being absolute in the sense that since all rights are equal, they must necessarily be non-contradictory. If the workers do, in fact, have the "right" to form labor associations and engage in certain activities, then *a fortiori* this does not violate the rights of employers or others in the community. Whatever legitimate interests employers or others have has already been taken into account in defining the exact parameters of the right—i.e., identifying the specific types of activities the right encompasses. And once that has been done, further balancing or accommodation is not only unnecessary, it also violates the right.

Likewise, in the Lockean tradition, rights were purely "negative" in character. That is, having a "right" simply meant being able to engage in an activity without coercive interference by others. The correlative duty was that of non-interference. Although other things, like a lack of money or opportunity, might make the full exercise of a right impossible, this in no way diminished the completeness and value of the right as such. In sum, natural rights were theoretically rather than pragmatically oriented. Thus, the miner had as much of a "right" to purchase the mansion on the hill as did the owner of the mine. The fact that one had the money to do it and the other did not was totally irrelevant. The second influence, the industrial revolution, was said to have been embodied in three concepts.

The three are (1) the concept of the individual "ennobled as a mine of energy, whose untrammeled activity would redound to the public weal"; (2) the concept of the state, "which was submerged under a theory of universal freedom of private competitive effort'; (3) the basis of wealth, which was industry, not land, and which in turn was based on "the free contract in the perfect market by the free man . . . a contract which . . . would redound to the benefit of each of the contracting parties, and thereby to the benefit of society."[38]

All of this pointed to a laissez–faire theory of government—not only as a matter of policy, but also as a matter of constitutional mandate.

The antislavery movement also had its influence. State–sanctioned slavery obviously violated the fundamental right of personal liberty. But the abolitionists were concerned with more than literal physical bondage. One commentator put it in these terms:

Another set of rights to which antislavery thought gave great attention were property and contract rights. Antislavery advocates urged that economic rights of property and contract be extended to all men, including slaves. One of "[t]he primary and essential rights of humanity [was] the right to occupy a portion of the earth's surface." Ownership of land, it was argued, would turn the dependent poor, such as slaves, into independent yeomen; "by giving them independent freeholds, [it would] incite them . . . to rear families in habits of industry and frugality, which form the real elements of national greatness and power." To deny men land, on the other hand, was to keep them dependent, and "to be dependent . . . [was] to be degraded."

Of course, the right to own land also included the "natural right to eat the bread" earned from the land "with [one's] own hands without asking leave of anyone else." The right of property, that is, "include[d], of necessity, [the] right to the products of [a man's] own industry, and his consequent right to dispose of those products, by barter or sale." All men were entitled to "the inalienable right of unrestricted free trade," and hence "all commercial restrictions . . . except the wise and needful prohibition of immoral and criminal traffic" and [a]ll monopolies, class legislations, and exclusive privileges" were "unequal, unjust, morally wrong, and subversive of the ends of civil government." And just as it was inappropriate for government to regulate lawful commerce, so too it was wrong to regulate the conditions of labor; [i]t emasculated people to be protected in this way," since they ought to "be used to protecting themselves."[39]

When battlefield and electoral victories put abolitionists into power, these views were destined to become law. The Thirteenth Amendment abolished slavery as such, and the Fourteenth Amendment guaranteed equal protection and due process of law to all persons. It is clear that at the time, the point of all this was to abolish government constraints on the right to work, or contract for work, or avoid doing so, as each individual saw fit. "It is idle," Representative Lawrence said, "to say that a citizen shall have the right to life, yet deny him the right to labor, whereby alone he can live," or "the right to make a contact to secure the privileges and rewards of labor."[40] Excessive regulation of the work relationship was seen by abolitionists in Congress as an incident of slavery, and in violation of the natural and inalienable rights of man.[41]

In sum, a natural law belief in the autonomy and sanctity of the individual required that he not only be released from the literal bonds of slavery, but that he also be unfettered by other coercive legal restraints on his freedom to pursue his chosen livelihood. A constitutionally–based, laissez–faire free–market system was viewed as the *consequence* of this belief, rather than something imposed directly by the literal words of the text itself.

In Support of Government Regulation. The influences and forces which built the pressure for increased government regulation of work and employment relationships are far more diverse and complex. The various strands of thought, however, can be identified as follows.

First, there was a growing sense of humanitarianism among the American public. Although exaggerated by the muckrakers and undoubtedly an improvement over the potato fields of Ireland, working conditions in early American industry were harsh by anyone's standards. Long hours, low wages (particularly for women), the use of child labor, dangerous equipment, and the alleged lack of adequate compensation for work-related injuries touched the conscience of many Americans.

The early 1900s thus saw the phenomenal growth of private charitable organizations and the growth of a Social Gospel among the churches—aimed in part at ameliorating the worker's plight. Economic pressure was also used. The National Consumers League, formed in 1899, promulgated "fair house" standards calling for decent working conditions and a $6 minimum weekly wage. Employers who complied were entitled to put the "fair house" label on their products—the theory being that sympathetic consumers would favor these brands. The perceived inadequacy of these approaches, however, simply increased the pressure for stronger measures.

Second, the era saw a growing tide of anti-individualism. The belief emerged that social conditions were not the responsibility of any discrete individual, and that the individual's self–realization was no longer regarded as the all-important value. Rather, society bore the responsibility for whatever conditions existed, and the collective good took precedent over the interests of any particular individual. Public spirit rather than private greed became the motivating force. One social historian described it this way:

Society rather than the individual was looked upon as being responsible for many of the evils and problems of a "highly civilized and complex community." Collective action was necessary to control and supplement individual economic activity—to correct or prevent its abuses and to make it an instrument of the general welfare.[42]

Third, as an extension of both humanitarianism and anti-individualism, there was also a new vision developing with respect to the power and potential of state action. Although the view had yet not been widely accepted at the time the following words were written, it did ultimately prevail.

Back in their minds the American public are still dominated by the dogmas of laissez-faire and individualism. . . . They still are influenced, though often unconsciously, by the doctrine that all resort to the state is to be deprecated. To the conception of the state as a powerful agent for the accomplishment of positive good they lend but a reluctant ear.[43]

A later commentator described the position of the Progressives in similar terms.

[The Progressives] viewed the government as an instrument to be used rather than shunned in their attempts to bring about economic and social justice. They believed the general welfare could best be promoted by substituting the positive state for the policy of laissez faire.[44]

Moreover, the coercive power of the state could be used to achieve humanitarian ends—whether the alleged beneficiaries wanted to be helped or not. Commenting on the failure of a German accident insurance law in which employee participation was voluntary, a United States Commissioner of Labor observed that "the most dependent class could only be reached by the strong hand of the state."[45] This paternalistic impulse was particularly strong with respect to female workers.

The concept of rights was also evolving. Under the old view, individual rights were regarded as inalienable, absolute, and negative in character. All of these notions came under attack during this period, since they served as a major stumbling block to enactment of economic regulation.

With respect to the inalienable and absolute nature of rights, the contrary view that ultimately prevailed was described by one proponent in these terms:

"Rights" are recognized as relative, not absolute, things—things that are of social creation, not "inalienable." To dismiss the possibility of wage regulations in such an economic system with the glib pronunciamento that it is contrary to "natural law" is as great an intellectual sin as is the antithetical one of uncritical espousal of attempts to control without recognition of the distributive forces striving to work themselves out in the system of capitalistic enterprise; to say that such attempts are a "manifest violation of sacred rights" of employer and employee is to expose oneself to the charge of a social romanticism ill becoming one who professes realistic concern in the economic problems of the 1930's.[46]

Similarly, negative rights were dismissed as often being without any practical value. A worker may have the "right" to contract with another employer for a higher wage, but that right was thought to be meaningless in a one-employer mill town. The terms "liberty" and "freedom" were undergoing a similar metamorphosis. One commentator put it this way:

> Modern liberalism, in the United States as well as in England, looks to state action as the means, and the only practicable means now in sight, of giving to the individual, all individuals, not merely a small economically strong class, *real freedom*. It holds that the so-called freedom of the dependent woman . . . to work at long hours and under any conditions, no matter what the danger to health and limb, is, in truth, but abject slavery masquerading under the name. Freedom means a *real liberty* to choose.[47]

The converse term, "coercion," was also undergoing definitional shifts. At common law, "coercion" (or "duress") had a fairly narrow meaning, referring only to physical force or the threat to commit some wrong if the victim did not comply. A more expansive notion of "coercion" was obviously involved in the English common law criminal conspiracy doctrine. But this is perhaps why that doctrine, as such, ultimately did not survive in this country. Ironically, however, the underlying conception did survive, to reappear in the context of being pro-employee rather than anti-employee. Thus, in the work context, the term "coercion" was often used to refer to any situation where a person's alternatives were all unattractive. Choice of the least unattractive was, however, regarded as a "coerced" choice. "Coercion" of this sort occurred, for example, whenever an employee's only choice was between being fired or resigning from the union.

There is much magic in words, and attaching the label "coercion" to the employer's conduct, in requiring that the employee make this choice, had enormous psychological and political impact. For some reason, however, the proponents of this new conception of "coercion" failed to see that it would equally apply to the situation facing a nonunion employee seeking a job in an industry with a "closed shop" agreement with the union—a situation they were perfectly willing to tolerate if not encourage.

Nevertheless, vis-à-vis the employer, most workers were thought to lack this "real liberty to choose" and were thus being "coerced" because of a perceived inequality of bargaining power. Speaking of the common law doctrine of assumption of risk, one early commentator put it in somewhat colorful terms.

Almost every element of unfairness in this law arises, I think, from one misconception; namely, that the two parties are on an equal footing. In the eyes of the law every working man, from the trained American locomotive engineer with a strong union behind him, to the newly-landed "Hunkie," tongue-tied and bewildered, is on an equal footing with the United States Steel Corporation in all its masterfully concentrated power. In the contract of hire, the law assumes that the workman is as free to accept or refuse a job as the employer is to take or drop him. In the matter of the release, the law assumes that the stricken and terrified widow of an ignorant laboring man is in a position of equal understanding and enlightenment in regard to the respective interests of the parties, with the hardened claim agent employed by the corporation. The law is behindhand, and the law makers have been blind. With their minds thoroughly steeped in old ideas of theoretical equality and freedom of contract, they have gone on, content with the "logic of the law," oblivious to actual facts.[48]

This quotation also reflects the influence that legal realism was beginning to play.[49] This growing school of American jurisprudence was generally impatient with the hoary abstractions of natural law, which seemed increasingly remote from the complexities and problems of an industrial society. The legal realists believed that both the "is" and the "ought" aspects of law, including constitutional law, are dictated by reality. And as "real world" situations change, so should the law.

In any event, since the negative right to be free of government coercion was itself inadequate to guarantee "real liberty" and "real freedom," the notion of positive rights began to take hold. Under this view, government has more than a duty just to leave you alone in certain respects. Rather, every person also has a right to have certain basic needs met, and the function of government is to provide affirmative assistance in that regard, directly or indirectly. In the words of a later Democratic Party platform, this included "the right to a useful and remunerative job in the industries or shops or factories or mines of the nation" and "the right to earn enough to provide adequate food and clothing and recreation."[50] And rather than providing these jobs itself, government was expected to vindicate the underlying right by imposing various "duties" on employers and prospective employers.

The final important influence was economic. A laissez–faire political/economic system was seen as producing great disparities in wealth, which were regarded as inequitable. And the boom-to-bust economic cycles that plagued this period had caused many hardships, with the Great Depression simply bringing it all to a shuddering climax.

Americans have always been an enormously practical people. When it was perceived that the system was not working, the impulse to fix it became overwhelming. Abstract theories of government and hollow rhetoric about "natural rights" were forced to give way to hard reality. Something had to be done, and government seemed to be the only institution that could do it. Legislatures became increasingly willing. The task was to get the legislation through the courts, and it was here that a somewhat uncertain resistance was encountered.

The Supreme Court Decisions

The economic due process era began shortly after the Civil War. The Supreme Court was initially reluctant to recognize a constitutional right to engage in work-related activities. Pre-war courts had often recognized the substantive, natural law aspects of "due process,"[51] but had never squarely faced the question of whether it encompassed work activities. They were soon to have the chance.

In 1869, the Louisiana legislature passed a law creating a corporation and giving it a monopoly to operate slaughterhouses and related activities in the New Orleans area for twenty years. Rival butchers challenged the legislation under the newly adopted Thirteenth and Fourteenth Amendments— specifically, the abolition of slavery provision, the privileges and immunities clause, the equal protection clause, and the due process clause. The issue was resolved by the Supreme Court in *The Butchers Benevolent Association of New Orleans v. The Crescent City Live-Stock Landing and Slaughter House Company*,[52] more commonly known as the *Slaughterhouse Cases*.

Writing for a bare majority, Justice Miller gave short shrift to the Thirteenth Amendment argument, holding that it prohibited all shades and forms of slavery but nothing more. Although he seemed to recognize that the purpose of the Fourteenth Amendment was, in part, to nullify the so-called "Black Codes" passed by states formerly in rebellion, laws by which blacks "were excluded from many occupations of gain,"[53] and although he admitted that the Fourteenth Amendment is not limited to a protection of "the colored race," he declined to invalidate the legislation in question. In a nutshell, the theory was that the "privileges and immunities" of Section 1 referred to those that a person had by virtue of national (rather than state) citizenship. And since the privilege of working was an incident of state rather than national citizenship, the privileges and immunities clause did not apply. Second, without extensive discussion, the Court held that under no plausible interpretation of the due process clause "can the restraint imposed by the State of Louisiana upon the exercise of their trade by the butchers of New Orleans be held to be a deprivation of property within the meaning of that provision."[54] And third, the Court held that the equal protection clause was more or less limited to discrimination on the basis of race.[55]

Three of the four dissenting justices filed opinions. In contrast to the majority's rather casual attitude toward the right of a person to engage in a lawful occupation, the dissenters were clearly outraged. Justice Field began the lead dissent by noting that the state's exercise of the "police power" (a term generally used to describe the inherent and plenary power of the state to legislate) and the individual's exercise of the "just rights of the citizen" are mutually exclusive. This is a tautology, but an important one, for it has served as the point of departure for most of the subsequent cases. Field then narrowly construed the scope of the police power, in this case finding its exercise only with respect to certain sanitation matters.[56]

Since the remainder of the legislation could not be justified as an exercise of the police power, it necessarily followed that the statute "presents the naked case . . . where a right to pursue a lawful and necessary calling, previously enjoyed by every citizen, . . . is taken away and vested exclusively . . . in a single corporation."[57] This only left the question, then, of whether it violated the Constitution.

In stating that it did, Justice Field relied on the Fourteenth Amendment. He was, however, sympathetic to the Thirteenth Amendment argument.

> The abolition of slavery and involuntary servitude was intended to make every one born in this country a freeman, and as such to give to him the right to pursue the ordinary avocations of life without other restraint than such as affects all others, and to enjoy equally with them the fruits of his labor. A prohibition to him to pursue certain callings . . . would so far deprive him of the rights of a freeman, and would place him, as respects others, in a condition of servitude. . . . He certainly would not possess the liberties nor enjoy the privileges of a freeman. The compulsion which would force him to labor even for his own benefit only in one direction, or in one place, would be almost as oppressive and nearly as great an invasion of his liberty as the compulsion which would force him to labor for the benefit or pleasure of another, and would equally constitute an element of servitude.[58]

Relying, however, on the Fourteenth Amendment as the basis of his opinion, Justice Field asserted that the rights and privileges of national citizenship "are those *which of right belong to the citizens of all free governments*. Clearly among these must be placed the right to pursue a lawful employment in a lawful manner, without other restraint than such as equally affects all persons."[59]

The dissents of Justices Bradley and Swayne are in a similar vein, except that the latter also made it clear that the due process clause of the Fourteenth Amendment was also implicated by the Louisiana legislation.

> Property is everything which has an exchangeable value, and the right of property includes the power to dispose of it according to the will of the

owner. Labor is property, and as such merits protection. The right to make it available is next in importance to the rights of life and liberty.[60]

It is ironic that in the very next case in the United States Reports, *Bradwell v. The State*,[61] Justices Bradley, Swayne, and Field stated that the Fourteenth Amendment property right to engage in a lawful occupation did not extend so far as to require the state to admit a woman to the bar, because "[t]he paramount destiny and mission of woman are to fulfill the noble and benign offices of wife and mother. This is the law of the Creator."[62]

Justice Field's less than total commitment to occupational freedom is also apparent in the 1885 cases of *Barbier v. Connolly*[63] and *Soon Hing v. Crowley*,[64] which involved the constitutionality of ordinances prohibiting the operation of public laundries from ten o'clock at night to six in the morning. The ordinances were probably passed for the purpose of driving Chinese laundry operators out of business, although the asserted justification was that of eliminating the danger of fires at night. Writing for the Court in *Soon Hing*, Justice Field denied that this violated any constitutional right to work.

> However broad the right of every one to follow such calling and employ his time as he may judge most conducive to his interests, it must be exercised subject to such general rules as are adopted by society for the common welfare. All sorts of restrictions are imposed upon the actions of men notwithstanding the liberty which is guaranteed to each. It is liberty regulated by just and impartial laws . . . [citing examples]. So, too, with the hours of labor. On few subjects has there been more regulation. How many hours shall constitute a day's work in the absence of contract, at what time shops in our cities shall close at night, are constant subjects of legislation. Laws setting aside Sunday as a day of rest are upheld, not from any right of the government to legislate for the promotion of religious observances, but from its right to protect all persons from the physical and moral debasement which comes from uninterrupted labor. Such laws have always been deemed beneficent and merciful laws, especially to the poor and dependent, to the laborers in our factories and workshops and in the heated rooms of our cities; and their validity has been sustained by the highest courts of the States.[65]

In the *Barbier* case, Justice Field conceded that the Fourteenth Amendment encompassed some degree of occupational liberty.

> But neither the amendment—broad and comprehensive as it is—nor any other amendment, was designed to interfere with the power of the State, sometimes termed its police power, to prescribe regulations to promote the health, peace, morals, education, and good order of the people, and to legislate so as to increase the industries of the State, develop its resources, and add to its wealth and prosperity.[66]

Together, these two cases would seem to suggest that the state's power to regulate work-related activities is virtually unlimited. As the Court put it in *Frisbie v. United States*,[67] the state "may restrain all engaged in any employment from any contract in the course of that employment which is against public policy."[68] The following year, however, the Court did recognize a Fourteenth Amendment limitation in this regard, albeit flowing from the equal protection clause rather than the due process clause.

Yick Wo v. Hopkins[69] involved the constitutionality of convictions under a San Francisco ordinance requiring permission of the board of supervisors in order to operate a laundry in a wooden building. Permission was routinely given to white applicants but not to those of Chinese ancestry, who were arrested in large numbers.

The Court reaffirmed *Barbier* and *Soon Hing,* stating that the laws in question there were constitutional, since they applied equally to all similarly–situated persons. But the Court held that an ordinance which gave unfettered discretion to the board of supervisors, who exercised it in a racially discriminatory fashion, violated the Fourteenth Amendment. As had the dissenting justices in the *Slaughterhouse* cases, Justice Matthews saw a clear connection between arbitrary deprivations of the right to work and the institution of slavery.

> For, the very idea that one man may be compelled to hold his life, or the means of living, or any material right essential to the enjoyment of life, at the mere will of another, seems to be intolerable in any country where freedom prevails, as being the essence of slavery itself.[70]

However, neither the Court nor its individual justices had yet settled on a consistent Fourteenth Amendment approach to economic regulation, and this continued to manifest itself in the cases relating to work and employment. Thus, in *Powell v. Pennsylvania,*[71] the Court held that the police power encompassed the prevention of fraud and the protection of public health and that, therefore, there was no Fourteenth Amendment liberty to manufacture and sell oleomargarine. Significantly, the Court refused to pass judgment on the wisdom of or need for the legislation, Justice Harlan finding that to be a legislative rather than judicial prerogative.

Reverting to his *Slaughterhouse Cases* position, Justice Field dissented. Rather than defining "liberty" in terms of the "police power," he simply reversed the approach and began with the concept of liberty.

> Liberty, in its broad sense, as understood in this country, means the right not only of freedom from actual servitude, imprisonment, or restraint, but the right of one to use his faculties, in all lawful ways, to live and work where he will, to earn his livelihood in any lawful calling, and to pursue any lawful trade or vocation.[72]

Justice Field then qualified that with the fundamental axiom of all classical liberal rights theories: "With the gift of life there necessarily goes to every one the right to do all such acts, and follow all such pursuits, *not inconsistent with the equal rights of others,* as may support life and add to the happiness of its possessor."[73]

Allgeyer v. Louisiana[74] is often identified as the case which marks the beginning of the substantive due process era. Although it did not involve a work-related issue, the Court did speak expansively of a Fourteenth Amendment right to work. This language was to be quoted many times in the following years.

> The liberty mentioned in that amendment means not only the right of the citizen to be free from the mere physical restraint of his person, as by incarceration, but the term is deemed to embrace the right of the citizen to be free in the enjoyment of all his faculties; to be free to use them in all lawful ways; to live and work where he will; to earn his livelihood by any lawful calling; to pursue any livelihood or avocation, and for that purpose to enter into all contracts which may be proper, necessary and essential to his carrying out to a successful conclusion the purposes above mentioned.[75]

The Court was soon given an opportunity to put those fine words into practice, but it failed to do so. Indeed, the next major employment case to come before the Supreme Court reflects nearly all of the regulatory influences discussed above. In *Holden v. Hardy,*[76] decided in 1898, the Court sustained the constitutionality of a Utah eight-hour workday law for certain mine workers. The Court, in an opinion written by Justice Brown, began with the premise of the legal realists that law, including constitutional law, is a "progressive science" and that it must "adapt itself to new conditions of society, and, particularly, to the new relations between employers and employees as they arise."[77]

The Court then conceded, by way of limitation, the existence of the due process clause as a superior positive law, containing "certain immutable principles of justice which inhere in the very idea of free government which no member of the Union may disregard."[78] Although the Court admitted that substantive due process included at least a general right to contract, it added that "this right of contract . . . is itself subject to certain limitations which the State may lawfully impose in the exercise of its police powers."[79] The Court then held that the exercise of the police power was in large measure a matter of legislative discretion and that as long as there were reasonable grounds for believing that long work days were detrimental to the health of employees, the federal courts would not interfere. In addition, the Court noted that

> The legislature has also recognized . . . that the proprietors of these establishments and their operatives do not stand upon an equality, and that

their interests are, to a certain extent, conflicting. The former naturally desire to obtain as much labor as possible from their employees, while the latter are often induced by the fear of discharge to conform to regulations which their judgment, fairly exercised, would pronounce to be detrimental to their health or strength. In other words, the proprietors lay down the rules and the laborers are practically constrained to obey them. In such cases self-interest is often an unsafe guide, and the legislature may properly interpose its authority.

[T]he fact that both parties are of full age and competent to contract does not necessarily deprive the State of the power to interfere where the parties do not stand upon an equality, or where the public health demands that one party to the contract shall be protected against himself. "The State still retains an interest in his welfare, however reckless he may be. The whole is no greater than the sum of all the parts, and when the individual health, safety and welfare are sacrificed or neglected, the State must suffer."[80]

In that one quote, one sees the influences of the practical over the theoretical, of paternalism, and of notions of collective rather than purely individual well-being.

In light of *Holden v. Hardy,* one would have thought that almost any maximum hour law could have withstood constitutional scrutiny. Yet, a scant seven years later in 1905, the Court struck down as unconstitutional a New York law limiting the hours of bakery workers to sixty hours per week. *Lochner v. New York*[81] is often thought of as the flagship of the substantive due process era. The case, however, is hardly an unqualified paean to liberty of contract and limited government. Indeed, the Court's concessions to regulation create an internal inconsistency, thus leaving it vulnerable to reasoned attack.

Justice Peckham, who had dissented without opinion in *Holden,* began the analysis in the traditional fashion, to wit: the Fourteenth Amendment generally encompasses a liberty to contract, but this is subject to limitation under a proper exercise of the police power. The issue, thus, was whether this was such an exercise.

The Court concluded that it was not. Viewed purely as labor legislation, the statute could not be justified in terms of any special need to protect bakers from economic exploitation.

> There is no contention that bakers as a class are not equal in intelligence and capacity to men in other trades or manual occupations, or that they are not able to assert their rights and care for themselves without the protecting arm of the State, interfering with their independence of judgment and of action. They are in no sense wards of the State.[82]

Viewing the statute as a health ordinance, the Court first concluded that there was no necessary connection between the hours that a baker worked and the enterprise of providing clean and wholesome bread to the public. Indeed, there was no contention to the contrary. With respect to the health of the bakers themselves, the Court rejected the *Holden v. Hardy* notion "that it is to the interest of the State that its population should be strong and robust, and therefore any legislation which may be said to tend to make people healthy must be valid health laws, enacted under the police power."[83] That, the Court recognized, would justify the regulation of everyone's hours of work, "lest the fighting strength of the State be impaired,"[84] and thus render liberty of contract a complete nullity. But without indicating what alternative state interest was involved, the Court recognized that the police power did allow a state to prohibit employment contracts that posed a threat to the health of the employee. However, the court concluded that the trade of a baker was "not an unhealthy one to that degree which would authorize the legislature to interfere with the right to labor, and with the right of free contract on the part of the individual, either as employer or employee."[85]

In sum, although the Court invalidated the legislation, it did so not because the statute violated some clear principle of constitutional liberty, but rather because the asserted factual justification was found to be lacking. In taking this approach, the Court thus opened itself up to two objections: first, that the Court was wrong in its factual determination, and second, that the Court was merely substituting its judgment for that of the legislature.

Justice Holmes wrote a trenchant and oft-quoted dissent.[86] He began by asserting that "[t]his case is decided upon an economic theory which a large part of the country does not entertain."[87] Presumably, what he had in mind was liberty of contract. He apparently recognized that liberty of contract is merely a part of the broader "liberty of the citizen to do as he likes so long as he does not interfere with the liberty of others to do the same."[88] That, however, he dismissed as a mere "shibboleth," noting that the "Fourteenth Amendment does not enact Mr. Herbert Spencer's Social Statics."[89] Indeed, he noted that "a constitution is not intended to embody a particular economic theory, whether of paternalism and the organic relation of the citizen to the State or of *laissez faire*."[90] And no matter how "injudicious" or "tyrannical" a statute may appear to be, when it is the "natural outcome of a dominant [public] opinion," Holmes suggested that it does not violate the Fourteenth Amendment unless it infringes "fundamental principles as they have been understood by the traditions of our people and our law"[91] — which apparently did not include the liberty to contract for more than 60 hours of work per day.

Despite *Lochner's* ambivalence over the scope of the Fourteenth Amendment liberty of contract and its relationship with the state's exercise of police powers, the Court continued to recognize the right of both employer and employee to contract for labor free from legislative constraints. In 1908, in *Adair v. United States,*[92] the Court confronted the issue in the context of federal rather than state law. Congress had made it a crime for a railroad or its agents to require its employees, as a condition of employment, to agree not to become a member of a labor organization (enter into so-called "yellow dog contracts"), or to fire or otherwise discriminate against employees because of union membership. Appealing a conviction under this statute, Adair claimed that the law violated his Fifth Amendment due process rights. The Court agreed, with Justice Harlan explaining it as follows.

> [The statute] is an invasion of the personal liberty, as well as of the right of property, guaranteed by that Amendment. Such liberty and right embraces the right to make contracts for the purchase of the labor of others and equally the right to make contract for the sale of one's own labor.[93]

The Court recognized that this liberty, like all others, is subject to the condition that it not be exercised in such a way as would be injurious to the health and safety of the public, but failed to find any such danger in this case.

In earlier cases, the Court had dealt with the relationship between fundamental liberties and the police power of states. The relationship is one of mutual exclusivity, with the key question being: "Which do you attempt to define first?" The federal government, of course, has no inherent police power. The government had argued, however, that the commerce clause empowered Congress to enact this legislation, "without regard to any question of personal liberty or right of property arising under the Fifth Amendment."[94] Although the Court held that the legislation was not within the scope of the commerce clause, it also rejected the government's Fifth Amendment argument. "We need scarcely repeat what this court has more than once said, that the power to regulate interstate commerce, great and paramount as that power is, cannot be exerted in violation of any fundamental right secured by other provisions of the Constitution." This seems to suggest that the proper analysis is first to identify those "fundamental" (presumably natural law) rights which are "secured" (not created) by the Constitution; from this it follows that whatever the scope of the commerce clause might be in the abstract, by definition it does not extend to cover any legislation which infringes those rights.

Subsequently, the Court confronted the question of whether a state law making it illegal for an employer to "coerce" employees into signing a yellow-dog contract violated the due process clause of the Fourteenth Amendment. Not unsurprisingly, the Court held that it did. The opinion in *Coppage v. Kansas*,[95] written by Justice Pitney, contains, however, some additional points worthy of mention.

First, the Court noted (with what seems to be tacit disapproval) that the term "coerce" in the statute had been construed by the state court as "applying to the mere insistence by the employer . . . upon its right to prescribe terms upon which alone it would consent to a continuance of the relationship of employer and employee."[96] There was no coercion in the traditional sense. And although the employee would lose certain benefits by resigning from the union, the Court found him to be "a free agent, in all respects competent, and at liberty to choose what was best from the standpoint of his own interests."[97] In sum, the Court refused to be influenced by the mere use of the label "coercion." The Court then evaluated the employer's conduct from the perspective of what it truly was, a simple refusal to continue to employ a person unless a certain condition was met.

The Court then held that such conduct was constitutionally protected. The Court reaffirmed the notion of a constitutional liberty of contract in very strong terms.

> Included in the right of personal liberty and the right of private property—partaking of the nature of each—is the right to make contracts for the acquisition of property. Chief among such contracts is that of personal employment, by which labor and other services are exchanged for money or other forms of property. If this right be struck down or arbitrarily interfered with, there is a substantial impairment of liberty in the long-established constitutional sense. The right is as essential to the laborer as to the capitalist, to the poor as to the rich; for the vast majority of persons have no other honest way to begin to acquire property, save working for money.[98]

The Court then confronted head-on the notion that this liberty could be curtailed because of the relative inequality of bargaining power between employer and employee.

> No doubt, wherever the right of private property exists, there must and will be inequalities of fortune; and thus it naturally happens that parties negotiating about a contract are not equally unhampered by circumstances. . . . Indeed a little reflection will show that wherever the right of private property and the right of free contract co-exist, each party when contracting is inevitably more or less influenced by the question whether he had much property, or little, or none; for the contract is made to the very end that each may gain something that he needs or desires more urgently than that which he proposes to give in exchange. . . . [Thus] it is from the nature of things impossible to uphold freedom of contract and the right of private property without at the same time recognizing as legitimate those inequalities of fortune that are the necessary result of the exercise of those rights.[99]

Finally, the Court refuted the notion that because workers have a constitutional right to organize, private employers have a duty to refrain from doing anything that would affect the exercise of that right.

> Conceding the full right of the individual to join the union, he has no inherent right to do this and still remain in the employ of one who is

unwilling to employ a union man, anymore than the same individual has a right to join the union without the consent of that organization. Can it be doubted that a labor organization—a voluntary association of working men—has the inherent and constitutional right to deny membership to any man who will not agree that during such membership he will not accept or retain employment in company with non-union men? Or that a union man has the constitutional right to decline preferred employment unless the employer will agree not to employ any non-union man? . . . And can there be one rule of liberty for the labor organization and its members, and a different and more restrictive rule for employers? We think not; and since the relation of employer and employee is a voluntary relation, as clearly as is that between the members of a labor organization, the employer has the same inherent right to prescribe the terms upon which he will consent to the relationship, and to have them fairly understood and expressed in advance.[100]

In sum, the Court was simply applying the theory and logic of *Commonwealth v. Hunt,* which had been regarded as the Magna Charta of the American labor movement. Refusing to enter into an employment relationship unless certain conditions are met does not amount to a legally recognizable "wrong" against the other party, regardless of whether the union supporters are insisting on a closed shop (as in *Hunt*) or the employer is insisting on an open shop (as in *Coppage*).

Justices Holmes, Day, and Hughes registered a strong dissent. Their position was that liberty of contract is not absolute and that it may be "circumscribed in the interest of the State and the welfare of its people,"[101] with the test being merely one of lack of reasonableness.[102] Because of the relative financial positions of employer and employee, the dissent refused to concede that the employer's action in this case was other than "coercive" in the literal sense. And since joining a union is itself encompassed by the constitutional right of free association, the dissenters thought the state has the power, if not the duty, to protect its citizens in the exercise of that right.

In sum, the majority and the dissenters simply had fundamentally different notions about the meaning of "coercion," the nature of constitutional rights (particularly with respect to who bears the correlative duty), and the proper function of the state in protecting those rights.

Despite the rhetoric and results in *Lochner, Adair,* and *Coppage,* the Court was not as firmly committed to individual liberty in the workplace as those cases might suggest—at least not in a principled sort of way. In *Muller v. Oregon,*[103] decided the same year as *Adair,* the Court sustained the constitutionality of a law limiting women to ten hours of work a day. In an opinion written by Justice Brewer, the Court adopted a new analytical approach. Rather than defining and limiting the scope of government power by reference to a fixed notion of individual rights, the court defined individual rights with reference to the proper scope of government power. That is, the Court rotely acknowledged, abstractly, the existence of a constitutional liberty to contract for work, shared equally by men and women. Without further defining it, the Court then also noted that this liberty is "not absolute"[104] and that it is thus subject to the state's police power. The Court then found that the need for the legislation brought it within the scope of the police power. From this, it necessarily followed that contracting for more than ten hours of work a day is not encompassed by the liberty in question.

The justification for this legislation was very simple. "That woman's physical structure and the performance of maternal functions place her at a disadvantage in the struggle for subsistence is obvious."[105] In this regard, the Court had the benefits of the famous "Brandeis brief," which provided extensive documentation of the deleterious effects of long hours of work for women. Thus, despite the theoretical equality of men's and women's liberty of contract, "some legislation to protect her seems necessary to secure a *real* equality of right."[106]

Protecting women from the greed and passion of male employers was thought to be necessary, moreover, not merely for her benefit alone, but also "in order to preserve the strength and vigor of the race."[107]

The Court's paternalism was not limited to women, however. In *McLean v. Arkansas*,[108] it approved a state law regulating the method by which miners' wages were calculated—a matter over which there had apparently been much disruptive dispute. The Court began with the oft-repeated litany that "liberty of contract is not universal, and is subject to the legislative branch of the Government in the exercise of its power to protect the safety, health and welfare of the people."[109] Presumably, it was the welfare of the miners themselves that the Court had in mind. Again, however, it was not pure paternalism, for the Court noted the public's interest in preserving "harmonious relations between capital and labor."[110]

Although *Muller* can be explained by the male chauvinism of the era and *McLean* by the notion that miners, like seamen,[111] are virtual wards of the state, the Court's lack of logical consistency is also evident in the 1917 case of *Bunting v. Oregon*.[112] It involved a statute which mandated a ten-hour day for anyone employed in a mill, factory, or manufacturing establishment, but further provided that employees could work up to thirteen hours if they were paid overtime. Justice McKenna's opinion, upholding the legislation, is a bit obscure, but it seems to say that since the legislature could limit the hours to ten absolutely, it could allow an employee to work more than that subject to the payment of overtime. The major premise of that argument is, of course, the significant one. Although the defendant argued that the legislation violated the liberty of contract and did not even relate to the health of employees, the Court upheld it essentially on the ground that the legislature's judgment could not be regarded as "unreasonable or arbitrary."[113] Under that constitutional standard, almost no work-related legislation could fail to pass muster.

The Court did not even bother to cite *Lochner*. But as Justice Taft noted later, "It is impossible for me to reconcile the *Bunting* and the *Lochner* cases and I have always supposed that the *Lochner* case was overruled *sub silentio*."[114]

Lochner was not to go away quite yet, but 1917 was apparently the year to ignore it.[115] In addition to *Bunting*, there was also *Wilson v. New*,[116] where the Court approved a federal statute setting both hours and wages on railroads. The legislation had been prompted by a series of crippling strikes over these matters. In a decision written by Justice White, the Court held that the legislation was justified by "the entire interruption of interstate commerce which was threatened, and the infinite injury to the public interest which was imminent."[117] What the Court had in mind, apparently, was the obvious economic inconvenience that a strike causes to the public. While this "harm" to specific third parties can certainly be very real, a rights theorist would not regard it as a harm that flows from a rights violation; the conduct causing this harm (here, the inability of the parties to agree and the strikes that result from this) is thus not a proper focus of the coercive power of the state. However, by recognizing the public's economic interest in the prevention of labor disputes, the Court put itself square in the camp previously occupied by the Hamiltonians in the *Pullis* case. The supporting theory is essentially the same; the only thing that is different is the remedy. Rather than using the coercive power of the state to prohibit strikes, Congress was now using its coercive power to eliminate the cause of strikes—low wages and long hours in railroading.

Justices Pitney and Van Devanter dissented. They alone were concerned about the implications of the decision on liberty of contract. The failure of parties to agree did not, in their opinion, justify state intervention.

> The right to contract is the right to say by what terms one will be bound. It is of the very essence of the right that the parties may remain in disagreement if either party is not content with any term proposed by the other. A failure to agree is not a waiver but an exercise of the right—as much so as the making of an agreement.[118]

Although litigation over yellow-dog contracts and the various kinds of wage and hour legislation occupied the bulk of the Court's employment law docket during this period, it did address other labor issues as well. The early 1900s had seen the passage of many workers' compensation statutes. These statutes abolished the fellow–servant rule (which had held that an employer is not liable when an employee is injured by a fellow employee) and the contributory negligence defense (which excused the employer's injury-causing negligence if the employee's negligence contributed to it in any degree), replaced the common law notion of liability based on fault (proof of negligence or intentional injury) with a form of strict liability, but in return limited the amount for which an employer would be liable when an employee was injured on the job.

Employers attacked these statutes on constitutional grounds, alleging a deprivation of property without due process of law. The argument was that this change in the common law rule and the imposition of liability in the absence of fault constituted a literal taking of the employer's property and giving to an employee. Although this argument was accepted by one influential state court,[119] the argument was rejected by the United States Supreme Court in *New York Central R.R. Co. v. White*.[120] Justice Pitney put it this way.

> The close relation of the rules governing responsibility as between employer and employee to fundamental rights of liberty and property is of course recognized. But those rules, as guides of conduct, are not beyond alteration by legislation in the public interest. No person has a vested interest in any rule of law entitling him to insist that it shall remain unchanged for his benefit.[121]

Moreover, worker compensation statutes were said to be within the scope of the police power, broadly defined, and in one case Justice Holmes regarded that alone as being dispositive of the issue.

> [I]f we have a case within the reasonable exercise of the police power, no more need be said.
>
> It may be said in a general way that the police power extends to all the great public needs. It may be put forth in aid of what is sanctioned by usage, or held by the prevailing morality or strong and predominant opinion to be greatly and immediately necessary to the public welfare.[122]

In sum, the debate over the constitutionality of workers' compensation statutes was rather drab in comparison with the controversies surrounding other employment issues—such as the use of injunctions in labor matters.

As was indicated earlier,[123] although the criminal conspiracy doctrine was gradually repudiated, its "spirit" lingered on in the law of injunctions. Believing, however, that peaceful concerted activity should be totally legal, Congress and many state legislatures passed laws broadly prohibiting the use of injunctions in labor disputes. Arizona had passed such a statute. When a restaurant with the unlikely name of "English Kitchen," located in Bisbee, Arizona, sought to enjoin the picketing that it was being subjected to, the statute was successfully interposed as a defense. The restaurant appealed, claiming that, so construed, the statute deprived it of property without due process of law in violation of the Fourteenth Amendment. The Supreme Court agreed. The case is *Traux v. Corrigan.*[124]

In an opinion written by Justice Taft, the Court began with the premise that "plaintiff's business is a property right . . . and free access for employees, owner and customers to his place of business is incident to such right."[125] The Court found that economic injury had occurred, and that it was intentional. The only question, thus, was whether the means used were illegal. The Court held that they were. In this regard, the means consisted of picketing close to the entrance of the restaurant, uttering loud assertions that the restaurant was unfair to labor, directing opprobrious epithets at the employees, making libelous charges against the owner, disparaging the quality of the food and the prices, attacking the character of the patrons, making veiled threats against patrons, and warning would-be purchasers that they would have to make a "donation" to the union before the picketing would stop.

The Court referred to this as "moral coercion by illegal annoyance and obstruction."[126] Although the Court's conception of "coercion" seems to be unduly broad, the theory of the case is essentially sound. It involves a very narrow and special kind of "positive right." The theory is that the state has an affirmative duty to protect the individual against rights-violations by other individuals. The state breaches that affirmative duty when it passes legislation which immunizes private right-violating activities. By thus failing to protect the rights of individuals, the state deprives them of property without due process of law.[127]

The difficult question in that case was whether the restaurant owner's rights had truly been violated and, conversely, why the striking employees did not have a First Amendment right to engage in at least some of the activity. This was the question in *Commonwealth v. Pullis.* As we shall see, it is still a question today.

In spite of the 1917 cases upholding wage and hour legislation, the Court was soon to return to the *Lochner* approach on those issues. In *Adkins v. Children's Hospital of the District of Columbia,*[128] the Court struck down a minimum wage law covering female workers in the District of Columbia. One of the plaintiffs was the hospital employer, but the other was a woman who had lost her job because the hospital could not afford to pay her what the statute required for the services she rendered.

The Court found that the legislation violated the due process clause. Justice Sutherland, writing for the Court, explained why.

> That the right to contract about one's affairs is a part of the liberty of the individual protected by this clause, is settled by the decisions of this Court and is no longer open to question. . . . Within this liberty are contracts of employment of labor. In making such contracts, generally speaking, the

parties have an *equal right* to obtain from each other the best terms they can as the result of private bargaining . . . [F]reedom of contract is . . . the general rule and restraint the exception; and the exercise of legislative authority to abridge it can be justified only by the existence of exceptional circumstances.[129]

Fitting into the "exceptional circumstances" category and thus distinguishing the plethora of legislation that the Court had previously sustained proved, however, to be no easy task. The Court characterized *Bunting* as merely holding that the law in question, which the state legislature and courts had found necessary for the preservation of health, was (in the absence of contrary facts) a "reasonable" one.

The Court attempted to distinguish *Muller* by reference to changed circumstances—i.e., the improved social, economic, and legal status of women. Obviously referring to bargaining power rather physical differences, the Court noted that "in view of the great—not to say revolutionary—changes which have taken place since [*Muller*] . . ., in the contractual, political and civil status of women, culminating in the Nineteenth Amendment, it is not unreasonable to say that these differences have how come almost, if not quite, to the vanishing point."[130] This led both dissents, perhaps tongue-in-cheek, to demur to the proposition that the Nineteenth Amendment repealed the biological differences between the sexes. But in a more serious vein, one commentator found it difficult to see why the greater civil liberties that women possessed by virtue of the Nineteenth Amendment "necessitated greater conservativism in extending legal protection [to them]."[131]

The Court also distinguished *Muller* on the grounds that wages go to "the heart of the contract," while hours do not.[132] This, of course, is inconsistent with any coherent theory of liberty of contract. As Justice Taft noted in dissent, "In absolute freedom of contract the one term is as important as the other, for both enter equally into the consideration given and received, a restriction as to one is not any greater in essence than the other, and is of the same kind."[133]

The remainder of the opinion is similarly unexceptional in its intellectual rigor. The Court, however, did make one additional point worth mentioning. As was noted earlier, this entire constitutional conflict was often viewed, at least in part, in terms of individual rights versus the common good. The Court believed they were one and the same thing.

To sustain the individual freedom of action contemplated by the Constitution is not to strike down the common good but to exalt it; for surely the good of society as a whole cannot be better served than by the preservation against arbitrary restraint of the liberties of its constituent members.[134]

The two dissents do not require extensive discussion. Justice Taft justified the legislation on the grounds that "employees, in the class receiving least pay, are not upon a full level of equality of choice with their employer and in their necessitous circumstances are prone to accept pretty much anything that is offered." The unstated and thus unsubstantiated minor premise is that this state of affairs justifies coercive intervention by the state.

Although Oliver Wendell Holmes is widely regarded as one of America's leading jurists, his notion of an "ordered liberty" clearly emphasized the former term rather than the latter. Nowhere is that more evident than in his dissent in this case. He summarized the previous due process cases in these terms.

> The earlier decisions . . . went no further than an unpretentious assertion of the liberty to follow the ordinary callings. Later that innocuous generality was expanded into the dogma, Liberty of Contract. Contract is not specially mentioned in the text that we have to construe. It is merely an example of doing what you want to do, embodied in the word liberty. But pretty much all law consists in forbidding men to do some things that they want to do, and contract is no more exempt from law than other acts. Without enumerating all the restrictive laws that have been upheld I will mention a few that seem to me to have interfered with liberty of contract quite as seriously and directly as the one before us.[135]

He then proceeds with a long catalog of regulations limiting the rights of individuals to contract, thus leaving one with the feeling that there is no constitutional right to contract or to do anything else that you might "want to do," if some legislature decides to pass a law against it.

In 1926, Congress passed the Railway Labor Act which, among other things, prohibited a railway employer from discriminating against union members and requiring it to recognize and bargain with the union selected by a majority of the employees. Despite its prior decisions in *Adair* and *Coppage*, the Court sustained the constitutionality of the legislation.

In *Texas & N. O. R. Co. v. Railway Clerks*,[136] the Court used a broad construction of the commerce clause to justify the act. But the case is more important as an illustration of the use of the notion of positive rights. Writing for the Court, Justice Hughes noted that employees have a constitutional right to organize, citing a case in which the issue came up in the context of the propriety of an injunction. The judicial repudiation of the criminal conspiracy doctrine also represents a vindication of that right. This right, however, was a negative right, with the duty being on the government not to interfere with its exercise. Congress and the Court turned it into a positive right. The Court noted that "Congress was not required to ignore this right of the employees but could safeguard it. . . . Thus the prohibition by Congress of interference with the selection of representatives for the purpose of negotiation and conference between employers and employees, instead of being an invasion of the constitutional right of either, was based on the recognition of the rights of both."[137] Of course, the statute did more than merely "recognize" an existing negative right against coercive interference by the government; it recognized it as a positive right which Congress vindicated by prohibiting employers from discriminating against employees who exercised it. The Court did not explain how this positive right was consistent with the employer's negative right to select its employees free from coercive government interference.

The *Slaughterhouse Cases* involved state legislation which, through the creation of a monopoly, limited entry into a particular occupation. Over the years, this had been a recurring issue. Women, of course, were not fit to practice law,[138] at least not under the constitutional view that regarded this, like other "economic regulation," a matter for the various local legislatures to "experiment" with. And the hapless public apparently needed similar protection from incompetent dentists[139] and itinerant drug peddlers.[140]

Icemaking, however, was obviously another matter. In *New State Ice Co. v. Liebmann*,[141] the Supreme Court invalidated a state law which required a license to manufacture and sell ice, obtainable only upon proof that an additional seller was "necessary" to meet public needs. In many respects, *New State Ice* represents the so-called substantive due process era better than *Lochner* does.

In an opinion by Justice Sutherland, the Court conceded that "all businesses are subject to some measure of public regulation."[142] The extent of that regulation, in turn, is determined by whether or not the business in question "has been devoted to a public use and its use thereby, in effect, granted to the public." The Court then determined that icemaking did not fit into that category.

One is left with one question: why? One is further left with the impression that this was more a matter of Supreme Court judgment prevailing over that of the Oklahoma legislature. And, finally, one is left with the uneasy feeling that this might not be a proper exercise of the power of judicial review. To many, that is economic due process in a nutshell.

The dissent of Justice Brandeis, however, is also a classic of the era. It lacks the ringing phrases and haughty brevity of a Holmes dissent. But in his plodding, factually meticulous way, Justice Brandeis spells out all the premises of the regulatory state. At its core is a profound antipathy to the free market—i.e., the notion that competition will not only provide the most efficient allocation of scarce resources (an economic theory), but also that such freedom is mandated by fundamental notions of individual liberty (a moral theory). Justice Brandeis, though purporting to adopt a position of economic agnosticism, is clearly sympathetic to the view that some kind of social control over the economy is both necessary and desirable. He notes that "there must be power in the States and the Nation, to remold, through experimentation, our economic practices and institutions to meet changing social and economic needs."[143]

Turning then to narrower constitutional issues, he asserts that "the police power commonly invoked in aid of health, safety and morals, extends equally to the promotion of the public welfare"[144] and that this "power extends to *every* regulation of *any* business reasonably required and appropriate for the public protection."[145] State "experimentation" in social and economic control is thus presumed valid, "unless clearly arbitrary, capricious or unreasonable."[146] However, few would quarrel with the notion that it is within the public's interest to be able to secure "a necessary service at reasonable rates."[147] And if the legislature reasonably concludes that limiting entry into the business is necessary to accomplish that, then the action is within the scope of the police power and not in violation of the due process clause. To hold otherwise, Justice Brandeis concluded, would assume that "the Federal Constitution guarantees to the individual the *absolute right* to enter the ice business, however detrimental the exercise of that right may be to the public welfare."

Except for the omission of massive amounts of factual data supporting the need for and reasonableness of certain legislation, subsequent Supreme Court decisions were to closely mirror Brandeis's philosophy and approach to questions of economic regulation. The public interest will always prevail over contrary assertions of individual rights. A legislative determination of what the public interest is and how it can best be served is presumed valid. And the legislation will be invalidated only if it is arbitrary, capricious, or unreasonable. The possession of such authority is, of course, the *sine qua non* of the regulatory state. However, we are getting slightly ahead of the game.

The next major case to come before the Supreme Court, *Morehead v. Tipaldo*,[148] involved a New York minimum–wage statute that was drafted in such a way that it would circumvent the *Adkins* decision. The Court, however, refused to read its prior decision narrowly and struck the legislation down.

Again, the most significant thing about this case is the length and vigor of the dissents by Justices Hughes, Brandeis, Stone, and Cardozo. These proponents of employment regulation were beginning to get their thesis into final shape. Liberty of contract was recognized, but only as "a qualified and not an absolute right,"[149] and thus subject to those restrictions "which reasonable men may think an appropriate means for dealing with any of those matters of public concern with which it is the business of government to deal."[150] They emphasized the inequality of bargaining power that exists between employers and female employees, thus making "real" liberty of contract nonexistent in this context. "There is grim irony," Justice Stone said, "in speaking of the freedom of contract of those who, because of their economic necessities, give their services for less than is needful to keep body and soul together."[151] And they argued that the lack of any specific reference in the Constitution to economic matters indicates that "a state is free to adopt whatever economic policy may reasonably be deemed to promote public welfare."[152]

These sentiments had powerful appeal in 1936. The nation was in a mood to "do something" about its economic problems, but "the nine old men" on the Supreme Court stood squarely in the way. The Court was not only willing to strike down legislation on substantive due process grounds; it also narrowly construed the scope of federal power under the commerce clause[153] and limited the power of Congress to delegate rule-making authority to the Executive Branch and its administrative agencies[154]—thus effectively crippling the New Deal. Criticism of the Court's opinions was mounting, and President Roosevelt finally seized upon a plan to "pack" the Court with additional justices sympathetic to the New Deal. These external pressures, coupled with the Court's own inconsistency on substantive due process issues and (according to some) the inherent weakness of the theory itself, led to the ultimate capitulation of the Court to the legislature's power to regulate virtually all facets of the employment relationship.

The case in which this turnaround occurred was *West Coast Hotel Co. v. Parrish*,[155] which involved another state minimum-wage statute for women. Although indistinguishable from the statute involved in *Adkins,* the Court sustained its constitutionality. The overall flavor of the majority opinion, written by Justice Hughes, is adequately demonstrated by the following quotation.

> In each case the violation alleged by those attacking minimum wage regulation for women is deprivation of freedom of contract. What is this freedom? The Constitution does not speak of freedom of contract. It speaks of liberty and prohibits the deprivation of liberty without due process of law. In prohibiting that deprivation the Constitution does not recognize an absolute and uncontrollable liberty. Liberty in each of its phases has its history and connotation. But the liberty safeguarded is liberty in a social organization which requires the protection of law against the evils which menace the health, safety, morals and welfare of the people. Liberty under the Constitution is thus necessarily subject to the restraints of due process, and regulation which is reasonable in relation to its subject and is adopted in the interests of the community is due process.

The Court's reasoning here is interesting. First, it seems to regard philosophical "liberty" in terms of an individual doing whatever he wants to do, regardless. No coherent theory of liberty takes that extreme view. Second, the Court correctly notes that the Constitution does not protect *that* extreme view of liberty. Third, the clause in the Constitution that had previously served as the source of liberty of contract is now used by the Court as the source of the limitations on that liberty. Finally, the Court then defines those limitations so broadly that almost any work-related legislation would pass constitutional muster.

The Court repeated many of the points it had made earlier in *Holden* and in *Muller*. It cited the inferiority, in bargaining power and psychological strength, of women; it reaffirmed the paternalistic function of the state in protecting people from their own indiscretions; it subscribed anew to the superiority of the interests of the community and of the race in the health and well-being of its component parts; and it again stressed the importance of real over purely theoretical rights.

Finally, in a revealing passage, the Court took judicial notice of the Great Depression, which it attributed in part to employer "exploitation" of defenseless employees who, unable to obtain a living wage, have thus become a burden on the community. The Court thus concluded that "the community is not bound to provide what is in effect a subsidy for unconscionable employers. The community may direct its law-making power to correct the abuse which springs from the selfish disregard of the public interest."[156]

Four justices dissented—Justices Sutherland, Van Devanter, McReynolds, and Butler—but theirs was now a losing cause. Although *Parrish* extended minimum-wage protection to women as a specially needful class, the theory of the case was significantly broader than that. Subsequently, in 1938, Congress passed the Fair Labor Standards Act, which covered the wages and hours of a significant portion of the American workforce. It was sustained in *United States v. Darby*,[157] where the court indicated that "it is no longer open to question" that it is within the legislative power to regulate hours and wages.[158]

In 1936, the Court also sustained the constitutionality of the National Labor Relations Act, which gave employees a statutory right to organize and imposed a duty on employers to not interfere with this right in any way and to recognize and bargain with the union that represented a majority of the employees. In *NLRB v. Jones & Laughlin Steel Corp.*,[159] it stated that employees have a right to organize and that "restraint for the purpose of preventing an unjust interference with that right cannot be considered arbitrary or capricious." That took care of the employer's due process argument, and the Court likewise had no difficulty justifying the statute under the commerce clause.

In sum, the forces and influences favoring regulation of the employment relationship recast the constitutional case law into its own ideological image. As a result, employment is currently one of the most heavily regulated of all human activities. Although the relationship is still essentially contractual in nature, an employer's "willingness" to enter into a contract is often compelled by law, and the terms and conditions of that contract are subject to numerous constraints. Debate continues over whether all of these laws are necessary or wise; but that they are generally constitutional is (for the time being, at least) apparently beyond dispute.

IV. Work-Related Constitutional Liberties from
the 1940s to the Present

One of the alleged defects in the 'liberty of contract' theory was that the Constitution does not expressly mention this liberty anywhere in the document—a point which undoubtedly contributed to its ultimate demise.[160] The Constitution, however, does expressly guarantee freedom of speech, freedom of religion, freedom from the establishment of religion, procedural due process, and the equal protection of the laws. Thus, although the Constitution provides very little protection to the private employer's now mainly theoretical "liberty" to contract with his employees on whatever terms the two of them can agree upon, these other express constitutional liberties continue to make their presence felt, albeit sometimes weakly, in the work and employment context.

Free Speech and Employer Opposition to Unionization

Prior to 1935, an employer had a constitutional right to condition employment on an employee's non-membership in a labor organization. Needless to say, an employer could similarly give his employees firm assurances that joining or supporting a union would result in termination. The death of economic due process and the birth of the National Labor Relations Act changed that. This statute made it an unfair labor practice for an employer to "restrain, coerce, or interfere with" an employee's statutory right to "form, join, or assist labor organizations." Consistent with the expanded notion of "coercion" that had firmly taken hold by then, the statutory prohibition was expressly intended to cover any form of economic retaliation by an employer against employees who supported unions. Since terminating an employee for union activity was illegal, "threatening" to do it was similarly illegal. And since the First Amendment clearly does not protect illegal threats, the statutory prohibition seemed to be secure against constitutional attack.

An overzealous administrative agency soon brought constitutional violations to the surface, however. The National Labor Relations Board (NLRB) initially took the position that because the employer possessed economic power over its employees, *any* voiced opposition to unionization carried with it a threat of employer retaliation and was thus inherently coercive.

The Supreme Court disagreed. In *NLRB v. Virginia Electric & Power Co.*,[161] the employer had posted bulletins and made a speech urging employees to organize without the assistance of an outside union. The Board found this to be an unfair labor practice. Before the Supreme Court, the employer argued that this finding was repugnant to the First Amendment. Although the Court seemed to resolve the issue on a statutory rather than a constitutional basis, its interpretation of the statute in this regard was undoubtedly influenced by the probability that any other interpretation would make the act unconstitutional. Thus, *Virginia Electric* is generally viewed as holding that the First Amendment protects an employer's right to express his opinion about unionization. On the other hand, the Court also made it clear that "coercive" speech is not protected, and that words which are otherwise innocuous in isolation may take on a coercive nature when viewed against the totality of the employer's conduct.

Subsequently, in 1947, Congress amended the National Labor Relations Act by declaring that an employer's speech cannot be an unfair labor practice "if such expression contains no threat of reprisal or force or promise of benefit." This was merely intended to restate the constitutional requirement and confirm the *Virginia Electric* holding, although in the Board's view the provision "appears to . . . grant immunity beyond that contemplated by the free speech guarantees of the Constitution."[162]

The problem then became one of determining when an "expression" could be construed as containing a "threat" of some kind. The Supreme Court squarely confronted the First Amendment aspects of the problem in *NLRB v. Gissel Packing Co.*[163] One of the employers in that case had suggested to its employees that unionization might result in strikes, loss of employment, and the possible closing of the plant. The NLRB found that the speech alone illegally restrained and coerced the employees. The employer challenged this on First Amendment grounds.

In an opinion written by Chief Justice Warren, the Court began with the premise that "an employer's free speech right to communicate his views to his employees is firmly established,"[164] and that the statutory provision quoted above merely implements the First Amendment guarantee—which is to say, albeit indirectly, that there is no First Amendment right to make a "threat of [economic] reprisal." With the real issue thus resolved by fiat, the only remaining issue before the Court was whether this employer's statements should be construed as an illegal threat of retaliation or a constitutionally protected prediction or expression of opinion about the probable economic consequences of unionization which are beyond the employer's control.

In creating a test to resolve the issue, the Court took a "balancing" approach. That is, it began with the premise that "an employer's rights cannot outweigh the equal rights of the employees to associate freely."[165] To the extent that the Court was talking about the employer's *statutory* right to make non-threatening speeches and the employees' *statutory* right to associate together in a union, the "balancing" approach is perhaps an acceptable way to achieve a reconciliation. However, more was involved here than two statutory rights. The employer was asserting its *constitutional* right of free speech. Although employees do have an implied constitutional right of association, this is a right—like any other constitutional right—that flows only against the government, not against other private persons.[166] Thus, the Court had to have been balancing the employer's *constitutional* right of free speech against the employee's purely *statutory* right.

If that is what the Court was doing, then it committed an egregious error. Constitutional rights are always superior to statutory rights. Indeed, the Constitution is the benchmark against which the statute must be measured. If what the statute prohibits (which should be independently determined under the rules of statutory interpretation) includes speech which the First Amendment protects (which should also be independently determined under the rules of constitutional interpretation, whatever they are), then the statute must necessarily fail. Accommodation through "balancing" is simply the abrogation of constitutional rights by the half-step.

The specific test the Court created for differentiating between "threats" and "predictions" is not important here. Suffice it to say that the application of the test has been fraught with difficulty and has precipitated an enormous amount of litigation. This suggests that it is hard, if not impossible, for an employer to know in advance what he can or cannot say when attempting to oppose the unionization of his employees.

In any other context, a statutory test that vague and unpredictable would be unconstitutional—because of its "chilling effect" if nothing else. In *Gissel,* the Supreme Court was aware of this difficulty, but not sympathetic. It noted that an employer "cannot be heard to complain that he is without an adequate guide for his behavior. He can easily make his views known without engaging in 'brinksmanship' when it becomes all too easy to 'overstep and tumble [over] the brink.' . . . At the least, he can avoid coercive speech simply by avoiding conscious overstatements he has reason to believe will mislead his employees."[167]

In sum, the Supreme Court continues to give lip service to an employer's constitutional right to voice his opposition to unionization. But the Court is far less protective of this kind of speech than it is of speech in other contexts. Moreover, even if the Court used the more traditional First Amendment mode of analysis here, a narrowing of the employer's speech rights is an unavoidable consequence of the antecedent narrowing of his economic right of contract. It goes without saying that no one has a First Amendment right to "threaten" to engage in conduct which is itself "illegal." Thus, by limiting the employer's liberty to insist upon certain terms as a condition of employment and otherwise curtailing the employer's exercise of economic power in response to unionization efforts, the law has necessarily also limited what the employer may say he will do in the event of unionization.

Strikes, Picketing, Boycotts, and Union Advocacy

The issue in *Commonwealth v. Pullis,* discussed earlier, was whether strikes, picketing, boycotts, and certain forms of vocal expression were "coercive" in the juridical sense of the word. That is still an issue today, and one with constitutional overtones.

Despite the demise of the criminal conspiracy doctrine as such, strikes and picketing were still frequently regarded as an illegal tort during most of the nineteenth century. Then, under the influence of Oliver Wendell Holmes's theory of social utility—i.e., resolving the issue by "considerations of policy and social advantage," rather than "merely by logic and the general propositions of law which nobody disputes"[168]—the courts began to take a more tolerant view. In 1940, in *Thornhill v. Alabama,*[169] the Supreme Court held that a state law which effectively outlawed every means of publicizing the facts of a labor dispute, including peaceful picketing, violated the First Amendment of the Constitution.

The Court in *Thornhill,* in the words of Justice Douglas in a later decision, implicitly "recognized that picketing might have a *coercive* effect"[170] in that it could induce actions inimical to the economic interests of the picketed employer. The Court, however, indicated that a higher degree or form of "coercion" than that would be required to overcome the immunity afforded by the First Amendment. Although the state argued that violence and breaches of the peace were a necessary concomitant of picketing, the Court rejected the equation and held that the statute did not identify with sufficient specificity the kinds of conduct that could be proscribed without running afoul of the First Amendment.

Nevertheless, the Court has recognized that picketing involves speech-plus-conduct, and that the constitutional analysis of picketing must take that into account.[171] Subsequently, in *Milk Wagon Drivers Local 753 v. Meadowmoor Dairies, Inc.,*[172] the Court was confronted with speech-plus-conduct picketing that clearly went beyond the protections of the First Amendment. In that case, there had been large-scale violence—windows smashed; trucks wrecked, burned, and pushed into the river; plants damaged by bombs; stench bombs thrown; stores set afire; and storekeepers and drivers threatened, shot at, held at gunpoint, and beaten. The Court, speaking through Justice Frankfurter, held that the state could enjoin all subsequent picketing (even though it was otherwise peaceful) because it would necessarily carry with it a threat of renewed violence.

On the other hand, the Court also cautioned that "the right of free speech cannot be denied by drawing from a trivial rough incident or a moment of animal exuberance the conclusion that otherwise peaceful picketing has the taint of force."[173]

In the 27 years since *Meadowmoor*, the courts have done little to further clarify the fundamental issue: under what circumstances does conduct loosely referred to as "picketing" go beyond the protections of the First Amendment and thus become "coercive" in the narrow, juridical sense of the word? Rather, we are left with a broad generality—that picketing involves speech-plus-conduct that is both protected by the First Amendment and subject to reasonable restrictions with respect to time, place, and manner.[174] And what a reasonable restriction is in that regard is apparently decided on a case-by-case basis.[175]

Traditional doctrine holds that the First Amendment not only does not protect picketing that is "coercive," it also does not protect picketing that has an "unlawful objective."[176] This latter exception has been applied most often in the context of so-called "secondary boycotts." This occurs when a union engaged in a labor dispute with a particular employer pickets the customers or suppliers of this employer in an effort to induce them to stop doing business with him, and thus causes this primary employer to capitulate to the union's demands. Because this tactic embroils a neutral party in a dispute not of his own making and often causes him severe economic harm, secondary activity is generally regarded with some degree of moral opprobrium. Moreover, since it expands the battlelines of the dispute and thus increases the disruption of commerce in the community, a secondary boycott can also be criticized on utilitarian grounds. Whether such conduct rises to the level of "coercion" in the narrow, juridical sense is another matter.

In 1947, Congress decided that it would generally outlaw secondary activity. Some senators were concerned, however, that a total ban on secondary activity might be unconstitutional. The statute thus exempted "publicity, other than picketing" that advised the public that the secondary employer was distributing nonunion products and that did not otherwise cause a disruption in deliveries or work.

Despite that attempt to narrow the scope of the prohibition, constitutional issues have arisen. With respect to picketing itself, the Court has relied on the "unlawful objectives" doctrine. That is, Congress has declared it unlawful to attempt to cause a secondary employer to cease doing business with a primary employer. Thus, even though it is a form of "expression," picketing with that objective warrants no constitutional protection.[177]

There is nothing wrong with the "illegal objectives" theory as such. If a stump-speaker urged his listeners to go out and immediately assassinate the mayor, that would certainly be an "expression," albeit one scarcely deserving of constitutional protection. The problem, however, is in narrowing the scope of the major premise—i.e., determining what is appropriately regarded as an "illegal" object for the purpose of the theory. As Justice Stevens has pointed out, if that includes anything that Congress has declared unlawful, then this means "the First Amendment would place no limit on Congress' power."[178]

With respect to labor matters, however, that seems to be precisely the case. In the absence of substantive due process constraints, Congress can regulate economic relationships at will. And if it can constitutionally prohibit secondary activity, then it can also constitutionally prohibit speech that is intended to achieve that objective.

This is true, moreover, even when the provisions of the labor statute are applied not in the context of a traditional labor dispute, but rather to a purely politically-motivated boycott. In *International Longshoremen's Assoc. v. Allied International, Inc.*,[179] the Court concluded that the union violated the statute when, in a protest over the Soviet invasion of Afghanistan, ILA members refused to handle any Russian goods in transit. Speaking through Justice Powell, the Court gave short shrift to the First Amendment argument.

> We have consistently rejected the claim that secondary picketing by labor unions in violation of Sec. 8(b) (4) is protected activity under the First Amendment. It would seem even clearer that conduct designed not to communicate but to coerce merits still less consideration under the First Amendment. The labor laws reflect a careful balancing of interests. There are many ways in which a union and its individual members may express their opposition to Russian foreign policy without infringing upon the rights of others.[180]

In other words, the "illegal objectives" test absolutely controls.

Moreover, the union's conduct involved "coercion," not communication. In any event, the employer's statutory right to be free from economic disruption prevails over the constitutional right of expression.[181]

The Supreme Court has yet to consider the really "hard case." It would consist of union handbilling or newspaper advertising, unaccompanied by any form of speech-plus-conduct picketing, that urged consumers to boycott a particular business until it stopped doing business with an employer with whom the union had a dispute. Assuming that the conduct would violate the statute and not fall within the "publicity, other than picketing" exception mentioned above, then the question would be whether such a prohibition is constitutional.

In *Florida Gulf Costs Building & Construction Trades Council v. NLRB,*[182] the Eleventh Circuit Federal Court of Appeals indicated, in a thorough and well-reasoned opinion, that if the statute did prohibit such handbilling, then the statute would be unconstitutional. But then, in an effort to avoid that result, the court construed the statute as not prohibiting the conduct in question.

On appeal, the Supreme Court only briefly noted the probable constitutional violation, and then avoided it by resolving the issue on a statutory basis. To do this, however, the Court had to torture the statutory language, read the legislative history imaginatively, and ignore or reconstrue a great deal of secondary boycott precedent. That is a high price to pay merely to avoid the appearance of 'Lochnerizing'.

The Freedom to Work, and to Require Employees to Work, on Sunday

Conservative Christians have traditionally held to some fairly narrow views about what one should and should not do on Sunday. Work is usually one of the proscribed activities. This belief has provided the impetus for Sunday closing or so-called "blue laws" in three ways. First, some of these people are not at all hesitant to impose this belief upon the community at large on the theory that it is a matter of "public morality" and thus within the purview of state action. Second, believers who happen to be business owners find that practicing the belief, when others do not, puts them at an economic disadvantage — and providing relief from competition is, apparently, a legitimate state function. Third, believers who happen to be employees of Sunday-working employers feel "coerced" when they have to make a choice between church and job — and the elimination of "coercion" is also a legitimate function of government.

But whether it flows through the conduit of "public morality" or a claim of insulating others from the result of making economic choices, the motivating force behind Sunday closing laws is clearly religious. The effect, moreover, is to provide direct support to a particular religious belief and indirect support to a particular religious faith. Unless one adopts the narrow view that the establishment clause of the First Amendment prohibits only the literal institution of a state religion, one would think that Sunday blue laws must necessarily be unconstitutional.

The Supreme Court has held otherwise. The general rule is that legislation which may tend to promote or retard religion will nevertheless be considered constitutional if it has some secular purpose and effect. In *McGowan v. Maryland*,[183] the Court held that providing a "uniform day of rest for all citizens" satisfied the secular purpose/effect requirement, and that the benefit to religion was remote and incidental—presumably because everyone, whether pursuing God or golf, equally enjoyed the liberty of choice.

The Court was apparently not at all embarrassed by the patent transparency of that explanation. However, even if the Court really believed that a legislature might choose to mandate a "uniform day of rest" even in the absence of any organized religious pressure to do so, a fundamental question remains. While that might be a "secular" purpose, what is the philosophical and constitutional justification for allowing a state to force a person to take a day of rest? Or conversely, why isn't working a full seven days a week a natural (and thus an inherently constitutional) right? However fundamental the question, *Parrish* rendered it moot in its repudiation of the underlying theory of economic due process.

The secular purpose and effect test does, however, impose some limits on how far a legislature can go in promoting religion over the right to work. In *Estate of Thronton v. Caldor, Inc.*,[184] the Court struck down a state statute which gave every employee the unqualified right to refuse to work on whatever day that employee observed as his Sabbath. The state supreme court found that neither the purpose nor the effect of the law was secular. The Supreme Court merely focused on the effect.[185] In an opinion written by Justice Burger, the Court found that since the statute "commands that Sabbath religious concerns [and only "religious" concerns] automatically control over *all* [emphasis added] secular interests at the workplace,"[186] the statute necessarily had more than a merely incidental or remote effect of advancing religion.

The Court, however, seemed even more concerned with the purely secular impact of the statute, noting that it would "cause the employer substantial economic burdens" and also "require the imposition of significant burdens on other employees required to work in place of Sabbath observers."[187] In this regard, the Court's opinion reads more like an economic due process case than an establishment clause case.

The Court also implicitly rejected the notion that the free exercise clause of the First Amendment is an inchoate positive right that legislation merely brought into fruition. Borrowing from Judge Learned Hand, the Court noted that "The First Amendment . . . gives no one the right to insist that in pursuit of their own interest others must conform their conduct to his own religious necessities."[188]

Freedom of and from Religion versus the Employment
Anti-Discrimination Statutes

Title VII of the federal Civil Rights Act of 1964 makes it illegal for an employer to discriminate on the basis of religion. In addition, an employer has an affirmative duty to "reasonably accommodate" an employer's religious observances and practices, unless doing so would cause the employer "undue hardship." On the other hand, although religious organizations are generally subject to the statute, they are exempt from these provisions.

Title VII's treatment of religious discrimination raises several important constitutional issues, especially in light of the *Thornton* decision. The primary ones are three. 1) Does a state-imposed duty to accommodate an employee's religious practices violate the establishment clause of the First Amendment? 2) Does the exemption of religious organizations violate the establishment clause of the First Amendment? 3) And, quite apart from the statute, does an employer (whether a religious organization or not) have a free exercise right to use religious criteria in selecting employees, even though it results in discrimination on some proscribed basis (race, sex, color, religion, national origin, age, and others)? These will be taken up in turn.

The Accommodation Requirement. The Supreme Court has never directly addressed the constitutionality of the accommodation requirement.[189] The argument, however, would be that it violates the establishment clause for the government to impose "a priority of the religious over the secular,"[190] especially when the accommodation would impose a tangible hardship on and result in discrimination against non-religious employees. The issue was raised in *Trans World Airlines, Inc. v. Hardison*,[191] with respect to an employee who, for religious reasons, would not work on Saturday. A majority of the Court, speaking through Justice White, avoided resolving the issue. They did this by construing the statutory duty narrowly and the exception broadly. That is, the Court held that if accommodation would cause anything more than *de minimus* cost to the employer or disadvantage to other employees, then this is an "undue hardship" and the employer is not bound to honor the employee's wishes. The Court found undue hardship, so defined, on the facts of that case.

Justices Marshall and Brennan dissented, claiming that the Court interpreted the statute as it did merely to avoid a constitutional issue that it did not need to avoid. They cited ample precedent involving religious exemptions from various duties owed the state, and concluded that "if the State does not establish religion over non-religion by excusing practitioners from obligations owed the State, I do not see how the State can be said to establish religion by requiring employers to do the same with respect to obligations owed the employer."[192]

To the extent that the *Hardison* case does have constitutional overtones, the significance lies in the Court's refusal to accept the parallel case argued by the dissent. Merely because the state may, without violating the Constitution, grant religious exceptions does not mean that the state may constitutionally compel a private employer to grant such an exception. Although the Establishment Clause is an odd vehicle for its expression, this may reflect a residual sensitivity to the autonomy of a private employer and his right to make employment decisions free from state interference.

The Exemption Issue. The second major constitutional issue that has risen under the religious discrimination provisions of Title VII is whether the exemption afforded religious organizations constitutes an impermissible establishment of religion. The Supreme Court has said that it does not. In *Corporation of the Presiding Bishop v. Amos*,[193] the Court upheld the application of the exception to a decision by the Mormon Church to terminate an employee working in a secular non-profit facility owned by the Church. In an opinion by Justice White, the Court applied the traditional three-pronged test of *Lemon v. Kurtzman*[194] and held that the exemption had a secular purpose, that its primary effect was neither to advance nor hinder religion, and that it did not foster excessive government entanglement.

The critical point of the analysis was in the Court's finding of a "secular" purpose. This, the Court said, consisted of the need to avoid excessive governmental entanglement with religious activities which might, thus, unconstitutionally interfere with a church's free exercise rights. This implicitly suggests that the Court felt that the Presiding Bishop of the Church of Jesus Christ of Latter-day Saints had a First Amendment right to discriminate against non-Mormons, a right which the exception merely vindicated.

The *Amos* decision reveals an enormous anomaly with respect to the First Amendment. It can be developed by reference to three relatively uncontroversial propositions. First, whatever the free exercise of religion means, it surely does not encompass the right to commit a "jural wrong" against another person—i.e., to engage in conduct which violates what *ought* to be considered that person's rights. Such conduct, rather, is a breach of what *ought* to be considered a duty. In this regard, it does not make any difference what legal or moral philosophy one uses to give definition to those rights and duties that *ought* to be honored—be it natural law, utilitarianism, or some sort of Rawlsian notion of "fairness." Thus, everyone would agree that no one has a First Amendment right to engage in the ritual sacrifice of virgins as a part of a religious exercise, or that a church has a right to commit fraud against its creditors on that basis.

Second, whatever norm of rights and duties is being relied on, that norm also provides the justification for a law which prohibits the rights-violating or duty-breaching misconduct. Conversely, if conduct is permissible under the controlling norm, then a law prohibiting it is itself without justification.

Third, to the extent that the norm is somehow also incorporated into the Constitution as both an authorization of and a limit on government power, then a law which prohibits rights-violating or duty-breaching misconduct is not only constitutional, it is constitutionally required. A law which prohibits permissible conduct, on the other hand, is unconstitutional.

From these three points, the anomaly emerges. If a religious organization has a constitutional right to discriminate against employees on a religious basis (which is what the *Amos* case implicitly holds), then *a fortiori* such conduct cannot be regarded as a right-violating or duty-breaching "jural wrong." But if that is the case, then one does not need to rely on the special provisions of the First Amendment. Rather, the law is unconstitutional under the third premise noted above. And if it is unconstitutional on that basis, then it does not make any difference whether it is being applied to a religious organization or not. It is unconstitutional in any event.

On the other hand, if employment discrimination on a religious basis is, under the controlling norm, properly regarded as a "jural wrong," as it is under Title VII, then *a fortiori* it cannot be regarded as a "right" protected by the First Amendment. Thus, a special exception for discrimination by religious organizations cannot be justified, as it was in *Amos,* by reference to the need to avoid governmental interference with free exercise rights. No such right exists!

This First Amendment anomaly is not new. Indeed, a slightly different form of it underlay some of the original opposition to the Bill of Rights as a whole. The argument was that since the federal government has no powers except those granted it by the Constitution, and since the Constitution does not empower the federal government to do any of the things that the Bill prohibits, the enumeration of rights was unnecessary. Indeed, it was felt that the very presence of the specific prohibitions would suggest that the federal government possessed inherent powers of general sovereignty. To overcome that implication, and thus gain the support of these detractors, the Framers included the Ninth Amendment which provides that "the enumeration in the Constitution of certain rights shall not be construed to deny or disparage others retained by the people."

In any event, what the anomaly reveals is that the First Amendment is essentially redundant or superfluous. The rights retained by the people already include everything that could legitimately be encompassed by the free exercise clause, and more.

Of course, the anomaly disappears if the critical third premise is rejected — namely, the notion that what government is constitutionally empowered or required to prohibit and what government can or must permit are mutually exclusive categories, with some extralegal concept of rights and duties serving as the divining rod. Rather, the government is free to prohibit whatever it wants to, unless the prohibition would run afoul of some specific constitutional provision. Indeed, this appears to be the approach that Holmes, Brandeis, and others urged the Court to take with respect to claims of substantive due process of an economic nature. It is likewise the approach currently favored by Judge Bork and certain other conservatives with respect to substantive due process claims of a personal nature (e.g., privacy and abortion).

The Right-to-Discriminate Issue. The third issue is whether a religious organization or individual has a free exercise right to discriminate, regardless of whether a statute grants an exception or not. The issue here could not only encompass employment discrimination based on conflicting religious beliefs, but also religiously motivated discrimination based on race, sex, and other grounds proscribed by statute.

Under the analysis developed above in connection with the anomaly, such a right might well exist — under the Ninth Amendment, if not under the First. The Supreme Court, however, has not yet addressed this issue. But it has arisen in the lower federal courts, and it is likely that one of these cases will eventually reach the Supreme Court. In *Dayton Christian Schools v. Ohio Civil Rights Commission,*[195] an employee who had given birth to a child was told that her contract would not be renewed, since the school believed that it was her Biblical obligation to stay at home with the child until it was of school age. The employee consulted an attorney, and was then terminated for failing to follow the Biblical "chain of command." She filed a complaint with the Ohio Civil Rights Commission, alleging sex (pregnancy) and religious discrimination.[196] The school sought an injunction and a declaratory judgment that the enforcement of the statute would violate the school's First Amendment right to the free exercise of its religious beliefs.

The federal district court denied the injunction.[197] After a comprehensive review of the confusing Supreme Court precedent, the court concluded that while enforcement of the Ohio statute would clearly impinge on the school's free exercise rights, "the state has a compelling and overriding interest in eliminating sex discrimination in the employment setting."[198] There is a close parallel between the approach the district court took here and the approach the Supreme Court ultimately took with respect to liberty-of-contract claims: the right (contract/religion) exists, but it is subject to limitation if the public interest (as defined by the legislature) requires it.

The Sixth Circuit Court of Appeals reversed. It also used a "compelling state interest" test, but construed it as meaning that the legislation must be "essential"—perhaps even to the point of being "constitutionally compelled." This suggests that the state has an affirmative duty and is thus "constitutionally compelled" to prevent and remedy rights violations (i.e., "jural wrongs"). The state, therefore, must prohibit natural law violations like murder, and the logical corollary of that is that such conduct is not encompassed by the free exercise clause. But discrimination in choosing one's work associates is not a violation of any natural law or inherent right. While the state may choose to prohibit it, it is not compelled to do so. There is, therefore, no "compelling state interest," and the employer's inherent or pre-constitutional right to engage in such discrimination, *at least when it can be fit into the positive protections of the First Amendment,* is entitled to prevail.

The Supreme Court agreed to review the case, but—perhaps because it did not want to confront this very difficult constitutional issue—reversed the court of appeals on totally unrelated grounds.

The issue, of course, will not die. However it is resolved, the resolution will still leave us with some fundamental questions. If the First Amendment does not protect this conduct, what does it protect and what function can it possibly serve? If the First Amendment does protect this conduct, does this mean that the First Amendment provides the religious with a cloak of immunity for their violations of other people's rights? There would seem to be no satisfactory answers to *either* question!

The Constitutional Right to Enter an Occupation

In medieval times, the various trades were organized into guilds. The guild regulated entry into the trade, imposed systems of training and apprenticeship, dictated standards of performance, fixed the price that could be charged, and otherwise controlled the practice of that trade. The modern equivalent of guilds is the multitude of state and federal licensing boards and agencies that currently controls the entry into and the practice of over 200 trades and occupations.[199] This includes not only the obvious professions such as medicine, law, dentistry, pharmacy, and the like, but also egg graders, tile layers, potato growers, yacht and lightning rod salesmen, beekeepers, tree surgeons, and a host of other common (and uncommon!) occupations. Although protection of the public is the asserted justification for licensing laws, it is rarely an aroused public that demands enactment of these occupational constraints. Rather, the pressure nearly always comes from the occupation itself, whose practitioners then occupy the boards that control who else can join the "club."[200]

Since the demise of economic due process, broad-based attacks on the constitutionality of occupational licensure laws have generally failed.[201] However, there has not been a total abdication by the Supreme Court in the matter of the regulation of occupational membership. Rather, the Court still recognizes that the individual has a constitutionally protected interest in being free from arbitrary and oppressive exclusion from life's common callings.[202]

The Supreme Court has held, for example, that the due process clause protects a person from being excluded from a profession for reasons which bear no rational relation to the applicant's fitness or ability to practice the occupation.[203] Indeed, the Court now seems to require more than mere rationality. In *Hampton v. Mow Sun Wong*,[204] the Court held that the asserted justification for excluding non-citizens from employment in the federal civil service was subject to a higher level of judicial scrutiny and proof than is usually used in economic regulation cases. The Court's approach in this case was not substantially different than the approach it took in the heyday of economic due process.[205]

The Supreme Court also continues to recognize certain procedural due process rights in the context of occupational licensing. For example, a person may not be excluded from an occupation without being afforded at least some kind of hearing, however informal.[206] Likewise, in *Gibson v. Berryhill*,[207] the Court held that due process requires impartiality and that a licensing board composed solely of practicing self-employed optometrists, whose pecuniary interests were thus directly at stake, could not constitutionally revoke the licenses of all optometrists who were employed by business corporations.

Although the degree of constitutional protection that exists in this regard is somewhat occupation-specific (the nuances of which need not concern us), the important thing is that these cases reflect the lingering beliefs that the ability to earn a living is too important to be left entirely to the whims of political influence, legislative notions of public policy, and majoritarian notions of social utility. Indeed, it is perhaps significant that in *Mow Sun Wong*, Justice Stevens quoted a leading *Lochner*-era case as follows: "It requires no argument to show that the right to work for a living in the common occupations of the community is of the very essence of the personal freedom and opportunity that it was the purpose of the [Fourteenth] Amendment to secure."[208]

Other Constitutional Issues

Other work-related constitutional issues have loomed large in recent years. For example, there has been a considerable amount of Supreme Court litigation over whether ostensibly private entities, like employers and labor unions, are in some circumstances agents of the state for constitutional purposes. Likewise, the substantive and procedural constitutional rights of public employees is a topic of enormous breadth and complexity. And there are others.

These issues, however, go beyond the scope of this paper. Its focus has been on the constitutional rights of admittedly private entities to engage in work-related activities free from prohibitions by the state.

V. Conclusion

This long review of Supreme Court decisions dealing with work-related constitutional issues yields no obvious conclusions—either about what has happened in the past, or what is likely to occur in the future. Some general observations, however, may be in order.

First, what happened in the mid-1930s was more than merely the repudiation of a specific doctrine of constitutional law, the so-called "liberty of contract." Rather, it represented a fundamental change in the philosophy of the Court, which manifested itself in constitutional law in an entirely different approach to economic and work-related issues—one with different results.

The *Lochner*-era Court was clearly operating from a natural rights premise. Although it never fully articulated (or perhaps even understood) its philosophy, and certainly never applied it in an entirely consistent fashion, that was nevertheless the base from which it operated.

The post-*Lochner* constitutional case law is harder to characterize, but it seems to consist of a loose mixture of utilitarianism and pragmatism. It can perhaps be synthesized into the following proposition: the current Court is likely to render decisions which it believes will tend to promote rather than retard work-related opportunities, security, and economic well-being—and which will thus inure to the stability and prosperity of society as a whole.[209]

The Court will thus recognize a constitutional right if it supports that result; it will ignore even express constitutional rights if their recognition would tend to negate that result.

If this is what the Court is doing, then it is no less a "super-legislature" then the *Lochner*-era Court was alleged to be. It is simply that the Court now tends to agree with what the real legislature is doing.

Second, I would suggest that the laws and decisions discussed in this historical overview are merely a paradigm of the broader principle that governmental power always tends to grow incrementally rather than diminish. The United States Constitution was designed, at least at the federal level, to reverse that historical fact. But as construed by the Supreme Court, it has not proved to be a very useful tool. The commerce clause is a classic example; originally designed to limit state interference with economic matters, it has now become the source of a general federal police power.

This suggests that the Constitution may be a slender reed on which to rely insofar as preserving individual liberty is concerned. Certainly, liberty of contract was once as firmly entrenched as a constitutional principle as the right of privacy currently is, if not more so. If the Supreme Court's constitutional-law methodology can be used to accommodate the growth of governmental power over economic activities, it can just as easily be used to justify the Leviathan's insatiable appetite in other areas. Thus, whether one subscribes to the liberty of contract doctrine or not, the circumstances surrounding its death should cause concern to those who value individual rights, whatever the substantive content happens to be.

Third, whether work-related constitutional liberties wax or wane will not be determined exclusively by the abstract principles of constitutional law. There are plenty of constitutional theories and doctrines that could be used to justify a rebirth of economic liberty—just as there are plenty to justify the continuation of extensive state regulation. The debate at that level is useful, important, and certainly contributes to the choice that is made. But history suggests that the Court's selection of an appropriate doctrinal tool is heavily influenced by factors which transcend the narrow and technical limits of legal discourse.

In the last analysis, it appears that American "constitutional law" consists of a particular moral philosophy permeating the social fabric and ultimately manifesting itself in a generally shared view as to where government power ends and individual rights begin, which is then pinpointed by a judicial decision. It occurred in the era following ratification. It occurred shortly after the Civil War. It occurred in the mid-1930s. It occurred in the early 1960s. And each occurrence produced its own version of "constitutional law," even though the words of the document often did not change.

Fourth, and finally, it is impossible to predict when another change in the public philosophy will occur, what direction it will take, or how it will affect the Supreme Court's resolution of work-related constitutional issues.

However, any reexamination of the rights and powers controversy must begin with the frank recognition of the true nature of law, for this is how the *power* of government is exercised and where the *rights* of the individual will be asserted. Although they disagree over the moral implications of this fact, most legal and political philosophers agree that in the last analysis that which we call "law" is merely the threatened or actual use of physical force by the political sovereign. Max Weber, for example, has said that the modern state is simple "a human community that (successfully) claims the monopoly of the legitimate use of physical force within a given territory."[210] Woodrow Wilson likewise defined governmental law-making power in terms of "organized force."[211]

In other words, whether it pertains to armed robbery or the payment of a substandard wage, the *ultimate* consequence of making something "against the law" is that a person who steadfastly refuses to comply with the command of the sovereign will eventually be visited by a police officer, who will then use whatever physical force is necessary to either compel the required compliance or punish the noncompliance. Recognition of that hard reality, by the public and officialdom alike, is absolutely essential before any meaningful reevaluation of the rights and powers dispute can occur.

Such recognition will also necessarily change the focus of the inquiry. When law is viewed in terms of coercive force, rather than merely as a set of abstract norms of socially-desired conduct, this considerably narrows the bases of justification that will be required. As the nineteenth-century French economist and philosopher Bastiat put it, "We must remember that law is force, and that, consequently, the proper functions of the law cannot extend beyond the proper functions of force."[212] In other words, there are *moral* limits on the use of physical force, even when it is by the political sovereign. Those limits thus define the proper scope of governmental *power;* where that power ends, the individual's *rights* begin.

Identifying those moral limits on the use of physical force, and applying them to the various laws which regulate work activities, is far beyond the scope of this paper. But even tentative speculation on the question leads one to suspect that many of our current labor and employment laws may have a hard time passing muster. Much of the currently regulated conduct is ethically offensive and socially dysfunctional, but this is not to say that it necessarily justifies a physically coercive response by the state.[213] And if that response is not justified, then the laws themselves are inappropriate.

This is not to say, however, that these laws are necessarily unconstitutional. That is a separate issue, and its resolution depends on whether these moral limits on the use of force have also been incorporated into the Constitution. That issue, too, is beyond the scope of this paper. However, a strong historical and contextual argument can be made that the Fifth and Fourteenth Amendment due process clauses, as well as the Ninth Amendment, do indeed contain implied moral limits on the use of coercive power by the state. To be sure, the process of implication will sometimes be difficult, uncertain, and even controversial. But as with the moral analysis itself, a constitutional analysis so predicated is likely to result in a substantial deregulation of work and employment relationships. And if that happens, then the words of Justice Douglas may finally be vindicated. He once said,

> The right to work I had assumed, was the most precious liberty that man possesses. Man has indeed as much right to work as he has to live, to be free, to own property. . . . It does many men little good to stay alive and free and propertied, if they cannot work. To work means to eat. It also means to live. For many it would be better to work in jail, than to sit idle on the curb. The great values of freedom are in the opportunities afforded man to press to new horizons, to put his strength against the forces of nature, to match skills with his fellow man.[214]

That quotation, however, reflects a far different allocation of *rights* and *powers* than currently exists. Whether it will change or not is too problematic to predict.

Notes

1. As will be evident throughout the paper, I am using the term "work" very broadly, to encompass whatever it is we do to obtain our subsistence. In that sense, "work" occurs on both sides of the employer-employee relationship.

2. The "regulations" that this paper deals with are limited mainly to restrictions on entry into certain occupations, controls over the terms and conditions of the employment relationship, and laws affecting organizational activities and employer responses to them.

3. The Supreme Court itself expressly recognizes this. In *Muller v. Oregon*, 208 U.S. 412, 420 (1908), the Court put it this way:

> Constitutional questions, it is true, are not settled by even a consensus of present public opinion, for it is the peculiar value of a written constitution that it places in unchanging form limitations upon legislative action, and thus gives a permanence and stability to popular government which otherwise would be lacking. At the same time, when a question of fact is debated and debatable, and the extent to which a special

> constitutional limitation goes is affected by the truth in respect to that fact, a widespread and long continued belief concerning it is worthy of consideration.

The "fact" in question was that woman's physical structure and her functions as wife and mother of the race justify special legislation limiting her freedom to work.

4. *See generally*, M. TURNER, THE EARLY AMERICAN LABOR CONSPIRACY CASES: THEIR PLACE IN LABOR (1967); Forkosch, *The Doctrine of Criminal Conspiracy and Its Modern Application to Labor*, 40 TEX. L. REV. 303 (1962); Nelles, *The First American Labor Case*, 41 YALE L.J. 165 (1931); Sayre, *Criminal Conspiracy*, 35 HARV. L. REV. 303 (1922); Witte, *Early Conspiracy Cases*, 35 YALE L.J. 825 (1926).

5. The Statute of Labourers, 1349, 23 Edw. 3.

6. *See* Forkosch, *supra* note 4, at 310–13. In *Charles Wolff Packing Co. v. Kansas*, 262 U.S. 522, 537 (1923), the Court noted that "it is true that in the days of the early common law an omnipotent Parliament did regulate prices and wages as it chose, and occasionally a Colonial legislature sought to exercise the same power. . . ." The Court, however, held that mandatory arbitration of wage disputes was unconstitutional under tenets of post-Revolution jurisprudence. *But see New State Ice Co. v. Liebmann*, 285 U.S. 262, 305–6 (1932) (J. Brandeis, dissenting) (noting with apparent approval the mercantilistic legislation of Parliament, the colonies, and even some states following the Revolution).

7. 2 & 3 Edw. 6. c. 15.

8. *See* Sayre, *supra* note 4, at 398–402.

9. HAWKINS, PLEAS OF THE CROWN (6th ed.), bk. I, c. 72, § 2, p. 348.

10. 8 Mod. 10, 88 Eng. Rep. 9 (K.B. 1721).

11. Although the name of the case is intriguing, the nature of the tubwomen/brewer controversy is unknown, as the cited case has never been located.

12. c. 726 (Jan. 21, 1777), 1 Laws of the Commonwealth of Pennsylvania 1700–1810, p. 429 (1810).

13. The transcript of the trial is contained in 3 J. COMMONS, DOCUMENTARY HISTORY OF AMERICAN INDUSTRIAL SOCIETY 58–250 (1958).

14. COMMONS, *supra* note 13, at 36–37.

15. Nelles, *supra* note 4, at 175.

16. COMMONS, *supra* note 13, at 111.

17. COMMONS, *supra* note 13, at 158.

18. COMMONS, *supra* note 13, at 150.

19. COMMONS, *supra* note 13, at 146.

20. BLACK'S LAW DICTIONARY 354 (5th ed. 1979).

21. COMMONS, *supra* note 13, at 147–48.

22. COMMONS, *supra* note 13, at 145.

23. COMMONS, *supra* note 13, at 236.

24. 45 Mass. (4 Met.) 111 (1982).

25. Nelles, *Commonwealth v. Hunt*, 32 COLUM. L. REV. 1128 (1932).

26. *Id.* at 123.

27. *Id.* at 133.

28. *Id.* at 130.

29. Although it is often said that *Commonwealth v. Hunt* marked the death of the criminal conspiracy doctrine, the doctrine actually lingered on until the end of the century; its underlying philosophy was evident in cases involving injunctions and damage actions against striking unions. *See* T. HAGGARD, COMPULSORY UNIONISM, THE NLRB, AND THE COURTS 17–24 (1977).

30. L. LEVY, THE LAW OF THE COMMONWEALTH AND CHIEF JUSTICE SHAW 183 (1957).

31. For an excellent and exhaustive study of all the slavery related cases, see P. FINKELMAN, AN IMPERFECT UNION—SLAVERY, FEDERALISM, AND COMITY (1981).

32. 60 U.S. (19 How.) 393 (1857).

33. The case itself is a monument to the complexity of the issue. There were nine separate opinions, covering 248 pages in the United States Report.

34. L. TRIBE, AMERICAN CONSTITUTIONAL LAW 356 n. 12 (2nd ed. 1988).

35. *See* B. SIEGAN, ECONOMIC LIBERTIES AND THE CONSTITUTION 16 (1980) (citing a variety of sources reflecting this point of view).

36. Although the United States Supreme Court has been roundly castigated for its substantive due process era decisions, state supreme courts were reaching virtually identical conclusions on the same labor issues. *See generally* A. PAUL, CONSERVATIVE CRISIS AND THE RULE OF LAW: ATTITUDES OF BAR AND BENCH, 1887–1895 (1976).

37. *See* L. TRIBE, *supra* note 34, at 567.

38. Turner, *supra* note 4, at 19, quoting from L. TELLER, LABOR DISPUTES AND COLLECTIVE BARGAIINING (1940).

39. Nelson, *The Impact of the Antislavery Movement Upon Styles of Judicial Reasoning in Nineteenth Century America*, 87 HARV. L. REV. 513, 537–38 (1974).

40. Cong. Globe, 39th Cong., 1st Sess. 1833 (1866).

41. Other evidence of this can be found in Vieira, *Of Syndicalism, Slavery and the Thirteenth Amendment,* 12 WAKE FOREST L. REV. 515, 674–81 (1976).

42. J. ANDERSON, THE EMERGENCE OF THE MODERN REGULATORY STATE 11 (1962).

43. 4 *Am. Labor Legis. Rev.* 45 (1914).

44. ANDERSON, *supra* note 42, at 8.

45. COMPENDIUM ON WORKMEN'S COMPENSATION 15 (1973).

46. H. MILLIS & R. MONTGOMERY, LABOR'S PROGRESS AND PROBLEMS 279 (1938).

47. 4 *Am. Labor Legis. Rev.* 39–40 (1914).

48. C. EASTMAN, WORK-ACCIDENTS AND THE LAW 188 (1910).

49. "Legal realism" is more an approach to the law than a distinct "philosophy." Its leading proponents have included Oliver Wendell Holmes, William O. Douglas, Jerome Frank, and Karl Llewellyn. It is characterized by one or more of the following attributes: 1) a separation of law and morality; 2) a distrust of deductive logic; 3) a suspicion of generalizations and abstract rules; 4) a belief that law should be used as an instrument for "social engineering"; and 5) an emphasis on what legal officials do rather than what they say. G. CHRISTIE, JURISPRUDENCE: TEXT AND READINGS ON THE PHILOSOPHY OF LAW 641–44 (1973).

50. Quoted and criticized in A. RAND, CAPITALISM: THE UNKNOWN IDEAL 324 (1967).

51. *See* SIEGAN, *supra* note 35, at 24–46.

52. 83 U.S. (16 Wall.) 36 (1873).

53. *Id.* at 70.

54. *Id.* at 81.

55. *Id.*

56. *Id.* at 87. This was consistent with a view prevalent at the time that the use of the police power was to be narrowly confined to the enforcement of the legal maxim *sic utere tuo ut alienum non laeda* (so to use your own as not to cause injury to another's). *See* C. TIEDEMAN, LIMITATIONS OF POLICE POWER (1886).

57. *Id.* at 88–89.

58. *Id.* at 90–91.

59. *Id.* at 97 (emphasis in original).

60. *Id.* at 127.

61. 83 U.S. (16 Wall.) 130 (1872).

62. *Id.* at 141 (Bradley, concurring).

63. 113 U.S. 27 (1885).

64. 113 U.S. 703 (1885).

65. *Id.* at 709–10.

66. 113 U.S. at 31.

67. 157 U.S. 160 (1895).

68. *Id.* at 165–66. "Public policy" is apparently anything the legislature says it is, as all that was involved there was a limit on the fee an attorney could charge for helping a person file for a pension under a federal statute.

69. 118 U.S. 356 (1886).

70. *Id.* at 370.

71. 127 U.S. 678 (1888).

72. *Id.* at 692, quoting from *In re Jacobs*, 98 N.Y. 98 (Ct.App. 1885).

73. *Id.* (emphasis added).

74. 165 U.S. 578 (1897) (holding unconstitutional a Louisiana statute which prohibited residents from obtaining marine insurance from out-of-state companies not licensed to do business in Louisiana).

75. *Id.* at 589.

76. 169 U.S. 366 (1898).

77. *Id.* at 387.

78. *Id.* at 389.

79. *Id.* at 391. This formula, which rings of moderation and reasonableness, was often evoked in subsequent years whenever the Court decided it would uphold a particular piece of legislation. *See, e.g.,* Knoxville Iron Co. v. Harbison, 183 U.S. 13 (1901) (law requiring employers to redeem "script" in cash); Muller v. Oregon, 208 U.S. 412 (1908) (maximum hours for female employees); McLean v. Arkansas, 211 U.S. 539 (1909) (law regulating the calculation of miner's wages).

80. *Id.* at 397.

81. 198 U.S. 45 (1905).

82. *Id.* at 57.

83. *Id.* at 60.

84. *Id.* at 60–61.

85. *Id.* at 59.

86. Justices Harlan, White, and Day also dissented, on the grounds that the physical well-being of bakers was a legitimate concern of the state, and that, because of an inequality of bargaining power, bakers were being compelled to work long hours. They felt that the New York legislature had made a reasonable judgment that this was unhealthy and that the Court should defer to that judgment.

87. *Id.* at 75.

88. *Id.*

89. *Id.* Spencer had articulated the maxim that "Every man has freedom to do all that he will, provided he infringes not on the equal freedom of any other man." H. SPENCER, SOCIAL STATICS 95 (Schalkenback Foundation ed. 1970). As was noted earlier, this maxim was the cornerstone of most theories of natural and individual rights.

91. *Id.* at 75 & 76.

92. 208 U.S. 161 (1908).

93. *Id.* at 172.

94. *Id.* at 176.

95. 236 U.S. 1 (1915).

96. *Id.* at 8.

97. *Id.* at 9.

98. *Id.* at 14.

99. *Id.* at 17.

100. *Id.* at 19–20.

101. *Id.* at 29.

102. This approach to the constitutional issue is itself a significantly different one, and it will be discussed more fully in the context of *Muller v. Oregon*, notes 103–7 *infra*.

103. 208 U.S. 412 (1908).

104. *Id.* at 421.

105. *Id.* at 421.

106. *Id.* at 422 (emphasis added).

107. *Id.* at 421.

108. 211 U.S. 539 (1909).

109. *Id.* at 547.

110. *Id.* at 550.

111. Anglo-American law has always regarded seamen as being totally infantile and incapable of looking after their own best interests, thus justifying a wide range of "protective" legislation. *See, e.g.,* Patterson v. Bark Eudora, 159 U.S. 169 (1903) (sustaining legislation prohibiting the payment of advance wages).

112. 243 U.S. 426 (1917).

113. *Id.* at 438.

114. Adkins v. Children's Hosp., 261 U.S. 525, 564 (1923) (Taft, dissenting).

115. The Court's 1917 tolerance of police power regulation was not without its limits, however. In *Adams v. Tanner,* 244 U.S. 590 (1917), the Court invalidated a law prohibiting employment agents from recovering fees from workers. "Happily for all," the Court said, "the fundamental guarantees of the Constitution cannot be freely submerged if and whenever some ostensible justification is advanced and the police power is invoked." *Id.* at 595.

116. 243 U.S. 332 (1917).

117. *Id.* at 347–48.

118. *Id.* at 386–87.

119. Ives v. South Buffalo Railroad Co., 94 N.E. 431 (N.Y. Ct. App. 1911).

120. 243 U.S. 188 (1917).

121. *Id.* at 197–98.

122. Nobel State Bank v. Haskell, 219 U.S. 104, 111 (1911).

123. See note 29, *supra.*

124. 257 U.S. 312 (1921).

125. *Id.* at 327.

126. *Id.* at 328.

127. A positive right to have the state protect you from rights-violations by other individuals is, of course, to be distinguished from a positive right to have the state provide you with something. One's "right to life" may involve a duty on the part of the state to stop other people from trying to take it away from you, but it does not necessarily imply a state duty to supply you with the food and shelter that are essential for survival.

128. 261 U.S. 525 (1923). Earlier, in *Hammer v. Dagenhart,* 247 U.S. 251 (1918), the Court had struck down a federal child labor law. The basis of the decision, however, was that the legislation was beyond the scope of the commerce

clause. There was no suggestion that anyone has a natural law right to work ten-year-old children fourteen hours a say.

129. *Id.* at 545–46. Although the Court did not dwell on it, it is significant to note that the reference was to the equality of the exercise of the right, not to the equality of the actual bargaining position. This suggests an emphasis on the theoretical rather than the pragmatic aspect of rights.

130. *Id.* at 553.

131. MILLIS & MONTGOMERY, *supra* note 46, at 331.

132. 261 U.S. at 554.

133. *Id.* at 564.

134. *Id.* at 561.

135. *Id.* at 568.

136. 281 U.S. 548 (1930).

137. *Id.* at 570.

138. See *supra* notes 61 & 62.

139. Douglas v. Noble, 261 U.S. 165 (1923); Dent v. West Virginia, 129 U.S. 114 (1889).

140. Baccus v. Louisiana, 232 U.S. 334 (1914).

141. 285 U.S. 262 (1962).

142. *Id.* at 273.

143. *Id.* at 311.

144. *Id.* at 304.

145. *Id.* at 303.

146. *Id.* at 285.

147. *Id.* at 304.

148. 298 U.S. 587 (1936).

149. *Id.* at 628.

150. *Id.* at 632.

151. *Id.*

152. *Id.* at 634.

153. *See, e.g.,* Carter v. Carter Coal Co., 298 U.S. 238 (1936) (Coal Conservation Act held unconstitutional because it regulated "production" rather than

"trade" or "commerce"); Railroad Retirement Board v. Alton R.R. Co., 295 U.S. 330 (1935) (compulsory retirement and pension system held unconstitutional because of a lack of a close relationship to interstate commerce); A.L.A. Schechter Poultry Corp. v. United States, 295 U.S. 495 (1935) (National Industrial Recovery Act held unconstitutional because it regulated activities after "the flow in interstate commerce had ceased").

154. See, e.g., supra note 153, A.L.A. Schechter Poultry Co. v. United States; Panama Refining Co. v. Ryan, 293 U.S. 399 (1935).

155. 300 U.S. 379 (1936).

156. Id. at 400.

157. 312 U.S. 100 (1941).

158. Id. at 125.

159. 301 U.S. 1 (1936).

160. It is perhaps ironic that the same "liberal" court that read liberty of contract out of the Constitution, on the grounds (in part) that it was not expressly mentioned there, nevertheless read into the Constitution the similarly unenumerated fundamental rights of privacy and association. See, e.g., Roe v. Wade, 410 U.S. 113 (1973); NAACP v. Button, 371 U.S. 415 (1963).

161. 314 U.S. 469 (1941).

162. 13 NLRB Ann. Rep. 49 (1948).

163. 395 U.S. 575 (1969).

164. Id. at 617.

165. Id. at 617.

166. On the other hand, some people argue that the right of association that the statute creates, with the duty of non-interference lying on the private employer, does have constitutional roots, on the theory that the constitutional right of association is a "positive right" and that the statute merely implements it. The balance, thus, is still between two constitutionally based rights—one negative and the other positive.

167. Id. at 620.

168. Vegelahn v. Gunter, 44 N.E. 1077, 1080 (1895) (Holmes, J., dissenting).

169. 310 U.S. 88 (1940).

170. Bakery Drivers Local 802, 315 U.S. 769, 776 (1942) (Douglas, J., concurring) (emphasis added).

171. See, e.g., Cox v. Louisiana, 379 U.S. 636, 555 (1965) (distinguishing picketing from "pure speech").

172. 312 U.S. 287 (1941).

173. *Id.* at 293. For a disturbing overview of the kinds of violence that have been regarded as mere "animal exuberance," and thus not a rights-violation that the state is constitutionally prohibited from granting affirmative protection to, see A. THIEBLOT & T. HAGGARD, UNION VIOLENCE: THE RECORD AND THE RESPONSE BY COURTS, LEGISLATURES, AND THE NLRB (1983).

174. *See, e.g.,* Police Dept. of Chicago v. Mosley, 408 U.S. 92, 98 (1972).

175. *See, e.g.,* Frisby v. Schultz, 56 U.S.L.W. 4785 (1988) (ban on residential picketing upheld).

176. *See, e.g.,* Giboney v. Empire Storage & Ice Co., 336 U.S. 490 (1949). This case involved an injunction against picketing designed to force Empire to sell only to union ice peddlers, in violation of the state anti-trade-restraint law.

177. *See, e.g.,* NLRB v. Retail Store Employees Union (Safeco), 447 U.S. 607, 616 (1980).

178. *Id.* at 618 (Stevens, J., concurring).

179. 456 U.S. 212 (1982).

180. *Id.* at 226–27.

181. This case should be compared with *NAACP v. Claiborne Hardware Co.,* 458 U.S. 886 (1986), which held that an economic boycott of white merchants was a constitutionally protected activity, despite its "coercive" impact.

182. 796 F.2d 1328 (11th Cir. 1986).

183. 366 U.S. 420, 445 (1961).

184. 472 U.S. 703 (1985).

185. This is perhaps because it would have been harder for the Court to have distinguished *McGowan* if it had invalidated the statute on "purpose" grounds, since a religious purpose is as obvious in a blue law case as it was here.

186. *Id.* at 709.

187. *Id.* at 710.

188. *Id.* at 710.

189. In *Estate of Thornton,* 472 U.S. at 712, Justice O'Connor's concurring opinion distinguished the state statute involved there from Title VII on the grounds that the latter requires "reasonable rather than absolute accommodation and extends that requirement to all religious beliefs and practices rather than protecting only the Sabbath observer."

190. Edwards & Kaplan, *Religious Discrimination and the Role of Arbitration Under Title VII*, 69 MICH. L. REV. 599, 628 (1971).

191. 432 U.S. 63 (1977).

192. *Id.* at 90–91.

193. 107 S.Ct. 2862 (1987).

194. 403 U.S. 602 (1971).

195. 766 F.2d 932 (6th Cir. 1985), *reversed on other grounds,* 477 U.S. 619 (1986).

196. The Ohio statute contains no exception for religious organizations.

197. 578 F.Supp. 1004 (S.D. Ohio, 1984).

198. *Id.* at 1037.

199. *See* Gelhorn, *The Abuse of Occupational Licensing,* 44 U. CHIL. L. REV. 6 (1976).

200. *See generally* M. FRIEDMAN, CAPITALISM & FREEDOM 137–60 (1962).

201. *See, e.g.,* North Dakota State Bd. of Pharmacy v. Snyder's Drug Stores, 414 U.S. 156 (1973); Village of Hoffman Estates v. Flipside, Hoffman Estates, Inc., 455 U.S. 489 (1982); Williamson v. Lee Optical of Oklahoma, 348 U.S. 483 (1955).

202. This is thus to suggest that *New State Ice Co. v. Liebmann,* 285 U.S. 262 (1932), discussed at some length earlier, may not have been totally swept under the *Parrish* rug of anti-economic due process.

203. Schware v. Board of Bar Examiners of New Mexico, 353 U.S. 232 (1957).

204. 426 U.S. 88 (1976).

205. The Court has also frequently used the privileges and immunities clause as grounds for striking down state attempts to limit occupational opportunities to residents of that state. *See, e.g.,* Supreme Court of New Hampshire v. Piper, 470 U.S. 274 (1985); United Building & Construction Trades v. Mayor of Camden, 465 U.S. 208 (1984); Hicklin v. Orbeck, 437 U.S. 518 (1978).

206. *See, e.g.,* Willner v. Committee on Character and Fitness, 373 U.S. 96 (1963).

207. 411 U.S. 564 (1973).

208. 426 U.S. at 102 n. 23, quoting from *Truax v. Raich,* 239 U.S. 33, 41 (1915).

209. Whether a decision over the constitutionality of a particular statute will have the beneficial effect it purports to have is a matter of disagreement. The "conventional" economic wisdom is that most labor legislation does in fact

accomplish that result, and the Supreme Court seems to have accepted that. However, if so-called "Chicago School" economists become popular with the Supreme Court, different results are likely to occur.

210. Weber, *Politics as a Vocation*, in FROM MAX WEBER 78 (1958).

211. W. WILSON, THE STATE 572 (1898). *See also*, H. KELSEN, WHAT IS JUSTICE? 289 (1957):

> Coercion is an essential element of law . . . because a careful examination of the social orders termed "law" in the history of mankind shows that these social orders, in spite of their great differences, present one common element, an element of great importance in social life: they all prescribe coercive acts as sanctions.

212. F. BASTIAT, THE LAW 28 (Foundation for Economic Education edition, 1972).

213. In 1963, Judge Bork wrote an article questioning the Civil Rights Act of 1964 on just those terms.

> Of the ugliness of racial discrimination there need be no argument. . . . But it is one thing when stubborn people express their racial antipathies in laws which prevent individuals, whether white or Negro, from dealing with those who are willing to deal with them, and quite another to tell them that even as individuals they may not act on their racial preferences in particular areas of life. The principle of such legislation is that if I find your behavior ugly by my stands, law or aesthetic, and if you prove stubborn about adopting my view of the situation, I am justified in having the state coerce you into more righteous paths. That is itself a principle of unsurpassed ugliness.

Bork, *Civil Rights—A Challenge*, NEW REPUBLIC, August 31, 1963, p. 22.

214. Barsky v. Board of Regents, 347 U.S. 442, 472 (1954) (Douglas, J., dissenting).

The Right to Organize Meets the Market

LEO TROY

I. Purposes and Scope

Government intervention in markets expanded extensively in this country over the last half-century, especially in the labor market. The reason for its continuing expansion is evident—concern for people. Currently, its regulatory scope covers over one hundred million persons in the labor force, encompassing all occupational categories—women and men, minorities and whites, the old and the young. It also extends to millions more who are not in the labor market.

Legal protection of workers' rights to organize and to bargain collectively stands in the forefront of the government's intervention in the labor market. Legislation conferred these economic rights piecemeal. The sequence began with the Railway Labor Act of 1926, which covered employees in railway and air transportation. Next was the Anti-Injunction Act of 1932, which was followed by the National Labor Relations Act of 1935 (NLRA). These extended legal protection of the right to organize and the right to bargain to workers generally. Significant extension of the right to organize and to bargain followed when the Supreme Court removed union activity from the antitrust laws, except in rare circumstances.[1]

The economic rights created by Congress and the courts in labor relations transformed constitutional law. as well as labor-management relations. In 1937, when the Court upheld the constitutionality of the NLRA, it opened new opportunities for congressional regulation by construing manufacturing to be within the scope of the commerce clause of the Constitution. Concurrently, states' powers shrunk under the Tenth Amendment. Since then, congressional regulation grew rapidly, simultaneously diminishing the constitutional power of the states. Indeed, the Tenth Amendment may now be no more than a truism. As we shall see, congressional power under the interstate clause has become so far-reaching that labor relations at the level of state and local government are now subject to congressional regulation.[2]

The new system of industrial relations created by these enactments made unions the beneficiaries of extensive legal immunities and privileges.[3] In economic terms, the new economic rights bestowed extensive monopoly bargaining power on unions in the labor market,[4] and helped to generate the largest and richest union movement in the free world.

Nevertheless, after more than a half-century under the NLRA (organized labor's basic charter), the unionized portion of the private-sector labor market is actually smaller than it was in 1935. After peaking in 1953 at 36 percent, today less than 13 percent of private sector workers are members of unions, slightly above the percentage on the eve of the National Labor Relations Act. By the beginning of the new century, it is likely that the extent of the labor market that is unionized will sink to the level of 1914. When the 21st century begins, union membership as a percentage of the labor market (union density) will probably have gone down to the level that it was at nearly a century ago.

What happened to unions and the economic rights which Congress created and the Supreme Court upheld under the National Labor Relations and Railway Labor Acts? After more than a half century of the NLRA, why is unionism, relative to the work force, back to where it was in 1935?

In brief, the answer is that the market and economic rights have collided, and the market has prevailed: the market has steadily repealed the economic rights Congress and the courts bestowed on unions, and it has relentlessly eroded union membership and union penetration of labor markets.

The process by which the market undermined union ranks and reduced union penetration of the work force is the subject of this essay. To explain that process, I shall answer four questions. (1) What are the market forces which diminished unionism in the private sector of the American economy? (2) Are union movements in the private sector abroad subject to the same forces, and are they declining as well? (3) How has American organized labor responded to the deterioration of its position in the labor market? (4) What will be the likely congressional response to that deterioration?

First, however, I will sketch the origin of the right to organize and bargain collectively in order to demonstrate that the enactment of organized labor's basic charter did, indeed, transform labor-management relations in this country. In addition to this qualitative assessment, I will also present the results of quantitative evidence on the transformation.

Next, I will show that a new labor market emerged in the mid-1950s, and that its emergence began the economic process of reducing union ranks and eroding the economic rights established by Congress under the National Labor Relations Act only two decades earlier. This change—structural change of the labor market—has continued and has simultaneously undermined unionism.[5]

II. The Right to Organize and Bargain Collectively: The Private Sector

The economic origins of the NLRA owe much to the Great Depression. Free-market dominance of economic policy in this century crashed with the Great Depression. Ironically, the Great Depression, historically cited as the example *par excellence* of the failure of private enterprise, can be more rightfully attributed to government intervention than to private enterprise. Government intervention probably converted what would have been a standard business downturn into a catastrophe.[6]

The aftermath of 1929–33 brought about expanding government intervention in the economy. New Deal interventionist policy was empirically, not theoretically, based. The theoretical basis for government intervention in the economy came with the triumph of Keynesian economic theory. Keynesianism justified government intervention in the economy to attain high levels of employment.

Legal protection of workers' rights was a corollary of the New Deal's empirical experience. No general theory motivated the transformation of labor-management relations in this country. Furthermore, the initial steps were undertaken before the New Deal (in the Railway Labor and the Anti-Injunction Acts), but the transformation was completed with the enactment of the NLRA.

Together, the Railway Labor Act, the Anti-Injunction Act, and the NLRA brought legal *protection* to the right to organize and to bargain collectively. Legal protection of the right to organize and bargain is the core of the transformation of labor relations and distinguishes it from its prior history. Unions and bargaining had been legal institutions in this country since the decision in *Commonwealth of Massachusetts v. Hunt* in 1842.[7] Before that decision, state and local judiciaries treated unions as conspiracies, and therefore regularly declared them illegal *per se*. The conspiracy doctrine denied any legal basis or right for workers to organize and bargain collectively.

After the Hunt decision, workers' rights to form a union and bargain became legal; their activities in forming unions and engaging in bargaining were not regulated by legislation. In the absence of legislative policy, the courts examined the means and ends of workers and unions in organizing and negotiating the terms and conditions of employment. Both means and ends had to pass judicial tests of legality. In economic terms, the success of unions' efforts to organize and bargain depended on the market power of the parties.

Typically, courts intervened in labor disputes through their injunctive power, making that legal device a particularly attractive target of organized labor. In 1932, organized labor achieved a goal it had believed it had achieved when the Clayton Act was adopted in 1914—exemption for the injunctive powers of federal courts in labor disputes. In 1932, President Hoover signed the Anti-Injunction Act (also known as the Norris-LaGuardia Act), passed by a Republican Senate and a Democratic House. This step was soon emulated in many important industrial states.

In 1947, Taft-Hartley amendments to the National Labor Relations Act of 1935 restored access to injunctions in labor disputes, but the access was limited to the government itself—the National Labor Relations Board and the President. The Board was permitted to seek injunctive relief to halt certain practices of unions violating the amended act; the President could petition for injunctive relief in strikes or lockouts affecting the national health, safety, and welfare.

It was widely believed that injunctive procedures were normally unavailable under the Railway Labor Act until the Machinists' Union strike against Eastern Airlines (which began March 4, 1989). However, a gap in that theory became apparent when attorneys for the affected railways obtained court orders which prevented unions representing employees of the Long Island Rail Road Company, Metro-North Commuter Railroad, the New Jersey Transit, and Amtrak from honoring pickets by the Machinists' Union. The Federal District Court's orders accepted the railroad companies' argument: sympathy strikes by the railroads' employees ensuing from the secondary picketing would constitute a dispute with the railroads that must be decided by procedures under the Railway Labor Act. The court therefore enjoined the defendant railway unions for honoring secondary picketing by the machinists.[8]

The origins of the legal *protection* of the right to organize, the step beyond the Hunt decision, date from experience under the Erdman Act of 1898, hearings before the Commission on Industrial Relations in 1914, labor policies of the Wilson Administration during the First World War, and the Transportation Act of 1920.

Legal protection of the right to organize first appeared in legislation governing labor-management relations on the railways. Because railway transportation was clearly subject to the commerce clause and was the first industry identified in the public mind as "big business," it was an early candidate for congressional regulation.

In the Erdman Act of 1898, Congress intervened to protect workers' right to join a union in two ways. It prohibited railway carriers from discharging or discriminating against an employee for membership in a union; it also forbade the carriers from requiring their employees, as a condition of employment, not to join or maintain membership in a trade union. (It banned what came to be known as the "yellow-dog" contract.) The "yellow-dog" agreement was, in effect, the mirror image of the contemporary closed shop—an agreement for a completely unionized work force. The "yellow-dog" agreement should be construed as a closed, nonunion shop. In contrast, a closed shop is a contractual agreement between an employer and a union that requires all employees to be union members as a condition of hire and tenure of employment. Currently, the union shop (a less restrictive agreement than the closed shop) is permitted on the railways. For all other workers, the Taft-Hartley Act of 1947 banned the closed shop, but permitted *de facto* closed shops (pre-hire agreements) in certain industries.

Congress's initial attempt to legally protect workers' right to join unions on the railways (and conversely, to limit employment at will) was struck down by the Supreme Court in 1908 as a violation of freedom of contract. In *Adair v. United States,* the Court voided the ban on a closed nonunion shop, the "yellow-dog" agreement, under the Fifth Amendment, declaring that:

> The right of a person to sell his labor upon such terms as he deems proper is, in essence, the same as the right of the purchaser of labor to prescribe the conditions upon which he will accept such labor from the person selling it.[9]

In *Coppage v. Kansas,* the Court applied this free labor market position to state regulation of labor relations as well. In this instance, the Court invalidated the state law banning the "yellow-dog" agreement under the due process clause of the Fourteenth Amendment. Echoing Adair, the Court wrote:

> Conceding the full right of the individual to join the union, he has no inherent right to do this and remain in the employ of one who is unwilling to employ a union man, any more than that same individual has a right to join the union without the consent of that organization.[10]

Antitrust violations served as the basis for the decision to once again uphold the legality of the "yellow-dog" agreement. In *Hitchman Coal & Coke v. Mitchell* in 1917,[11] the Court upheld the issuance of an order enjoining the United Mine Workers from seeking to induce miners to join the union who had previously signed a "yellow-dog" agreement. It stated:

> The same liberty which enabled men to form unions and the union to enter into agreements with employers willing to agree, entitles other men to remain independent of the union and other employers to agree with them to employ no man who owes allegiance or obligation to the union.[12]

Protection of the right to organize made a significant advance when, in 1917, the government seized the railways in furtherance of the war effort. The U.S. Railroad Administration, which ran the roads, initiated labor relations policies to encourage unionization. Even though they were terminated when the railways were returned to private control in March of 1920, these policies had a long-term impact and helped to set the pattern for what eventually became legislatively sanctioned rights.

By the time the railways were returned to private control by the Transportation Act of 1920, union organization had grown immensely. Leo Wolman estimated that membership on the railroads had jumped from 315,000 in 1910 to 640,000 in 1920, and the percentage of employment organized changed from 27.6 percent to 53.2 percent.[13]

The Transportation Act of 1920 enacted, among other goals, the right to organize and bargain collectively—a goal similar to that of the wartime U.S. Railroad Administration. However, the law provided limited administrative power to interpret and apply the legislation. Strife between the carriers and the unions of non-operating employees, exacerbated by the short but sharp recession of 1921–22, led in 1922 to the largest strike to that date; some 400,000 nonoperating workers were involved. The unions lost the strike, blaming their defeat in part on the ineffectiveness of the law. Dissatisfaction with the Transportation Act among employers as well as unions led to joint acceptance of the Railway Labor Act in 1926 to replace the 1920 statute.

Legal protection of the right to organize and bargain began *de facto* with the enactment of the Railway Labor Act of 1926 and the Supreme Court's decision upholding the act in 1930.[14] The legislation forbade "any limitation upon the freedom of association among employees or any denial, as a condition of employment or otherwise, of the right of employees to join a labor organization"; to underline its point, it explicitly forbade the "yellow-dog" agreement. In upholding the statute, the Court wrote:

> The Railway Labor Act of 1926 does not interfere with the normal right of the carrier to select its employees or to discharge them. The statute is not aimed at this right of the employers but the interference with the right of the employees to have representatives of their own choosing. As the carriers subject to the act have no constitutional right to interfere with the freedom of the employees in making their selections, they cannot complain of the statute on constitutional grounds.

Building on this and the experience of World War I, the New Deal extended legal protection of the right to join unions and bargain collectively in Section 7(a) of the National Industrial Recovery Act (NIRA) of 1933. A companion section, 7 (b), permitted the establishment of company labor organizations. In theory, these organizations were viewed as consistent with the rights expressed in 7(a). However, the provision led to a substantial increase of company-wide organizations established by employers as substitutes for unions.

Company-wide labor organizations, principally employee-representation plans, were initiated by employers as early as the beginning of this century. They flourished during the war years and the following decade, and received further impetus under Section 7(b) of the NIRA. Later, under the original National Labor Relations Act, many became independent unions. However, most company-wide organizations were uprooted by the national Labor Relations Board or were overcome or absorbed by unions in organizing drives. Nevertheless, over fifteen hundred such independent (legal) organizations exist to this day.

The National Recovery Administration, which administered the National Industrial Recovery Act, required companies and industrial groups to adopt the text of Section 7 of the NIRA as part of their codes of fair competition. A tripartite National Labor Board (NLB) was set up to administer Section 7(b) under the chairmanship of Senator Robert Wagner. Panels were established for specific industries as well.

One method used by the NLB to implement protection of the right to organize was the representation election. Its impact on union organization was immediate. The most important election involved the United Mine Workers. As a result of representations elections conducted by the NLB, the captive coals mines (the coal mines owned by vertically-integrated steel companies) became organized—a goal which had long eluded the United Mine Workers. The captive coal mines were regarded as especially significant by management and unions alike, because they were rightly seen as the path with the fewest obstacles to the unionization of the steel industry.

The anticipated consequences soon followed. The UMW's victory set the stage for the unionization of the U.S. Steel Corporation, and eventually most of the steel industry, by the Steel Workers' Organizing Committee-CIO, an organization established, funded, and staffed by the United Mine Workers. In addition, the victory also reversed the United Mine Workers' defeat in the *Hitchman* case. The legal implications of *Hitchman* faded with the enactment of the Anti-Injunction Act in 1932.

The NIRA was declared unconstitutional in May 1935, for reasons unrelated to Section 7. Two months later, the National Labor Relations Act (or Wagner Act) was adopted. In retrospect, it is amazing that the basic charter of organized labor—which would in the future revolutionize labor-management relations in the United States—was enacted so speedily. The most likely explanation is that employers believed the opinions of many leading constitutional lawyers, who suggested that the legislation would not get past the Supreme Court.

However, much to their surprise, in April of 1937 the Supreme Court upheld the Act. The Court's constitutional grounds for validating the NLRA construed manufacturing to be in the flow of interstate commerce, and therefore within the reach of congressional authority. The decision initiated both a new era in industrial relations in this country and a new era of expanding government regulation of the labor market.

The goal of the NLRA was to foster the growth of union organization in the United States in order to decrease industrial conflict (over the issue of unionization) and to strengthen the economy. In its findings and policies, Congress concluded that the denial of workers' rights to form unions and to bargain collectively by some employers "led to strikes and other forms of industrial strife or unrest," and caused "the diminution of employment and wages." It also found that the inequality of bargaining power between unorganized workers and corporately-organized employers "tends to aggravate recurring business depressions, by depressing wage rates and the purchasing power of wage earners . . . and by preventing the stabilization of competitive wage rates and working conditions within and between industries." Congress declared that the activities of these employers, as well as their consequences, impaired or disrupted interstate commerce—and thus brought labor-management relations within the range of congressional authority.

The economic rationale of Congress's regulation of labor-management relations was rooted in a popular, but analytically incorrect, reading of the causes of the Great Depression. As I pointed out above, three decades after the start of what became the Great Depression, Milton Friedman identified government itself as the culprit. Perverse monetary policy, coupled with counterproductive fiscal tightening by the federal government, was responsible for converting what might have been a standard downturn into a catastrophe. In its analysis of the Great Depression, Congress attributed it, in part, to an under-consumptionist theory of the business cycle. Another economic misconception lurking in the congressional language, which encouraged unionism and collective bargaining, was the notion that wages could be taken out of competition. This remains an article of faith among unionists and many academics, despite economic theory and fact.

For these economic reasons, and for ideological reasons as well, the original NLRA was constructed as a one-sided, pro-union law regulating labor relations. Only employers could violate the NLRA; only employers could commit unfair labor practices. This imbalance was addressed 14 years later by the Labor Management Relations Act (LMRA) of 1947—the Taft-Hartley Act. The LMRA amended the original NLRA and added policy: including, as previously noted, a procedure which enabled the government to intervene in strikes and lockouts affecting the national health, safety, and welfare.

Taft-Hartley also made important changes in workers' rights: this time, Congress addressed the rights of individual workers in an organized labor-management relationship. I refer here to the amended Sections 7 and 8 of the NLRA. The amended Section 7 affords individuals the right not to join a union, provided that there is no valid contractual agreement requiring membership in a union as a condition of employment. The right not to join was given additional support by the well-known Section 14(b), which permits states to adopt laws (known generally as "right-to-work" laws) which prohibit clauses in bargaining agreements requiring membership in a union as a condition of employment. Taft-Hartley banned closed shops in theory, but permitted them in pre-hire agreements for certain kinds of work—notably, for construction workers and longshoremen.

Other changes in the NLRA also aimed at bolstering individual rights. Taft-Hartley introduced unfair practices which unions could commit which might interfere with the right of workers to join or refrain from joining a union. It became a violation of the act for unions to demand and for employers to agree to the dismissal of an employee for any reasons other than the non-payment of dues if all parties were under agreements requiring membership as a condition of employment. In addition, employers were forbidden to discharge individuals to whom union membership was not available under the same conditions that it was to all others. These provisions were intended to protect individuals from arbitrary denial of membership by unions (who might be therefore subject to immediate discharge under a union shop agreement). Arbitrarily high initiation fees and dues were also banned; these, too, were efforts to protect individual workers in an organized setting. Another was to allow individual employees to present their own grievances, although the bargaining representative had to be notified of the action.

Despite the changes made by Taft-Hartley, the NLRA retained the powerful economic rights that Congress had bestowed on organized labor. And organized labor's subsequent decline cannot be laid at the doorstep of the amended act, as some have contended.[15] The transformation in labor relations wrought by the National Labor Relations Act remained intact.

That the National Labor Relations Act inaugurated a new era in labor relations in the U.S. is indicated by quantitative as well as qualitative analysis. A contrary view has been asserted in statistical models of union growth. These models claimed that union growth in the United States during the 20th century could be explained by compact and structurally stable models.[16] However, two colleagues and I found structural instability associated with the Court's approval of the NLRA in 1937.[17] In other words, our findings showed that enactment of the NLRA was consistent with the qualitative conclusion that the Act had changed the environment of union growth and transformed labor-management relations in this country.

Subsequently, one of my associates investigated the speed of the transition to the new era brought on by the NLRA.[18] He found that the speed of the transition to the new labor-management environment depended upon the year that one judges the NLRA to be effective. Should it be 1937, the year it was upheld by the Supreme Court? Or should it be 1935, the year it was enacted by Congress? If one chooses 1937, then the transition to the new environment created by the act came in one year, and was completed in 1938. If one chooses 1935, then the transition took from three to four and one-half years; that is, the transition came between mid-1938 and the end of 1939. The results of the two analyses are not inconsistent because, for nearly two years (from July 1935 to April 1937), the statute was widely ignored in the belief that the Supreme Court would invalidate it.

Howard Dickman's scholarly analysis of the NLRA offers a qualitative assessment of the NLRA's impact on employees' economic rights and the industrial relations system in this country.[19] His central thesis is that our national policy toward labor organization engendered "quasi–syndicalism" — "private governments" in the organized sectors of the private sector labor market—which were monopoly conditions inconsistent with free markets. The new "private governments" of syndicates are unions exercising rights prescribed by the National Labor Relations Act and extended by interpretations of the National Labor Relations Board and the judiciary.

The inconsistency between markets and national labor policy described by Dickman began to make itself evident in the mid-1950s. Dickman's study may be said to conclude chronologically in 1947, so his work does not deal with the results of the collision of the market and national labor policy—the subject of this essay.

III. The Decline of Private Sector Unions

Markets function incessantly, but their effects—often unseen in the short run or temporarily thwarted by government policies—nevertheless accumulate until, one day, they are so evident that they cannot be ignored. The cumulative effects of markets on the economic right to organize (and therefore on unions) exemplify this regular, unremitting behavior of markets.

In the case of private-sector unionism in this country, the process consisted of the slow but steady substitution of nonunion for union production from inside and outside the country, the rise of new (nonunion) industries, the decline of older (unionized) industries, changes in the geographic location of industries, and changes in occupations and the composition of employment—particularly, increases in women's participation in the labor market. The set of these changes shifted the labor market toward nonunion employment and away from union jobs and union membership.

The most profound aspect of structural change in the labor market in the United States was the switch from a goods- to a service-dominated labor market. It began in the mid-1950s.[20] In union terms, the switch meant the swap of employment in growing nonunion markets for relatively diminishing employment in unionized industries and occupations. Put another way, as the number of employees grew in the service group of industries, the number of jobs remained stable among the goods group, thereby reducing the *relative importance of goods employment in the labor market*. This shift—the shift to services and the relative decline of goods—reduced unions' *penetration of labor markets (density), but not their membership*. As already noted, the peak of private-sector union penetration of the labor market was registered in 1953 (at 36% of nonfarm employment). Since that time, unions' penetration rate of the private labor market has steadily fallen, receding to a level below 1935—the eve of the NLRA. Currently, 13.4 percent of the private labor market is unionized; in 1935, it was 14.2 percent.

The impact of the structural shift to services on union growth was found by another quantitative study. This study found a second structural break in union growth. (It will be recalled that the first structural break in the process coincided with the NLRA.) The second break occurred during the mid-1950s, coincident with the emergence of the service-dominated labor market.[21] Again, quantitative analysis was consistent with the qualitative assessment that the service economy introduced a new (and unfavorable) era for union trends in this country.[22]

Based on this record, it can be said that while the new economic rights of workers embedded in the NLRA heralded the transformation of labor relations during the late 1930s, the change of the labor market in the mid-1950s ushered in yet another new era of labor-management relations— one which is undoing the transformation produced by the NLRA. The new regime is characterized by the growing dominance of nonunion labor-management relations: that is, relations outside the NLRA.

As previously noted, while the shift to services reduced union density, it did not reduce union membership in the private sector. Private sector density peaked in 1953, as already pointed out; private sector membership peaked much later, in 1970. From then to date, the number of private sector members fell because of other structural changes in the labor market: structural changes in the composition of goods employment, particularly manufacturing.

The structural change in manufacturing hit the industrial heartland of union membership: steel, autos, textiles, clothing, shoes, and leather goods. Employment in these industries shrunk drastically—and, along with it, union membership. Meanwhile, employment in nonunion "high-tech" manufacturing rose sharply:[23] this rise, coupled with the absolute decline in union ranks, sharply reduced the unionized percentage of the labor market over the last two decades. Thus, the industrial changes within manufacturing—the rise in employment of nonunion industries and companies—replicated the general switch from unionized goods to nonunion services, and compounded it by actually reducing membership.

This changeover from highly unionized to unorganized manufacturing has been mischaracterized as the "deindustrialization" of America. The term was coined to depict the loss of employment—specifically, manufacturing employment in the United States—in order to justify a protectionist trade policy. The AFL-CIO has shifted to a protectionist position, citing deindustrialization as the reason.

Actually, instead of a loss of manufacturing jobs, there has been virtually no change in the total number of employees in manufacturing industries. The total has been maintained at an average of about 19 million over the past two decades, because of the exchange of jobs between the nonunion high-tech industries and the older, unionized manufacturing industries. Given, also, that the share of real Gross Domestic Product originating in manufacturing has changed little over the past decades, it is, therefore, a misnomer to describe recent trends in manufacturing as the deindustrialization of America. In reality, the term has less to do with the loss of industrial employment than with the decline in union membership. Deindustrialization has really been the extensive "de-unionization" of much of American manufacturing.

The market-induced shift in the industrial composition of the economy—the switch from goods to services and the growth of high-tech and the decline of traditional manufacturing—has been accompanied by occupational shifts: the substitution of white-collar for blue-collar workers. This changeover is not only associated with the switch from goods to services, but *is taking place within manufacturing* as well. To illustrate this shift, note that white-collar employees of General Motors in auto manufacturing are counted as employed in manufacturing, and their share of employment in the corporation has grown—while the work of blue-collar workers has declined, both in numbers and in share.

Like the industrial changes, the occupational change has further reduced union ranks. Since the labor market shifted toward the industries and occupations in which unions have been historically weak, the question arises: why hasn't the new labor force, blue- and white-collar, embraced unionism?

Briefly, the answer is that the majority of nonunion employees do not wish to join. While, on its face, this may seem to be a tautology, polls have shown that a majority of nonunion workers reject unions in private surveys and in official government (National Labor Relations Board) representation elections. The Institute for Social Research at the University of Michigan surveyed private-sector nonunion workers as to whether they would vote for a union in a secret ballot election in 1977, and over two-thirds (67 percent) replied "no." Among white-collar workers, the most rapidly growing segment of the labor force, 72 percent opposed unions; among blue collar workers, 61 percent would vote against union representation. Only among nonwhites did a majority reply "yes" to union representation.[24]

A Lou Harris poll in November 1984 on behalf of the AFL-CIO's self-analysis of declining unionism queried nonunion workers, and found similar results: 65 percent responded that they would not vote for a union if an election were held in their workplace. Again, a majority of minorities replied "yes." Among occupational groups, only a majority of service workers replied that they would vote for a union.[25]

The Harris survey went into the reasons for nonunion workers' rejection of unions. Of twenty responses, three accounted for over 80 percent of the explanation: nonunion employees said they had no need for a union, that unions didn't make sense for their job, or that they disapproved of unions. Employee opposition to unions in the 1980s mounted with the growing unemployment in unionized industries (particularly steel, auto, and clothing manufacturing), and these responses reflect that unease.

Over the last decade, unions have lost the majority of votes in representation elections conducted by the NLRB. These elections are, of course, the type referred to in the two private surveys. What is remarkable about the official polls is that unions do better in NLRB elections than the private polls would predict. While the private surveys showed about two-thirds of nonunion workers reporting that they would not vote for a union, the average percentage of nonunion votes since 1974 is only just over 50 percent! In the face of that result, it would seem that employers' campaigns to defeat unions, denounced by some academics as responsible for so much of the unions' decline, are not only not as effective as claimed, but may be counterproductive. Of course, another reason may be that union election campaigns may be more effective than generally realized.

For considerable time, little notice was taken of the eroding position of organized labor; those who did take notice, as I did, were denounced as doctors of gloom and doom. The reasons for the unwillingness or inability of many to recognize the erosion in union penetration of the private labor market was the boom in public-sector unionism. Because of the explosion of public-sector unionism and the typical error of many to note only total membership, without breaking the figure down into private and public sectors, the decline of private-sector membership was obscured. The combined public and private union membership peaked in 1975 in the United

States.[26] Thereafter, the continued decline of private-sector membership swamped the slowing rise (and eventual stability) of public-sector membership, until it became evident that union membership, as a whole, was falling because of the sharp declines in the private sector.

Public-sector unionism began to grow in earnest after President Kennedy's Executive Order 10988 of 1962. Although limited, of course, to federal employees, it set an example for state and local governments. (Actually, Wisconsin and the city of New York anticipated the federal government.) The truly remarkable growth of public-sector union membership and density rose sharply until it peaked in 1976. Since then, it has remained fairly stable. Meantime, private sector union membership, which edged up during the 1960s because of the Vietnam War, turned down as America disengaged from that conflict—peaking, as I have already noted, in 1970.

It was not until 1984 that the AFL-CIO commissioned a study of shrinking union membership and density. Its results, published in early 1985, acknowledged that there were problems and proposed remedies.

It identified the 1982–83 recession as a major factor in the decline of the 1980s, and structural change in the labor market as a long-run problem. However, the AFL-CIO reserved major blame for the decline to management opposition and to the failings, as they saw it, in the NLRA and its administration by the Reagan-appointed National Labor Relations Board.[27]

The AFL-CIO contended that in contrast to the 1950s and 1960s, when, the Federation said, employers had given "some measure of acceptance" to workers' rights to organize and bargain under the NLRA, this measured acceptance had been withdrawn in recent years and replaced by determined opposition. (This fatuous analysis was the product of the AFL-CIO's academic consultants.) Facilitating employer opposition, according to the AFL-CIO's analysis, were "persistently high levels of unemployment," as well as the federal government's (Reagan Administration's) encouragement of that opposition "by providing less and less protection to workers who exercise their right to organize and setting an example for the most virulently anti-union employers."[28] The example given was President Reagan's firing of air traffic controllers because of their illegal strike. The strike took place in the public sector; it was over wages, not recognition. The union's existence was not jeopardized by the policy of the Reagan Administration; it became jeopardized by continuing an illegal strike—one which received little, if any, support from rank-and-file union members throughout the country. Only leaders and academics were vociferous in denouncing the action of the government.

There is no doubt that employer opposition to the unionization of their employees is an important factor in warding off union organization, but it is not unique to our era. Unions faced employer opposition throughout their existence, including the 1950s and 1960s, contrary to the AFL-CIO's observations. Indeed, their largest advances, during the early years of this century and during the 1930s and 1940s, came in the face of very determined employer opposition.

The AFL-CIO and its academic advisors have also confused the issue of union decline by their emphasis on employer opposition. Unions have lost membership for reasons which have little, if anything, to do with employer opposition. Membership losses are associated with the shrinkage of employment in unionized industries buffeted by economic change and competition. Unions have not been ousted from industries and companies wholesale, as they were in the 1920s. The decline in density is the result not only of the membership loss over the last two decades, but also the long-run employment changes beginning with the rise of the service-dominated labor market in the mid-1950s.

In the contemporary arena of labor-management relations, employer opposition applies primarily to the organization of new workers, and hardly at all to existing membership. Its importance in deterring new organization is exaggerated, while the genuine opposition of nonunion workers to joining unions is ignored—despite poll results. Employer opposition also serves as a convenient reason for amending the NLRA to commit government more fully to the organization of new employees. It is also a substitute for the recognition of the underlying economic reasons for unions' decline in this country.

The AFL-CIO's proposed remedies, largely the product of academic consultants, were to offer union members and nonunion workers benefits (such as, for example, credit cards with interest rates lower than the usual rates), and to set up halfway houses in union membership: that is, associations. Since these proposals were adopted in 1985, union membership and density have continued to fall.

The accelerated decline of private-sector unions in the 1980s is often compared to earlier episodes of union decline: in particular, the union decline of the 1920s. Are the 1980s a rerun of the 1920s? Both share the common factor of employer opposition—employers are economic actors, after all—but they differ substantially for many reasons, not the least of which is public policy that protects workers' right to self-organization and bargaining. In the 1920s, there was no federal law sanctioning the right of workers in the private sector to join unions, except in the case of the railways. In the 1980s, the NLRA governs employee relations in most of the private labor market, and the railways function under an act far more protective of unions than its original version. Nevertheless, can it be that the AFL-CIO is correct—that the NLRA and its administration are responsible for the current decline of unions—making the decline of the 1980s no different than that of the 1920s?

My answer to these questions is no. Public policy that protects the right to organize and bargain has become increasingly ineffectual: less because of the content or administration of the NLRA, but (as previously pointed out) because of economic change and competition. The effort of Congress to create workers' rights in the domain of labor-management relations has run head-on into the marketplace, a collision which first became evident with the structural change in the labor market that began in the mid-1950s. Increased competition in manufacturing by the 1970s and 1980s, as the economies of West Germany and Japan revived and flourished, accentuated the pressure on the NLRA's ability to shield union organization from market forces as it had during its first two decades of its existence. Economic forces, competition and economic change, have eroded the power of the National Labor Relations Act, just as economic forces have always undermined regulation of markets throughout history.

It is not surprising, therefore, that economic reasons explain the decline of private-sector unions that became so spectacularly visible in the 1980s. Employer opposition must be understood as the product of intensified competition. After all, employers are economic actors. Yet it must be pointed out that if employers' opposition to unions was as effective as claimed, it is hard to understand why the results of the NLRB's representation elections show nonunion workers' voting record against unions so far below the percentages revealed by the two surveys reported above. Alternatively, the unions' election campaigns have successfully whittled down the nonunion workers' opposition to unions.

The impact of the structural and competitive forces on unionism are not unique to the United States; they are visible in other countries. Although timing and amplitudes differ, private-sector unions in all Atlantic Community nations but Sweden have declined as well. In fact, the Netherlands appears to have preceded the United States in the decline of private-sector density. Most importantly, Canada, held up as the exemplar for the United States, has been said by the AFL-CIO (based on the claims of some academics) to have escaped the decline of unionism which has taken place in the U.S.[29] Factually, this is wrong; private sector unionism (both membership and density) has been declining in Canada since 1975. (Private membership peaked in 1970, and density in 1953, in the United States.) Canada lagged behind the American decline because of differences in the timing of the switch to a service economy and in the composition employment in both the goods and service sectors.[30]

IV. The Public Sector

Union trends in the public sector strongly contrast with the private-sector labor market. As in the private sector, government has protected public employees' right to organize,[31] although not as comprehensively as in the private sector. Unlike the private sector, however, membership and union penetration in the public labor market has grown or remained stable.

What sets the two sectors apart? In a word, the market. In the public sector, unions are shielded from market forces: because of limited market pressures, public-sector unionism has flourished while private-sector unionism has languished.

Differences between the two sectors of the labor market were always recognized legislatively as well. Public policies to create economic rights for public-sector workers in labor-management relations were always separated from the private sector. For example, when the National Labor Relations Act was adopted in 1935, government employees at all levels were exempted. Federal employees were excluded because few believed that government employees should be organized—and even fewer believed that they ever ought to strike. State and local employees were exempted because, in that era, few believed the federal jurisdiction could include them—a view which has now changed, and which I shall address later in this paper.

Federal policy protecting the right of federal employees to join unions began with the enactment of the Lloyd-Lafollette Act of 1912. The right of all executive-branch federal employees to organize was sanctioned under the law, but was applied only to postal employees. Congress distinguished between postal and other federal employees because, at the time, there was little union organization outside the Post Office. In fact, postal union membership was the only discernible union membership in the federal service from 1897 (when records of total union membership begin) until 1917, when the First World War brought unionism to other units of the federal government. The policies of the Act were eventually applied to non-postal federal employees.

Under Lloyd-Lafollette, union membership did not constitute grounds for discharge or for reduction in pay or rank; to be eligible for the protection of the Act, a union had to forgo the right to strike. Employees in departments and agencies other than the Post Office were permitted to petition Congress individually or in groups. When unions were formed in agencies other than the Post Office, agency management extended the provisions of the Lloyd-Lafollette Act to them, provided they, like the postal unions, renounced the right to strike.

Because of Lloyd-Lafollette, postal unions grew steadily. In 1912, there were 57,000 union members in the postal service; by 1939, there were 235,000 members, and they constituted 74 percent of the total employment. In 1962, when President Kennedy announced a new policy on the right of federal employees in the executive branch of government to organize and enter into collective negotiation in Executive Order 10988, there were 447,000 union members in various postal unions. Their share of employment was about the same as their pre-World War II rate: 75 percent.

Obviously, public policy establishing the economic right of postal workers to organize, even though the tone of the legislation was more tolerant than activist, was sufficient to give postal unionism a helping hand in taking advantage of that right. In addition, it should be pointed out that post offices are to be found in every Congressional district, a circumstance which established a mutually helpful association between politicians and postal unions. The geographic dispersion of membership is one of the strengths of postal unions (and many other public sector unions) which followed— notably, the teachers' unions.

Public policy bestowing the right to organize is common to public- and private-sector labor-management relations, and it has been decisive in the growth of unions in each sector. In the public sector, Richard Freeman also believes that public policy is the crucial factor responsible for the surge of public sector unionism:

> What caused the spurt of public sector unionism in the late 1960's through the 1970's? . . . First and foremost were changes in the laws regulating public sector unions. In the federal sector, Executive Order 10988, which President Kennedy announced in 1962 and which was later strengthened by ensuing presidents, was the principal cause of the rapid organization of federal employees. . . . Before 1962 unionization of federal employees was going nowhere; then suddenly, it shot upward. At the state and local level there were a variety of changes in the law occurring mostly in the 1960's and 1970's . . . which were followed by a rapid growth in unionization.[32]

Following President Kennedy's Executive Order, the postal unions quickly gained recognition rights under that Order; they prospered further as federal labor relations policy moved closer toward the private-sector model, a process I identify as "convergence." In the case of the postal workers, reorganization of the Post Office Department into the U.S. Postal Service and placement of its employees under the jurisdiction of the National Labor Relations Board in 1970 were the next steps toward convergence. The Board can conduct elections, determine bargaining units, and consider unfair labor practices, just as it can the private sector. The Postal Reorganization Act of 1970 continued the ban on strikes by postal workers; however, it also authorized postal workers to negotiate on the same issues as in the private sector, except for compulsory membership and pensions. Given that postal workers' unions had a penetration rate near 100 percent, compulsory membership was not much to give up; likewise, their pensions were (and are) among the best in both public and private sectors, so taking this item off the bargaining table imposed no costs on the postal unions. In fact, the unions probably prefer their exclusion.

For postal unionism, which began with three-quarters of all postal employees already organized in 1962, the new policy added more members and further increased their penetration of the postal service to beyond 90 percent. This puts American postal unionism on a par with public-sector unionism in the Scandinavian countries and the British postal system. According to a recent survey of the postal and telecommunications systems in Britain (prior to the privatization of telephones), 95 percent of all employees in these industries were organized.[33]

The record of unionism in the postal service shows that public policy has a decisive impact on union organization. It also indicates that Freeman erred when he declared, "Before 1962 unionization of federal employees was going nowhere." It was obviously going somewhere for postal workers, although it lagged for other federal employees.

After 1962, favorable public policy promoting the economic rights of federal employees in labor-management relations stimulated rapid gains in organization among federal employees. Many states emulated the federal example, often with policies far more interventionist in labor relations and more supportive of union organization.

Although public- and private-sector workers are subject to similar public policy with respect to the right to organize, there are marked differences in the protection afforded and the results of the application of these policies. As previously pointed out, government protection of the right to organize is more extensive in the private sector, yet the rate of unionization among public sector workers is over 2.6 times as great as it is among private sector workers.

The basic reason for the gap in union penetration between the two sectors is the degree to which each is exposed to competition. Domestic competition, enhanced by the growing intensity of international competition, and structural changes in the labor market have eroded the right to organize in the private sector. In contrast, the virtual absence of competition in the public sector has sheltered public employees' legal right to organize. The competitive threats faced by public employees are limited—privatization and contracting-out. Of the two, the latter is the more important in the United States, but neither is, as yet, a serious challenge to public-sector unions in this country.

Among the reasons contributing to the success of the right to organize in the public sector is the implementation of that policy. Unlike business management, political leaders and public managers are not "accountable" to the market. In contrast to business management, public authorities often encourage the organization of public employees because they see public-sector unions as natural political allies, and rarely as a factor in cost. Indeed, by raising costs, unions provide public managers with a justification for a larger budget, an outcome often devoutly wished by both parties to collective negotiations. Instead of competing interests, the parties, at least up to a point, share a joint interest.

The situation is comparable abroad. In Britain, for example, "[t]he role of the employer in actively or passively encouraging union organization is . . . marked in the public sector. From the First World War onwards, Government has taken on the role of model employer . . . [and] joint employer/employee bodies have a long tradition in the public sector, and these traditions were incorporated into those parts of the private sector nationalised after 1945."[34] The association and collaboration of socialist and labor parties and unions throughout Europe is a fact of life: one hand has fed the other.

Public administrators' support of unionism among public employees, whether activist or permissive, substitutes for the organizational strife and costs—including strikes—in the private sector. The strike has not been used by unions to organize in the public sector. Typically, it is illegal. More importantly, however, it has not been necessary. For example, with little to do, a new successor union has replaced the air traffic controllers' union, whose illegal strike (over wages, not recognition) led to their demise.

State and government policies to establish the right to organize and bargain vary substantially around the country. One of the objectives of organized labor will be to bring all state and local government within the jurisdiction of a single national policy. Congress can now enact legislation to bring state and local government employees, as well as all federal employees, under an amended national Labor Relations Act, or it can adopt new legislation covering all public employees. Either change would be a bonanza for public-sector unions, because of the limited competitive pressures faced in the public domain. It would be even more significant than revisions of the NLRA desired by unions in the private sector—because, at the end of the day, private-sector unions will still have to face the effects of accelerating competition, particularly from Japan and Germany.

The goal of a federal law covering all public employees has been constitutionally possible even since the decision in *Garcia v. San Antonio Metropolitan Transit Authority* in 1985.[35] The central issue in *Garcia* was the jurisdiction of the Fair Labor Standards Act of 1938: did it extend to local government employees (in this instance, to employees of a publicly-owned and -operated mass transit system)?

The message from *Garcia* was that it did. By a five-to-four decision, the Court ruled that the Tenth Amendment did not preclude the application of the Fair Labor Standards Act to employees of state and local governments. One of the most telling conclusions of *Garcia* was the majority view: although the states do "unquestionably retain a significant measure of sovereign authority, . . . [t]hey do so, however, only to the extent that the Constitution has not divested them of their original powers and transferred those powers to the Federal Government."[36] Another way of putting this is to say that the states retain whatever power Congress chooses to leave them. From that perspective, the Tenth Amendment has become only a truism.

As Justice Powell wrote in dissent, "Despite some genuflecting in [the] Court's opinion to the concept of federalism, . . . [the] decision effectively reduces the Tenth Amendment to meaningless rhetoric when Congress acts pursuant to the Commerce Clause."[37]

Justice O'Connor echoed these concerns in her dissent. She wondered "whether any area remains in which a state may act free of federal interference." In response to her own speculation, she wrote that, conceptually, "the essence of federalism is that the States have legitimate interests which the National Government is bound to respect even though its laws are supreme."[38]

Justice Powell saw the extension of the federal minimum-wage and maximum-hour law to the San Antonio Metropolitan Transit Authority as perhaps leading to other aspects of labor relations. Specifically, it would permit Congress under the commerce clause to exercise control "over the terms and conditions of employment of all state and local government employees . . . [rejecting] the distinction between public and private employers that had been drawn carefully in 'National League of Cities'."[39]

Justice Blackmun, in the majority opinion, noted that the jurisdiction of federal regulation of state and local governments had not included those governments under the National Labor Relations Act or the Labor Management Reporting and Disclosure Act, as well as other pertinent legislation. However, with the Democrats in control of Congress, the stage is set for legislation to bring federal, state, and local employees under the reach of one law. At stake are over fourteen million state and local government employees and about another two million federal employees—a significant part (about 16 percent) of the nation's labor market.

The implications of *Garcia* are even more far-reaching. *Garcia* also implies the possibility of nationalizing all labor policies, so as to combine all levels of government employment with the private labor market. Justice Stevens spelled out the potential of such a nationalization in his opinion in

EEOC v. Wyoming: "Because of the interdependence of the segments of the economy and the importance and magnitude of government employment, a comprehensive congressional policy to regulate the labor market may require coverage of both public and private sectors to be effective."[40]

V. Conclusions

Public policy in protecting workers' right to organize and bargain collectively, epitomized by the National Labor Relations Act, inevitably collided with market forces. The result was to slowly, but steadily, counteract government intervention, fostering the decline of private-sector unionism. Structural changes in the labor market and competition, international and domestic, have steadily eroded the size and strength of American unions. Nor is that experience unique to the United States: private-sector union movements in Canada and Western European countries have followed the pattern of America.

The role of market forces is underscored by the contradictory experience of private- and public-sector unions in the United States. Because of the limited degree of competition affecting the public sector, legislatively created rights and union strength in the public sector have remained virtually untouched, while those in the private sector have eroded.

Notes

1. Apex Hosiery Co. v. Leader, 310 U.S. 469.

2. Garcia v. SAMTA, 105 S. Ct. (1985). TROY, *State and Local Government Employee Relations After* 'Garcia', GOV'T UNION REV. (Summer 1986).

3. R. POUND, LEGAL IMMUNITIES OF LABOR UNIONS (1957). *See also* R. POUND, *Legal Immunities of Labor Unions,* J. LAB. RES. (Fall 1979), reprint series no. 1.

4. H. DICKMAN, INDUSTRIAL DEMOCRACY IN AMERICA: IDEOLOGICAL ORIGINS OF NATIONAL LABOR RELATIONS POLICY (1987).

5. By structural change I mean the change in the composition of employment in terms of industry, occupation, gender and age. The most notable structural change is the switch from a goods dominated to a service dominated labor market.

6. M. FRIEDMAN, FREE TO CHOOSE 70–90 (1980); M. FRIEDMAN & A.J. SCHWARTZ, A MONETARY HISTORY OF THE UNITED STATES 1867–1960, ch. 7 (1963).

7. 4 Metcalf. (Mass.) 111 (1842).

8. U.S. District Court, Southern District of New York, Opinions and Order, 89 Civ. 1536, 1535, 1516, 1504 (RPP)(1989).

9. Adair v. United States, 208 U.S. 161 (1908).

10. Coppage v. Kansas, 236 U.S. 1 (1915).

11. Hitchman Coal and Coke Company v. Mitchell, 245 U.S. 229 (1917).

12. *Id.* at 229.

13. WOLMAN, EBB AND FLOW IN TRADE UNIONISM 219 (1936).

14. Texas & New Orleans Railroad Company v. Brotherhood of Railway and Steam Ship Clerks, 281 U.S. 548 (1930).

15. S. BARKIN, THE DECLINE OF THE LABOR MOVEMENT (1961).

16. O. Ashenfelter & J. Pencavel, *American Trade Union Growth: 1900–1960,* 83 Q. J. ECON. 13 (August 1969). G. BAIN & F. ELSHEIK, UNION GROWTH AND THE BUSINESS CYCLE: AN ECONOMETRIC ANALYSIS (1975).

17. Sheflin, Troy, and Koeller, *Structural Stability in Models of American Trade Union Growth,* 96 Q. J. ECON. (February 1981).

18. N. SHEFLIN, *Transition Function Estimation of Structural Shifts in Union Growth,* 16 APPLIED ECON. 81 (February 1984).

19. H. DICKMAN, *supra* note 4.

20. V.R. FUCHS, THE SERVICE ECONOMY 19 (1968).

21. J. KEDDY, ECONOMETRIC ANALYSIS OF AMERICAN TRADE UNION GROWTH: NEW EVIDENCE (1988) (unpublished manuscript).

22. L. TROY, IS THE U.S. UNIQUE IN THE DECLINE OF PRIVATE SECTOR UNIONISM? (1989) (unpublished manuscript). L. Troy, *The Decline of the Labor Movement: A Comment,* I BRIT. J. INDUS. REL. (1963). L. Troy, *Comments: Bernstein's Growth of American Unions, 1945–1960,* 2 LAB. HIST. (1961).

23. The designation of an industry as "high tech" depends upon the ratio of professional and technical employees to total employment, research expenditures, and product sophistication. Some examples are computer equipment (where the number of jobs now exceeds that in motor vehicle production), radio and TV communication equipment, semiconductors, electronic equipment, measuring and controlling devices, and medical instruments and supplies.

24. J. MEDOFF, THE PUBLIC'S IMAGE OF LABOR AND LABOR'S RESPONSE 10, table 4A (December 1984) (mimeo).

25. L. HARRIS & ASSOCIATES, A STUDY ON THE OUTLOOK FOR TRADE UNION ORGANIZING 63, table 20 (1984).

26. L. TROY & N. SHEFLIN, UNION SOURCEBOOK (1985).

27. AFL-CIO, THE CHANGING SITUATION OF WORKERS AND THEIR UNIONS 10–11 (1985).

28. Id. at 11.

29. R.B. Freeman, Contraction and Expansion: The Divergence of Private and Public Sector Unionism in the United States, 2 J. ECON. PERSP. (1988).

30. L. Troy, Is the U.S. Unique in the Decline of Private Sector Unionism? (1989) (unpublished manuscript).

31. There are important differences in the nature and scope of legislative protection of public employees' right to organize and bargain among local, state, and federal governments. In the text, I refer to the protection in a generic sense.

32. R.B. Freeman, Unionism Comes to the Public Sector, 24 J. ECON. LITERATURE, 1986, quoted by J.F. Burton & T. Thomason, The Extent of Collective Bargaining in the Public Sector, in B. AARON, J.M. NAJITA AND J.L. STERN, PUBLIC SECTOR BARGAINING 18–19 (1988).

33. Incomes Data Services, PUB. SERVICE DIG. 5 (May 1987).

34. Id. at 4, table 5.

35. Garcia v. San Antonio Metropolitan Transit Authority, et al., 105 S. Ct. 1005 (1985).

36. Bureau of National Affairs, Public Sector Overtime Pay: The Impact of 'Garcia' on State and Local Governments, BNA Special Report, GERR 1117—pt. II, at 44 (June 10, 1985).

37. Id. at 48.

38. Id. at 56.

39. Id. at 55.

40. EEOC v. Wyoming, 460 U.S. 226, 248 (1983).

Contributors

ELLEN FRANKEL PAUL is Deputy Director of the Social Philosophy and Policy Center and professor of political science at Bowling Green State University. She received her doctorate from the Government Department at Harvard University in 1976. She is the author of numerous scholarly articles and is, also, the author or editor of eighteen books, including MORAL REVOLUTION AND ECONOMIC SCIENCE (1979), PROPERTY RIGHTS AND EMINENT DOMAIN (1987), and EQUITY AND GENDER: THE COMPARABLE WORTH DEBATE (1989).

HOWARD DICKMAN is a Research Associate at the Social Philosophy and Policy Center. He received his Ph.D. in history from the University of Michigan in 1977. He has been Research Director of the Manhattan Institute for Policy Research and Senior Editor of *Harper's* magazine. He has written many articles and is the author of the book INDUSTRIAL DEMOCRACY IN AMERICA: IDEOLOGICAL ORIGINS OF NATIONAL LABOR RELATIONS POLICY (1987).

JAMES M. BUCHANAN is Harris University Professor and Advisory General Director, Center for Study of Public Choice at George Mason University and winner of the 1986 Nobel Prize in economics for his contributions to the theory of political decision-making and public economics. He is the author or coauthor of twenty-five books, including THE CALCULUS OF CONSENT: LOGICAL FOUNDATIONS OF CONSTITUTIONAL DEMOCRACY (with Gordon Tullock, 1962), THE LIMITS OF LIBERTY: BETWEEN ANARCHY AND LEVIATHAN (1975), and WHAT SHOULD ECONOMISTS DO? (1979), and several hundred articles in professional journals.

MARK TUSHNET, Professor of Law at the Georgetown University Law Center, received a J.D. and M.A. (history) from Yale University in 1971. After serving as a law clerk to Justice Thurgood Marshall of the United States Supreme Court, he taught at the University of Wisconsin from 1973 to 1981. Professor Tushnet is the author of AMERICAN LAW OF SLAVERY, 1810–1860: CONSIDERATIONS OF HUMANITY AND INTEREST (1981), THE NAACP'S LEGAL

STRATEGY AGAINST SEGREGATED EDUCATION, 1925–1950 (1987), RED, WHITE AND BLUE: A CRITICAL ANALYSIS OF CONSTITUTIONAL LAW (1988), and CENTRAL AMERICA AND THE LAW: THE CONSTITUTION, CIVIL LIBERTIES, AND THE COURTS (1988). He is the coauthor of two casebooks, FEDERAL JURISDICTION: POLICY AND PRACTICE (1987), and CONSTITUTIONAL LAW (1986), and is the author of numerous law review articles on constitutional law and history.

WILLIAM H. RIKER is Wilson Professor of Political Science at the University of Rochester. He is the author of, *inter alia,* THE THEORY OF POLITICAL COALITIONS (1963), LIIBERALISM AGAINST POPULISM: A CONFRONTATION BETWEEN THE THEORY OF DEMOCRACY AND THE THEORY OF SOCIAL CHOICE (1982), and THE ART OF POLITICAL MANIPULATION (1986). He is a fellow of the American Academy of Arts and Sciences and of the National Academy of Sciences, and he has served as President of the American Political Science Association.

LINO A. GRAGLIA is the A. Dalton Cross Professor of Law at the University of Texas School of Law. He is a graduate of the City College of New York and Columbia Law School. He practiced law for twelve years with the United States Department of Justice and private law firms in Washington, D.C. and New York City. As a member of the University of Texas law faculty, which he joined in 1966, he teaches constitutional law, civil rights, and antitrust. He is the author of DISASTER BY DECREE: THE SUPREME COURT DECISIONS ON RACE AND THE SCHOOLS (1976) and numerous articles on affirmative action and judicial review in legal periodicals and *Commentary, National Review, The American Spectator,* and *Public Interest.*

STEPHEN MACEDO is assistant professor in the Government Department at Harvard University. He is the author of THE NEW RIGHT V. THE CONSTITUTION (1987) and several articles on American constitutionalism and political theory. His forthcoming book, LIBERAL VIRTUES: A LIBERAL THEORY OF CITIZENSHIP, VIRTUE, AND COMMUNITY, will be published by Oxford University Press.

FRANK MICHELMAN has been teaching since 1963 at Harvard Law School, where he is currently professor of law, specializing in the fields of property and constitutional law. He is the author of numerous articles dealing with intersections among property, constitutional law, political theory, and general legal theory. Most recently, his work has focused on the possible significance for contemporary constitutional-legal argument and understanding of the "civic republican" strain that recent historiography has found, along with nascent liberalism, in American constitutional foundations.

RICHARD A. EPSTEIN is the James Parker Hall Distinguished Service Professor of Law at the University of Chicago, where he has taught since 1972. He has been the editor of the *Journal of Legal Studies* since 1981, and a member of the American Academy of Arts and Sciences since 1985. His books include TAKINGS: PRIVATE PROPERTY AND THE POWER OF EMINENT DOMAIN (1985), CASES AND MATERIALS ON TORTS (4th ed., with C. Gregory and H. Kalven, Jr., 1984), and MODERN PRODUCTS LIABILITY LAW (1980). He has taught courses in civil procedure, contract, land development, property, torts (including defamation and privacy), jurisprudence, legal history, Roman law, and workers' compensation. He has written extensively in these areas, as well as in those of constitutional and labor law. Before joining the University of Chicago faculty, he taught at the University of Southern California Law School from 1968 to 1972. He is a graduate of Columbia College, Oxford University (Juris.), and the Yale Law School.

R. SHEP MELNICK is associate professor of politics at Brandeis University and a member of the Brookings Institution affiliated staff. He is the author of REGULATION AND THE COURTS: THE CASE OF THE CLEAN AIR ACT (1983). His articles on administrative law and environmental regulation have appeared in *The Public Interest, Public Administration Review,* and *The Brookings Review.* He taught at Harvard University, where he received his B.A. and Ph.D. He is currently completing a book for the Brookings Institution on the courts, Congress, and social welfare programs.

THOMAS R. HAGGARD holds the David W. Robinson Chair at the University of South Carolina School of Law. He graduated from the University of Texas with a B.A. in political science in 1964 and an LL.B. with honors in 1967. For two years, he practiced law as an associate with Covington and Burling in Washington, D.C. In 1969, he joined the law faculty of the Rutgers-Camden Law School in New Jersey. He joined the University of South Carolina law faculty in 1975, where he teaches labor and employment law. Professor Haggard has written numerous articles and books in this field.

LEO TROY is Distinguished Professor of Economics at Rutgers University, where he specializes in labor economics and industrial relations. His research has been published in such leading journals as the *Journal of Political Economy,* the *Review of Economics and Statistics,* the *Quarterly Journal of Economics,* and the *Industrial and Labor Relations Review.* He received his Ph.D. from Columbia University in 1958; taught previously at Rutgers, Columbia, New York University, and Bard College; and has twice been a visiting Fulbright Professor to the United Kingdom.

Index